## Praise for
## *Best of* CALIFORNIA'S Missions, Mansions, and Museums

This guide is essential for anyone who wants to experience California's missions, mansions, and museums. It is full of little vignettes that inspire, educate, and enlighten the reader. Dahlynn and Ken McKowen have done a masterful job.

*—Donald Murphy, former director, California State Parks*

This comprehensive travel guide to California's rich diversity of historic and cultural treasures is a must for anyone interested exploring the Golden State in-depth. It will prompt locals and tourists alike to not only read about these scenic and historic attractions, but to visit them as well.

*—Christopher Craig, editor, Encyclopedia of San Francisco, a project of the San Francisco Museum and Historical Society*

Wilderness Press's new publication, *Best of California's Missions, Mansions, and Museums*, is a wonderful addition to their list of well-known publications. This is the best guide I have seen on a behind-the-scenes look at the Golden State's historic and cultural treasures. This book will make you want to get off your butt, jump into your car, disregard gas prices, and take a long sabbatical to check out all the wonders that California has to offer. A wonderful addition to a traveler's collection.

*—Jay Aldrich, Tourism & Public Relations, Autry National Center*

Californians have always looked within themselves, beyond themselves, and to each other for inspiration. This book will help you find the true heart of California—yesterday, today, and tomorrow. Even California natives will find someplace new to discover and explore in this book. In its pages you come to realize that art, architecture, and inspiration are all around us.

*—Joe D'Alessandro, president and CEO, San Francisco Convention & Visitors Bureau*

# Best of
# CALIFORNIA'S
# Missions
# Mansions
## and Museums

**Ken & Dahlynn McKowen**

**WILDERNESS PRESS** · BERKELEY, CA

**Best of California's Missions, Mansions, and Museums:**
**A Behind-the-Scenes Guide to the Golden State's Historic and Cultural Treasures**

**FIRST EDITION September 2006**

Copyright © 2006 by Ken & Dahlynn McKowen

Front cover photos copyright © 2006 by Ken McKowen *(left and middle)*
and Ed Cooper *(right)*
Back cover photos copyright © 2006 by Ken McKowen
Interior photos, except where noted on page vii, by Ken McKowen
Maps: Bart Wright (Lohnes + Wright)
Book and cover design: Larry B. Van Dyke
Book editor: Eva Dienel

Library of Congress Card Number: 2006022076
ISBN-13: 978-0-89997-398-2
ISBN-10: 0-89997-398-1
UPC: 7-19609-97398-0

Manufactured in Canada

Published by:   **Wilderness Press**
**1200 5th Street**
**Berkeley, CA 94710**
**(800) 443-7227; FAX (510) 558-1696**
**info@wildernesspress.com**
**www.wildernesspress.com**

Visit our website for a complete listing of our books and for ordering information.

*Cover photos:*   La Purisima Mission, San Francisco Cable Car Museum,
Governor's Mansion *(front, left to right);* Mission San Diego
de Alcala, Filoli, de Young Museum *(back, top to bottom)*
*Frontispiece:*   Top to bottom: Mission San Antonio de Padua, Adamson House,
Turtle Bay Exploration Park

**Library of Congress Cataloging-in-Publication Data**

McKowen, Ken.
    Best of California's missions, mansions, and museums : a behind-the-scenes guide to the Golden State's historic and cultural treasures / Ken and Dahlynn McKowen.
       p. cm.
    Includes index.
    ISBN 0-89997-398-1
    1. Historic buildings—California—Guidebooks. 2. Historic sites—California—Guidebooks. 3. Spanish mission buildings—California—Guidebooks. 4. Mansions—California—Guidebooks. 5. Museums—California—Guidebooks. 6. California—Guidebooks. 7. California—History, Local. I. McKowen, Dahlynn. II. Title.
    F862.M38 2006
    917.9404'54—dc22
                                                                              2006022076

*We dedicate this book to our children, Dahlynn's son, Shawn, and daughter, Lahre, and Ken's son, Jason, all of whom are native-born Californians. We also dedicate this book to those die-hard travelers who love the open road as much as we do.*
*Enjoy!*

# Acknowledgments

When we embarked on our journey to write *Best of California's Missions, Mansions, and Museums*, we were aware that it would be a collaborative effort. And we were right. During our total of nearly four months on the road driving some 10,000 miles, we met many dozens of wonderful, dedicated people and visited more missions, mansions, and museums than most people will in their lifetimes.

Our collaboration began with the talented staff at Wilderness Press. We'd like to thank managing editor Roslyn Bullas, who quickly understood what we wanted to accomplish with our book, and Eva Dienel, for her skillful editing and concise attention to detail, always asking for just a little more background or explanation when we "over-assumed" that our readers would *certainly* know about some piece of California's history. Of course, we can't forget the sales and marketing savvy of Heather Harrison and Laura Keresty, who are helping to make our book successful, as well as the creative talents of Larry Van Dyke, this book's designer, and the rest of the staff at WP.

*Best of California's Missions, Mansions, and Museums* wouldn't exist if it weren't for the hundreds of historical destinations in California. And the hundreds of missions, mansions, and museums would not exist if it weren't for the thousands of dedicated professionals, docents, volunteers, and the local communities who keep the collections protected and the doors open. Staff from so many of the historic homes, missions, and museums that we included were especially helpful providing tours, fact checks, photos, and other assistance as we developed the manuscript. Museum closures, traffic worse than we had planned for in Southern California, late-season Sierra snowstorms, or, quite often, a new mansion or museum that we discovered during our travels frequently changed our planned travel schedule. The result was that many people became our collaborators on very short notice, with some going well beyond the call of duty, including Clancy D'Angelo, for his help in securing photo releases for the many missions operating under the Diocese of Monterey; Joanne Steele, for her die-hard assistance with Siskiyou County officials; and last, the Franciscan Friars of the Old Mission San Luis Rey, for their help and permission in using the photos of their mission.

We would especially like to thank Roy Stearns and John Arnold at California State Parks for helping us gain access to the many state historic parks, and Lynette Hernandez for greatly simplifying the photography requirements within most of the state park units.

Considering we were on the road for a total of nearly four months visiting more than 200 destinations, we cannot forget to thank our good neighbor Bill Falkenstein for watching our home and feeding our two dogs. It was wonderful to come home to a well-watered, green yard and two happy and well-fed dogs! (Bill spoils them.)

A special thanks to Shayla Johnson for jumping in during the final frantic days of proofing galleys, creating the index, and checking photo captions. Her attention to detail was a great help!

We would be remiss if we didn't thank Dahlynn's two children, 9-year-old son, Shawn, and 14-year-old daughter, Lahre, who were "forced" to visit dozens of missions, mansions, and museums when they were out of school and traveling with us. They provided their personal kids' view of what was fun and interesting for them, and although they are reluctant to admit it, they actually learned much about California's history along the way, even if occasional bribes were required.

For readers of *Best of California's Missions, Mansions, and Museums*, you become our final collaborators. Our wish is that you enjoy and find useful our family's efforts to help your family and friends navigate the modern by-roads of California's fascinating history. Please, let us know how we did.

—*Ken and Dahlynn McKowen*

## PHOTO CREDITS

All interior book photos were taken by Ken McKowen, except for the following:
  page 45:    Bottom photo courtesy of the Luther Burbank Home and Gardens
  page 91:    Photo courtesy of Kevin Hunsanger
  page 107:  Photo courtesy of Kevin Hunsanger
  page 133:  Photo courtesy of the Crocker Art Museum
  page 164:  Photo courtesy of California State Park
  page 217:  Photo courtesy of the Ronald Reagan Presidential Library Foundation
  page 234:  Photo courtesy of the California African American Museum
  page 236:  Photo courtesy of Shawn Shiflet
  page 276:  Photo courtesy of the Richard Nixon Library & Birthplace
  page 286:  Photo courtesy of the Museum of Making Music
  page 313:  Photo courtesy of Shawn Shiflet
  page 315:  Photo courtesy of the National Park Service

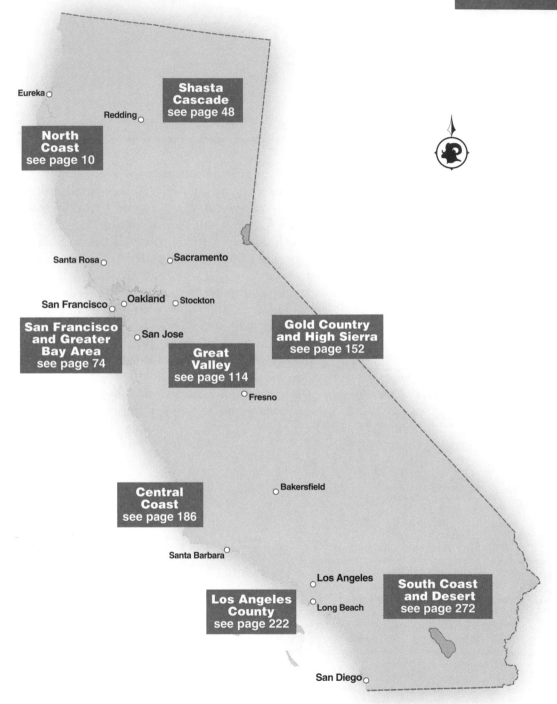

**California**

Eureka

Shasta Cascade
see page 48

Redding

North Coast
see page 10

Santa Rosa

Sacramento

San Francisco
Oakland
Stockton

San Francisco and Greater Bay Area
see page 74

San Jose

Great Valley
see page 114

Gold Country and High Sierra
see page 152

Fresno

Bakersfield

Central Coast
see page 186

Santa Barbara

Los Angeles

Los Angeles County
see page 222

Long Beach

South Coast and Desert
see page 272

San Diego

# Contents

## SHASTA CASCADE

# SAN FRANCISCO AND GREATER BAY AREA

## GREAT VALLEY

# GOLD COUNTRY AND HIGH SIERRA

## CENTRAL COAST

# LOS ANGELES COUNTY

# SOUTH COAST AND DESERT

# TRIVIA ANSWERS

# INDEX **333**

# ABOUT THE AUTHORS **343**

# Destinations by Category

## NORTH COAST

### Missions
Sonoma Mission and Barracks

### Mansions
Guest House Museum
Kelley House Museum
Lachryma Montis (General Mariano Vallejo Home)
Jack London State Historic Park
Luther Burbank Home and Gardens

### Museums
Battery Point Lighthouse and Museum
Del Norte County Museum
Samoa Cookhouse Museum
Clarke Historical Museum
Humboldt State University Natural History Museum
Fort Humboldt State Historic Park
Fortuna Depot Museum
Ferndale Museum
Kinetic Sculpture Museum
Point Cabrillo Light Station
Fort Ross State Historic Park
Mendocino County Museum
Charles M. Schulz Museum

# SHASTA CASCADE

## Museums

Siskiyou County Museum
Weed Historic Lumber Town Museum
Lava Beds National Monument Visitor Center Museum
Fort Crook Museum
Modoc County Historical Museum
Lassen Historical Museum
Plumas County Museum
Portola Railroad Museum
Weaverville Joss House State Historic Park
Shasta State Historic Park Museum

# SAN FRANCISCO AND GREATER BAY AREA

## Missions

Mission Dolores

## Mansions

Pardee Home Mansion
Winchester Mystery House
Filoli

## Museums

Benicia Capitol State Historic Park
Alcatraz Island
Angel Island State Historic Park
Fort Point National Historic Site
San Francisco Maritime Museum
SS Jeremiah O'Brien
San Francisco Cable Car Museum
San Francisco Museum of Modern Art
Asian Art Museum
De Young Museum
San Francisco Fire Museum
Oakland Museum of California
USS Potomac
USS Hornet Museum

# GREAT VALLEY

## Mansions

Bidwell Mansion State Historic Park
Leland Stanford Mansion State Historic Park
Governor's Mansion State Historic Park
Crocker Art Museum
The Meux Home
Kearney Mansion

## Museums

Turtle Bay Exploration Park
The California Museum for History, Women, and the Arts
Sutter's Fort State Historic Park
State Capitol Museum
California State Railroad Museum
The Sacramento Museum of History, Science, Space, and Technology
Towe Auto Museum
Folsom Prison Museum
Folsom Powerhouse Museum
Castle Air Museum
Colonel Allensworth State Historic Park

# GOLD COUNTRY AND HIGH SIERRA

## Mansions

Ehrman Mansion
Vikingsholm
Tallac Historic Site

## Museums

Marshall Gold Discovery State Historic Park
Columbia State Historic Park
Empire Mine State Historic Park
El Dorado County Historical Museum
California State Mining and Mineral Museum
Donner Memorial State Park Museum
Bodie State Historic Park
Laws Railroad Museum and Historical Site
Manzanar National Historic Site

# CENTRAL COAST

## Missions
Mission San Juan Bautista
Carmel Mission
Mission San Antonio de Padua
Mission San Luis Obispo
La Purisima Mission State Historic Park
Mission Santa Ines
Mission Santa Barbara

## Mansions
Cooper-Molera Adobe
Larkin House
Hearst San Simeon State Historical Monument

## Museums
Custom House and Pacific House Museums
Colton Hall
Monterey Maritime Museum and History Center (Stanton Center)
National Steinbeck Center
Monterey County Agricultural & Rural Life Museum
Ronald Reagan Presidential Library and Museum

# LOS ANGELES COUNTY

## Missions
San Fernando Mission

## Mansions
Workman and Temple Family Homestead
Rancho Los Alamitos
Los Cerritos Ranch House
Adamson House
William S. Hart Mansion
Will Rogers State Historic Park
Fenyes Mansion
The Gamble House
Banning Residence Museum

## Museums
The Getty Center and The Getty Villa
California African American Museum
Page Museum at La Brea Tar Pits

Petersen Automotive Museum
Natural History Museum of Los Angeles County
Museum of the American West
Southwest Museum of the American Indian
Wally Parks NHRA Motorsports Museum
Huntington Museum
Los Angeles Maritime Museum
Pio Pico State Historic Park

# SOUTH COAST AND DESERT

### Missions
Mission San Juan Capistrano
Mission San Luis Rey de Francia
Mission San Diego de Alcala

### Mansions
Leo Carrillo Ranch Historic Park
Marston House
Scotty's Castle (Death Valley Ranch)

### Museums
Richard Nixon Presidential Library and Birthplace
International Surfing Museum
Newport Harbor Nautical Museum
Museum of Making Music
Old Town San Diego State Historic Park
San Diego Museum of Man
San Diego Air and Space Museum
San Diego Automotive Museum
San Diego Model Railroad Museum
San Diego Natural History Museum
San Diego Museum of Art
Maritime Museum of San Diego
San Diego Aircraft Carrier Museum (USS Midway)
Twenty Mule Team Museum
Colonel Vernon P. Saxon Jr. Aerospace Museum
US Naval Museum of Armament and Technology

San Fernando Mission

Fenyes Mansion

Kinetic Sculpture Museum

# Introduction

With its mountain forests and arid deserts, world-renowned cities and living ghost towns, ocean beaches and valley farmlands, California is more diverse in geography, culture, and history than most nations. Since its earliest times, California has attracted immigrants, newcomers looking for economic opportunities, and refugees seeking freedom.

This diversity is reflected in an equally diverse collection of missions, mansions, and museums, each celebrating and memorializing its small part of California's human history. While we can't replay history in order to satisfy our curiosities, California's missions, mansions, and museums provide the best opportunities to see, experience, and occasionally touch our past. They also allow us to come to "know" the people who shaped that history.

California history begins with the Native Americans who documented what was important to them with their carved petroglyphs and painted pictographs on desert rocks. Today, hundreds of California museums feature some aspect of our earliest residents. From projectile points to baskets, pottery to dugout canoes, some of the best Native American collections can be seen at places such as the Southwest Museum of the American Indian in Los Angeles.

The next great era in California's history began even before the US became preoccupied with its Revolutionary War against the British. In 1769, Father Junipero Serra followed orders from the Spanish monarchy and founded the first of what ultimately became a series of 21 missions along California's southern and central coasts. The mission program was designed to convert thousands of local Indians to Christianity, to proclaim them as Spanish citizens, and to allow Spain to legitimately claim title to having settled California. In 1833, a dozen years after Mexico's successful war for independence against Spain, the Mexican government secularized and took control of the missions' vast lands. Over the next half century or more, most of the missions were abandoned and fell into severe disrepair.

Since that time, all of the missions have undergone various levels of restoration, and you can visit them today. Mission Santa Barbara, for instance, is one of the more spectacular missions, featuring a wonderful museum inside its soaring adobe architecture. La Purisima Mission, today a state historic park, has been restored to capture its original ambiance, with its gardens, farm animals, and wonderful living-history programs.

Twenty years after the Mexican government dismantled the mission system, California's 1849 Gold Rush ushered in a new age for the Golden State. James Marshall's discovery of gold at what is today the Marshall Gold Discovery State Historic Park in Coloma brought dramatic and irreversible changes, especially to California's Mother Lode landscape. Mining towns sprang to life almost overnight as thousands of miners rushed to the next big find near places like Columbia State Historic Park and Bodie, one of the most notorious mining cities of its day, and what today is a real ghost town—and also a state historic park.

The Gold Rush marked only the beginning of what was to become the new California. Statehood quickly followed, and with that came the constant flood of immigrants. New industries grew, creating great cities, railroads, harbors, and ground-transportation systems. California's love affair with the automobile is characterized not only by thousands of miles of freeways, but by museums such as the Petersen Automotive Museum in Los Angeles and the Towe Auto Museum in Sacramento, among many more dedicated to cars, trucks, motorcycles, and the need for speed and style. California's tie to the railroads is documented at the beautiful California State Railroad Museum in Sacramento, and its link with ocean transportation can be found in every major port city. San Diego, Los Angeles, Monterey, and San Francisco each has a splendid maritime museum, with the ones in San Diego and San Francisco featuring 19th and 20th century merchant ships and ships of war.

As gold, oil, transportation, and industry in general created the state's first multimillionaires, many of those early entrepreneurs began giving back to the citizens of California by creating great museums through rich endowments and donations. The Huntington Museum in San Marino, the Crocker Art Museum in Sacramento, and the Getty museums in Los Angeles and Malibu are but a few examples.

Every aspect of the human condition is likely covered by at least one mission, mansion, or museum in California. Each place takes its own special peek at one small part of California's history: The US Naval Museum of Armament and Technology at China Lake looks at the technology of war, the International Surfing Museum in Huntington Beach checks out surfing, LA's Page Museum at La Brea Tar Pits celebrates tar-covered fossils, and the San Diego Air and Space Museum explores the history of aircraft. The best of California's missions, mansions, and museums are out there waiting for you and your family to stop by and experience firsthand the stories of the Golden State's history.

## THE "BEST" SELECTIONS

Our intention with this book and with the selections we have made is to provide a broad geographic and subject-matter selection of California's missions, mansions, and museums, primarily as they relate to California's history and culture. But with such a large selection of missions, mansions, and museums in California, we needed to narrow the field for this book, so we tasked ourselves with selecting the best.

Ultimately, our selection was subjective, but it was based on extensive research and visits to many destinations across the state. Not everyone will agree with all of our choices, and we certainly weren't able to include every worthy destination. For instance, some geographic regions, such as Los Angeles, have a dozen or more major art museums, so we had to narrow them down for the book. On the other hand, when a wide geographic area has but one small history museum, we generally included it to ensure coverage of important parts of California's history. We also chose some places because they were just plain quirky and we liked them—or because our kids had fun there.

We began by recalling a few dozen years of trips throughout California as travel writers, photographers, and tourists, visiting its historic homes, the missions, and many of its hundreds of museums. We ran thousands of Internet searches, reviewed volumes of travel and history books, and read through stacks of promotional brochures. We then drove a few thousand miles and walked what felt like a few hundred miles visiting the most promising sites. Dahlynn's two children, Lahre, age 14, and Shawn, age 9, accompanied us for many of those miles, occasionally with a dual refrain of "not another museum!" They were able to provide us with an age-relevant kids' perspective on what excites the younger generation and what bores them to tears, which, fortunately, didn't happen often.

Even after researching several hundred potential candidates and visiting more than 250 sites, attempting to choose the "best" of anything in California is a challenge; one person's daffodil is another's poison oak. Obviously, we weren't writing an encyclopedic listing of California museums and historic sites, and we were limited to the number of pages we could fill. And, to be fair, we didn't visit every site and thus didn't consider them for inclusion. (Even as we write this, we are continuing to discover new sites that could be considered among the "best," but we'll save those for future editions.)

While it's possible to disagree with some of the places we chose to include—and probably easier to disagree with some of the missions, mansions, or museums that we chose not to include—we are confident that if you visit the sites we have written about here, you will not be disappointed. It's likely that if we went through the same process again, even we would not end up with the exact same list of the "best" missions, mansions, and museums; however, it is likely that the great majority of our final choices would remain unchanged.

## The Best Missions

The Native American population and cultures had flourished for thousands of years when the Spanish padres arrived in the 18th century. Father Junipero Serra founded the first California mission, Mission San Diego de Alcala, on July 16, 1769, in what is today the city of San Diego. Each of California's 21 missions is unique and each has become an integral part of California's history. Indeed, every year, thousands of fourth-graders throughout the state visit the missions as they embark on studying their home state's past.

While the king of Spain's plan to populate his claimed lands in North America by establishing the missions resulted in settlements as far north as Sonoma, the Native American population suffered significantly. Spanish padres and soldiers inadvertently introduced European diseases that decimated the native populations. While tens of thousands of Indians converted to Christianity and worked at the missions as what the padres called "neophytes," tens of thousands also died from diseases ranging from measles to influenza that seldom proved fatal to their European carriers. Over the decades, this loss of life proved detrimental to the missions because the padres needed hundreds of Indian workers to raise the thousands of cattle and other livestock and to tend the crops required to support the missions.

Spain's North American colonies began their revolt against the homeland in 1810, finally gaining independence in 1821. In 1833, an independent Mexico passed a law that secularized the original Spanish missions. Essentially, the government confiscated the lands that the missions supposedly had held in trust for the Indians working under the mission system. Ultimately, the land ended up in the hands of local well-to-do Mexican landowners, political leaders, and members of the military.

All of the missions have undergone some level of restoration, and for most that has meant major reconstruction. California's environment was not only hard on the missionaries, but it took a heavy toll on the mission buildings. A very abbreviated and generalized history for all of the missions looks something like this: A mission was founded by Father Serra or his successor; many were moved a year or so later to better locations; earthquakes destroyed numerous mission buildings; the missions were rebuilt (though many were destroyed again by subsequent earthquakes, and at least one burned in an Indian revolt); secularization took the missions' land holdings, with most acquired by wealthy landowners or politicians; abandoned by the church, the mission buildings deteriorated and often their parts were scavenged; President Lincoln returned the missions to the Catholic Church; restoration and sometimes complete reconstruction efforts began to rebuild the missions to what you see today. Add to these problems droughts, fires, deaths, administrative transfers, poor leadership, great leadership, varying levels of support and mostly nonsupport from either Spain or Mexico, and during the 70 years that the missions were active, they experienced both prosperous years and disastrous years.

While all of California's missions are worth visiting, we found that some offer more than others. Our final choices came down to 13 missions that we felt included not only wonderful museums, but retained much of their original or at least their early 20th century restored historic fabric. Santa Barbara is one of the premier missions. The Carmel Mission is most noted for its location in the city of Carmel, but perhaps more importantly, it is the final resting place of Father Serra. Some of our selections were based on how much our kids enjoyed visiting them. La Purisima is one of our favorites for many reasons. It has been restored almost completely from its crumbling state of decay, and today La Purisima Mission (and its adjacent hillsides, which are empty of fancy modern homes and businesses) most resembles how the missions originally appeared, including the presence of livestock and gardens.

## *The Best Mansions*

We chose our favorite mansions in much the same way as the missions, but we added accessibility—how frequently they are open to the public for tours. In deciding what constituted a mansion, size was only one of the determining factors; most of our chosen 19th century homes would have been considered mansions during their time, even though they are smaller and significantly less fancy than many of today's suburban castles. So rather than allowing a home's size or value be the deciding factors, we chose instead to look at how these homes were viewed during their prime eras. A 2000-square-foot ranch house, such as novelist Jack London's ranch house, built in the small rural community of Glen Ellen in the early 1900s, may have been viewed as a mansion by many people back then, although not so much as his nearby Wolf House, which was destroyed by fire just days before the Londons planned to move in. A large adobe constructed in 1820 may more closely resemble a primitive mud hut when compared with today's colossal homes, but the elegance of those early mansions and the influence that their owners enjoyed during their times easily exceeds that of most of today's two-income wage earners and their big suburban "mansions."

What constituted a mansion selection for this book had more to do with its place in history, its elegance, its uniqueness—or its quirkiness, such as with the Winchester Mystery House in San Jose—and its level of preservation, restoration, and historic interpretation. Often, our selections included historic homes that also have become museums. The Crocker Art Museum in Sacramento is the perfect example. The home itself easily qualifies as a mansion, but add the fact that it became an art museum (the oldest art museum west of the Mississippi), and it qualifies as one of the best mansions *and* museums.

There are numerous mansions that we chose not to include. It's also likely that there are some we never identified in our many travels. Others may be reasonably well-known, such as Pasadena's Wrigley Mansion, but we felt that public access was limited. Many others, such as the Carson Mansion in Eureka, one of California's grandest Victorians, are privately owned, and public tours are not available. There are also dozens of bed-and-breakfast inns, such as the beautiful Gingerbread Mansion in historic Ferndale, that we chose not to include. Even though some level of public access may be available at many B&Bs, most limit the opportunity to wander their hallways and other rooms only to paying overnight guests.

With our final selections, we have attempted to provide a representative balance across the state. Those who could afford to own mansions during the 19th and early 20th centuries tended to live near major metropolitan areas where their businesses were also located. With most of California's larger cities located in central and southern California, there are significantly fewer homes that can be classified as historic mansions found in the northern reaches of the state, especially mansions that are open to the public.

## The Best Museums

There are hundreds of museums in California. Some are massive, built by the megarich. Often, these places began as their homes and, following their deaths, were transformed to museums to share their private collections with the rest of us. Some of these museums, such as the Getty Center and Villa in Los Angeles and Malibu, and the Huntington Museum in San Marino, likely have annual budgets larger than some third-world nations, and they employ hundreds of paid professional staff and train cadres of docents. The majority of museums in this book do not fall into this category; most are much smaller and depend on grants and donations to continue operating. Most of the artifacts in their collections consist of donations from families who have lived in the area for generations, and they require dedicated volunteers and docents to keep their doors open.

We didn't choose our best museums based strictly on their ability to meet anyone's standards. We didn't choose them because of their size or the value or rarity of their collections, although we certainly considered those things. We looked at many attributes. We considered their uniqueness, not only in the types of collections and the variety of artifacts, but also in how they relate to California's overall history or to their local community's history. We looked at their ties to historical events and the importance of the people responsible for their collections or the significance of the museum building itself. And sometimes we chose a museum simply because of its eclectic collections of fun or weird or unique stuff, such as the International Surfing Museum in Huntington Beach.

California's cultural and economic interests are as varied as its people. There are museums representing nearly every aspect of its historic, cultural, and economic interests. We have museums dedicated to one of California's strangest "athletic" races (Kinetic Sculpture Museum), to a cartoonist (Charles M. Schulz Museum), to US presidents (Nixon and Reagan), to historic aircraft (Castle Air Museum), to historic aircraft carriers (*USS Hornet* and the *USS Midway*), to railroad history (California State Railroad Museum), and to a gaggle of governors (Governor's Mansion State Historic Park, Pardee Home Mansion, and Leland Stanford Mansion State Historic Park).

While we visited many fine "high-tech" museums, such as San Jose's Tech Museum of Innovation and San Diego's Reuben H. Fleet Science Center, ultimately, we decided not to include this category of museum. These institutions are great for hands-on science education exhibits, but they are often short on historic collections representing California's history and culture, which is the focus of this book.


## ABOUT THIS GUIDE

Since the earliest days of statehood, special interests have attempted to divide California into two states, north and south. They haven't yet succeeded. We chose instead to divide California into eight regions (which we use as chapters) based mostly on geography, with consideration for population tossed in. One of the things you will notice is that the more densely populated the area (Los Angeles County vs. Modoc County), the more museums and mansions you will find. We began our great tour in the northwest part of California (Crescent City), and as we made our way to southern California, we crossed back and forth, east and west. Our geographic dividing lines may cause heartache for a few people, at least those who insist that their particular mission, mansion, or museum has been assigned to the "wrong" region.

The **North Coast** region begins at the Oregon border and heads south all the way to Marin County, and it includes portions of the coastal mountains to the east. **Shasta Cascade** is one of our most "gerrymandered" regions, similar to the voting districts our politicians like to create. It swings a crescent-shaped swath around the northern third of the Great Valley, touching the east side of the North Coast region and reaching east to the Oregon and Nevada borders, finally resting at the northern end of the Sierra Nevada. Next comes **San Francisco and Greater Bay Area**, which includes Oakland and goes as far south as San Jose. The **Great Valley** follows and includes the northern Sacramento Valley and the southern San Joaquin Valley, a great swath of farmland and rapidly growing cities.

The **Gold Country and High Sierra** region is about 400 miles long, parallel with much of the east side of the Great Valley. It includes the gold-bearing foothills, better known as the Mother Lode, along Hwy. 49. Back across to the west side of the Great Valley, the **Central Coast** region picks up near the inland city of San Jose and just north of Santa Cruz along the coast. This region includes the inland portion of the coastal mountains, following US 101 along the east side of that range, much as the Spanish missionaries did when establishing this stretch of missions. The Central Coast, for our purposes, ends in the south were Ventura County butts against Los Angeles County just past Point Mugu.

**Los Angeles County**, with its plethora of people, cars, mansions, museums, and a couple of missions, is its own chapter. We've tried to move north to south, east to west within most of the regions, although, for ease of use, we chose to list these destinations alphabetically by their home city. The **South Coast and Desert** is the second of our gerrymandered regions, beginning south of Los Angeles County, encompassing San Diego, and then sweeping east and finally north through the desert region all the way to Death Valley.

Fortunately, we also have included maps (the trip numbers, not trip names, are listed on the maps), cross references, and an index to help everyone find their favorite missions, mansions, and museums. In writing the text, we have attempted to point out the numerous historical links between many of our sites—such as the connections between Sutter's Fort, Bidwell Mansion, Lachryma Montis, and Fort Ross.

## Special Features

Describing more than 135 missions, mansions, and especially museums would be tedious if all we did was talk about their collections. After all, hundreds of California museums hold at least one or two Native American baskets, dozens include collections of art by European masters, and one can describe only so many gold nuggets. In our descriptions of each destination, we decided to focus not just on the collections—although we do cover the contents, collections, and furnishings of these missions, mansions, and museums.

We also devote quite a few words to the history that surrounds these missions, mansions, and museums. Our goal was to place each destination in the context of California's human, cultural, and natural history. That way, in addition to learning about California's unique history by visiting some of its best cultural and historical places, you'll also learn quite a bit just by reading this book. We hope that by reading about the characters behind these places—folks like Huntington, Crocker, Banning, Pio Pico, Lucky Baldwin, and the Temples—you'll begin to see a picture emerge of the people who created California, and how their influence developed the state we know today. And if you're up for a challenge, check out the trivia questions at the start of each chapter and see if you can come up with the answers after reading about the missions, mansions, and museums in that region. If you're stuck, there's a cheat sheet with the trivia answers starting on page 323.

We also have included some special features throughout the book to help you choose the destinations that best suit your particular interests. If you're most interested in seeing a certain type of institution, simply turn to the section "Destinations by Category" (page xix), find the perfect mission, mansion, or museum in the region you'd like to explore, and plan your trip.

If you have more time and would like to travel the state to explore some of these places, each chapter offers a selection of tours (daylong to weeklong) tailored to families, couples, and other individuals with specific interests, such as visiting the missions or seeing homes of famous Californians. These tours include institutions in the book, as well as other sites to visit and activities to do along the way. Each chapter ends with a listing and contact information of the regional travel bureaus where you can obtain additional information on accommodations and more.

## A Final Word

Things change, and that certainly includes the institutions covered in this book. Even during the year we researched, visited, and wrote about these destinations, several changed their prices and hours of operation, and one even changed its official name. Others were planning moves within the next couple of years, and one large museum closed its doors just as we were completing the manuscript.

You should always check websites or call ahead to confirm any of the information we have included in this book. This is especially true regarding admission prices and hours of operation, as most organizations don't advertise price increases very loudly or broadly. During winter, you should also check in advance of your visit whether museums located in the Sierra snow country are open. A few close through part or all of the winter and others shut down during heavy snowfalls when roads are closed awaiting the plow trucks.

Mission San Juan Bautista

Jack London's Wolf House

Fort Crook Museum

9

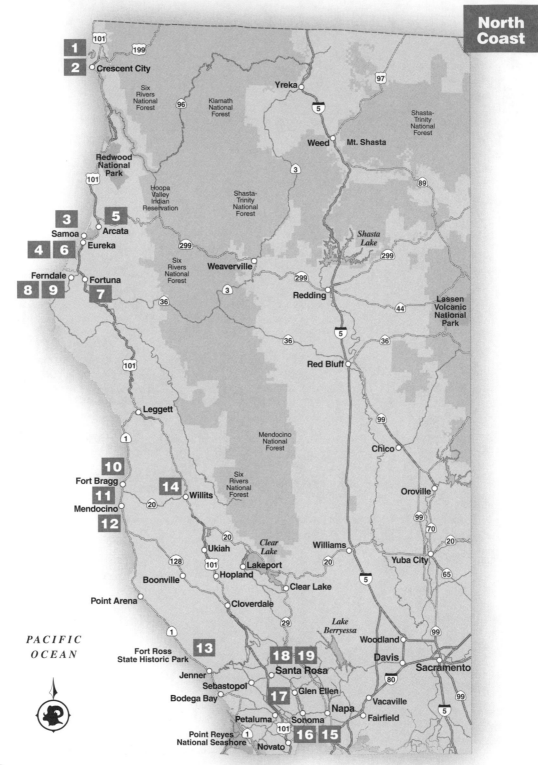

**1**
**2** Crescent City

Yreka

Six Rivers National Forest

Klamath National Forest

Shasta-Trinity National Forest

Weed    Mt. Shasta

Redwood National Park

**3**
**5** Arcata

Samoa

**4**  **6** Eureka

Hoopa Valley Indian Reservation

Shasta-Trinity National Forest

Shasta Lake

Ferndale

**8**  **9**  **7** Fortuna

Weaverville

Six Rivers National Forest

Redding

Lassen Volcanic National Park

Red Bluff

Leggett

Mendocino National Forest

Chico

**10**
Fort Bragg

**11**
Mendocino

**12**

**14** Willits

Six Rivers National Forest

Oroville

Clear Lake

Williams

Ukiah

Yuba City

Boonville    Lakeport
Hopland

Clear Lake

Point Arena    Cloverdale

Lake Berryessa

Woodland

Fort Ross State Historic Park

**13**

**18**  **19**

Santa Rosa

Davis    Sacramento

Jenner
Sebastopol    Glen Ellen
Bodega Bay

**17**    Napa    Vacaville
Petaluma    Sonoma    Fairfield

Point Reyes National Seashore

**16**  **15**

Novato

*PACIFIC OCEAN*

10

# North Coast

Towering redwoods, salmon-filled rivers, eternal fog and rain—California's North Coast remains a place of mystery and beauty. The Native Americans who first settled these lands thrived in a world where food was plentiful and the climate mild. It was a land rich in natural resources, from furs to whales, which first brought the Russians to Fort Ross and later the Americans and others to the great redwood forests spawning generations of loggers who built today's cities and towns.

The North Coast remains relatively isolated, even today. There are no large commercial airports, only a single main highway, US 101, and even its largest cities, Eureka, Arcata, and Crescent City, are reminiscent of small-town America. Traveling almost anywhere along the North Coast is free of LA-type traffic, and its scenic roads, such as Hwy. 1 along the coast and Hwy. 299 that crosses the mountains from east to west, are bordered by the spectacular beauty of towering trees, mountains, and sheer cliffs pounded by ocean waves.

Battery Point Lighthouse

The missions, mansions, and museums along the North Coast are more widely scattered, fewer in number, and smaller in size than those found in the more populated areas of California. Their scarcity does not, however, make them less interesting. Indeed, considering the very different lifestyles and attendant cultural aspects of the North Coast, there often is a special quaintness to the collections found in many of the museums. In Crescent City, you can climb to the top of the town's historic lighthouse. In Eureka, you can dine at the Samoa Cookhouse, where generations of loggers ate their fill, or wander though Fort Ross, which the Russians originally built.

Unfortunately, while there are certainly mansions of significant size and beauty, such as the spectacular Victorian Carson Mansion in Eureka and the stately Victorian mansions of Ferndale, nearly all remain in private ownership, so there is no public access. Yet there are historic homes open to the public. You can visit the ranch home of novelist Jack London, tour the home of Mexican General Mariano Vallejo, or walk the grounds and see where horticultural pioneer Luther Burbank lived. For mission lovers, California's last and most northern mission is located in the wine country town of Sonoma.

## TRIVIA

1 Which lighthouse can be visited only during low tide?

2 Where can you get up close and personal with a living honeybee hive—and not get stung?

3 Where is the only active historic cookhouse for lumberjacks and the public?

4 What military assignment convinced Ulysses S. Grant to resign his commission early in his career?

5 Which museum is devoted to a goofy race that doesn't guarantee the fastest finisher first place?

6 Where can you see a giant slice of Mendocino County's largest redwood ever cut?

7 What fancy home originally came with an octagon-shaped privy?

8 Which fort was built by the Russians?

9 Which California horticulturist created a potato that McDonald's now uses for its famous French fries?

10 Name the childhood pet of Charles Schulz that became the inspiration for Snoopy.

*For trivia answers, see page 323.*

# 1  Battery Point Lighthouse and Museum

**WHAT'S HERE:**  Furnished historic lighthouse and small gift shop
**DON'T MISS THIS:**  The climb to the very top of the lighthouse

Several historic lighthouses in California are open to the public, but the 150-year-old lighthouse in Crescent City is unique in that tours are offered only during low tide. This is because the walk from the mainland parking lot to the rock outcropping that supports the lighthouse requires crossing a stretch of rocky beach submerged during high tide. But the tours of this restored 19th century lighthouse are well worth the strategic waiting.

Originally known as the Crescent City Light Station, Battery Point began operation on December 10, 1856, when an oil lamp first illuminated the fourth-order Fresnel lens. The multifaceted glass lens was designed to greatly extend the power of the early lights, allowing seafarers ample warning of coastal hazards. In 1953, the US Coast Guard automated the light system, installing a drum lens illuminated by a 1000-watt electric bulb. The relatively small light was rated at 20,000 candle power, and in clear weather it could be seen from more than 14 miles away.

During the first century of the lighthouse operation, many of the light keepers who lived on the tiny outpost brought their families. Having school children living at the lighthouse posed a timing problem; often the kids would have to get up very early to make the low tide, and stay in town with friends or relatives if the afternoon tides were not conducive to safely getting home.

Today, the Coast Guard no longer tends the light. In 1982, the Battery Point Lighthouse was leased to the Del Norte County Historical Society, which now is responsible for keeping the light running. The society does this by allowing volunteer light keepers to live in the old lighthouse, maintain the light, and provide public tours.

These tours take visitors inside the early light keepers' living quarters, including the two bedrooms with their great views of the harbor and ocean. Much of the furniture has been in the lighthouse throughout its 150 years of operation, including the government-issued banjo clock that hangs in the living room. Manufactured by the Howard-Davis Company, the key-wound, weight-driven clock is still running.

On the tour, guides may even share stories about the lighthouse's ghosts. According to some, several ghosts haunt the property, including the ghost of Captain Samuel de Wolf, whose ship, *Brother Jonathan*, sank nearby in 1865 with significant loss of life. Another

Lighthouse keeper's master bedroom

13

ghost may be John Jeffery, the keeper who lived at the lighthouse for almost 40 years, beginning in 1875.

Unlike most other lighthouse tours, this one allows visitors to climb up the narrow spiral stairway to the very top of the light tower. The view is spectacular, especially on a clear, fogless day. It apparently provided a great view of the damage wrought by the 1964 tsunami that devastated Crescent City but did no damage to the lighthouse.

When visiting the lighthouse, check the tide schedule and use the restroom facility in the A Street parking lot, as there are no public restroom facilities on the lighthouse grounds.

> **HOURS:** April through September, Wednesday through Sunday, 10 AM to 4 PM, when low tides permit safe pedestrian access to the lighthouse island.
> **COST:** Adults, $3; 12 and under, $1.
> **LOCATION:** At the end of A Street, Crescent City
> **PHONE:** 707-464-3089 or 707-464-3922
> **WEBSITE:** www.delnortehistory.org

# 2  Del Norte County Museum

**WHAT'S HERE:** Indian baskets and 19th century local history exhibits

**DON'T MISS THIS:** The St. George lighthouse first-order Fresnel lens

Often, historical buildings find new life as museums; such is the case in Crescent City, the largest community in Del Norte County and the last major California city before the Oregon border. The old County Hall of Records building, constructed in 1926, also served as the county jail during its official days. The county vacated the building in 1963, and it became the county museum just two years later. Today, the museum offers a look at the county's history, much of which involved lumber and the fishing industry. Several of the old cells remain on the second floor, serving as extra exhibit space.

Prior to the arrival of the Spanish (and later, the Americans) in California,

Balcony view of the first-order Fresnel lens

Native Americans had lived relatively easy lives in this area for thousands of years. The museum's collections of primarily Tolowa and Yurok baskets, tools, and other ephemera is reasonably representative of other regional museum collections. With the prevalence of fishing along the North Coast, the collection includes various fishing nets and traps, in addition to numerous baskets of various sizes designed for many different uses, from food gathering to storage.

Many of the displays include information about the small town's history. Today, logging and fishing are on the wane, and the biggest employer in the area is the infamous Pelican Bay State Prison, which houses many of California's most notorious convicted criminals. Yet the prison is not what first brought worldwide attention to Crescent City; that title belongs to the 1964 tsunami. That year, the Anchorage earthquake set off a fast-moving and powerful wall of water that devastated much of the downtown commercial area before receding. The museum has numerous before-and-after photos and newspaper articles about this tragedy.

This is one of those museums that collects and provides exhibit space for just about anything old. While that may create a cluttered appearance for some of the exhibits, it also provides an opportunity to see a lot of the personal memorabilia—the stuff that ordinary people found useful or sentimental during their lives, from war souvenirs to quilts to personal photos and official documents.

One of the biggest and rarest artifacts is the first-order Fresnel lens that is mounted in the rear of the museum. The lens originally came from the St. George Reef Lighthouse, which sits precariously on a reef jutting from the Pacific Ocean about 9 nautical miles northwest of Crescent City. When the lighthouse was operational with this lens, mariners could see its warning light up to 18 miles away. The lens rises from the museum's first floor through the second floor, offering easy viewing of the entire prism structure that was originally invented by Augustin-Jean Fresnel (1788–1827) during the early 1820s. The concentric glass prismatic rings surround a central glass bull's-eye, which redirects the light into a powerful, focused beam.

For those who think that life along the North Coast was all work and no fun, one exhibit dispels such notions. On the second floor, you'll find early stills, bottles, jugs, and other tools required to produce less-than-fine sipping whiskey, although the concoction likely accomplished the job for which it was intended.

Other exhibits include farm and creamery equipment, 19th century clothing, musical instruments, and furniture. Inside one of the jail cells are saddles, cattle brands, woodworking tools, and locksmiths' tools. There is more than enough here to keep anyone busy for an hour or more wandering among the hundreds of artifacts.

**HOURS:** May through September, Monday through Saturday, 10 AM to 4 PM.

**COST:** Adults, $3; under 12, $1.

**LOCATION:** 577 H Street, Crescent City

**PHONE:** 707-464-3922

**WEBSITE:** www.delnortehistory.org

# 3 Samoa Cookhouse Museum

**WHAT'S HERE:** Many exhibits on early logging equipment
**DON'T MISS THIS:** The food!

The North Coast's history revolves around logging, and to some extent a logger's best friend is good food and lots of it. The more successful logging companies knew that their loggers worked best on full stomachs, and the Samoa Cookhouse, located in Samoa, just across the bridge from Eureka, is the last remaining logging company cookhouse in the West. Built in 1885, the cookhouse served some of the best food a logger could get anywhere, a sure way of retaining its employees. The great thing about this place is that the cookhouse still serves hearty meals, but now to the general public.

The first thing you'll likely notice as you pass through the front door and into the covered entryway is the large menu written on a blackboard. Just like during its time as a lumberjack cookhouse, each day brings a different menu for breakfast, lunch, and dinner, along with a set price for each meal. No large menu to ponder, no difficult decisions to make. It could be ham, eggs, pancakes, rolls, gravy, and toast for breakfast, with equally hearty meals for lunch and dinner, plus dessert. And as long as you can keep eating, they'll keep bringing you food.

Inside the historic cookhouse, you sit at one of the dozen or more long tables, each covered with a red-and-white-checkered oil cloth, and your food is served family style. But eating is only half the fun. You are surrounded by dozens of photos and hundreds of logging-related artifacts from the old days. Company hardhats hang from the wall as do well-worn utensils from meals prepared here 50 to 100 years ago. Take time from eating to wander to the far end of the dining hall, and you are greeted by a plethora of the company's 19th and early 20th century office machines and logging equipment. While this may not be considered a "true" museum by some, it certainly draws you back to the 1890s with its ambiance, its food, and the surrounding historic artifacts.

Very few of the items are labeled, but they are fascinating in their own right. One area is filled with early chain saws, many of which are bigger than any two men could move. And there are old saw blades, including a big circular mill blade, and many designs of the long, narrow blades, some 10 and 15 feet long, that attached to seemingly ancient gasoline-powered saws used before the introduction of chain saws. There's one of the original wood-fired stoves from the cookhouse, a piano, a safe, office adding machines, and old invoices from past transactions.

Since the main focus of the cookhouse was and remains food, one specialty item

Samoa Cookhouse logging tool collection

draws locals into the cookhouse daily—fresh bread made by the cookhouse bakers nearly every day. The loaves are sold, usually very quickly, as they come hot out of the oven. Since the daily supply is limited, it's wise to arrive early if you'd like to share in one of the locals' favorite gastronomical secrets.

**HOURS:** Monday through Saturday: breakfast, 7 AM to 11 AM; lunch, 11 AM to 3:30 PM; dinner, 5 PM to 9 PM. Sunday: breakfast, 7 AM to noon; lunch, noon to 4 PM; dinner, 4 PM to 9 PM. Closed Christmas and Thanksgiving.

**COST:** Museum free; meals are moderately priced.

**LOCATION:** From US 101 in north Eureka, take the Hwy. 255 (Samoa Blvd.) bridge over Humboldt Bay. The road dead-ends into Samoa Blvd; turn left, then take the first left at the driveway (follow the signs) that will take you up the hill to the cookhouse.

**PHONE:** 707-442-1659

**WEBSITE:** No official website; information is available at www.humboldtdining.com/cookhouse.

# 4  Clarke Historical Museum

**WHAT'S HERE:** Re-created and furnished Victorian rooms

**DON'T MISS THIS:** The dugout canoe exhibited at the New York World's Fair in the 1940s

This museum, situated in Old Town Eureka, is located in what was once the Bank of Eureka building. The museum tells the story of Eureka's prominent place in the history of California's North Coast through a series of panels and exhibits on the gold, lumber, farming, and maritime history that brought jobs and homes to many and riches to few.

As was the case for so many of California's early and more prominent homes and commercial buildings, the bank building was designed by San Francisco architect Albert Pissis. Constructed in 1912, this corner landmark building, with its formal columns and glazed terra-cotta facade, is unusual in appearance for the North Coast.

The bank building served its intended purpose until 1960, when local teacher Cecile Clarke purchased the structure to house her extensive collection of artifacts related to Eureka's early history. An annex was added in 1979 for her significant Native American collection. Today, that gallery holds an impressive array of artifacts ranging from fishing nets and projectile points to ceremonial blades and drums. There is also an extensive collection of Pacific Northwest Indian baskets.

Not seen in most museum collections are traditional bows fashioned from yew by the local Karuk, Yurok, and Hupa Indians. Their rather stubby bow design, about 3 inches wide and 3 feet long, shares only the rudimentary appearance and operation of modern bows. Another much larger wooden item displayed here that was commonly constructed and used by the Native Americans throughout the Pacific Northwest is the dugout canoe. This dugout, originally built by a local Yurok who was born in 1900, was exhibited at the New York World's Fair during the 1940s.

The museum's main gallery, which is essentially the entire original bank building, holds numerous exhibits related to the area's history. Within the large gallery, the Clarke Historical Museum staff regularly change several of its exhibits, an uncommon practice in many small-town museums. Here, you will find re-creations of Victorian rooms filled with furnishings, right down to the papers and books that would have appeared in homes during the late 19th and early 20th centuries. There is a tea set that belonged to H.H. Buhne, who owned one of Eureka's first commercial buildings and was the first ship's pilot to enter Humboldt Bay in 1850. Buhne's building, about two blocks away, houses a small maritime museum today.

The 1940s dental office that has the original x-ray machine may bring back old fears for some. The museum's other numerous exhibit cases hold everything from 19th century cookbooks and toys to antique guns and minerals.

**HOURS:** Tuesday through Saturday, 11 AM to 4 PM. Closed Thanksgiving, Christmas, and New Year's Day.

**COST:** Free

**LOCATION:** 240 E Street, Eureka

**PHONE:** 707-443-1947

**WEBSITE:** www.clarkemuseum.org

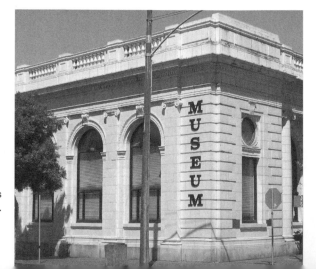

A 1912-era bank now serves as Eureka's Clarke Historical Museum.

# 5 Humboldt State University Natural History Museum

**WHAT'S HERE:** Fossil and bug collections, and microscopes for kids to explore nature

**DON'T MISS THIS:** The living honeybee hive

Rich and relatively unspoiled, California's North Coast is ideal for natural history research, and Humboldt State University takes advantage of this environment through its many resource-management courses and programs. One offshoot of the university's work is their small but kid-friendly museum located in Arcata. If you've ever wondered how fossils came to be, or which butterflies call California home, or what lives in the coast's rocky tide pools, this museum has exhibits that solve those mysteries—and more.

The fossil exhibit explains the different kinds of fossils and the many ways in which dead plants and small animals are transformed into something much more resilient. Some are turned to stone, such as petrified wood, others are carbonized through burial where the soft tissue decays, leaving a thin film of carbon, and some are created through burial and hardened by surrounding sediments that penetrate their cells. The accompanying fossil exhibit covers 1.9 billion years of life on earth. Fossil displays include the more commonly found trilobites, relatively small marine creatures that lived as long as 600 million years ago. Other fossils include less common crinoids, pygmy mammoth teeth, and insects trapped in amber—really ancient dead bugs that in past decades have driven creative minds into making dinosaur movies.

The museum also houses extensive bug collections, with tiny beetles and giant beetles and tons of bugs in between. The butterfly collection features more than 70 percent of all the species of butterflies that either live year round in California or pass through on migrations between North, Central, and South America.

Another exhibit reveals what most of us never see while exploring the North Coast's rocky beaches: There are representative invertebrates found in local tide pools or often

washed up dead on the beaches, from purple sea urchins and blood stars to rock snails and hoof snails. Although they are not alive, there is an exhibit of some 15 different crabs found in this part of the Pacific, ranging from the very common red crab that often outnumbers the more desirable Dungeness crabs in local crab pots (traps), to the much less common red king crabs and moss crabs.

This museum explores North Coast natural history, from prehistoric to present.

Kids will especially appreciate this hands-on museum. There are microscopes that allow them to get up close and friendly with butterfly wings, paper wasp nests, whale baleen, and fossils. An extraordinarily fascinating exhibit that isn't actually interactive, at least with people, is the beehive. It's a real, active hive with clear windows on each side that reveal the bees' honey-making activities. Honeybees come and go as they would in the wild, but not to fear—the hive's entrance and exit is through a small, protected pipe that opens to the outside of the building.

> **HOURS:** Tuesday through Saturday, 10 AM to 5 PM. Closed state and federal holidays.
> **COST:** Free, but a donation is requested.
> **LOCATION:** 1315 G Street, Arcata
> **PHONE:** 707-826-4479
> **WEBSITE:** www.humboldt.edu

# 6  Fort Humboldt State Historic Park

**WHAT'S HERE:**  Historic logging equipment and reconstructed military buildings

**DON'T MISS THIS:**  The steam donkeys, especially on steam-up days

Taking the high ground has always been a good military strategy. When the US Army arrived in Eureka in 1853, ostensibly to ease the tensions between the local Indians and the settlers and gold seekers streaming into the county, they chose a hill overlooking the bay as their high point. Here they constructed Fort Humboldt, which would become California's most northern coastal military headquarters.

The isolation that the soldiers encountered made Fort Humboldt one of the less-desirable assignments. The misery of the place caused at least one young officer to resign his commission, at least temporarily, after only six months. That officer was Captain Ulysses S. Grant, who had been sent here following his more illustrious and decoration-producing assignment in the Mexican-American War. He later became one of the Civil War's most famous generals.

The Army eventually abandoned Fort Humboldt and its 14 buildings. Today, only the original hospital building remains, although several others, including the surgeon's quarters, have been reconstructed on the site. The buildings are spread out around a large, open area, a great place for the kids to run across the field and carve out shortcuts between the pathways to the different buildings, while adults enjoy the incredible views of Humboldt Bay.

A small museum is situated near the north end of the parking lot. Although the Army fort had nothing to do with logging, most of the museum is dedicated to the local logging industry. Inside, you can view photos and interpretive panels depicting and explaining historic logging operations, old saws and axes, and even the special caulk boots that had spiked soles, which allowed loggers to walk on wet, slippery logs.

Outside, a walkway meanders through another display, where the really big equipment sits. There is also a log cabin, railroad tracks, a rail car, and a logging bobbie. The logging bobbie, a trailer used for transporting logs, could be adjusted to carry any size log. It was used at the Holmes Eureka Sawmill, which was located just down Hwy. 1 on land now occupied by the sprawling Bayshore Mall. Among the many pieces of equipment are Dolbeer steam donkeys, invented by Eureka's own John Dolbeer in 1882 and designed to replace oxen as the favored means of moving giant redwood logs. The "portable" steam-powered wench pulled itself through the forests on cables, dragging cut logs over "skid roads."

During the last weekend in April, staff and docents fire up some of the old equipment, including a Dolbeer steam donkey, for the annual Dolbeer Steam Donkey Days and Logging Contest. There are also summer steam-ups scheduled for the third Saturday of May through September. This is the perfect time to see locally famous "Lucy," the Bear Harbor Lumber Company's Gypsy Locomotive #1.

**HOURS:** Park open daily, 8 AM to 4:30 PM; museum may be closed during winter if staff is unavailable to open.

**COST:** Free

**LOCATION:** 3431 Fort Street, just off US 101, near the south end of Eureka.

**PHONE:** 707-445-6567

**WEBSITE:** www.parks.ca.gov/parkindex

Gypsy Locomotive #1 is just one of the museum's steam-era logging machines.

# 7 **Fortuna Depot Museum**

**WHAT'S HERE:** Collections of all kinds, from fishing gear to spark plugs

**DON'T MISS THIS:** The personal items of Paul Hill, who charged San Juan Hill with Teddy Roosevelt in 1898

Just a few blocks from US 101 in the small town of Fortuna, a historic train depot now serves as a museum. An active depot for the Northwestern Pacific Railroad from 1893 until 1965, it was originally constructed at the foot of 7th Street, near the Eel River. The building was moved to land donated for a public park by the descendents of pioneer Heinrich Rohner. The land's original purchase document, a government letter patent signed by President Lincoln, is displayed in the museum.

The museum is painted the typical cream-yellow with brown trim that is found on so many early train depots. Walk through the front door, and you've entered a restored waiting room that includes exhibits of early railroading. Stroll through the doorway toward the back where the clerks would have worked and the baggage would have been checked, and you've enter a different world. Here, panels tell the story of some of the more prominent locals and their families, including Swiss immigrant Heinrich Rohner. Born in 1829, Rohner immigrated to California during the 1849 rush for gold and then headed north on the advice of fellow Swiss settler John Sutter (see Sutter's Fort State Historic Park, page 123). Rohner was a miner, farmer, and newspaper printer, which was a job he held until a disgruntled reader shot his boss, the editor, convincing Rohner to change careers.

The back room houses collections that are amusing, amazing, and eclectic, most having little or nothing to do with railroading, but much to do with local community life and the history of Fortuna. For mechanics, there is a display of old engine spark plugs—probably more than 100 different brands, sizes, and vintages—and a wall of wrenches. For fishermen, dozens of very old fishing rods, reels, and lures line a portion of one wall and a shelf. And for ranching history buffs, the collection of early barbed wire is one of the largest to be found anywhere, each sample piece dated and its manufacturer identified; there are probably more than 300 samples, most from the 19th century, but also some that were used by the Germans and Allies during the World Wars. And the museum doesn't leave out locksmiths, with a very large and varied collection of old padlocks.

Among the other artifacts are various steel animal traps, farming and logging equipment, and a huge brass Swiss

The restored Fortuna Depot is typical of early train station architecture.

cheese kettle for making cheese. In one corner is a collection from Paul Hill, one of the locals, who in 1898 rode with Teddy Roosevelt's Rough Riders on their famous charge up San Juan Hill during the Spanish-American War in 1898. His shooting jacket, shotgun, and shell-reloading equipment are exhibited.

**HOURS:** June through August, daily, noon to 4:30 PM; September through May, Thursday through Sunday, noon to 4:30 PM.

**COST:** Free

**LOCATION:** 4 Park Street, Rohner Park

**PHONE:** 707-725-7645

**WEBSITE:** gov.sunnyfortuna.com/museum/index.htm

# 8  Ferndale Museum

**WHAT'S HERE:** Re-created 19th century rooms, from bedrooms to kitchens

**DON'T MISS THIS:** The active seismograph

The Victorian town of Ferndale is a visual delight, with its gaily painted 19th century homes. Unfortunately, the famous architecture is nearly all privately owned, so thousands of visitors each year can only look, never tour. But just a block off Main Street sits a museum that provides a trip back 100 years and more into the town's past.

The Ferndale Museum offers splendid historical exhibits and provides a make-believe town street, which you can stroll down and peek through windows and doors of what could have been homes and businesses in early-day Ferndale. The museum is filled with items that have survived the past century or more; a kitchen, dining room, bedrooms, and a parlor allow a look at the furniture, tools, and more that Ferndale's ancestors used in their daily lives.

The last of Pacific Telephone's switchboards, used between 1952 and 1983, where operators actually rearranged corded plugs to connect callers, is housed here. For those whose only experience in life is with cell and push-button phones, there's an old crank telephone you can use to call from one of the museum's rooms to another.

More "old" technology awaits in a room with the original Bosch-Omori seismograph. It is actually two seismographs with one set to measure north to south and the second to measure seismic activity from east to west. It is still active—you can see what kind of earth-shaking activity has been occurring for the last week or so anywhere in the region. For fun, kids can compare the current activity with the length of the seismic lines on the accompanying graph from the 1906 San Francisco earthquake.

In the annex, which is just through an inside door on the left of the main building, there are more exhibits. The collection spans much of Ferndale's earlier history, from blacksmithing exhibits to everything related to the ranching and dairy industries, including cattle brands.

Situated close to the ocean, Ferndale also has a rich nautical history, which is represented in the museum. There are also artifacts from whaling, another popular industry in early California. And if you thought that Bakersfield or the Southern California beaches were where the first of California's commercial oil wells were drilled, you'd be wrong. The very first oil well in California was drilled in 1865 about 35 miles south of Ferndale in the tiny community of Petrolia, and there are parts of that first well on display here.

Since Ferndale is noted for its milk and cheese—perhaps the reason some people referred to the town's Victorian houses and commercial buildings as "buttermilk palaces" —the museum houses a collection of farm implements such as cow-milking equipment from previous generations of dairy farmers.

For those professional and amateur woodworkers who can remember the day when large pieces of fine-grained wood were relatively easy to come by, a little nostalgia awaits. Hanging on a wall is something seldom seen anymore–a solid, 3-inch-thick board that is 6 feet wide and 12 feet long.

**HOURS:** February through December, Wednesday through Saturday, 11 AM to 4 PM; June through September, Tuesday through Saturday, 11 AM to 4 PM, and Sunday, 1 PM to 4 p.m; closed Mondays and the month of January.

**COST:** Adults, $1; 6–16, $0.50; under 6 (must be accompanied by an adult), free.

**LOCATION:** 515 Shaw Street, about one block north of Main Street, Ferndale

**PHONE:** 707-786-4466

**WEBSITE:** www.ferndale-museum.org

From butter churns to washboards, the museum is a slice of 19th and early 20th century life.

# Kinetic Sculpture Museum

**WHAT'S HERE:** Human-powered race car art vehicles

**DON'T MISS THIS:** The "Old Lady and the Shoe" race car

Eclectic is certainly one term and weird is another, but you may have to invent a new word to accurately describe what is inside the Kinetic Sculpture Museum. Partially hidden in the back of a building on Ferndale's Main Street, this museum requires a little history to explain why anyone would create such a place.

In 1969, so the unofficial story goes, Ferndale artist Hobart Brown made "artistic augmentations" to his son's tricycle, rearranging the pedals, replacing the handlebars with a small steering wheel, and adding high-rising extensions to the seatback. Inspired by this newly minted human-powered transportation device, Brown's neighbors decided to borrow their own kids' tricycles and do the same. In the good old American spirit of competition, a challenge quickly followed, and a race was set. By the time their scheduled Memorial Day race arrived, a few thousand people showed up to witness the art-to-art competition. And the rest, they say, is history.

Every year since then, artists, mechanical engineers, and just fun-loving crazily creative people show up with their art contraptions for what is now a three-day, 40-mile race of pedal-powered vehicles that bear little resemblance to those simple tricycles that started the whole craze. The race begins north in Arcata, where the human-powered vehicles travel over back roads and US 101, crossing sandy beaches, dunes, and mud. The real test comes when they reach the water crossing. Suddenly, the competitors must push pedals that somehow turn props or paddles or something that will propel them through water. And then those slick wheels must again gain traction on equally slick mud as they attempt to get back to dry land. Mechanical breakdowns and sinking pieces of art are the norm.

But engineering excellence, physical strength, stamina, and crossing the finish line first on Ferndale's Main Street do not guarantee the championship. Points are added for the

creative aspect of the competing "kinetic sculptures." So while the giant yellow duck whose racers spent the previous night camping in the bushes (camping is required to win a trophy) might power past the lumbering dragon and the oversized crab just yards before reaching the finish line, it may not be declared the ultimate winner. The fourth place whimsical whammy machine could be declared the grand trophy winner. The race begins at noon on Saturday of the

One result of creative minds combining art with mechanical locomotion

Memorial Day weekend at the Arcata Plaza, and by Sunday most have made it to the water crossing that begins in Eureka on Humboldt Bay. Monday brings the contraptions to the finish line in Ferndale. Even if you can't make this entertaining event, don't miss the museum, which holds numerous old and retired race machines. Here's your chance to see up close how artists and engineers work together to create race-day masterpieces. Among other "artifacts" is a real car, its engine removed and replaced by pure pedal power, a giant shoe, and other mechanical conveyances that defy description.

> **HOURS:** Daily, 10 AM to 5 PM. Closed holidays.
> **COST:** Free
> **LOCATION:** Ink People Center, 580 Main Street, Ferndale
> **PHONE:** 707-845-1717
> **WEBSITE:** www.kineticsculpturerace.org

# 10 Guest House Museum

**WHAT'S HERE:** Fort Bragg's most elaborate historic Victorian mansion and museum

**DON'T MISS THIS:** The giant slice of Mendocino County's largest logged redwood tree in front of the house

Mendocino County's gold rush wasn't for the yellow metal but the giant redwood and Douglas fir forests that covered nearly every mountain along the coast. Fort Bragg became one of the key lumber mill and shipping towns in the county. In 1882, an ambitious 23-year-old from Michigan, Charles Russell Johnson, arrived in the area. He soon owned his own lumber mill and prospered selling his prime redwood lumber to the new cities born out of the Gold Rush. Johnson laid out the streets for the new town, and in 1889, he was elected mayor of his newly founded city of Fort Bragg. It didn't hurt that he had the financial backing of his father and business friends back in Michigan.

By 1891, Johnson was becoming richer, having merged his company with others to create the Union Lumber Company. But as many newly successful businessmen were prone to do, Johnson wanted to exhibit his success in a more obvious manner. "C.R.," as he was often called by friends and family, decided to build an elaborate Victorian mansion on a knoll overlooking the city's main street. The mansion was to serve as a guest house for out-of-town business executives, friends, and for himself when he traveled to Fort Bragg from his company's new San Francisco headquarters.

The Guest House was constructed from 67,000 board feet of lumber—and not just any lumber. He used the finest old-growth redwood and Douglas fir that Union Lumber Company could cut and mill. More concerned about appearance than practicality, Johnson built 12-foot ceilings. They were designed to impress visitors, not to reduce heating costs—although, with seven fireplaces and a company that owned thousands of acres of timber, firewood was never a problem. Over the years, the number of fireplaces has been reduced to just three, some destroyed by the 1906 San Francisco earthquake and not replaced, others removed when a more modern heating system was introduced.

Johnson spared no expense in finishing the house, with its beautiful redwood stairway banisters, elaborately carved and milled window and door moldings and trim, and the colorful leaded-glass windows. He included electric lighting in all of the rooms except the kitchen. It was a time when many men drank alcohol yet considered it inappropriate to be kept in one's home, so Johnson had a wet bar designed on the first floor that could be concealed. He often brought his male guests to the third floor, with its commanding views of the city, where they could meet, talk, smoke, and play billiards—but apparently not drink.

The historic mansion also displays many photographs of Johnson's Union Lumber Company facilities and its operations in the Fort Bragg area. The second floor exhibits focus on the shipping problems and solutions along this rugged coast, as well as some of the other coastal lumber mills and the railroad that pulled everything together.

Near the Main Street entrance to the mansion grounds is a slice of a giant redwood tree, thought to be the largest redwood tree ever to grow in Mendocino County. In 190 AD, it was a mere seedling; when finally cut in 1943, the redwood was 1800 years old and 334 feet tall. It took about 60 hours to cut the tree with the 22-foot-long Spaulding scale hand saw.

**HOURS:** May through October, Monday though Thursday, 11 AM to 2 PM, and Friday through Sunday, 10 AM to 4 PM; November through April: Friday through Sunday, 10 AM to 4 PM. Call to confirm, as hours during May and October may be changed and winter hours are occasionally extended to midweek. For groups of six or more, please call ahead for a reservation.

**COST:** Donation requested.

**LOCATION:** 343 North Main Street, Fort Bragg

**PHONE:** 707-964-4251 or 707-961-2840

**WEBSITE:** None

Built originally as a showpiece, the 19th century home has not lost its status.

# 11 **Point Cabrillo Light Station**

**WHAT'S HERE:** Lighthouse that was built to protect ships supplying lumber to rebuild San Francisco following the 1906 earthquake

**DON'T MISS THIS:** Whale-watching during winter and spring

Following the 1906 San Francisco earthquake, the high demand for lumber to rebuild the city spurred a significant increase in maritime lumber trade up and down California's coast. That increase in sailing ships braving California's treacherous coast prompted the government to build additional lighthouses, including the Point Cabrillo Light Station, to help assure safe passage for the ships.

Although initial surveys had been made in 1873 for the Point Cabrillo Light Station to be located about 6 miles south of Fort Bragg, construction of the light station—and its all important lighthouse—was completed on June 10, 1909. Support buildings included three light keepers' residences, carpenter and blacksmith shops, an oil house, barn, water towers, and pump house. Some of these structures, such as the barn and two water towers, have since been removed, but the lighthouse, most of the outbuildings, and the keepers' homes are still here.

The lighthouse contains a third-order Fresnel lens that is still operating today, its light is visible from up to 15 miles away. It has been updated over the years, though, with its lantern wick replaced by a light bulb, and its rotation powered by an electric motor instead of the original weighted chain that had to be reset every two hours. It also has the distinction of being one of only three operating Fresnel lenses that were manufactured in Great Britain. The other two are bigger and brighter first- and second-order lenses at Heceta Head lighthouse in Oregon and on Staten Island, New York. Each lighthouse is assigned a distinctive timed pattern of light flashes, controlled by its rotational speed; Point Cabrillo's light flashes every 10 seconds. This assures that ship captains can identify their locations along the coast even in the heaviest of fog, as long as they can see the lighthouse lights.

From the parking lot and visitor center, it is a half-mile walk out to the light station. Anyone with a handicapped license plate or permit may drive out to the light station parking area. The walk is pleasant and provides an opportunity to see numerous birds, deer, and other wildlife along a narrow dirt road.

Point Cabrillo Light Station is a restoration work in progress. The lighthouse itself is now a small museum and gift shop. The museum's exhibits tell the story of shipping along the California coast in the 19th century. One account describes a ship named *Frolic* that was built in Baltimore in 1844 and was assigned to run opium from India to China, a profitable and, at the time, legal business. The vessel was designed to be fast enough to outrun pirates and others interested in stealing its cargo. In 1850, while heading to San Francisco from China, the 97-foot brig struck a reef near Point Cabrillo and sank. The crew abandoned ship and the local Indians acquired its cargo as it washed ashore. In more recent years, the wreck was rediscovered by divers, and research continues on the ship.

Although all of the light keepers' homes remain, so far, only the East House has been restored. Its exterior appears as it did when constructed in 1909, but inside, several of the rooms have been kept as they likely were in the 1930s, primarily so electricity could be retained in the home. Early artisans used many tricks to make common construction materials appear more like their more expensive counterparts. An example here is the "subway tile" that is actually plaster that has been grooved and painted to appear as the real thing. It was copied from a technique used in the New York subway, thus the name.

Today, the light station is operated by the nonprofit Point Cabrillo Lightkeepers Association. Several of the reconstructed and restored historic buildings are part of a bed-and-breakfast facility, open to the public. It's a great opportunity to spend time on a truly beautiful part of the California coast, after everyone else goes home.

**HOURS:** Park is open daily, 8 AM to 6 PM; light station is open daily, 11 AM to 4:30 PM; Farmhouse Visitors Center (at main parking lot) is open Thursday through Monday, 10 AM to 4 PM; light keeper's home and museum is open Saturday and Sunday, 11 AM to 4 PM.

**COST:** Free

**LOCATION:** Two miles north of Mendocino on Hwy. 1, turn onto Point Cabrillo Road at Russian Gulch and follow the signs about 1.3 miles.

**PHONE:** 707-937-0816

**WEBSITE:** www.pointcabrillo.org

The Point Cabrillo Light Station beacon lights the way on a typical North Coast foggy day.

# 12 **Kelley House Museum**

**WHAT'S HERE:** Restored and furnished Victorian home and museum
**DON'T MISS THIS:** The balloon architecture of the home

Compared with the inflated prices for land along the Mendocino coast today, you could get a bargain in 1854. That was the year William Kelley purchased most of the Mendocino peninsula for $2650. Kelley came by way of ship from Prince Edward Island, Canada, just two years earlier. He soon made his fortune in the retail business and as part owner of the local lumber mill. Kelley decided to bring his new wife, Eliza, to the wilds of this northern California lumber town in 1855. Here, she lived below her Victorian status for the first few years, until her husband completed their new home in 1861.

From either outside or inside the two-story home, it is difficult to see the pre-1930s balloon construction technique used. Unlike today's multistory homes, which are built one level at a time with a new sub-floor and a new set of wall studs added for each level, balloon construction dictated that the wall studs run from ground level to the second-floor roof level, about 20 feet or so. Back in Kelley's time they could easily mill 20-foot-long two-by-fours that were straight–something of a problem with today's second- and third-growth trees. The west-facing wall, which must deflect the heavy winter storms, is constructed with more expensive and weather-proof tongue-and-groove redwood.

During the home's construction, Eliza Kelley required some level of adherence to Victorian design values. Most of the interior walls were covered with wallpaper, but likely the absence of large oak trees in redwood and pine country dictated the use of random-width pine boards for the floors. Nonetheless, with only three other families in Mendocino deemed of acceptable social standing, there were not a lot of people to impress.

Today, the home's interior is part museum and part restored Victorian home. Photos of early logging show how the big redwood logs were cabled down from the high coastal cliffs and loaded onto waiting ships, most for transport south to San Francisco. Much of the history of Mendocino awaits those who visit the mansion, which is home to the Mendocino Historical Research, Inc., a nonprofit organization that runs the house.

Some of the upstairs bedrooms have been restored and filled with Victorian-era furnishings. The master bedroom, although not furnished as such, provides a spectacular view overlooking the bay. The Kelley's four children, two boys and two girls, had bedrooms with lesser views.

The original home did not come with indoor toilets, but the octagon-shaped privy outside could accommodate five at a time. Today, the privy is used for storage.

The backyard view of this 19th century lumber mill owner's home

Gardens and lawn surround the home, which sits behind the white picket fence on its south-facing side. Actually, the south side offers the best view of the home, even though it is the back of the house. It can be accessed from Main Street, near old town Mendocino's business district.

> **HOURS:** June through September, daily, 1 PM to 4 PM; October through May, Friday through Monday, 1 PM to 4 PM.
>
> **COST:** Suggested donation is $2.
>
> **LOCATION:** 45007 Albion Street, Mendocino
>
> **PHONE:** 707-937-5791
>
> **WEBSITE:** mendocinohistory.org/index.html

# 13 Fort Ross State Historic Park

**WHAT'S HERE:** Museum of California's Russian history

**DON'T MISS THIS:** The rebuilt Russian church and the bell outside

In the early 1800s, a Russian fur trader named Ivan Kuskov built Russia's first and only fort in what was to become California—on a bluff overlooking the Pacific Ocean just north of what is today the sleepy seaside town of Jenner, along Hwy. 1. As early as 1742, Russian fur traders in search of valuable pelts had begun to move both south and east from Siberia, arriving in Alaska by 1784 and establishing settlements there. In 1809, the adventurous Kuskov sailed down the West Coast of North America to the Bodega Bay area, and the 40 Russians and the 150 native Alaskans who accompanied him triumphantly returned to their Alaskan settlements with more than 2000 sea otter pelts. Two years later, Kuskov returned to establish a permanent settlement that he named "Ross."

Constructed as a prominent and protective fort with stout redwood walls and cannons aimed out its corner blockhouses, the colony's main purpose was to grow wheat and fruit and raise other foods that could be sent north to the Alaskan settlements where short growing seasons prohibited most agricultural endeavors. They continued to harvest sea otter pelts, but the mammal's population was decimated by 1820, essentially ending the fur trade.

By 1839, the Russians decided to abandon what they called the Ross colony, hoping to sell it to the Hudson's Bay Company, the oldest operating corporation in North America at that time. After attempts to sell failed, John Sutter, who in 1839 had come to California and founded New Helvetia (also called Sutter's Fort) near the confluence of the

31

Sacramento and American rivers to the southeast (see Sutter's Fort State Historic Park, page 123), agreed to purchase the fort in 1841. The Russians soon left, and Sutter sent his trusted business associate, John Bidwell (see Bidwell Mansion State Historic Park, page 119), to Fort Ross to secure everything of value, including herds of livestock.

In 1843, Wilhelm Otto Benitz took over management of Fort Ross for Sutter and eventually purchased the property. Through the remainder of the 19th century, the property passed through other owners, including James Dixon and Lord Fairfax, who ran a lumber operation until 1872. George W. Call acquired the property as part of the 15,000-acre Call Ranch. He added a wharf and a 180-foot-long chute that moved various products, including lumber, from shore to ships waiting safely out from the shoreline cliffs and rocks. The Call family owned Fort Ross until 1903, when the California Historical Landmarks Committee purchased it; it became a state historic park a few years later. Over all those years, settlers and others stripped away most of the fort's timber.

Today, the main fort has been reconstructed, including the heavy redwood stockade walls. Adjacent to the parking lot and nearby the actual fort is a small museum that is one of the most comprehensive Russian, Alaskan, and native Kashaya cultural museums in the state. Its displays, which include artifacts from archeological digs on the fort grounds, provide an excellent overview of this period of Russian occupation.

It's a short walk from the museum past the gardens and into the fort. There are only five buildings inside the tall redwood walls, but they have been reconstructed and filled with items that make it appear as though the Russians aren't far away. Supplies are stored in some rooms, simple furniture similar to what the Russians likely used is in others, and tools cover work tables and the walls where the fort's craftsmen worked.

Kuskov's two-story house, sitting prominently next to the fort's small chapel, includes exhibits such as an armory filled with rifles, powder, and cannonballs for the blockhouses' artillery. There is also a room that contains samples of late 18th and early 19th century scientific instruments, as well as numerous plant and other samples. They may seem out of place here, but the items are appropriate; the Russians were leaders throughout the region in early scientific research that included geology, ethnography, botany, cartography, meteorology, and geology. Unfortunately, geology as a science at that time was not far enough advanced for them to understand plate tectonics and the fact that California's infamous San Andreas Fault slices back ashore just 2 miles south of the fort, passing right through the original location of the fort's orchard.

During the summer, park docents and staff periodically offer special tours and other interpretive programs. Across the highway, about a quarter mile away, is the historic Russian orchard where some of the original trees still grow. Check at the visitor center about visiting the orchard, as there are periodic access restrictions.

**HOURS:** Daily, 10 to 4:30 PM. Closed Thanksgiving, Christmas, and New Year's Day.

**COST:** Vehicle day-use fee is $6.

**LOCATION:** 11 miles north of Jenner on Hwy. 1; the park is visible from the highway.

**PHONE:** 707-847-3437

**WEBSITE:** www.parks.ca.gov/parkindex

# 14 Mendocino County Museum

**WHAT'S HERE:** Collection of more than 100,000 county artifacts
**DON'T MISS THIS:** Pieces of the sunken ship *Frolic*

Mendocino County's human history began with the Native Americans, who were followed by a few early European and American trappers, explorers, and settlers, and then the loggers and other entrepreneurs from commercial offshoots such as the railroads. The small community of Willits, which straddles US 101 along part of its north-south journey, hosts the county's history museum, which covers all of these human transitions.

The large museum complex shares space with Mendocino College and is across the street from a large public park. The museum's most recent 7500-square–foot addition has provided additional exhibit space for its 100,000-plus collection of Mendocino artifacts. The majority of the added square footage is used to house the double tracks and the museum's collection of railroad equipment.

Although allotted museum space tends to favor huge locomotives and their associated rolling stock, before the railroads, people traveled long distances by horse or by stage. During the 1890s, Fountain Ledfort instituted a horse-drawn wagon freight business over the mountains to Cloverdale. Ledfort was able to expand his freight business to include a passenger stage line to the coast when the US Postal Service awarded him the mail contract in 1902. One of the route's original horse-drawn coaches is preserved and displayed in the museum. The coach's "open" design subjected passengers to significant levels of horse-kicked dust as it passed between the inland valley and the coastal towns on its route (roughly today's Hwy. 128). The stage line lasted until the 1920s, when motorized transportation was introduced and the business was sold.

The collections here are as diverse and eclectic as any of the small county museums. Descendent families of early Mendocino pioneers have donated much of artifacts, which include Pomo baskets, domestic home furnishings, mercantile hardware, and maritime collections.

One sunken ship whose parts surface at several museums along the coast is the *Frolic*, a brig that met its watery fate not far from Point Cabrillo (see Point Cabrillo Light Station, page 28) in 1850. Pieces of the ship and its cargo are still being brought to the surface by archeologists. Much of its lost cargo, including bolts of silk cloth, a prefabricated house, and more than 6000 bottles of Edinburgh ale, was lost, except for some that washed

This steam-powered spool donkey was a vital tool for the early logging industry.

ashore and was scavenged by the local Pomo Indians. Bits of ceramics, broken and formed into beads and arrow points, have been found in Native American archeological digs. The museum collection includes portions of the ill-fated ship, including its broken rudder, which was the primary cause of the accident. There are also pieces of jewelry, old gold coins, wax-coated rope that survived more than a century underwater, and broken pieces of porcelain.

Since so much of the *Frolic*'s cargo was lost or destroyed, and that which remains is broken and tarnished, the museum has gathered a collection of historic artifacts that range from fans to porcelain that, while not from the *Frolic*, are identical to those on the ship's manifest. The display includes small, broken pieces of the ship's cargo exhibited next to unbroken pieces of the time period that exactly match the patterns and materials of the originals.

**HOURS:** Wednesday through Sunday, 10 AM to 4:30 PM. Closed Thanksgiving, Christmas, and New Year's Day.

**COST:** Suggested donation is $2 per person or $5 per family.

**LOCATION:** 400 Commercial Street, a few blocks east of US 101, Willits

**PHONE:** 707-459-2736

**WEBSITE:** www.co.mendocino.ca.us/museum

# 15 Sonoma Mission and Barracks

**WHAT'S HERE:** California mission and Mexican army barracks

**DON'T MISS THIS:** Collection of 61 paintings depicting California's missions between 1903 and 1905

Under the authority of the Spanish crown, Father Junipero Serra founded the first California mission in San Diego in 1769. While Serra looked to Christianize California's Indian populations, the king of Spain's ultimate goal was to "civilize" the new Christian converts into makeshift Spanish citizens, thus adding legitimacy to the Spanish colonial empire claims. Both goals served as the impetus for expanding the missions north, especially following the Russian's entry into California with the establishment of Fort Ross (see Fort Ross State Historic Park, page 31), just 60 miles north of Sonoma.

The situation changed substantially in 1821, when Mexico gained its independence from Spain. Suddenly, the Spanish missions were no longer a government priority. The last mission was founded in Sonoma that same year. Father Jose Altimira, a disgruntled padre from another mission, did so by bypassing church authorities and working directly with Governor Don Luis Arguello. Father Altimira wanted to close two older missions (Mission Dolores and Mission San Rafael) and move their operations to a new mission in Sonoma, a plan he knew church authorities would not allow. When the church leaders discovered the devious plot, they reprimanded both the governor and Father Altimira, but ultimately allowed the mission's development to continue.

In 1834, Mexican Governor Jose Figueroa ordered Sonoma resident General Mariano Vallejo to move forward with the mission's secularization. This ended the Franciscan missionaries' authority, and the government took control of the extensive and valuable land holdings around the mission. While much of the confiscated land was supposed to go to the mission Indians, in the end, the Indians received next to nothing, while the local Mexican citizens—the Californios—received most of the property

Following secularization, the mission was soon abandoned as a church and turned over for other uses, such as storing hay and making wine. The buildings eventually fell into disrepair and collapsed. In 1841, Vallejo built a small chapel on the mission site for use by his soldiers, and that structure remains today as part of Sonoma State Historic Park. Of the mission's original 27 rooms built around a center quadrangle, only five remain today. The chapel and its adjacent structure serve as a small museum with exhibits about the history of California's missions. These include a wonderful collection of 61 paintings by Norwegian-born landscape artist Chris Jorgensen that depict many of California's missions between 1903 and 1905. A resident of San Francisco, Jorgensen and his wife, Angela, spent several years traveling through California by horse and buggy, painting the 21 missions.

Just across the street from the mission is Sonoma Barracks. In the 1830s, General Vallejo began construction of the adobe barracks to house his troops next to the mission and the town square. The last section of the barracks wasn't completed until 1840 or 1841. Unfortunately, the Mexican government failed to provide wages and supplies for Sonoma's small military contingent. When General Vallejo tired of paying his soldiers from his own pocket, he disbanded the last of the army, by this time numbering about 30 soldiers.

Sonoma Barracks is part of Sonoma State Historic Park, and several of its rooms have been restored and others include exhibits about Sonoma's early history. Exhibits include a look at how the Mexican soldiers lived during their 10-year enlistments in the Mexican Army, along with their required equipment, much of which they had to buy with their own meager wages.

There are also exhibit cases that hold some of the artifacts discovered during archeological digs in the area. Those include a US half-dollar coin that is dated

This chapel is a small remaining part of the last mission built in California.

1840 and was found near the west end of the barracks. For a short time, the barracks also served as headquarters for an American detachment following the US takeover of California from Mexico.

A small theater in the barracks shows a 22-minute movie about General Vallejo and Sonoma's early history.

> **HOURS:** Daily, 10 AM to 5 PM. Closed Thanksgiving, Christmas, and New Year's Day.
> **COST:** 17 and older, $2.
> **LOCATION:** 20 East Spain Street, at the corner of 2nd Street West, across the street from the plaza park, Sonoma.
> **PHONE:** 707-939-9420
> **WEBSITE:** www.parks.ca.gov/parkindex

# 16 Lachryma Montis (General Mariano Vallejo Home)

**WHAT'S HERE:** Visitor center, home, and gardens

**DON'T MISS THIS:** The small gardens and historic pond

Mexican General Mariano Guadalupe Vallejo built his first home, La Casa Grande, near the Sonoma Mission in 1840, during a time when he was directing the development of Sonoma. His home often served as an official meeting place when government representatives and other dignitaries visited.

Vallejo strongly supported the movement to make California part of the US, although his stance didn't deter a group of Americans from arresting and imprisoning him for a time at Sutter's Fort during Sonoma's short-lived 1846 Bear Flag Revolt (see Sutter's Fort State Historic Park, page 123). Once California officially became part of the US, Vallejo fully participated in the constitutional convention held in Monterey's Colton Hall, and he was elected a state senator in 1850. That same year, he purchased 500 acres a short distance west of Sonoma's main plaza for his new home and farm. His original home, which had been one of the finest in California (much of which fire destroyed in 1867), had overlooked the town's plaza and the soldiers' barracks. His new "Yankee" home, as he called it, was a Gothic-style American-Victorian house that was prefabricated in the Northeast and shipped around the Horn. He added another prefabricated building nearby to store fruit from his orchards and wine from his vineyard. This storage house serves as today's visitor center.

Vallejo named his new home "Lachryma Montis," a Latin translation for what the Indians called "Chiucuyem," or Tears of the Mountain. The name referred to the property's free-flowing spring, one of the reasons he chose this site. He built a stone reservoir on the hill just behind his home to capture the spring and provide fresh water directly to the house. Today, a trellis-covered walkway surrounds a portion of the pond, providing a shady spot for visitors to rest.

The furnished home is open for tours with or without a guide. Barriers at each room's entrance allow for easy viewing, while protecting the valuable artifacts. Most of the home's furnishings originally belonged to the Vallejo family, providing a first-hand look at 19th and early 20th century family living in California—at least the living enjoyed by those with money and power. The parlor, the first room seen upon entering the home, features a rosewood piano that belonged to Vallejo's daughter Epifania, and there is a needlepoint that his wife, Francisca, made for the wedding of Maria, one of their 15 children.

The first-floor study offers a look at a small portion of what was thought to be the largest personal library in California at the time. The chess set given to Vallejo by his wife is also in the study, along with the general's globes and paintings. The long wooden dining room table and Blue Willow china belonged to the Vallejo family, as did the mantle clock.

One of the second-floor bedrooms belonged to their daughter Luisa, who was their youngest child. Luisa Vallejo was born and lived in this house. She also married here and later returned to give birth to and rear her three children. Luisa inherited the home following her parents' deaths and lived here until her own death in 1943 at the age of 87. She, however, sold the property to the state of California in 1933 and was allowed to continue living in the home, serving as the historic site's first curator.

**HOURS:** Daily, 10 AM to 5 PM. Closed Thanksgiving, Christmas, and New Year's Day.

**COST:** 17 and older, $2.

**LOCATION:** 363 3rd Street West, Sonoma

**PHONE:** 707-938-9560

**WEBSITE:** www.parks.ca.gov/parkindex

General Mariano Vallejo's prefabricated "Yankee" home was shipped around the Horn.

# 17 **Jack London State Historic Park**

**WHAT'S HERE:** Historic homes, buildings, ruins, and a visitor center

**DON'T MISS THIS:** The Wolf House ruins and London's gravesite, under a large, volcanic rock

Tucked into the hillsides of Sonoma County's Glen Ellen is the home of one of the world's most beloved and widely read 20th century authors. Although Jack London was born in 1876, some of his most famous books, *Call of the Wild* and *The Sea Wolf*, were published just after the turn of the century. His works have been translated into 70 languages and many remain popular even today.

London wrote prolifically to support his desire to travel and experience life to its fullest—adding more to his experiences about which he could write. Nearly every morning, he wrote at least 1000 words. Between 1900 and 1916, London wrote more than 50 fiction and nonfiction books, in addition to hundreds of short stories and thousands of letters. It wasn't unheard of for him to receive 10,000 letters each year. He also entertained a constant stream of guests in his home, and in his spare time, he oversaw construction of his sailboat, *Snark*, on which he spent 27 months sailing the South Pacific.

In 1911, London and his wife, Charmain, purchased land above Glen Ellen that included a dilapidated farm and cottage. The couple named their property Beauty Ranch, and the small cottage—which is found near the center of today's park—served as their home and London's writing office. Over time, London acquired more land. He expanded and significantly improved his ranch's operations, constructing what he dubbed "Pig Palace." His innovative "piggery" included a fancy, circular pen that reduced the labor needed to raise large numbers of pigs. London also began construction of the couple's new home, and by 1913, he had spent $80,000 (in pre-World War I dollars) on the Wolf House. In August 1913, just days before moving from the small cottage into the completed mansion, it burned to the ground. The shell of its stone walls remains not too far from the cottage, which continued to serve as their home. Depressed about the loss, London quickly went back to work, using an advance to add onto the cottage, bringing it to a total of nearly 3000 square feet.

In 1915, London and his wife went to Hawaii, an attempt by Charmain to get Jack to slow down and take better care of himself. His proclivity toward too much

In 1919, following Jack's death, Charmain London built her House of Happy Walls.

alcohol, too much good food, and too little exercise was taking a toll on his health. Yet his financial obligations drove him even harder. Unfortunately, on November 22, 1916, at the age of 40, Jack London died of gastrointestinal uremic poisoning. In the end, London lived up to his words: "The proper function of man is to live, not to exist. I shall not waste my days in trying to prolong them. I shall use my time."

Beginning in 1919, Charmain, now a widow, couldn't bring herself to live in the cottage any longer, so she began construction nearby of what would be her own home, the House of Happy Walls. It was reminiscent of the Wolf House, but smaller, and much of its furniture had originally been custom designed by the Londons for the Wolf House. Charmain lived here until her death in 1955. Today, the home serves as a visitor center and museum, displaying photos and collections of artifacts from the couple's many adventures throughout the world, especially in the South Pacific.

From the House of Happy Walls, it is about a half-mile walk down a sometimes steep trail to the ruins of the Wolf House. Many of the huge stone walls, now covered in moss and ferns, remain. Just a short distance away, on top of a small knoll near the graves of two pioneer children, is London's grave site. His ashes were placed in the ground and a large volcanic rock rolled over them.

Visiting the historic site requires walking. From the western parking lot, it is about a five-minute walk to the cottage where London did most of his writing. On the way are the farm buildings that he either constructed or improved upon, including the silos, sherry barn, winery ruins, and the distillery. The original cottage remains much as it did when London lived here, including his office, which looks almost identical to a photograph taken in the early 1900s. The home had no cooking facilities, so London added another building adjacent to the cottage that served originally as part of the winery, but became a kitchen and dining room where he entertained his many guests. In the front of the house are two "sleeping" porches, one for himself and the other for Charmain. Apparently, his working schedule, which included reading well into the night, conflicted with Charmain's sleeping schedule.

London's cottage and the kitchen-dining room addition have been restored and are open for docent-led tours.

---

**HOURS:** Park: daily, 9:30 AM to 5 PM. Visitor center: daily, 10 AM to 5 PM. Closed Thanksgiving, Christmas, and New Year's Day.

**COST:** Park day-use fee is $6 per vehicle.

**LOCATION:** 2400 London Ranch Road, Glen Ellen

**PHONE:** 707-938-5216

**WEBSITE:** www.parks.ca.gov/parkindex

# 18 Luther Burbank Home and Gardens

**WHAT'S HERE:** Historic home and gardens of horticultural pioneer

**DON'T MISS THIS:** The glass greenhouse that survived the 1906 San Francisco earthquake

Famed horticulturalist Luther Burbank, born in 1849 in Lancaster, Massachusetts, was not college educated, but during his lifetime—much of it spent in Santa Rosa—Burbank developed more than 800 varieties of plants. They included fruits, grains, grasses, and flowers, with his Shasta daisy being the most famous.

The Burbank potato, which he developed, had the potential to make him a very wealthy man. A natural sport or natural mutation from his Burbank potato became the Russet Burbank. Today, that potato is the most widely cultivated potato in the world—and McDonald's uses it exclusively for their French fries. But in 1871, Burbank sold the rights to the potato for $150 and took his money to Santa Rosa, where he purchased 4 acres and began his plant crossbreeding experiments that would continue for 50 years. Later, he purchased 18 acres in nearby Sebastopol, where he conducted many more of his plant experiments. The inspiration for his lifetime of experiments was Charles Darwin's book *The Variation of Animals and Plants Under Domestication*.

It was an unfortunate fact that during Burbank's lifetime there was no legal protection for his hundreds of new plants. The ability to patent and thus financially benefit from new plants didn't occur until four years after his death in 1926. It was his friend Thomas Edison whose testimony in Congress helped pass the 1930 Plant Patent Act. Following the passage of the new law, Burbank was posthumously awarded more than a dozen plant patents.

Today, Burbank's modest home—including its glass greenhouse, which survived the 1906 San Francisco earthquake undamaged, and more than an acre of gardens—is maintained in Santa Rosa. Many of the plants that Burbank developed are growing around the home, and some of the plants, such as the huge spineless cactus, are quite impressive. Apparently, Burbank hoped the spineless cactus would offer a way to provide cattle feed in very arid regions that could support nothing more than drought-tolerant cacti. Unfortunately, the cattle loved eating the spineless cactus so much that it had to be fenced off in order to give the succulent plant a chance to grow. That extra fencing cost made it cheaper to bring in cattle feed.

Burbank died in 1926 at the age of 77, and his body was buried under a Cedar of Lebanon tree that he planted in front of his cottage in 1893. Unfortunately, the tree had to be removed in 1989. Elizabeth Burbank, his second wife, continued living in the home until her death in 1977. She was significantly younger than Burbank when they married. She, too, is buried on the grounds. Upon her death, Elizabeth Burbank gave the property, including the home, to the city of Santa Rosa.

The fully furnished, Greek Revival home is open for tours beginning each spring. The best time to visit is during late spring and summer when most of the flowers, trees, and other plants are at their growing peak, although many of the plants are perennials and can be seen throughout the year. The property also includes the carriage house that now serves as a museum and gift shop, offering many plants for sale.

**HOURS:** Gardens: April through October, daily, 8 AM to 7 PM; November through March, daily, 8 AM to 5 PM. Home and museum tours: April through October, Tuesday through Sunday, 10 AM to 4 PM, with the last tour starting at 3:30 PM.

**COST:** Adults, $4; 65 and older, $3; 12–18, $3; under 12, free; audio tours, $3.

**LOCATION:** At the corner of Santa Rosa and Sonoma avenues, Santa Rosa

**PHONE:** 707-524-5445

**WEBSITE:** www.lutherburbank.org

# 19 Charles M. Schulz Museum

**WHAT'S HERE:** The cartoon collection and history of *Peanuts*
**DON'T MISS THIS:** The short video shown on Schulz's old television set

With the obvious exception of presidential libraries and museums, there are not many California museums dedicated to single individuals. And in reality, the Charles M. Schulz Museum, located in Santa Rosa, is dedicated not to one person, but to the many *Peanuts* characters that this venerable cartoonist created over his lifetime of making people laugh.

Charlie Brown greets visitors outside the museum's entrance.

The museum explores Schulz's creative process for developing his cartoon strips. He often began by doodling different rough sketches, which frequently led to the creation of his cartoon characters. Numerous samples of his cartoon frames are on display, from beginning notes and doodles to more finished pencil drawings and examples of completed inked art. When he made a mistake or didn't care for an idea, Schulz did what most of us do with our mistakes—he simply crumpled the paper and tossed it into the trash can. Fortunately, his secretary often pulled his "mistakes" out of the trash, took them home and ironed the sheets of paper flat. She kept hundreds over the years and donated them to the museum when it opened. Sometimes, as one of those saved examples attests, Schulz forgot a single letter when writing the finished captions, and, without room to squeeze it in, he simply started over with a new cartoon.

Schulz maintained his working studio in his Santa Rosa home. He felt that going to the same studio each day was the only way he could focus. Much of his studio, from his drawing table, desk (a gift from his wife in 1973), the family photos pinned to the wall, and the old Sears color television (that shows a video of Schulz drawing and talking about his cartooning) has been moved into a corner of the museum. About 200 books have been selected from the 2000 in his library and are shelved as part of the office exhibit, providing a look at the breadth of subjects that Schulz read about. One is a history of the Red Baron—not Snoopy's escapades atop a dog house, but the real German Red Baron of World War I fame, perhaps the inspiration for Snoopy's great misadventures.

Schulz was very competitive during his life, playing ice hockey at the local rink, and golf, as well. It wasn't unheard of for Schulz to fly a couple friends down to Monterey in a private jet to play a round or two of golf at the famed Pebble Beach course. While Schulz didn't mind paying the several hundred dollars per round for green fees, he despised losing a hole to one of his playing partners and being out their 25¢ bet.

A Minnesota native, Schulz was born in 1922, and within a few days of his birth, an uncle tagged him with the nickname Sparky, after a character in a cartoon strip. The nickname stuck throughout his life. In 1934, the Schulz family was given a black and white dog. The dog was named Spike, and it would become the inspiration for one of the most famous cartoon dogs—Snoopy. In 1952, Schulz's first *Peanuts* comic was published in 40 newspapers, and by 1969, *Peanuts* had become famous enough that *Apollo 10* astronauts named their command capsule Charlie Brown and the lunar module Snoopy.

When Schulz announced his retirement in December 1999 due to health issues, his *Peanuts* comic strip was being published in more than 2600 newspapers around the world and more than 20,000 different *Peanuts* character products had been developed. The last original *Peanuts* comic strip was published in January 2000. Schulz died the following month.

The museum's first-floor gallery features temporary exhibits related to cartooning and cartoonists. The exhibits are rotated about four times each year. The museum also periodically offers cartooning classes for kids.

**HOURS:** Weekdays (closed Tuesday), noon to 5 PM; weekends, 10 AM to 5 PM. Closed most major holidays.

**COST:** Adults, $8; seniors and youth, $5.

**LOCATION:** 2301 Hardies Lane, Santa Rosa

**PHONE:** 707-579-4452

**WEBSITE:** www.schulzmuseum.org

# North Coast Tours

## Romantic Tour

**ESTIMATED DAYS:** 2
**ESTIMATED DRIVING MILES:** 10

**B**egin your day in the coastal town of Mendocino with its quaint shops and restaurants and make your first stop at the **Kelley House Museum** (page 30). It's a great opportunity to wander through a mid-19th century Victorian home that was built by one of this early lumber town's most successful businessmen.

Afterward, head north on Hwy. 1 about 4 miles to the **Point Cabrillo Light Station** (page 28). You can actually spend the night here in one of the restored lightkeepers' houses that is now a **bed and breakfast** (707-937-0816; www.pointcabrillo.org). Or hike out to the lighthouse for a picnic and enjoy the ocean views, and perhaps even see a few whales.

Another mile or so north of the light station on Hwy. 1 is the **Mendocino Coast Botanical Garden** (707-964-4352; www.gardenbythesea.org). This is another great place for a hand-in-hand stroll before you head to Fort Bragg to visit the **Guest House Museum** (page 26), the town's largest and most elaborate historic mansion. If you visit any of these destinations during the winter or early spring months, try to plan your stay around one of the whale festivals.

Interior of the restored Point Cabrillo
lightkeeper's residence

# Family/Kids Tour 1

ESTIMATED DAYS:  1
ESTIMATED DRIVING MILES:  8

Start the family's day just like the lumberjacks did, with a belly-filling breakfast at the historic **Samoa Cookhouse Museum** (page 16), where you can fill your plates with all-you-can-eat pancakes, eggs, biscuits, and more. After your meal, stroll through the cook-house, which also serves as a lumberjack museum. From here, head north (right) on Samoa Blvd. about 7 miles to the **Arcata Marsh** (707-829-2359; www.arcatacityhall.org/arcata_marsh.html). Turn right on South G Street just before you cross over US 101. Here, the kids get a little exercise on the trails while viewing some of the many birds, with a short stop at the visitor center that is focused on teaching kids about the marsh environment.

From here, head north on G Street across Samoa Blvd. and continue several blocks, where you'll pass the **Arcata Town Square** (8th and G streets), a park that, on clear days, often looks like a young hippies' encampment of local college students. Continue north to 13th and G streets, and stop at the **Humboldt State University Natural History Museum** (page 19), a very kid-friendly place.

Samoa Cookhouse dining room

# Family/Kids Tour 2

ESTIMATED DAYS:  1–2
ESTIMATED DRIVING MILES:  16

The ocean tide schedule will dictate whether you can begin your day trip at Crescent City's **Battery Point Lighthouse and Museum** (page 13), located just north of the harbor—or somewhere else. You must wait until low tide to walk over to the 150-year-old lighthouse's "island," but the wait is worth it! Just a few blocks away on H Street is the **Del Norte County Museum** (page 14), with two floors of exhibits, including a look at Crescent City's famous 1964 tsunami that destroyed much of the city. If you happen to be up here in February, be sure to plan you trip around the great annual **World Championship Crab Races** (707-464-3174; www.delnorte.org). The crab races are a hoot, and the cooked crab is even better. As a side trip, drive to the **Trees of Mystery** (800-638-3389; www.treesofmystery.net), about 16 miles south of Crescent City on US 101. Besides Paul Bunyan's giant blue ox, Babe, standing prominently in the main parking lot, there are dozens of strange and beautiful redwood trees to see along a short trail (fee), and a free Native American museum inside the gift shop.

Del Norte County Museum

# Famous Californians Tour

ESTIMATED DAYS: 2
ESTIMATED DRIVING MILES: 34

This tour is best done over two days because there are too many side trips (restaurants, specialty shops) and some hiking to be done to squeeze this into a single enjoyable day.

Begin with a morning stroll through the **Luther Burbank Home and Gardens** (page 40) in Santa Rosa to see the life's work of this famous horticulturalist. From there, it's less than 3 miles to the **Charles M. Schulz Museum** (page 41), the creator of the comic strip *Peanuts*. The second day's tour begins in the wine country city of Sonoma, just about 22 miles from Santa Rosa. From the park in the center of **old town Sonoma** at Broadway, Napa Street, and West Spain Street, it's only few blocks west down West Spain Street to **Lachryma Montis**

Luther Burbank Home and Gardens

(page 36), better known as the General Mariano Vallejo Home. It won't take long to tour the home and its small visitor center, which leaves much more time to wander through **Jack London State Historic Park** (page 38). From Sonoma, it is about 9 miles to Glen Ellen, where the park is located. It includes London's cottage, where he wrote many of his most famous books, his grave site, the burned hulk of his mansion, Wolf House, and his wife's home, built after his death.

At Jack London's cottage home, London often slept on the enclosed porch on the left side of the front door, and his wife, Charmain, slept on the right porch.

# North Coast Travel Information Centers

Redwood Empire Association/Northern California Visitor's Bureau
www.redwoodempire.com
415-292-5527 or 800-619-2125

California Welcome Center (Arcata)
www.arcatachamber.com
707-822-3619

Crescent City Chamber of Commerce (Del Norte County)
www.northerncalifornia.net
707-464-3174

Humboldt County Convention & Visitors Bureau
www.redwoods.info
1-800-346-3482

Mendocino County Alliance
www.gomendo.com
707-462-7417 or 866-466-3636

Sonoma County Tourism Program
www.sonomacounty.com
707-539-7282 or 800-576-6662

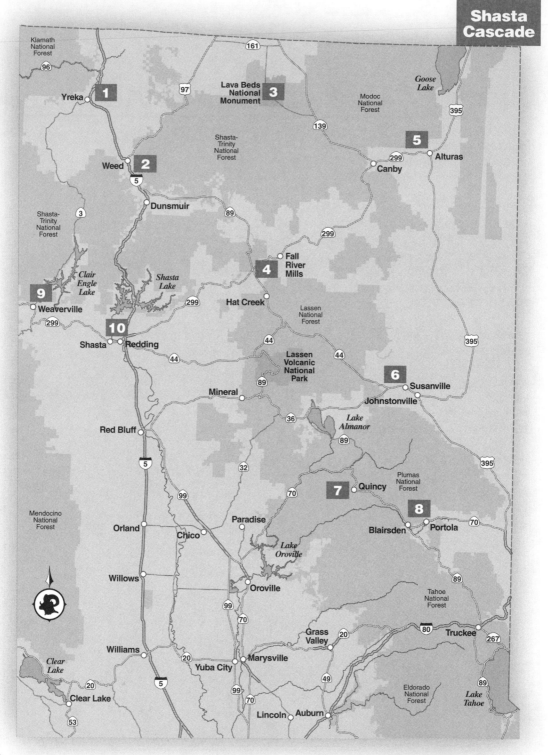

Shasta
Cascade

Klamath National Forest

96

Yreka **1**

97

Lava Beds National Monument **3**

161

*Goose Lake*

Modoc National Forest

395

Weed **2**

5

Shasta-Trinity National Forest

139

**5** Alturas

299

Canby

Dunsmuir

89

299

3

Shasta-Trinity National Forest

*Clair Engle Lake*

*Shasta Lake*

Fall River Mills **4**

299

**9**

Weaverville

299

5

299

Hat Creek

Lassen National Forest

395

**10**

Shasta Redding

44

44

Lassen Volcanic National Park

44

395

89

Mineral

**6**

Susanville

Johnstonville

36

*Lake Almanor*

89

Red Bluff

32

**7** Quincy

Plumas National Forest

5

99

70

**8**

395

Mendocino National Forest

Orland

Chico

Paradise

Blairsden

Portola

70

89

*Lake Oroville*

Tahoe National Forest

Willows

Oroville

99

70

Grass Valley

20

80

Truckee

267

Williams

20

Marysville

49

89

5

Yuba City

99

70

*Clear Lake*

20

Eldorado National Forest

*Lake Tahoe*

Clear Lake

53

Lincoln Auburn

# Shasta Cascade

The early settlers here needed stout hearts, self-determination, and an occasional sense of humor to thrive in the wild lands that fill this crescent-shaped region surrounding the northernmost quarter of the Great Valley. With vast mountain forests and open grasslands punctuated by towering volcanoes and their lava-covered wastelands, Shasta Cascade is much different than the rest of California. The communities are often isolated, especially during winter when snow can close roads, creating a special bond among the people who live in towns like Portola or Weaverville or Alturas.

Those bonds, built over more than 150 years, continue today as the early pioneers' grandchildren, great grandchildren, and their children are busy saving the histories of

Interior of Coburn-Variel Home

their pioneer families. Even though the larger towns such as Susanville, Oroville, Alturas, Quincy, and Portola have neither the populations nor large budgets of the big cities to the south, the townspeople are determined to preserve the culture and history of their respective communities.

Timber, cattle ranching, and farming have always been the primary industries in this region. You can see evidence of these activities in most of the area's museums. The Weed Historic Lumber Town Museum focuses much of its attention on early lumbering, while the Siskiyou County Museum in Yreka takes a broader look at the history of the area, from the Native Americans and early trappers to role of the US military in settling this land. The Modoc County Museum in Alturas also takes a wider view of the area's history, from the Native Americans to 20th century artifacts and events that shaped nearby communities. Travel the west side of the Shasta Cascade area, and the importance of gold mining and the resulting diverse communities, such as the Chinese, become obvious in places like Shasta State Historic Park.

Driving in the Shasta Cascade region is a joy, with its brilliant blue skies, breathtaking mountain vistas, beautiful rivers, and traffic to match the population—sparse. Whether you are into bird-watching, photography, or fishing, in addition to history, there are unlimited opportunities to pursue your interests while touring the area's mansions and museums. Today, it's much easier to travel in the Shasta Cascade area during winter than it was during the 19th century when many of the towns were founded, yet winter snow storms can prove to be a challenge. Some of the museums and mansions close during winter, so it is always good to call ahead if you're planning to travel here during that time of year.

# TRIVIA

1 Name the museum where you can see a 1940s-era iron lung.

2 Which museum has a large collection of famous early California art?

3 Name the museum that houses one of the state's largest collections of antique firearms.

4 Which home was built in 1878 by a husband and wife who first passed through the area by way of Beckwourth Pass in 1852?

5 What is the name today for the region where the Modoc Indian War took place?

6 Name the museum where it is possible to drive a real locomotive.

7 Name the park that includes the oldest continuously used Chinese temple in California.

8 Where can you see a stuffed mountain lion that once ate the local district attorney's dog?

*For trivia answers, see page 324.*

# 1  Siskiyou County Museum

**WHAT'S HERE:** Three galleries showcasing the county's history and an outdoor museum

**DON'T MISS THIS:** The historic schoolhouse and miner's cabin in the outdoor museum

Within a single museum complex, two very different museum experiences await you in Yreka. The first is the more formal and beautiful indoor museum, with glass-encased exhibits of Siskiyou County's history. Outside, the second part of the complex reproduces what the old days more closely resembled, at least in the pioneers' daily lives, with five historic buildings that have been moved here.

The main museum's exhibits are exquisitely designed and maintained. There are three primary galleries—covering Native American history, gold mining, and the trapper and early military history—each with its own sub-themes and carefully chosen artifacts. The Native American gallery is composed of a representative collection of clothing, tools for hunting and fishing, and ceremonial regalia from the local tribes, including the Achomawi, Karuk, Konomihu, Modoc, Okwanuchu, and Shasta. The basket collection includes samples of the plants used in their construction. Exhibits touch on trade, not only among the local tribes, but also the inclusion of European goods the Indians found they could incorporate into their own cultures. The mystique and power of the American Indian is made evident by the thousands of commercial products that have been produced over the years using native names and logos, many of which are on display.

As shown in the gold mining gallery, mining in the 19th century was not a pleasant way to make a living. These early miners endured great hardships, considering the small handful who got rich. Besides the tools and other miners' provisions in the collection, there are numerous photos depicting their daily lives and the different mining methods employed by these industrious people. A reproduction of the gold nugget found by an early miner may get your prospecting juices flowing. It weighed more than 15 pounds, and even though gold sold for just $16.50 per ounce at that time, finding it was still a productive day's work.

The miners had other problems besides hard work, bandits, and miserable living conditions. Food was expensive since it was brought in primarily by packhorse. But where miners saw problems, others saw opportunity. The first grist mill in the county was erected in 1853 and others soon followed. By 1880,

Several historic buildings are part of the Siskiyou County Museum.

five mills, powered either by water or steam, were producing 9000 barrels of flour annually.

In the trapper and early military history gallery, you will find those famous Hudson Bay blankets, along with an explanation as to how the trading "points" system worked in pricing blankets to beaver pelts. Early trappers depended mostly on their own skills, courage, and luck, and exhibits include personal clothing items, such as their great coats or "capotes," and weapons, from a tiny pepperbox pistol to a .50-caliber flintlock rifle. There is also an exhibit illustrating the necessary survival skills, along with a re-creation of local trapper Stephen Hall's 1830s Scott Valley spike camp.

The US military played a role in attempting to keep peace between the local Indians and the miners and ranchers. Nearby Fort Jones was their home and several pieces of that history are shown, including a uniform, bugle, and weapons. The museum also includes Chinese artifacts, because the Chinese settled and worked throughout Siskiyou County just as they had in other Gold Rush-era towns. Cloths, tools, and other items they brought with them are included.

Across the small parking lot from the main museum is the entrance to the outdoor museum. On the grounds are several historic buildings moved here from their original locations within Siskiyou County. These buildings give visitors the opportunity to learn how people worked, lived, and prayed in a much earlier time. Many of the county's children attended one-room schools such as the Spring Schoolhouse, which was used from 1890 to 1949 and moved to the museum after being abandoned. Mary M. McCraig taught just 10 students during the school's first year.

Nearby is the reconstructed blacksmith barn. In the days when transportation was by horse and people depended on local farms for most of their food, the town blacksmith was an indispensable part of every community. In addition to shoeing horses, this small business was responsible for making and repairing myriad metal objects, from door hinges to plows, shovels, and wagon wheels.

The grounds also include the mostly reconstructed Callahan Church and the small cabin built in 1856 by Henry Levi Davis, who came to find gold but stayed to ranch. While his cabin has been moved to the museum grounds, his ranch remains in family hands. Another cabin, built of logs that were originally hand hewn with a broad axe, provides a good look at this early construction technique used by many 19th century miners.

**HOURS:** Main museum: Tuesday through Friday, 9 AM to 5 PM; Saturday, 9 AM to 4 PM. Outdoor museum: May through September, Tuesday through Saturday, 9:30 AM to 4:30 PM.

**COST:** Adults, $2; ages 7–12, $0.75; 6 and under, free.

**LOCATION:** 910 South Main Street, Yreka

**PHONE:** 530-842-3836

**WEBSITE:** www.co.siskiyou.ca.us/museum/index.htm

# 2  Weed Historic Lumber Town Museum

**WHAT'S HERE:** Exhibits ranging from lumbering to the old jail and booking room

**DON'T MISS THIS:** The 116-year-old white fir that has grown around an axe someone left in the tree many years ago

This small Siskiyou County town gained its name from its founder, Abner Weed, who arrived in the 1890s to make his mark on the new but growing lumber industry. Weed had noticed that nearby Black Butte, a prominent extinct landmark volcano, caused winds to swirl with tremendous force and clouds to form over and around the peak of nearby Mt. Shasta. He reasoned that such winds could be used to quickly dry newly cut, wet lumber. In 1879, Weed launched his company after purchasing nearly 300 acres, along with the existing Siskiyou Lumber and Mercantile mill, for only $400. His company and its ability to quickly dry newly cut lumber spawned the booming mill town that he named after himself.

Today, Weed's Lumber Town Museum celebrates the lives of those who, like Abner Weed, helped settle this town. The building that houses Weed's museum has gone through several phases, beginning as a barn that was transformed into a courthouse and jail before maturing into today's museum. As its name implies, its focus is on the county's lumber industry, but as you wander through its numerous rooms, surprises await.

In addition to the jail, booking room, and police department memorabilia such as badges, handcuffs, and even a pair of thumb cuffs, there is an exhibit on Charlie Byrd, who, in 1986, became the first African American county sheriff in California. Jail cells have been turned into exhibit rooms, one of which highlights women's fashions.

Other rooms include everything from boring bits to millwright tools, bucking saws, and numerous kinds of axes, from double-bit to brush-clearing. If you're old enough to remember the days of home milk delivery, the museum includes a collection of milk bottles. Throughout the building, there are photos that provide insights into the town's old lumber mills and what life was like in Weed during the 20th century.

Walking to the rear of the museum, you can visit the old courtroom, and farther back, the museum opens into a large gallery filled with historical logging

A look at the tools many late 19th century women used in their kitchens

53

equipment, including a 104-inch-diameter saw blade donated by lumber giant Weyerhaeuser. The chainsaw exhibit makes modern tree-fellers very happy they no longer have to depend on some of the antiques displayed. Portable, many of them were not!

The museum houses a couple of old fire trucks, including a bright red 1923 La France with an attached wooden ladder that you can walk up to and actually touch. One of the more peculiar artifacts is a large piece of a 116-year-old white fir that had grown almost completely around an axe someone long ago stuck in the tree. The find even made the local newspaper.

A somewhat surprising exhibit displays wooden produce boxes with such names as Sunkist Oranges, Tri-Valley Growers, and Country Boy. It was the dried lumber from mills such as Weed's that produced many of these packing boxes used to ship California produce all over the world. The exhibit includes some of the equipment that was used to print the fancy words and art on these bygone pieces of commercial art.

**HOURS:** Memorial weekend through September 30, daily, 10 AM to 5 PM. Closed during winter, but may be opened by appointment. The museum is staffed by volunteers and occasionally may be closed if one is not available.

**COST:** Free

**LOCATION:** 303 Gilman Ave., Weed

**PHONE:** 530-938-0550

**WEBSITE:** www.siskiyous.edu/museum/about.htm

# 3  Lava Beds National Monument Visitor Center Museum

**WHAT'S HERE:** Exhibits on volcanism and the Modoc Indian War

**DON'T MISS THIS:** The short hike up to Captain Jack's stronghold, where the Modoc Indians and 50 fellow warriors held off up to 1000 US Army troops for months

This museum, located on the lava beds south of Tule Lake, is small, yet it represents one of the most tumultuous times in northeastern California—both in its natural history and in its cultural conflicts. For millions of years, volcanoes spewed lava across the landscape and sent poisonous gasses and cinders high into the atmosphere. And for thousands of years after that, the Modoc Indians lived in this land of jagged volcanic rocks, where nearby lakes and forests provided abundant fish and game.

When settlers began arriving following the Gold Rush, the Modoc battled the intruders, until reluctantly agreeing to move to a reservation. But reservation life did not suit the Modoc, and by 1867, many escaped and returned to their ancestral lands. In late 1872, the US Army arrived, and in their first battle, which marked the beginning of the Modoc War, the Modoc, led by Captain Jack, defeated the soldiers. Captain Jack and 160 of his fellow Modoc men, women, and children quickly retreated to the lava beds' natural fortifications, where, for months, more than 50 warriors held off the Army, whose numbers eventually grew to more than 1000 troops. Finally, in May of the following year, with most of his men killed or captured, Captain Jack surrendered. He and two others were later hanged.

The museum holds only a few artifacts left from the Modoc Indian War. One of those is a Koehorn mortar that lobbed a 12-pound explosive shell up to 900 yards. Following a two-day bombardment of these mortar rounds on Captain Jack's stronghold, only one Modoc was killed, attesting to the effectiveness of their natural volcanic defenses.

At one point during the Modoc Indian War, Lt. William Sherwood and another officer walked out to meet several Modoc Indians who approached them under a white flag. Without warning, the Modoc pulled out weapons and fatally wounded Sherwood. A chest belonging to Sherwood was preserved and is on display at the museum. It provides some insight into the personal effects that Army officers in the West may have carried. His included a powder horn, bullets, and a "break-down" rifle that could be separated into its barrel and wooden stock for easier storage.

J.D. Howard, a local miller, in 1916 became the first person known to have explored and documented many of the caves found in the park, although it's likely that the Modoc Indians had been aware of them for centuries. His camera and typewriter are part of the museum exhibits. The cave names that he painted on many of their walls remain visible today. After seeing the visitor center and museum, it's time for you to experience what Howard first saw. From the parking lot, a road leads directly to Cave Loop, which will take you to more than a dozen volcanic tubes or caves waiting to be explored. Be sure to take a flashlight and a hard hat (available at the visitor center) for each person, and don't go exploring alone.

To get a first-hand look at Captain Jack's stronghold and how his small band of Indians was able to hold off the Army for months, drive to the north side of the park. Two loop trails lead around and through his stronghold, where you can walk among the natural fortifications and caves that protected them even from artillery bombardments.

While most of the lava flows you will see throughout Lava Beds may appear similar, there are actually numerous kinds of volcanic rock. The museum shows samples of the park's volcanic

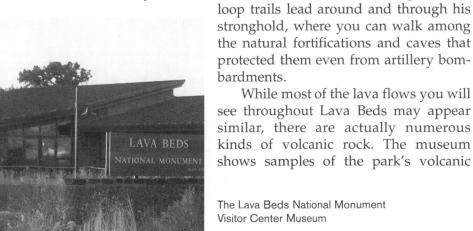

The Lava Beds National Monument
Visitor Center Museum

rocks, including andesite, which comprises only about 10 percent of the lava found here. Ninety percent of the rock in Lava Beds is basalt. There are lesser amounts of pumice and obsidian, the smooth, glass-like black stone that most people associate with Indian projectile points.

The museum offers a short movie that illustrates the power of volcanoes similar to the Medicine Lake volcano. Medicine Lake is a low and wide shield volcano, not a composite or stratovolcano such as Mt. Shasta and Mount St. Helens. Despite the absence of that typical cone-like volcano appearance, Medicine Lake is the largest volcano in the Cascades, but fortunately it is inactive. The park covers only about 10 percent of Medicine Lake's 700 square miles of surface area.

**HOURS:** The park and museum are open all year, although winter snow may close some southern access roads. Museum: Memorial Day through Labor Day, daily, 8:30 AM to 6 PM; the rest of the year, daily, 8:30 AM to 5 PM. Closed Christmas Day.

**COST:** Museum is free; park entrance fee, $10 per vehicle, good for seven days.

**LOCATION:** About 10 miles south of Hwy. 161 on the Modoc Volcanic National Scenic Byway that parallels the west side of Tule Lake.

**PHONE:** 530-667-2282

**WEBSITE:** www.nps.gov/labe

# 4  Fort Crook Museum

**WHAT'S HERE:** Exhibits of local artifacts going back 150 years, including a look at Fort Crook, which no longer exists

**DON'T MISS THIS:** The collection of wedding dresses showing that the all-white gown hasn't always been essential to marital bliss

The Fort Crook Museum, located near Fall River Mills, is, unfortunately, not a fort, but a replica of a round barn, something rare in California. It does, however, serve as a repository for what little of the fort's history remains, along with an abundance of tools, photographs, and clothing that have been used by locals during the past 150 or so years.

The original fort was established in July 1857, on Fall River, about 7 miles from the present-day museum. Captain John W.T. Gardner's Company A, 1st Dragoons, constructed the pine-pole stockade and its more than 25 buildings to help protect travelers along the Shasta-Yreka Road. The fort was originally named Camp Hollenbush, after the company's surgeon. It soon was renamed for Lt. George Crook, who became one of the surgeon's patients after taking a poison arrow in his hip. Crook would later gain national fame as a Civil War general and advocate for the Plains Indians. Fort Crook was abandoned shortly after the Civil War, and most of its parts were scavenged by local farmers and ranchers or they simply rotted away. The single exception is one of the fort's recently discovered cookhouses that has been moved to the museum grounds.

Most of the museum is essentially an eclectic collection of many things common to homes and businesses during the late 18th and early 19th centuries. You can see early dental chairs, barber chairs, and guns, including Winchester and Savage rifles. A rare item in the collection is the Bilhorn telescope organ, made in Chicago and brought to northeast California in 1898. It has a much reduced keyboard that can fold down into a small suitcase-sized carrying case. For today's kids who are only familiar with computers, there is a large collection of early to mid-20th century Underwood typewriters and a circa 1939 Burroughs wide-carriage electric typewriter used in one of the local sawmills.

One of the museum's more intriguing collections includes a representation of local wedding dresses from the 1860s to the 1880s. Only one is today's traditional white. The others, including the hats and veils, are black or gray or some other color, including one with red polka dots.

When you finish wandering through the many more displays on the main floor, head to the upper floors. More surprises await, including a wheelchair that appears to be a century old, but nobody is certain, and numerous cameras from bygone eras. Head up another level to the barn's cupola for a great view of the surrounding land.

Outside, several historic buildings from the surrounding community have been donated and moved to the museum site, including an 1860s log cabin, a school built in 1884, and the town's 1930s-era jail. The jail is solid concrete, built by a seven-man WPA crew. One of the jail's first occupants was also one of its builders, who was arrested shortly after he and his crew had completed construction.

The James family, longtime residents of the area, had another building constructed adjacent to the museum to house their donated collection of family heirlooms. It holds Victorian furniture, an organ, stoves, sewing machines, tables, glassware, quilts, and a collection of 233 teapots. Next door is a barn with carriages, tools, wooden skis, a barbed wire collection, an old fire truck, and a working blacksmith shop in back. Local schoolchildren learn blacksmithing skills here, and some of what they make, from candle holders and hooks to fire pokers and nails, is available for purchase in the

The Fort Crook Museum features pianos that sailing ships brought around the Horn.

57

museum gift shop. There's also a 1911 Wichita truck that served as the local motor transport for supplies beginning in 1918.

The museum also has acquired the only remaining structure from Fort Crook. Apparently, the rancher who owns the land once occupied by the fort was going to demolish an old shack on his land. As work began, they discovered that it was actually one of the fort's original cookhouses that had been added onto over the years. The non-original parts were removed and the remaining building was moved to the museum grounds, where it is undergoing restoration.

---

**HOURS:** May 1 through October 31, Tuesday through Sunday, noon to 4 PM.

**COST:** Donations accepted

**LOCATION:** 43030 Fort Crook Ave., just west of the town of Fall River Mills, near the corner of Glenburn Road and Hwy. 299 east. Look for the sign.

**PHONE:** 530-336-5110

**WEBSITE:** www.ftcrook.org

---

# 5  Modoc County Historical Museum

**WHAT'S HERE:** Varied collections representing local history

**DON'T MISS THIS:** Monster shotguns that commercial waterfowl hunters once used

So many special collections and even entire museums have come about because of the initial efforts of a single person or two dedicated to saving pieces of history. The Modoc County Historical Museum, located in Alturas, is a perfect example of what a few dedicated people with limited funds can accomplish.

Marc and Myrtle Belli, longtime Alturas residents, began collecting historic artifacts in 1926. Over the years, they gathered a large collection of Native American artifacts, historical photos and documents, and pioneer tools and other items. In 1932, they acquired an impressive gun collection from the son of Nathan Rogers, who had begun his collecting in 1870. Thousands of valuable artifacts were housed in the Bellis' private museum—their home's attic, where they identified and preserved their growing collection.

Finally, in 1966, a group of Alturas businessmen purchased the Bellis' collection in hopes of creating a museum, which became reality when Modoc County purchased the collection a year later. The collection was moved into the Veterans Memorial Building in Rachael Dorris Park and opened to the public the following year. A building addition in

1984 doubled the museum's exhibit space. Since its opening, hundreds of additional historical items have been donated to the museum.

The museum is dedicated to preserving and exhibiting the history of Modoc County's pioneers. It houses one of the largest gun collections in California and is a destination for firearm aficionados. The collection ranges from a 15th century blunderbuss to numerous shotguns. After all, Alturas does sit in the middle of a major migratory waterfowl flyway. When hunting laws were changed in the early years to outlaw shotguns larger than the 10-gauge monsters that commercial hunters used, the hunters got creative. In order to get enough lead into the sky, they simply built 10-gauge guns with two and four barrels. As such, hitting more than one bird per shot was almost guaranteed. There are examples of both guns in the collection. One of those outlawed monster three-gauge shotguns also hangs on the museum's display wall, along with numerous muskets, revolvers, and a Marlin Ballard 40-90-caliber, single-shot rifle. Its cartridge is nearly 4 inches long.

The museum's Native American exhibit is significantly larger than its gun collection. The thousands of artifacts represent the three groups who lived in the area—the Pit River, Modoc, and Paiute tribes—as well as those living farther away in southern Oregon and eastern Nevada. Artifacts date from the 19th century to more than 8000 years ago. The biggest share of the collection consists of displays of various arrow and spear points, but there are also bows, arrows, stone tools, beadwork, baskets, and clothing.

Perhaps counter to the Native American artifacts is the small collection of US Cavalry items such as a uniform and a very uncomfortable-looking bunk. Keeping with the military theme, other items include uniforms and rifles from World Wars I and II. Loosely associated with war is the collection of purple, green, and clear glass bottles and jars. What's the war connection? The glass, originally clear, turns purple when subjected to extended periods of sunlight. It was the clarifying agent manganese dioxide that reacted to the sunlight and caused the color change. Most of the chemical came from Russia, but German blockades in World War I created shortages. Glass makers turned to selenium, which doesn't react with sunlight, as an alternative. Following the end of the war, they never went back to the manganese dioxide. As such, war collectors prize 19th and early 20th century purple glass.

Other pieces of Modoc history fill the museum, from railroad clocks to a beautiful oak Estey organ. Tobacco lovers will enjoy the display of pipes and lighters, while the tobacco disparagers will likely chuckle at the irony of having an old iron lung displayed nearby. The iron lung was actually invented in 1928 at Harvard and used extensively during the 1940s to aid polio victims. There are also exhibits of

Modoc County Historical Museum features a large Native American artifact collection.

early woodworking tools and Chinese bottles and jugs, some more than 100 years old. For kids who are easily bored with museums, there is a "touch-me" display of animal skins, including silver fox, skunk, rabbit, deer, and wolverine. And finally, don't be startled by the woman dressed in her 1940s business suit, operating the old phone switchboard. She's a dummy—or perhaps mannequin is a better choice of words.

**HOURS:** May through October, Tuesday through Saturday, 10 AM to 4 PM.

**COST:** Adults $2; 16 and under, free.

**LOCATION:** 600 South Main Street, Alturas

**PHONE:** 530-233-6238

**WEBSITE:** www.alturaschamber.org/modoc-museum.htm

# 6 Lassen Historical Museum

**WHAT'S HERE:** A varied collection of artifacts, including a cannon, Indian baskets, and a violin brought around the Horn in 1852

**DON'T MISS THIS:** The small and very old wood building known as Roops Fort, located just outside the museum overlooking the meadow where early immigrants often camped

This part of California is probably best known for Lassen Peak, one of California's most active volcanoes. At 10,457 feet above sea level, it is also the second tallest mountain in the Cascade Range inside California; only Mt. Shasta is higher. The mountain and its national park, the county, and the museum took their names from one of the area's earliest pioneers, Denmark native Peter Lassen.

Two other locally notable men were William Nobles and Isaac Roop, who arrived in the area about the same time as Lassen. Nobles began leading settlers over a new immigrant trail that he established between Humboldt Sink (an intermittent dry lake in northwestern Nevada) and Shasta City in 1851—a trail he named after himself. Roop was one of the first settlers to pass along Nobles Immigrant Trail. He decided to stay and take advantage of the business possibilities by establishing a trading post where travelers could restock their supplies, feed their animals, and make needed repairs.

Roop named his little trading settlement Rooptown, but later renamed it Susanville in honor of his daughter. Peace and tranquility were not always part of this idyllic setting. In 1856, Roop and Lassen joined forces with a group of fellow citizens in a small tax revolt against county officials. With state boundaries still up for grabs, or at least not yet surveyed, they were not interested in being part of the newly established Nevada Territory. Because the boundary between Nevada and California was not yet settled, both states claimed Susanville and the Honey Lake area as theirs. Roop, Lassen, and a group of conspirators formed a short-lived separate territory, which they called "Nataqua." Their new republic never became as well known as the equally short-lived California Bear Republic (see Sutter's Fort State Historic Park, page 123, and Lachryma Montis, page 36), and their efforts were rendered mute when Nevada Territory was established without Susanville, and Roop became territorial governor. Lassen's once proud Nataqua Republic became known as Lassen County.

Today, Roop's Fort—a small log cabin in need of restoration work—remains on its original site next to the museum, still overlooking the meadow area (now a park) where settlers camped. The museum next door celebrates Lassen County's early days with stories and artifacts—many donated by local families—from those who lived during the time of Lassen and Roop. The Lassen History Museum goes a step farther than most museums with its Native American basket exhibit, which shows, in detail, the different weaving techniques that the Maidu used in their basket making. The collection also includes a cannon, apparently never fired in anger, and not likely ever to be fired, considering that a cannonball is welded partway down the barrel. Also featured is a violin that one of the local settlers, Lefe McDow, brought around the Horn in 1852 and played at local dances. He was apparently quite the fiddler until a sawmill accident severed several fingers. The instrument was last played by his grandson in the 1930s before making its way to the museum's collection.

One peculiar item is a set of snowshoes for horses. Given the weight of the shoes, it's a wonder how these steel contraptions could possibly have aided a horse tromping through deep snow. There is a fulgurite, created when lightning strikes the ground, melting sand and small stones together forming a rough, tube-like recreation of the bolt's image.

Considering that the Lassen Historical Museum is named for Peter Lassen, it's appropriate that some of Peter Lassen's personal property would be included in the collection. Few things belonging to Lassen remain, but the museum has his tobacco pipe, in addition to an official US government document appointing him postmaster.

**HOURS:** May through October, Monday through Friday, 10 AM to 4 PM.
**COST:** Free
**LOCATION:** 1115 N. Weatherlow Street, Susanville
**PHONE:** 530-257-3292
**WEBSITE:** There currently is no museum website.

# 7 Plumas County Museum

**WHAT'S HERE:** Inside: numerous collections, from Indian baskets to an 1895 Steinway piano; outside: mining, blacksmithing, and logging equipment

**DON'T MISS THIS:** The strong box that apparently was stolen by the famous outlaw and self-proclaimed "P8" (poet) Black Bart

This museum, located in the town of Quincy, on the street directly behind the town's imposing 1920 county courthouse, features three distinct parts: The first is the main museum with its historic collections; just outside are re-created historic exhibits including a miner's cabin; and next door is a historic home. Most of the artifacts have been donated over the years by locals whose families have lived in Plumas County for generations.

The museum houses a superb collection of Maidu Indian baskets, a beautiful 1895 Steinway square grand piano, a collection of early firearms, and Chinese clothing. One of the more intriguing artifacts is a strong box that was once stolen by famous outlaw and self-proclaimed "P8"(poet) Black Bart. There is also a corner in the museum that has been set up as a taxidermy shop, with numerous birds and an unfortunate mountain lion as exhibits. Years ago, the lion was making meals of the local sheep, but apparently it didn't get the Fish and Game Department's attention until it was caught sitting in a tree munching the local district attorney's dog.

Walk out the back door of the main museum, and you'll find a small exhibit hall filled with rock specimens and mining equipment, as well as an old railway luggage wagon, complete with luggage. Outside there are also numerous larger pieces of mining and logging equipment and a 100-year-old log cabin that was moved here and subsequently outfitted with the meager furnishings a miner may have owned. There is a fully equipped blacksmith shop that actually gets used during special events and an agricultural tool exhibit, as well.

## Coburn-Variel Home

The museum's Coburn-Variel Home, located next door, is a restored two-story house that was likely considered a mansion locally when it was built in the 1890s by one of Quincy's well-to-do settlers. Joshua Variel and his wife, Mary, were two of the original settlers in the Quincy area, having come over the famed Beckwourth Pass in 1852. Before they lived in Quincy, though, the family spent

The 1870s-era Coburn-Variel Home

some time in Yuba County, returning to the area in 1878. That same year, Joshua, an attorney, and his son, Will, constructed the family's two-story home. It has since been owned by several families, including an early sheriff.

The home has been through significant restoration, including the removal of add-on rooms and structures, and now it appears as it did in early photos. With the home passing through so many owners over the years, its original furnishings have long since disappeared. Inside the home today is a wonderful collection of late 19th and early 20th century furnishings and artifacts. From furniture, lamps, and rugs to kitchen gadgets, clothing, and musical instruments, this is a trip back to a more simple time.

One of the best things about this house tour is the informality. There are no schedules; if you arrive at the Plumas County Museum and a docent is available, he or she will be happy to take you and a small party through the home. You even get to go up the narrow stairs to the second-floor bedrooms, something that isn't always possible in some historic homes because of fire-safety concerns.

The home is handicap-accessible, with a sloped entrance along the cement driveway, and all ground-floor doors are wide enough to accommodate wheelchairs. There is no wheelchair access to the second floor.

**HOURS:** All year, Tuesday through Saturday, 8 AM to 5 PM; from April through October, it's also open Sunday, 10 AM to 4 PM. Closed all legal holidays.

**COST:** Adults, $1; ages 12–17, $0.50; under 12, free.

**LOCATION:** 500 Jackson Street, Quincy

**PHONE:** 530-283-6320

**WEBSITE:** www.countyofplumas.com/museum

# 8 Portola Railroad Museum

**WHAT'S HERE:** Lots of locomotives and other historic rolling stock from the Western Pacific Railroad

**DON'T MISS THIS:** An opportunity to ride the trains and, for an extra fee, operate a real locomotive

You will likely notice two things as you walk from the parking lot to the main museum entrance. The first is that there are a lot of parallel tracks to cross, and museum trains move on them regularly, although slowly, so don't let young kids run too freely. Second, most of the locomotives sitting on the tracks are from the Western Pacific Railroad (WP).

If you know anything about railroading history, you'll know that WP no longer exists, having merged with the larger Union Pacific Railroad (UP) in the early 1980s.

Fortunately, a number of railroad enthusiasts understood the importance of creating a museum and acquiring pieces, albeit large pieces, of WP's history. Long an innovator in the railroad industry, relatively small WP helped introduce diesel power and turbo-charging for locomotives, freight cars that used more efficient roller bearings, and concrete ties to replace the old wood ties.

Railroads tend to be generous to museums, and UP has certainly followed tradition, providing the Portola Railroad Museum with numerous WP and UP pieces of rolling stock. You won't find much in the way of steam locomotives here. This is diesel country, and the museum houses mostly diesel locomotives built after 1950. There are several older diesel locomotives, including a very rare Foley Bros. 1-110 that was built by GE/Ingersoll-Rand in 1929.

It may seem odd that such a large railroad museum is located in this small town, but back in the days of steam power, Portola was the halfway point between Oakland and Salt Lake City. WP built a large facility here that included a roundhouse for servicing and a turntable that allowed the old steam trains to be turned around for trips back down the Feather River Canyon to Oroville or across the desert to Winnemucca, Nevada.

Unfortunately, the roundhouse and turntable are gone. WP replaced them in 1953 with the 228-foot-long, two-track, diesel-electric, locomotive-servicing building. That structure has been repaired and now houses the museum's collections and gift shop, as well as a working repair and restoration shop. So don't be surprised if you see and hear volunteers running heavy power equipment or working among grease-covered locomotive parts scattered around the concrete floor.

Much of the collections found here are old photos of WP's history. One of its more fascinating, dangerous, and difficult operations was clearing snow over the Sierra Nevada. Outside of the museum, don't miss the large locomotive with a huge rotary snowplow mounted on its front. Other items around the museum include old lanterns, safes, and other railroad equipment.

Unlike most other museums, this one offers a unique program allowing visitors to operate some of these big diesel locomotives over a mile of track. With an instructor in the cab with you, you can actually pull the switches and levers that make these monsters move. The adventure, available from mid-March to mid-November, will cost you about $100 per hour, which includes the instructor who will be with you the entire time. This is a

The Portola Railroad Museum features a large collection of operating rolling stock.

very popular program and usually sells out fast, so if your heart is set on this adventure, be sure to call ahead for reservations.

For those more interested in riding in than driving a train, "caboose train" rides are offered on weekends between Memorial Day and Labor Day, generally every half hour between 11 AM and 4 PM. There is a small, per-person charge, but for about $12, an entire family can ride all day long.

Because the snow in this region sometimes creates problems for all forms of transportation, including trains, the museum and its operations are open seasonally. Typical downtimes occur in the months of December and January. You may want to call if you're planning to visit during those months, especially if there have been some big snow storms recently.

**HOURS:** February through mid-December, daily, 11 AM to 4 PM.

**COST:** Suggested donation: 17 and older, $5; 11–16, $2; 3–10, $1.

**LOCATION:** 700 Western Pacific Way, Portola

**PHONE:** 530-832-4131

**WEBSITE:** www.wplives.org

## 9  Weaverville Joss House State Historic Park

**WHAT'S HERE:** A Chinese place of worship in continual operation since it was built in 1875, as well as a small museum dedicated to the local Chinese history

**DON'T MISS THIS:** The Chinese writing on the interior walls

The discovery of gold attracted thousands of newcomers to California. In January 1848, about the time James Marshall found his first gold nuggets, there were 54 Chinese men and one Chinese woman living in California. By the end of the decade, several thousand, most from Kwangtung Province, had immigrated to the state, along with tens of thousands of other fortune seekers. While many searched for gold, others gathered in settlements and created businesses. Weaverville was one of those Gold Rush-era settlements, and the Chinese who settled here owned several businesses, including stores, a bakery, a restaurant, and an opera house.

Around 1852, the Chinese townspeople constructed a Taoist temple. Unfortunately, the original temple met the fate of so many Gold Rush-era wooden buildings and burned to the ground in 1873. The local Chinese donated generously to the construction of new temple, which was completed in 1875. That temple—the Weaverville Joss House—is the oldest continuously used Chinese temple in California. Today, in addition to being a place of worship, the Joss House and an adjacent museum are part of a state historic park and open for public tours.

The museum is small, but it offers a look at the Chinese culture in Weaverville starting more than 150 years ago. Photos, panels, and documents help tell the story of who these people were and from where they had come. Items that Chinese locals used day to day, from clothing to smoking pipes, help add understanding to their ways of life, which the Anglos who lived here found "foreign," even though many practices were similar. For example, the Chinese had their brothels just as were found in most Gold Rush towns, and they had gambling parlors, with the only difference being that they served cigars and tea, not alcohol. By 1865, gold mining was losing its profitability, and the town's citizens began moving on. Many Chinese left Weaverville to work for the Central Pacific Railroad, constructing the transcontinental railroad. In 1906, with fire protection little improved from the previous century, accidental fire struck once again, destroying a large portion of the community. As a result, more Chinese left.

Fortunately, that last fire missed the Joss House. Today the Joss House is an active place of worship for the Chinese, and it is also open to the public by way of guided tours, which offer insights into the history of the Joss House and into this very peaceful religion. Nearly every aspect of the temple, from its form and especially to its bright colors, holds special meaning: red for good luck and good fortune, gold for wealth and prosperity, and green for health and longevity. The bright blue painted on the front of the building represents heaven.

Among the temple's many very colorful items is the ornately painted wooden alter. The three canopies above the alter hold images of special gods thought to be ancestors from some 2800 years ago. The gods represent the best examples of people who lived the correct life, in part by helping their communities prosper. The three groups represent longevity and good health; wealth, prosperity, and protection; and mercy, understanding, and forgiveness.

Beyond the temple's tall entrance doors are two additional doors—spirit doors meant to keep out evil spirits. According to traditional beliefs, evil spirits can travel in only straight lines, never around corners. Taoism is closely connected with nature and the environment; the parade banners hanging on the side walls represent good luck and good fortune, they dispel evil spirits, and they protect the four seasons of the year.

Three side rooms in the temple were once business areas. The largest room

Weaverville Joss House

was occasionally used as a courtroom. Written and painted on its walls are numerous Chinese characters; some are records of the temple's upkeep costs, while others are public documents. A full-time caretaker lived in the other two smaller rooms. His job was to maintain the temple and raise funds for its upkeep. Sometimes donations were lacking, so the more enterprising caretakers told fortunes, sold Chinese teas, and ran the Weaverville Shanghai Keno Palace at night.

> **HOURS:** Wednesday through Sunday, 10 AM to 5 PM; tours leave on the hour until 4 PM. Closed Thanksgiving, Christmas, and New Year's Day.
>
> **COST:** Adults, $2; children, free.
>
> **LOCATION:** Southwest corner of Hwy. 299 and Oregon Street, Weaverville
>
> **PHONE:** 530-623-5284 or 530-225-2065
>
> **WEBSITE:** www.parks.ca.gov/parkindex

# 10 Shasta State Historic Park Museum

**WHAT'S HERE:** Museum, art gallery, restored general mercantile, and historic working bakery

**DON'T MISS THIS:** The basement jail, hologram prisoner, and gallows

James Marshall was not the first to discover gold in California, but his discovery in January 1848 marked the beginning of the Gold Rush, although the real rush didn't begin in earnest until 1849. The few Americans already living in California got the jump on the hundreds of thousands who came during the next few years. One of those lucky early settlers was Pierson B. Reading, who discovered gold nuggets in Clear Creek. By 1849, a community of tents had sprung up around the main gold diggings, and it was called Reading Springs. The developing town quickly became a transportation hub, with settlers constructing permanent buildings and homes. In 1850, it was given the new name of Shasta.

In December 1852 and again just six months later, major fires destroyed the town's wooden buildings, but business owners rebuilt a third time, using fireproof brick and iron shutters. Even with such improvements, Shasta's boom times lasted only a dozen years. As the gold fields played out, the miners left, as did the town's businesses, including the stage lines. When the Central Pacific Railroad laid tracks in the nearby valley town of Redding, Shasta's fate was sealed.

Today, many remnants of the old brick business buildings still line Hwy. 299, the town's main street. A few of the buildings have been restored and now function as active parts of the historic park and museum. The Courthouse Museum, much of it constructed in 1853, has been restored to its 1861 appearance. It's a great place for kids, who can try all sorts of activities, including weighing gold-colored rocks on an old assay scale. Then they can take the unlucky 13 stairs to the basement and jail cells, where the courthouse looks much as it did in the 1860s, when it was used for marriages, hearings, and trials. The jail has been restored, and you can spend a little time behind bars or try on the leg irons attached to a chain secured to the floor. During the jail's use, convicted murderers walked out the back door to the gallows, where they where "hanged by the neck until dead." The gallows, reconstructed for the museum, has a staircase to the top, but no access to the gallows' trap doors. And kids will love the spooky hologram prisoner in one of the cells—he spins quite a yarn as to why he's being held prisoner.

The museum also holds a collection of California Indian baskets, mortars and pestles, and other tools used for food preparation. In contrast is the exhibit dealing with living conditions of the early settlers and gold miners. The chamber pot and handgun speak volumes about the comfort and safety of guests in one of the local hotels.

Some of the bigger mining towns acquired nicknames, and Shasta was no exception. Its long row of brick buildings and the large population that once lived here brought it the title of "Queen of the North." It was the largest town in the area, and it attracted people from all over the hills in need of supplies, their equipment repaired, and a little social interaction and entertainment.

The museum also hosts one of the most extensive collections of early California art. There are nearly 100 paintings by 71 artists, mostly from the 19th and early 20th centuries. Subjects include pastoral settings, portraits, and early cityscapes. Some of the artists and their works are well known both in this country and abroad, where many worked and studied art, and paintings from the collection are often borrowed by bigger art museums for special showings. The collection's portrait of John Augustus Sutter (see Sutter's Fort State Historic Park, page 123) was painted in 1859 by Emmanuel Leutz, who was very popular for his historical scenes. Leutz is probably best known for his 1851 painting *Washington Crossing the Delaware* (which isn't part of the museum collection).

The best part about this museum is the historic park. Just across the street

The Shasta State Historic Park Museum provides an overview of the town's history.

from the main museum are two stores and a working bakery from the 1870s. The Litsch General Store is a museum; even though some of the merchandise is available for sale, much of the store is filled with tools, supplies, and foodstuffs that would have been found here 130 years ago. Back then, most merchandise was displayed behind the counter and shown to inquiring customers by the store clerk.

The Blumb Bakery, with its working 1870s wood-fired oven, is next door. If your timing is right, you can actually help bake cookies—and enjoy the fruits of your labor hot out of the old brick oven. This is great fun for kids who often tire of touring museums.

**HOURS:** Wednesday through Sunday, 10 AM to 5 PM. Closed Thanksgiving, Christmas, and New Year's Day.

**COST:** Adults, $2; 15 and under, free.

**LOCATION:** Hwy. 299 West, in the town of Shasta, about 6 miles west of Redding

**PHONE:** 530-243-8194

**WEBSITE:** www.parks.ca.gov/parkindex

# Shasta Cascade Tours

**T**

## Family/Kids Day Tour 1

**ESTIMATED DAYS:** 1

**ESTIMATED DRIVING MILES:** 7

This is a great trip to begin in the morning at **Shasta State Historic Park Museum** (page 67), located along Hwy. 299 in the foothills west of Redding. Here is an opportunity for the kids to see an old jail, wagons, and more. And if the historic bakery is operating that day, the kids will have an opportunity to help the master baker make and bake cookies the old-fashioned way—and to taste their work! From here, head east on Hwy. 299 about 7 miles, crossing into the Great Valley region, where the family can spend the remainder of the day at **Turtle Bay Exploration Park** (page 117). After running around the expansive park, exploring, learning, and having loads of fun, you can stop for a snack or late lunch, whether you bring your own or enjoy Turtle Bay's small restaurant (good, reasonably priced food). Adjacent to the restaurant is the artistically impressive Sundial Bridge, Turtle Bay's special attraction that spans the Sacramento River. It's a pedestrian-only bridge, so there is no worry about having to dodge speeding cars and trucks.

Young visitors at Shasta State Historic Park make their own cookies in the historic bakery's brick oven.

# Family/Kids Day Tour 2

ESTIMATED DAYS: 1
ESTIMATED DRIVING MILES: 10

**D**epending on your starting destination, it may take a while to get to the **Portola Railroad Museum** (page 63), located about 50 miles northwest of Reno and 150 miles northeast of Sacramento. Hwy. 70 ultimately leads to the town of Portola, and it does so by following the scenic Feather River, where there are plenty of **campgrounds** (www.east-

ernplumaschamber.com) should you wish to spend more time exploring this beautiful part of California. If you don't camp, start out early in the morning and stop at one of the many **trout-fishing spots** along the way (www.eastern-plumaschamber.com). At the museum, spend a couple of hours wandering around and riding old Western Pacific trains—and perhaps driving one of the big locomotives (for an extra fee) if you've made prior arrangements.

Portola Railroad Museum

# Family Camping Tour

ESTIMATED DAYS: 5–7
ESTIMATED DRIVING MILES: 170

**I**t's best to take a week for this tour and to wander and explore along the way. There are plenty of camping opportunities because two of the stops are in a state park and a national park. To help wear out the kids, head to **Lava Beds National Monument Visitor Center Museum** (page 54) first, where the family can camp out among the stunted forest growing on the ancient lava flows. You can easily spend a couple of days here exploring dozens of lava caves, hiking through Captain Jack's stronghold, and visiting the museum and visitor center. Then it's off for a three-hour drive south along any one of several roads, but most likely Hwy. 49 to Hwy. 89 for a few days of relaxing beneath the tall pine and fir trees at **McArthur-Burney Falls Memorial State Park** (www.parks.ca.gov/parkindex). Besides seeing the park's spectacular waterfall, **Lake Brittton** awaits you with its cool water, swimming beaches, fishing opportunities, and boat rentals. If you happen to be in the neighborhood during the last weekend in July, don't miss the **Annual McCloud Lumberjack Fiesta** (530-964-3113; www.mccloudchamber.com), which is only about 40 miles away in the town of McCloud.

Exploring one of the many lava tubes at
Lava Beds National Monument

# Shasta Cascade
# Travel Information Centers

**?**

Shasta Cascade Wonderland Association
www.shastacascade.com
530-365-7500 or 800-474-2782

California Welcome Center (Anderson)
www.shastacascade.org
530-365-1180

Mt. Shasta Chamber of Commerce
www.mtshastachamber.com
530-926-4865 or 800-926-4865

Redding Convention & Visitors Bureau
www.visitredding.com
530-225-4100 or 800-874-7562

Plumas County Visitors Bureau
www.plumascounty.org
530-283-6345 or 800-326-2247

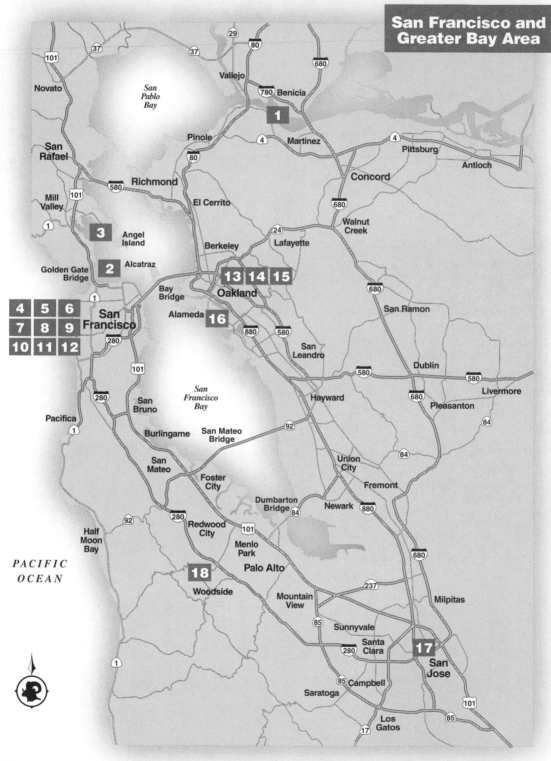

**San Francisco and Greater Bay Area**

San Pablo Bay

Novato

101

37

37

29

80

Vallejo

680

780 Benicia

**1**

San Rafael

Pinole

4 Martinez

Pittsburg

4

Antioch

101

Mill Valley

580 Richmond

80

El Cerrito

Concord

680

Walnut Creek

1

**3** Angel Island

24

Berkeley

Lafayette

Golden Gate Bridge

**2** Alcatraz

Bay Bridge

**13** **14** **15**

Oakland

680

San Ramon

**4** **5** **6**

**7** **8** **9**

**10** **11** **12**

San Francisco

1

Alameda

**16**

880

580

San Leandro

Dublin

580

280

San Bruno

San Francisco Bay

Hayward

580

680

Livermore

84

101

Pacifica

1

Burlingame

San Mateo Bridge

92

Pleasanton

San Mateo

84

PACIFIC OCEAN

Foster City

Union City

Fremont

Half Moon Bay

92

280

Redwood City

Dumbarton Bridge

84

Newark

880

101

Menlo Park

Palo Alto

680

**18**

Woodside

Mountain View

237

Milpitas

85

Sunnyvale

Santa Clara

**17**

280

San Jose

1

85 Campbell

Saratoga

101

17

Los Gatos

85

# San Francisco and Greater Bay Area

Ask most travelers to name their favorite California city, and San Francisco will invariably be at the top of their lists. Known for cable cars, the Golden Gate Bridge, steep hills, a notorious prison, and an occasional earthquake, the city is as vibrant and fun today as it was during the beginning of the great California Gold Rush in 1849, when hundreds of sailing ships clogged the bay, abandoned by hopeful gold seekers.

In may be difficult to believe, but the San Francisco Bay, a perfect haven from Pacific storms for early sailing ships, was discovered relatively late. Spanish explorer Juan Rodriguez Cabrillo sailed right past the bay in 1542, as he headed north to Oregon. More than 200 years later, Gaspar de Portola's expedition stumbled onto San Francisco Bay during his search for Monterey. It was another six years, in 1775, when Juan de Ayala sailed his ship into San Francisco Bay, finally becoming the first non-Indian boat to ply the

Filoli

waters that today are often filled with dozens of sail-boats dodging huge ocean-going freighters.

In 1776, a year when the original 13 colonies were declaring their independence from Great Britain, Mission San Francisco de Asis was founded. The town that grew up around the mission was officially dubbed Yerba Buena in 1835, but the name was changed to San Francisco after the Mexican-American War began and the US took possession of California in 1848.

San Francisco has proven to be of strategic importance; originally, it was a key entry point for gold seekers; later, it was a military defensive outpost. In February 1846, the US military completed Fort Point, designed to guard the bay from trespassing foreign warships.

Today, San Francisco has captured most of its early history in its many museums and its preserved forts. Within this region there are a couple of missions and dozens of mansions and museums. Just as we have done in other areas of California where museums are numerous, we chose those that we most enjoyed, while attempting to select those that have strong connections with California's history and also cover a wide range of interests.

Of course, we chose some of San Francisco's biggest museums, such as the de Young and the San Francisco Museum of Modern Art. Because this area has had such a strong Asian influence since the earliest days of the Gold Rush, we included the Asian Art Museum. But we also included some of the small, specialty museums such as the USS Potomac, Alcatraz Island, and the Cable Car Museum. And we couldn't ignore the oldest building in the city, Mission San Francisco, which even withstood the 1906 earthquake. Across the bay, Oakland has its share of fine museums and mansions, including the Oakland Museum of California and the home of George Pardee, who was governor of California during the 1906 earthquake.

If you're a first-time visitor, getting around San Francisco (and finding parking) can be challenging. But having good maps and possessing a sense of adventure will guarantee a memorable visit.

# TRIVIA

1 What is San Francisco's oldest building?

2 Which museum holds one of California's largest collections of Asian art based on Buddhism?

3 Where can you see the giant wheels that pull all the cables that power San Francisco's cable cars?

4 Which museum looks like a big white boat?

5 Where in San Francisco can you find the remnants of a Cold War missile site?

6 What ship picked up the *Apollo 11* astronauts following their historic first walk on the moon?

7 What is the name of one of the only two remaining World War II Liberty Ships?

8 On which mansion did carpenters work for nearly 40 years?

9 Which mansion was home to the governor who was in office during San Francisco's great 1906 earthquake?

10 Which fort was built as part of California's Civil War defense?

*For trivia answers, see page 325.*

# 1  Benicia Capitol State Historic Park

**WHAT'S HERE:** Original capitol building with historic exhibits about California's efforts to decide on a permanent state capital location

**DON'T MISS THIS:** The historic Fischer-Hanlon House next door

As a historic site, Benicia Capitol holds a significant place in California's early statehood. Benicia served as California's capital from 1853 to 1854, and it is the only early state capital whose capitol building is still standing. While Monterey served as California's capital during Mexico's rule, it didn't rate with those first legislators as a place where the new state of California should locate its capital. San Jose was awarded that honor from 1849 to 1851.

In 1849, Robert Semple had served as the president of the California Constitutional Convention, held in Monterey's Colton Hall (see Colton Hall, page 198). It was even before this time when Semple and his business partner, Thomas Larkin (see Larkin House, page 197), began plans to make Benicia the state capital, hoping that success would bring them even more prosperity. Semple and Larkin had founded the city of Benicia in 1847 after purchasing 5 square miles of land from General Mariano Vallejo (see Lachryma Montis, page 36). Semple had met Vallejo when he helped capture the Mexican general at Vallejo's home in Sonoma during the Bear Flag Revolt the year prior. But before the capital landed in Benicia, the legislature moved it from Monterey to San Jose, then to Vallejo, then to Sacramento, and finally back to Vallejo.

Always planning, Semple and other city fathers managed to raise $25,000 to build a two-story, red brick city hall, with the secret hope that the building would become the state capitol building. Finally, on February 4, 1853, after a long and much-heated debate among the legislators, they passed a resolution designating Benicia as California's capital. To Semple's delight, Benicia's city hall did, in fact, become the new state capitol, when legislators convened here later that same year.

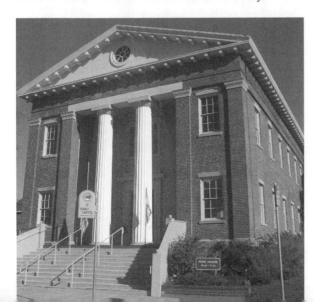

During its first 90 days, the capitol's 27 senators and 63 assemblymen introduced 460 pieces of legislation and passed 180, all of which Governor John Bigler signed into law. Some of those first laws included one that established a 10-hour workday; the first Woman Suffrage Act, which permitted women to own property under their own names; and one bill that named San Quentin as the first state prison, at a cost not to exceed $153,315. A flour inspection program was

Benicia Capitol

established that created penalties for false branding or counterfeiting brand names; flour was to be officially graded as "superfine, fine, middling, bad, or condemned."

There was also significant debate over whether California would be a free or slave state; the issue nearly split the state in two. This was to be Semple's downfall, as the issue over slavery was resolved by some backroom deals, one of which included moving the capital back to Sacramento—permanently. Governor John Bigler signed the legislation for the move the day following its passage by the legislature.

After the legislature headed east to Sacramento in 1854, the Benicia capitol went through numerous changes over the next century, including becoming the county courthouse, a place for church services, a recreation center, a firehouse, library, jail, and its so-called original intention, as city hall. The building came to State Parks in 1951, and several years later, it was restored to its original 1853 condition.

Today, the old capitol sits quietly as a small museum dedicated to its short but lively history. The largest part of the first floor appears as though the legislature just adjourned from the building, leaving their papers and white quill pens on their desks in the main chamber. A short video in the back of the room tells the story of the old capitol, and several early documents are displayed on the wall, including a map of California's original 27 counties, as they appeared in 1854.

Some of the other small rooms have been restored as offices, including one with the elaborate but simple hand stamp for the official California state seal. Exhibits include a look at California's other state capitals and why they didn't quite make it; excuses ranged from too much mud to too many fleas.

Directly next door to the capitol is the historic 14-room Fischer-Hanlon House that once served as a hotel, but at a different site in town. It was damaged by fire in 1856, and subsequently was purchased by Joseph Fischer, a Swiss merchant and cattleman, who moved it to its present location and made it his home. Successive generations of the Fischer family lived in the home until 1969, when his two granddaughters, Raphaelita and Catherine Hanlon, donated it to State Parks. The historic house provides a look at a 19th century family's home, but, unfortunately, it is open only on special occasions. For information regarding the Fischer-Hanlon House, contact Benicia Capitol. There is a small, park-like lawn and gardens separating the capitol from the home.

**HOURS:** Wednesday through Sunday, 10 AM to 5 PM. Closed Thanksgiving, Christmas, and New Year's Day.

**COST:** 17 and older, $2

**LOCATION:** 115 West G Street, Benicia

**PHONE:** 707-745-3385

**WEBSITE:** www.parks.ca.gov/parkindex

# 2  Alcatraz Island

**WHAT'S HERE:** Cell blocks and great views of San Francisco

**DON'T MISS THIS:** Exhibit about Frank Morris and his escape attempt that became a Clint Eastwood movie

Alcatraz Island, just a 10-minute ferry ride from San Francisco's Fisherman's Wharf, is best known for its days as a federal prison (1934 to 1963), during which time it incarcerated some of the country's most notorious bad guys. But it had been used as another kind of prison before the likes of Al Capone and "Creepy" Karpis took up their involuntary service on this desolate island.

Spain and Mexico ignored the island, and it wasn't until the Gold Rush that the new owners, the US government, decided to build a lighthouse to help direct the massive number of ships coming and going through the Golden Gate. In 1853, the Army built a small outpost for additional artillery that could help protect the bay from marauding foreign ships. When the Civil War broke out, the island's battery was increased to 111 smoothbore cannons, along with other defenses. The biggest gun was a 25-ton Rodman cannon that fired 440-pound cannonballs.

Even though it wasn't designated as a prison at the time, the island housed Indians who were captured during the different Indian wars in the mid- to late 19th century. It held the first US military prisoners in 1859, when 11 soldiers were placed in confinement at the garrison. During the Civil War, soldiers who had been convicted of serious crimes such as desertion, rape, and murder, along with the crew of a captured Confederate ship, were held on the island.

The advent of modern artillery made San Francisco's forts, including Alcatraz, obsolete, and the island's defensive role was decommissioned in 1907. But that only marked the beginning of the island's expanded role as a military prison. Alcatraz soon became the US Disciplinary Barracks, Pacific Branch. In 1934, the military transferred the island jail to the US Department of Justice, thus beginning its role as a federal penitentiary.

Part of Alcatraz's intrigue is its reputation, "enhanced" by Hollywood, as being the escape-proof holding place for the country's most notorious criminals. The island prison did live up to its reputation; only one of the 14 attempted breakouts may have been successful. As portrayed in the 1979 Clint Eastwood movie *Escape from Alcatraz*, Frank Morris and two brothers attempted to escape in 1962 by floating across the channel. They were never seen again. Of the 1545 men (there were no women) who served time on the "Rock," only a handful, such as Capone, Karpis,

San Francisco Bay's infamous Alcatraz Island

"Machine Gun" Kelly, and Robert Stroud (better known as the "Birdman of Alcatraz"), met the definition of "notorious." Most of the others were sent to Alcatraz because of behavior or attempted escape problems.

Alcatraz closed in 1963, and the remaining prisoners were transferred elsewhere. The following year, Native American activists occupied the island for several hours, attempting to bring attention to their many issues. Five years later, more Indians returned to Alcatraz, demanding that the government sell it to them for $26 in beads, cloth, and other trinkets (just like the 1626 purchase of Manhattan Island). They stayed for 19 months, until federal agents finally removed them in 1971. Then the General Services Administration began bulldozing the island's buildings, but demolition was halted in 1972 when the island became part of the new Golden Gate National Recreation Area.

Today, the National Park Service manages the island, most of which is open to the public for tours. Ferries drop people at the floating dock facility and everyone is ushered up to the main office area. There, a park ranger provides a quick orientation that includes a little of the prison's history, warnings about staying out of closed areas, and most importantly, a request that you return to the dock in time to catch the last ferry back to the mainland. The guardhouse and sally port building sit adjacent to the dock and, besides a couple of old cannons from its role as a harbor defense point during the Civil War, there is now only a visitor center and small museum inside that shows a 12-minute orientation film.

The cellblock offers a look at the tiny cells that became homes for so many convicted felons. You can even "lock" your kids in one of the isolation cells, but you aren't allowed to leave them. A few of the cells have beds and examples of the personal effects that prisoners were permitted to have. One of the cells includes exhibits that tell the story of the famous 1962 escape attempt, which the *San Francisco Chronicle* headlined "Out of Alcatraz—by a Spoon," and which subsequently became the aforementioned film, *Escape from Alcatraz*.

There is much more to see, including the walled-in exercise yard, the remnants of the warden's house, and the gardens. The military brought in topsoil by barges, and over the years, residents and convicts introduced and raised hundreds of different plants. The island also is home to one of northern California's largest colonies of western gulls, and on clear days, the views of San Francisco and the Golden Gate Bridge are spectacular.

The only access to the island is by ferry, and the tours can fill a week in advance, especially during summer and holiday weekends. Reservations are advised in order to avoid certain disappointment. The tours take about 2.5 hours, but you can return on any ferry. There is no food service on the island and if you bring your own, the dock area is the only place where picnicking is allowed. For anyone unable to walk the

Alcatraz guard tower near the tour boat dock

quarter mile up the 12 percent grade from the dock to the main cellblock, a shuttle is available, and the ferries will accommodate wheelchairs. You may not ride a bike on the island, but if you're taking the ferry tour with Angel Island as your next stop, there are bike racks (bring your own locks) at the docks for your use.

**HOURS:** Ferries from the Blue and Gold Fleet leave about every 30 to 40 minutes, beginning at 9:30 AM. The island closes at 6 PM during summer and 4:30 PM the remainder of the year.

**COST:** Includes ferry ride and audio tour: Adults, $16.50; ages 62 and older, $14.75; 5–11, $10.75

**LOCATION:** Pier 41, San Francisco

**PHONE:** For reservations, contact the Blue and Gold Fleet: 415-705-5555 or www.blueandgold-fleet.com. For information, contact the National Park Service: 415-561-4700.

**WEBSITE:** www.nps.gov/alcatraz/welcome.html

# 3  Angel Island State Historic Park

**WHAT'S HERE:** Historic military buildings, bike trail, and mountaintop views of San Francisco and the Golden Gate Bridge

**DON'T MISS THIS:** The tram ride around the island

Angel Island is one of those great San Francisco side trips. Originally, the island was used by the Coast Miwok Indians, but in 1863, the US Army took over the strategic island and established Fort Reynolds in response to its Civil War needs for defending the bay. Angel Island later served military needs during World War I and II, and also during the Cold War.

The island is loaded with history that you can explore in its museum and many historic buildings. There are also 12 miles of roads and trails; since the public isn't allowed to drive on the island, it's a great place for a day of hiking or bicycling (helmets are required). Some people reach the island in their own boats, landing at Ayala Cove, but most come over on ferries from either San Francisco's Pier 41 or from the much closer community of Tiburon.

The island wasn't always so welcoming. Similar to Alcatraz, its infamous and much smaller neighbor, Angel Island served as a military outpost beginning in 1863. But unlike the inhospitable Alcatraz, the Coast Miwok Indians had inhabited Angel Island for 2000 years. That began to change when, in 1775, Lt. Juan Manuel de Ayala sailed his tiny ship into the bay and anchored near what is today the island's Ayala Cove. He named the island "Isla de Los Angeles." With the advent of the local missions and with a decreasing Indian population, the island became less important and less accessible as one of their fishing and hunting sites. By the time the US Army arrived in 1863, the Miwok had ceased using the island.

In 1900, the Army renamed the island Fort McDowell, and the Civil War-era Camp Reynolds became the island's West Garrison, with the East Garrison constructed later. East Garrison continued as an Army recruitment and replacement depot through the 1920s, processing 40,000 soldiers each year. Throughout World War II, Angel Island served as an embarkation point for troops headed to the Pacific, as well as a processing center for enemy troops lucky enough to live, but unlucky enough to be captured.

The island also served as a quarantine station beginning in 1891. Foreign ships and their cargo, along with their crews and passengers suspected of carrying diseases, were inspected and fumigated when necessary. When medical technology later improved, the US Public Health Service closed the 400-bed detention barracks, disinfecting plant, and laboratories, and moved their operations to San Francisco.

One of the island's most historical roles was as an immigration center beginning in 1910 and continuing until 1940. Following the Chinese Exclusion Act of 1882, Chinese desiring entry into the country were detained on the island anywhere from two weeks to six months, as long as it took to fully scrutinize and process their applications. The Chinese were generally required to have relatives already in the country in order for them to be admitted, and even that was no guarantee. Prejudice ruled and their stays were not free from stress and harassment. During a 1970 restoration of the immigration station barracks, workers discovered poetry that some of the Chinese detainees had carved into the wooden walls about their lives on Angel Island. These can still be seen today on tours.

The Army finally abandoned Angel Island in 1946, but it returned during the Cold War to build a Nike missile battery near the island's southeastern corner. Nike missiles were designed to intercept Russian bombers, but by 1962, the technology had become obsolete, and the Army decommissioned the base. Once again, the island was free of military control, but remnants of the missile site can still be seen near the top of a hill on the southeast corner of the island.

Ayala Cove is where nearly everyone first enters the island. It's a five-minute walk on the pathway from the ferry dock past the food concession, bicycle-rental stand, and island tour tram staging area to the visitor center and museum. They are housed in the historic bachelor officers' quarters at the top of the grassy rise just above the picnic tables. Inside, among a few artifacts, is a timeline exhibit of the island's history. One of the best ways to get a sense for the island's 700-plus acres and the many historic homes, military facilities, and ruins is either to ride a bike or take the paid tram tour around the island.

The historic bachelor officers' quarters serves as a visitor center and museum.

Picnicking is encouraged on the island, and tables are available in several areas. Open fires are not allowed, but there are barbecue grills available, or you can bring your own. Dogs aren't allowed, and since there is poison oak, staying on trails is wise. It's a good idea to check the different websites associated with Angel Island for special events that feature tours of the historic homes that generally are not open to the public on a daily basis. There are also living history days and Civil War reenactments. Anytime you visit Angel Island, dress in layers, as it can be warm and sunny, or windy, foggy, and cold, all within the same hour.

**HOURS:** Day use generally begins with the first ferry arrivals, about 10:30 AM, and ends with the departure of the last ferry, usually from 3:20 PM to 3:50 PM. For those using their own boats, the park is open from 8 AM to sunset. Limited overnight camping is available. For camping information, contact the park; for camping reservations call 800-444-7275.

**COST:** Round-trip ferry fees range from $10 for adults and $7.50 for children from Tiburon, to $13.50 for adults and $8 for children from San Francisco's Pier 41. For the Tiburon ferry, call 415-435-2131 or visit www.angelislandferry.com; for the Blue and Gold (San Francisco) Ferry, call 415-773-1188 or visit www.blueandgoldfleet.com.

**LOCATION:** San Francisco Bay, access from Pier 41 in San Francisco or 21 Main Street in Tiburon.

**PHONE:** 415-435-1915 or 415-435-5390

**WEBSITE:** www.angelisland.org

# 4 Fort Point National Historic Site

**WHAT'S HERE:** Exhibits on 1860s military life at Fort Point

**DON'T MISS THIS:** The view of the Golden Gate Bridge from the fort's top level

This Civil War-era fort is located directly beneath the south end of the Golden Gate Bridge, where the US Army saw the importance of protecting this narrow entrance into San Francisco Bay from marauding ships and potential enemy navies. On the West Coast, Fort Point is the only "third system" fort, a designation given to these heavily fortified forts specifically designed to defend major US harbors. Several had been built on the East Coast following the War of 1812.

The Army started construction of Fort Point in 1853, but it wasn't completed and the first of its artillery wasn't in place until 1861, at the start of the Civil War. Much of the initial construction work was spent cutting the cliff down to just 15 feet above the water's surface where the fort would be constructed, and then securing enough granite to complete the fortifications. Workers began construction using quarried granite for the fort's walls, but they soon found that sources of the hard stone were limited, so they switched to using brick. A nearby brickyard produced 8 million bricks to complete the fortifications.

The introduction of rifled cannon barrels during the Civil War had demonstrated that brick walls couldn't withstand the new, more powerful and accurate artillery. As a result, following the war, Fort Point was demoted from its role as a key defense location, although it continued to function as a military fort. It was renamed Fort Winfield Scott in 1882. In 1892, new breech-loading rifled cannons were installed and the remaining smooth-bore cannon was removed. The Coast Guard manned the fort during World War II to protect the bay from enemy attacks in part by guarding the anti-submarine net that spanned the bay's opening, monitoring the mine fields, and protecting the entrance with their rapid-fire cannon.

When the Golden Gate Bridge was being planned for in the 1930s, the fort was identified for removal. Fortunately, chief engineer Joseph Strauss redesigned the bridge supports so that the historic fort could remain. He was enamored with the brick work and felt strongly that the fort should be preserved and restored as a national monument. This occurred when it became a national historic site in 1970, and it is now managed by the National Park Service.

Most of the fort is open to visitors' wanderings, including the top Barbette tier, where sod once helped to protect the fort from the force of enemy artillery rounds. Today the sod is gone and the Golden Gate Bridge has been added overhead, offering a much different perspective of the span. Inside the fort are several exhibit spaces, mostly old photos and drawings. A portion of the barracks has been restored—note the differences between the space allocated for officers versus that for the enlisted men. Also note that the enlisted men were housed on the third level, and the officers were below on the second, likely affording the officers a little more protection from ship artillery bombardments. There is a small mess hall kitchen exhibit that features some of the meals fed the soldiers.

The lower-level rooms, where all the gun powder was stored, has been reconstructed and filled with powder kegs that include markings indicating where the East Coast factories were located that shipped the power to the West Coast. Out in the now empty casemates, those individual sections where each cannon was mounted, all of the half circles on the floors behind each of the cannon firing ports were where steel rails were mounted that allowed the cannon to be moved and aimed either left or right. The rails have been removed.

Rangers offer periodic talks about the history of the fort and also demonstrations on how the big guns were loaded and fired—although they don't fire the weapons. There is also a small gift shop and a small theater that shows history-related videos.

The top of Fort Point offers a different view of the Golden Gate Bridge.

HOURS: Daily, 10 AM to 5 PM; the fort will be closed Monday through Thursdays while the Golden Gate Bridge undergoes a five-year earthquake retrofit. Check the website for updates. Closed Thanksgiving, Christmas, and New Year's Day.

COST: Free

LOCATION: Beneath the southern end of the Golden Gate Bridge; from Lincoln Blvd., turn left onto Long Ave., which turns into Marine Drive and ends at the fort's parking lot.

PHONE: 415-556-1693

WEBSITE: www.nps.gov/fopo

# 5  San Francisco Maritime Museum

**WHAT'S HERE:** Exhibits on San Francisco's maritime history, especially the ship's radio room

**DON'T MISS THIS:** The walk to the Hyde Street Pier to see the historic ships

The San Francisco Maritime Museum, located at the far west end of Fisherman's Wharf near Aquatic Park, is part of the San Francisco Maritime National Historic Park. Built to resemble a large, white ship moored on the beach, the museum overlooks a historic park with numerous old ships and a small visitor center, just a stroll away at the nearby Hyde Street Pier. The museum exhibits cover California's maritime history, the Gold Rush, sailing around the Horn, the whaling industry, and the move to steam technology.

From wonderfully detailed large-scale models of sailing ships to the intricately carved, full-size figureheads that adorned the bows of many 18th and 19th century ships, the museum offers three floors of historic maritime artifacts. Remnants of sunken ships and wall-sized photographs of early San Francisco blend well with the maritime exhibits that cover everything from the Chinese shrimp industry in San Francisco Bay to the founding of the San Francisco Yacht Club.

The bay's Chinese shrimp industry was very successful, and it even survived, although at a lesser extent, after the US government banned Chinese from shrimp fishing in 1911. In 1850, there also

The *Balclutha*, built in 1886, is part of the San Francisco Maritime Museum.

SAN FRANCISCO & GREATER BAY AREA

85

was a lively and profitable ferry business on the bay between Oakland and San Francisco, but just as politics, money, and new technology manage to kill long-time successful businesses today, in 1863, the railroads had taken control of the major transportation links between the San Francisco peninsula and the mainland at Oakland, lessening the need for water travel.

Another exhibit tells about the Alaskan Packers Association, which moved its fleet of fishing vessels each year to Alaska for the salmon season, and then back to San Francisco at its close. They formed in 1893 and initially depended on wooden-hulled boats, but by 1901, they were using steel-hulled vessels.

The museum offers numerous bits of maritime trivia, such as the fact that the *USS California* was the only battleship ever built at the nearby Mare Island shipyard. From 1916 to 1919, workers constructed the 624-foot-long warship. Another bit of trivia is that during the late 19th century, about a quarter of all the captains of American merchant ships carried their wives and children onboard while they sailed to different ports around the world.

Be sure to wander up to the museum's top floor, where there are more exhibits and great views of the bay, then head over to the Hyde Street Pier. The most prominent ship at the pier is the three-masted *Balclutha*, a 256-foot-long, square-rigged vessel built in 1886 in Glasgow, Scotland. It was originally designed to carry wheat from California to Europe. Below deck offers an opportunity to see how sailors lived while spending months onboard sailing around the Horn. Their accommodations were not spacious, especially when compared with the captain's quarters.

Nearby, the *C.A. Thayer* is also three-masted, but it's a schooner and 100 feet shorter than the *Balclutha*. She and hundreds just like her were used to haul everything from timber to concrete up and down the West Coast. Climb down below and see where freshly caught salmon and other fish were packed in salt and stacked to the ceiling. Most people who have spent time near large port cities such as Seattle have seen ferries that move people across water just as the *Eureka* did for decades. The biggest difference is that the *Eureka* is a 300-foot long, side-wheel-powered ferry built in 1890. It was originally named the *Ukiah*, but as happened with many vessels when they changed owners, its name was changed in 1922 to *Eureka*. Several other vessels, including tug boats and smaller sailing craft, are moored at the Hyde Street Pier.

**HOURS:** Daily, 10 AM to 5 PM. Closed Thanksgiving, Christmas, and New Year's Day.

**COST:** Maritime Museum is free; to board the Hyde Street Pier ships, 16 and older, $5.

**LOCATION:** Museum is at 900 Beach Street; Hyde Street Pier is at the end of Hyde Street at Jefferson; Pier 45 is at the end of Taylor Street and Jefferson Street, San Francisco.

**PHONE:** 415-447-5000

**WEBSITE:** www.nps.gov/safr

# 6  SS Jeremiah O'Brien

**WHAT'S HERE:** World War II memorabilia, docents who served on these ships, and a chance to go on a cruise aboard the ship

**DON'T MISS THIS:** The tight sleeping quarters for the crew, the flying bridge, or the weekend engine operations

Docked at San Francisco's famed Fisherman's Wharf is a floating museum, one of the few of the 2751 remaining Liberty Ships that were crucial to the Allies winning World War II. The *SS Jeremiah O'Brien* takes it name from a Scots-Irish lumberjack from coastal Maine. Captain O'Brien became a naval hero, winning the first American naval victory against the British during the American Revolution.

As war loomed for the US during the late 1930s, America knew that having large numbers of supply ships would prove critical. The government began a ship-building program meant to launch 100 of these new, cheap freighters annually. That number was soon doubled, and then doubled again. New construction techniques were developed, such as welding the ships rather than using the time-tested but time-consuming rivets. Shipyards developed new ways to prefabricate entire sections of the ships that could then be dropped into place by huge cranes, welded, and launched. Soon, American ingenuity was turning out supply ships faster than the deadly German U-boats could sink them.

The ships originally were designed to last just five years, assuming they managed to elude the German U-boats that long. The assembly techniques built quality ships that instead operated for decades. Originally predicted to take 100 days to build a single ship, they were churned out in just 40 days. The generic name, Liberty Ship, was a great public relations move designed to add status to what most mariners considered an ugly ship, and to focus the public's attention on the vital role these ships would play in the war. The first Liberty Ship was launched in November 1940.

The 441-foot-long *SS Jeremiah O'Brien* was built in South Portland, Maine, and launched on June 19, 1943. She served as a supply carrier, crossing the Atlantic as part of the great convoys to Great Britain and participating in the Normandy D-Day invasion, before heading to the Pacific. The *O'Brien* saw many ports, including the Philippines, India, and China, and was attacked several times,

World War II Liberty Ship *SS Jeremiah O'Brien*

but it never received any significant damage. When the war finally ended, one of her last duties was steaming back to San Francisco with nine Australian war brides who were coming to the US to meet their husbands.

The *SS Jeremiah O'Brien* became one of the ships that the US Navy was preserving should they be needed for future actions. Finally, in 1963, the Navy determined that the old Liberty Ships would not be needed. Most were cut into scrap, but the *O'Brien* survived, and a hearty group of volunteers set about restoring the old ship. In 1978, she was placed on the National Register as a historic object and, finally, in 1979, the *O'Brien* was able to steam away for the first time in 33 years.

Today, the old Liberty Ship still goes on short cruises, taking paying passengers around the bay and occasionally on longer voyages up the Sacramento River to the city of Sacramento or to San Diego. But most of the time, the *O'Brien* remains in port and is open for tours. You can board the ship and wander among its decks, including the main deck, where the old 3-inch gun that offered very little real protection is still pointed skyward— toward the city. There are also great views of San Francisco from the main deck. You can head down to the engine room, where, on Steaming Weekends (usually the third weekend of each month), the boilers are "lit off" and the 2500-horsepower, triple-expansion reciprocating steam main engine is operated. Or you can head up to the flying bridge, where the captain spent much of his time.

In 1994, the *SS Jeremiah O'Brien* steamed beneath the Golden Gate, through the Panama Canal, and back to England and France as part of the 50th anniversary of Operation Overlord and the Normandy invasion in World War II. Of the 5000 ships that took part in the June 6, 1944, D-Day invasion, she was the only Liberty Ship to make the return voyage. Only one other Liberty Ship exists today as a museum, and it is located in Baltimore, Maryland.

**HOURS:** Daily, 10 AM to 4 PM. Closed Thanksgiving, Christmas, New Year's Day, and when actively cruising.

**COST:** Adults, $9; seniors, $5; ages 6–14, $4; people with military ID, free. Family discounts are available, and there are additional fees to join one of the cruises.

**LOCATION:** Pier 45, Fisherman's Wharf, San Francisco

**PHONE:** 415-544-0100

**WEBSITE:** www.ssjeremiahobrien.org

# 7  San Francisco Cable Car Museum

**WHAT'S HERE:**  Exhibits about cable car history overlooking the actual, operating cable-pulley system

**DON'T MISS THIS:**  The close-up view of the cables that provide the pull for all of San Francisco's cable cars

Every tourist who comes to San Francisco likely takes at least one ride on the city's famous cable cars. Yet for most, how the cars are able to operate on such steep hills and turn corners remains a mystery. The San Francisco Cable Car Museum, located in the historic Washington/Mason cable car barn and powerhouse, offers a first-hand look at what drives all those bell-ringing cable cars. This is a working museum—the observation deck overlooks 510-horsepower electric motors and huge, winding wheels that pull miles of heavy steel cable at a constant 9.5 miles per hour beneath San Francisco's streets. Each of the cables is labeled to show which cable line is at work. The lower observation level offers a great view of how the pulleys work underground to redirect the cables as they operate beneath the streets of San Francisco.

The cable car concept is simple: The cars have a lever-operated, grip-like device that extends through the bottom of the cable car and into the slot that runs the length of the street. When the grip man pulls on the grip, it grabs hold of the constantly moving cable beneath the street and moves forward. To stop, the grip man simply releases the grip on the cable and applies the brakes. More than one person has wondered what kind of brakes stop these cars from hurtling down one of the steep hills. But there is little to fear, because each cable car is equipped with three separate braking systems, one on the wheels, another that can be pressed against the tracks, and the third, a steel wedge that is jammed into the street slot and is used only for emergency stops.

In addition to showing what powers the cable cars, this free museum features numerous exhibits, including the only car that remains from the very first cable car company in San Francisco, the Clay Street Hill Railroad. Andrew Smith Hallidie founded the Clay Street Hill Railroad; it was his British father who invented and had the patent for "wire rope" cable. Hallidie, who developed systems in the 1850s for hauling ore from mines and for building suspension bridges, established the line in San Francisco in 1873. His success was the driving force behind others beginning their own cable cars in other parts of the city, signaling an end to horse-drawn wagons.

This new mode of transportation became more popular in the 1880s—considered cable car's glory days—when eight separate companies operated cars over many more of San Francisco's

The giant wheels that power San Francisco's cable cars can be seen from the museum's balcony overlook.

streets than are currently in operation today. Most ran only a few years; the California Street Cable Railway, founded in 1878, was purchased by the city and county of San Francisco in 1952 and became one of the three remaining routes for the city.

Just 10 years after that purchase, the electric streetcar was developed in 1888 and cost significantly less to construct and maintain. Many in the city government wanted the electric system to be the city's first choice for transit services, as both systems were being utilized in the city. By the late 1940s, most of the cable car systems had faded away, prompting San Francisco Mayor Roger Lapham to declare, "The city should get rid of all cable car lines as soon as possible." Fortunately, the mayor lost his bid to rid the city of its historic cable cars. In the end, others, including the city's voters, saw the importance of maintaining the famed cable cars; for the tourism industry, they had become a symbol of San Francisco, right along with the Golden Gate Bridge.

There is a cable car stop at the corner of Washington and Mason streets, right in front of the museum. Both the Powell-Hyde or Powell-Mason lines will get you to the museum from near the waterfront (Powell-Hyde stops at the San Francisco Maritime Museum, see page 85). If you're not sure which car to catch or where to get off, ask one of the cable car operators or grip men.

> **HOURS:** April through September, daily, 10 AM to 6 PM; October through March, daily, 10 AM to 5 PM. Closed New Year's Day, Easter Sunday, Thanksgiving, and Christmas.
> **COST:** Free
> **LOCATION:** 1201 Mason Street, on the corner of Washington and Mason streets, San Francisco
> **PHONE:** 415-474-1887
> **WEBSITE:** www.cablecarmuseum.org

# 8  San Francisco Museum of Modern Art

**WHAT'S HERE:** Wide array of art from the 20th century's most creative minds
**DON'T MISS THIS:** The furniture made from corrugated cardboard

SF MOMA was the first museum on the West Coast to focus on modern art, although "modern" wasn't officially added to its name until 1975. Founded in 1935, the museum's emphasis is on 20th century art, and its diversity of media is as wide as the imaginations of the best artists who have worked in the past 100-plus years. The museum today is a work of art in itself, with four levels of exhibits and a lobby entrance ceiling that soars to the top of the building.

With more than 22,000 pieces in its permanent collection, which is added to each year, there are limits to what can be exhibited at any one time. The exhibits fall into four general categories: architecture and design, media arts, painting and sculpture, and photography. Architecture and design brings a collection of many things, from building plans to furniture. Its pieces range from a chair that artist Frank O. Gehry fashioned from corrugated cardboard to the ceramic vase that Frank Lloyd Wright created in 1905 that resembles a 1930s skyscraper, which he aptly named *Skyscraper Vase*. Other pieces include many additional furniture designs from throughout the 20th century, such as the couch made from telephone directories and lamps that look like fish and lamps that look like…lamps.

Go to the media arts gallery, and you've entered the realm of digital video, multi-channel stereos, film clips, and more. Digital animation is one of today's most popular electronic mediums, and most of the exhibits are composed of viewable screens of different sizes. Sometimes it's the actual delivery system that is the piece of art, at least as much as what is projected.

Wander into the museum's world of paintings and sculptures, and you've entered another very different arena. Some of the pieces are wall-sized canvases painted a single solid color; others, such as Anselm Kiefer's *Osiris und Isis* (Osiris and Isis), which the German artist completed between 1985 and 1987, includes the use of oil and acrylic emulsion "with additional three-dimensional media." Accurately describing the image he created is another matter entirely, but it is nonetheless fascinating to see.

The photographic gallery covers everything from the artistic and avant-garde to documentary images taken during the past 150 years. Photographic processes have evolved over those years, and many of the processes that have changed the face of photographic prints are presented here. There's Carleton E. Watkin's 1861 albumen print of *Yosemite's Nevada Fall* and Edward Weston's gelatin silver print of *Pipes and Stacks, Armco, Middletown, Ohio* image from 1922. No matter what the medium, the images all offer peeks

into the past, whether it is a 1906 city street scene in San Francisco following the earthquake, two brightly painted ladies in a New York City taxi, or an Egyptian pyramid taken in 1858.

This is a great place to spend a couple of hours simply wandering the floors and perusing the art. And with the ever-changing temporary exhibits, it's worth coming back anytime the opportunity arises, even if it's just to browse the expansive gift shop.

San Francisco Museum of Modern Art

**HOURS:** Friday to Tuesday, 11 AM to 5:45 PM; Thursday, 11 AM to 8:45 PM (opens at 10 AM from Memorial Day through Labor Day); closed Wednesday, except on the Wednesday between Christmas and New Year's Day. Closed July 4, Thanksgiving, Christmas, and New Year's Day; closes at 4:45 PM on Christmas Eve and New Year's Eve.

**COST:** Adults, $12.50; students age 13 and older (with ID), $7; age 62 and older, $8; 12 and under, free; first Tuesday of each month, free.

**LOCATION:** 151 Third Street San Francisco

**PHONE:** 415-357-4000

**WEBSITE:** www.sfmoma.org

# 9  Asian Art Museum

**WHAT'S HERE:** A large collection of art, much of which is based on Buddhism's expansion throughout Asia

**DON'T MISS THIS:** The beautiful and expansive Samsung Hall

San Francisco is an appropriate venue for the Asian Art Museum. The city served as the primary entry point for thousands of Chinese following the discovery of gold in California, and today, the imprint of Asian cultures throughout San Francisco is evident from the Chinese, Japanese, and other "towns" found here.

For those who may have visited the Asian Art Museum in its old location in Golden Gate Park, you are in for a pleasant surprise. The museum is now housed in the Chong-Moon Lee Center for Asian Art and Culture in San Francisco's Civic Center, just across the park from City Hall. The museum collection includes more than 15,000 artifacts, making it one of the largest museums in the western world dedicated to Asian art. Each year, the museum rotates up to 3000 different pieces from its collection into the exhibits, providing opportunities to see new art.

The museum's numerous galleries are found throughout its three floors. The museum staff recommends that you begin your tour on the third floor and work your way through the timeline "path" to the second floor and then back to the first floor. This allows you to follow the collections through the general path of Buddhism, one of the strongest influences in Asian art, as it spread throughout the continent and beyond. Pieces from as early as 100 to 300 AD can be found here, such as the Bodhisattva Maitrreya, a statue of what is sometimes described as a hypothetical being that has gained total enlightenment. There are slightly different versions of this, depending upon what culture you are ascribing the Bodhisattva to.

The many other pieces in the third floor's several galleries provide a look at art from Pakistan, India, Iran, Burma, Indonesia, and even Nepal and Tibet. Their ages are equally diversified, with many of the pieces dating from 1000 AD through the 20th century. You can find the Hindu deities Shiva and Parvati, popular with many artists, dating back 1000 years or more.

Some of the more curious pieces include a collection of Indonesian puppets dating from sometime after 1800. The brightly painted and clothed puppets representing people from various stations in life are rotated through the exhibit regularly.

On the second floor, Japanese contributions to the art world are represented through several galleries that cover the entire wing. The collection ranges from Japanese Buddhist art to beautiful paintings and screens, and porcelain and tea-related pieces. The war arts of the samurai warriors are included, at least with respect to their clothing, from helmets to leather armor. The second level also includes a small Korean section with exquisite pieces of pottery, and a continuation of the Chinese galleries (from the top floor) that fill the remaining second-floor wing. Much of the Chinese exhibits on the second level consist of paintings from various periods of the different dynasties.

The first-floor galleries feature changing exhibits, a gift shop, and an Asian cafeteria-style cafe. There is also a coat-check room. If you bring in backpacks, umbrellas, and large bags or parcels, they must be checked. You can also check at the information desk for the periodic free guided tours of the museum. If you'd like more information than is found on the museum labels for many of the art pieces you will see, free audio wands are available at the information desk

**HOURS:** Tuesday through Sunday, 10 AM to 5 PM; open until 9 PM on Thursdays. Closed Thanksgiving, Christmas, and New Year's Day.

**COST:** Adults, $10; 65 and older, $7; college students with ID and ages 13–17, $6; 12 and under, free. Thursdays after 5 PM, adults, $5; children, free.

**LOCATION:** 200 Larkin Street, San Francisco

**PHONE:** 415-581-3500

**WEBSITE:** www.asianart.org

Asian Art Museum

# 10 **De Young Museum**

**WHAT'S HERE:** Art from Africa, the Pacific Islands, the Americas, and more

**DON'T MISS THIS:** The elevator to the glass-walled tower for spectacular San Francisco views

San Francisco's Golden Gate Park is home to the "new" de Young Museum and its extensive collections of art from around the world. The redesigned museum was completed and reopened to the public in 2005. Its distinct cinnamon-colored copper walls will eventually change to a rich green patina designed to blend with the surrounding park environment.

The museum's namesake is M.H. de Young who, in 1893, was the publisher of the *San Francisco Chronicle*. The idea for a museum likely began when de Young decided that San Francisco should sponsor a huge exposition. He quickly convinced the powers-that-be, and, in January 1894, the California Midwinter International Exposition, featuring "exotic Eastern themes," opened in Golden Gate Park. The six-month fair proved to be so popular and such a financial success that he pushed for a permanent museum to memorialize the fair. Successful in his efforts, the first museum building was designed in an Egyptian Revival-style architecture, and it opened in 1895.

Many of the museum's exhibits came from the 1894 International Exposition, but de Young was determined to add to the collections. When confronted with the extraordinarily high price demanded for a collection of antique knives and forks owned by Tiffany's of New York, he decided to put together his own collections. De Young spent the next 20 years gathering nearly anything that struck his fancy: paintings, sculptures, birds' eggs, handcuffs, and an extensive selection of knives and forks. In 1929, de Young's Egyptian museum was declared unsafe and was replaced by yet another building.

During those early years, there was little focus to the museum's eclectic collections. The replacement museum opened in 1931, and by 1933, the de Young had a new director, Walter Heil, who gave direction to the museum's collection policy, refusing to accept every piece of art or curiosity that was offered. The museum continued to grow, merging with the California Palace of the Legion of Honor (about 3 miles away) to become the Fine Arts Museums of San Francisco. Over the years, many prominent people, such as John D. Rockefeller III, have donated extensive and important collections of art to the museum.

The new de Young museum has two levels. The entry court area exhibits located on the concourse level focus on 20th century and contemporary art. Included are some of the 100 paintings donated by the late John D. Rockefeller III, including those done by Winslow Homer and John Singleton. There is a selection of pieces designed to represent American art from the early 20th century modernism through the 1950s and '60s. Georgia O'Keeffe, Diego Rivera, and Wayne Thiebaud are just three of the dozens of artists represented.

The de Young also features a representative sampling of beautiful works from tribes known for their exquisite basketry, such as the California North Coast Yurok. The exhibited collection also includes the works of peoples from Mexico, Central America, and South

America. A carved stone Maya stele is one of the museum's featured pieces; an extensive collection of ceremonial and religious sculptures shows the skills possessed by these early artisans.

African art also intrigued the de Young's collectors. Ceremonial masks, shields, carved wooden religious icons, and other pieces fill the exhibits. The ceremonial masks feature teeth, horns, and other attributes that were often included in exaggerated forms in terms of size and often numbers. They were done to accent the attributes of power or what was perceived as power. One piece in particular that draws attention is the Dogon sculpture carved in about 1200 AD. The bearded nude figure is carved from wood and appears anatomically to be a cross of a man and a woman, likely representing a primordial ancestor. It is speculated that the figure's upraised arms (although broken) may be reaching toward the heavens as a prayer or perhaps as a plea for rain.

The Pacific Islands are also represented, with artifacts ranging from carved masks to headdresses, shields, and human skulls that have been artfully transformed into ceremonial holders. The collection numbers more than 400 works of New Guinea art, and considering the range and rarity of the art pieces, it is one of the finest collections in the world.

The photo gallery, while not extensive, does include works from such renowned 20th century photographers as Edward Weston (1886–1958), Imogen Cunningham (1883–1976), and Paul Strand (1890–1976). The collection features photographs from the advent of the art form, spanning the 1840s to more contemporary works.

The textiles gallery on the upper level offers a look at the broad range and history of textiles. While the exhibits are changed periodically to protect the fragile nature of the fabrics and dyes, pieces can range from the fragments of a Chinese woman's dress (265–400 AD) made of red and blue dyed wool, to 11th and 12th century Asia fabrics, along with intricately woven carpets from Afghanistan, Iran, and Turkmenistan.

One thing not to be missed while at the museum is the view from the museum's tower. An elevator rises to the top floor of the tower, where the full-length glass walls offer a 360-degree view of San Francisco. Much of the city is visible, including peeks at the Pacific Ocean, San Francisco Bay, the top of the Golden Gate Bridge, and many of the city's more prominent buildings.

In addition to rotating portions of its permanent collections, the museum offers extensive temporary exhibits and programs. There is also a cafeteria and a large museum gift store.

The de Young Museum's tower provides spectacular views of San Francisco.

**HOURS:** Tuesday through Sunday, 9:30 AM to 5 PM; Fridays, 9:30 AM to 8:45 PM.

**COST:** Adults, $10; ages 65 and over, $7; 13–17, $6.

**LOCATION:** 50 Hagiwara Tea Garden Drive, at the intersection of John F. Kennedy Drive in Golden Gate Park, San Francisco

**PHONE:** 415-863-3330

**WEBSITE:** www.deyoungmuseum.org

# 11 San Francisco Fire Museum

**WHAT'S HERE:** Everything from historic hand- and steam-powered water pumpers to century-old firemen's hats

**DON'T MISS THIS:** The collection of 19th century portable fire extinguishers

Fire was the nemesis of most 19th and early 20th century towns in California—and San Francisco was no exception. Its first major fire started on December 24, 1849, and the only fire-fighting engines at that time were three hand-pumpers that had to be rushed from the docks. Six more fires devastated the city before the Gold Rush ended, which prompted the city's early leaders to expand its firefighting capabilities. By 1855, with a small budget, the city depended on 950 volunteer firefighters manning 17 different volunteer fire departments. The museum highlights these early days of firefighting in San Francisco, with a look at some of the changes that followed over the years.

The city's tall buildings and steep hills created problems that most other big cities of the time didn't share. Those challenges spurred many of the early fire department's maintenance chiefs into creative action. They invented such things as the Hayes Aerial Ladder in 1868 and the Gorter Nozzle in 1886, both of

This large fire bell was recovered from the 1906 earthquake rubble.

which proved themselves in action and soon spread to other fire departments around the world. The Gorter Nozzle, given enough water through hoses connected to nearby fire hydrants, could shoot a steady stream of water out 300 feet from its one-man-operated water cannon.

When the 1906 earthquake struck, igniting San Francisco's most destructive fire ever, much of the equipment spread around the city was useless; the jolt had destroyed many of the city's water pipes that supplied its fire hydrants. Without water, desperate firefighters used dynamite in an attempt to level buildings and create fire breaks that could slow the fire's advance. The tactic didn't work, and in some cases it started more fires.

There is a lot of history in this relatively small building, from a collection of fireman hats that identified the beginning of professional rather than volunteer fireman in 1866, to small pieces of household dishes taken from the 1906 earthquake. There is also a display of early chemical fire extinguishers. You'll no longer find any of these in use, as their active ingredient was the poisonous chemical carbon tetrachloride.

Of special interest is Engine Protection Co. #2, which was one of the city's first three fire engines, and one of those that fought the December 1849 fire. It had been shipped around the Horn that same year. The 1893 "steamer" La France No. 270 is also on display. It was shipped from New York and was stationed in the city's Richmond District near the Cliff House when the 1906 earthquake hit.

There is much more to see here in the way of firefighting equipment and history, including photographs. Near the museum entrance desk is a large bronze fire bell that fell during the great quake. It was cast in 1853 and managed to survive the fire with only some damage around its base. Look carefully and see if you can find the misspelled word cast into the bell's dedication message.

The museum occupies a couple of bays of an active fire department, so tours may be occasionally interrupted by sirens blaring as modern trucks head out to real emergencies. The firefighters in the active station are usually more than happy to show you around and let kids and their parents sit in some of the fire equipment.

HOURS: Thursday through Sunday, 1 PM to 4 PM. Closed major holidays.

COST: Free

LOCATION: 655 Presidio Ave., San Francisco

PHONE: 415-563-4630

WEBSITE: www.sffiremuseum.org

## 12 **Mission Dolores**

Father Junipero Serra established Mision San Francisco de Asis, better known as Mission Dolores, on June 27, 1776. It was only the sixth mission to be established, following the first in San Diego, founded just six years earlier. The church was completed in 1791, making it the oldest intact mission of the original 21 (the others were either moved to new locations or have undergone significant restoration or reconstruction, some several times). The Mission Dolores chapel was also San Francisco's first building, and it remains the city's oldest structure, having survived the 1906 earthquake.

Unfortunately, the 1906 earthquake destroyed the original and larger parish church that had been constructed next to the original mission chapel. The destroyed church was replaced by today's basilica, completed in 1918. The two structures couldn't contrast more in design. The original chapel possesses some of the simplest architectural lines of all the missions. The most elaborate part are the half-pillars set into the wall of the front facade. Even the bells are original to the church, having been rung now for well over 200 years.

After Gaspar de Portola's party discovered San Francisco Bay in 1769 and provided a description to the Spanish crown, Spain saw the importance of the port. They established a presidio near the entrance and a mission nearby. This was not, however, a place where most mission padres wished to be assigned. The windy, cold, damp weather proved unhealthy for everyone, especially for the Indians needed to work the fields and care for the livestock. In 1817, with sickness prevalent, a hospital was established across the bay at San Rafael to care for the sick in a warmer, drier climate.

Following the mission's secularization by the Mexican government in 1834, the mission operations declined rapidly. In 1845, the mission was sold to a private owner, but, like many of the other

The diminutive Mission Dolores sits in the shadow of the larger basilica.

missions, it was ultimately returned to the Catholic Church in the mid-1800s by US presidential proclamation.

Today, Mission Dolores, which means "sorrow," is one of San Francisco's favorite tourist attractions. Inside the historic chapel, the gold and red color scheme adds life to the dark and somber interior. The pattern, although redone, resembles the original Ohlone Indian design painted with vegetable dyes. The ceiling beams are original redwood tied together with rawhide, although steel beams were added following the 1906 earthquake to further strengthen the roof.

Outside, in the covered walkway between the chapel and the basilica, is a large diorama that shows the mission and its surrounding lands as they were more than 200 years ago. At the back of the chapel is a small one-room museum that houses several exhibits related to the mission's history. One explains the rediscovery of an original mural behind the alter that had been covered at some time in the past.

Both the exterior and especially the interior of the basilica are very much the opposite of the old mission church. The newer basilica dwarfs the original mission chapel, and the stained-glass windows cast their glow across the open interior. The art glass images include Saint Francis of Assisi, along with angels on the upper windows, and the 21 missions are presented in stained glass along the side windows.

On the opposite side of the chapel from the basilica is a small cemetery that had been used until the 1890s. The original cemetery was much more expansive, but over the years, the old unmarked graves of the unknowns were consolidated into a single common grave.

**HOURS:** Daily, 9 AM to 5 PM; occasionally closes early for special services. Closed Christmas Day.

**COST:** Adults, $5; 6–18, $3; 65 and older, $3.

**LOCATION:** 3321 Sixteenth Street, San Francisco

**PHONE:** 415-621-8203

**WEBSITE:** www.missiondolores.org

# 13 Oakland Museum of California

**WHAT'S HERE:** Exhibits and artifacts that you can practically touch

**DON'T MISS THIS:** The Dorothea Lange photo exhibit

One of the first things you will notice about the Oakland Museum of California (OMCA) is the artistry of its design. The many lines and levels of the different galleries work to soften the hard concrete walls and walkways. The design also creates a sense of intimacy with the collections as you wander through the museum. Some of the exhibits are so close you could touch them, but please don't. Even those artifacts that are protected by glass allow a closeness not found in many large city museums.

The OMCA features relevant pieces of art and artifacts related to its mission that focuses on California's environment, history, people, and art. Like most museums with collections too large and diverse to exhibit at one time, the Oakland Museum's permanent exhibits showcase its most important artifacts, such as those related to California's history. They include 19th century fire pumpers, remnant records and clothing from the hippie era, an assay office from the Gold Rush and more. The museum also hosts temporary national touring exhibits that add a little spice of a different flavor to its permanent exhibits.

An example of its large collection is the photography of Dorthea Lange (1895–1965), one of the most prominent documentary photographers ever. In 1935, President Franklin Roosevelt's Farm Security Administration hired Lange to document the plight of migrant farm workers escaping the Dust Bowl for the promised land of California. Her career took her through World War II, from internment camps to shipyards. Her husband and collaborator donated more than 25,000 images from her personal file, along with 6000 vintage prints. Different pieces from her collection are rotated through the photo gallery.

Nearly every museum in California has an Indian basket collection, but the OMCA is one of the best in exhibiting and interpreting California's Native Americans and their cultures. Few other museums include information on the significance and differences in basket artistry and the quality control that Indians employed as an integral part of their basket-making. Display panels delve deeper into the hows and whys of Indian practices. Here, you can learn that a shaman gained his powers in the form of a dream, with his body taken over by the spirit that actually did the healing of the sick. Shamans charged high fees for their services because only half went to the shaman, while the remainder was destroyed in the name of the spirit. Along with the story are shaman baskets, a shaman doctor's kit, feather wands, ceremonial rattles, pipes, and the plant roots ground for medicines.

Many of the large galleries are divided by timeline themes such as "The Founders," "The Organizers," and "The Builders." Each focuses its collection and their interpretive stories on a segment of California's development, from primitive land to modern cities. You can see mid-19th century wagons and tools that helped build the state's towns and economies. One exhibit shows the working space of the first gold assayer in California, along with explanations about how gold was mined from its different sources, such as river gravels and hard rock ores buried deep beneath the earth.

The Natural History Center re-creates California's many eco zones, from ocean

Oakland Museum of California

tide pools to redwood forests. It does an excellent job of presenting the state's plants and wildlife relationships. There is a "slice of earth," offering a look at what lives on the surface and also beneath the surface. The interpretation of wildlife goes beyond simply including species that live in each habitat; it also covers behaviors such as which are night animals and which can be found at dawn or mid-afternoon. You walk away with a much better understanding of how and why the state's animals live where they do and how the plants have adapted to climates ranging from dry desert to snow-capped mountains.

Within the art galleries, including the exhibit of Dorthea Lange's photography, is an impressive collection of California art and artists. The collection includes artists who were either born or reared, or have studied in, moved to, or worked in California.

**HOURS:** Wednesday through Friday, 10 AM to 5 PM; Saturday, 10 AM to 8 PM; Sunday, noon to 6 PM. Closed Monday and Tuesday and most major holidays.

**COST:** Adults, $8; 65 and older, $5; students (children and adults with school ID), $5; under 6, free.

**LOCATION:** 1000 Oak Street, Oakland

**PHONE:** 510-238-2200

**WEBSITE:** www.museumca.org

# 14 Pardee Home Mansion

**WHAT'S HERE:** Original furniture from the Pardee family

**DON'T MISS THIS:** The three formal front parlors

Enoch Pardee built his multistory Italianate villa estate in Oakland in 1868–69 after having given up gold mining to become a successful eye doctor in San Francisco. Although he would become involved in East Bay politics, getting elected as mayor of Oakland and also a state senator and member of the state assembly, it was his son, George C. Pardee, who would gain fame as California's earthquake governor.

George Pardee was born in San Francisco in 1857, and he also became an eye doctor and mayor of Oakland. He was involved in Republican politics and was elected governor of California, assuming office in January 1903. His strong leadership skills came into play in the days and months that followed the April 6, 1906, San Francisco earthquake. He worked tirelessly from his office in Sacramento (see State Capitol Museum, page 125) to advance relief efforts for the beleaguered city and its citizens.

Following his father's death in 1897, George and his wife, Helen, moved into the family home in Oakland. Helen had a penchant for collecting fine art objects from around the world. Over the years, she turned many of their home's public rooms into small museum galleries exhibiting such things as Alaskan scrimshaw and Chinese alter pieces. She gave tours of her home to friends and acquaintances, including George's business and political partners, eager to share the beauty of her art collection.

The Pardees had four daughters, only two of whom, Madeline and Helen, survived to adulthood. Both continued living in the home as single women well after their parents' deaths in the 1940s. Following daughter Helen's death in 1981, the home became a public museum dedicated to sharing more than a century of the extended Pardee family's life with the world. Since the home went directly from the Pardee family to the foundation that operates the historic home, all of the furniture, including the elder Helen's many fine collections, remain intact.

Docent-guided tours will take you through nearly all of the home, including the main parlor and two additional parlors—part of Helen Pardee's personal museum exhibit spaces—and the dining room. Tours continue up the 22-step stairway (there is no elevator) to the second floor's three bedrooms, billiard room, and the hallway where Helen Pardee placed cabinets to hold more of her fine art pieces. Visitors are generally allowed to climb to the top of the cupola to enjoy the view of the surrounding estate.

Outside, the tour continues to the Pardee carriage house. The redwood building was nearly razed when the adjacent freeway was constructed. A planner apparently thought it was the perfect place for an off-ramp. Fortunately, the off-ramp was moved instead of the historic carriage house. Today, the structure still has its horse stalls and tack room.

Group "tour and tea" outings can be arranged at almost any time of the year by calling the home in advance. The cost of these special outings can range from $10 per person for simple tea and crumpets to $25 per person for more elaborate meals, both with special tours of the home.

**HOURS:** Wednesday, Friday, and Saturday, 1 PM, 2 PM, and 3 PM; for groups of four or more, tours can be scheduled any day of the week from 10 AM to 3 PM; out-of-town visitors can call to arrange tours. Closed major holidays.

**COST:** 13 and older, $5

**LOCATION:** 672 Eleventh Street, Oakland

**PHONE:** 510-444-2187

**WEBSITE:** www.pardeehome.org

Future California governor George Pardee built the Pardee Home Mansion in 1868-69.

# 15 USS Potomac

**WHAT'S HERE:** Restored 165-foot yacht used by FDR during his presidency

**DON'T MISS THIS:** The radio room where FDR broadcast one of his famous "fireside chats"

In 1934, the *USS Potomac* was launched as a Coast Guard cutter, and its name then was *Electra*. But President Franklin D. Roosevelt had other plans for the 165-foot vessel, transferring it to the US Navy in 1936 and converting it to his presidential yacht.

FDR disliked flying and preferred the comfort of either trains or ships for his traveling. After contracting polio at the age of 39, FDR became a paraplegic and was confined for the most part to a wheelchair. For this reason, what he feared most was fire, and the existing presidential yacht, the *Sequoia*, was constructed of wood. The new *Potomac*, as it was renamed, was made of steel with wood trim and set up to accommodate FDR's wheelchair. A pulley-operated elevator was built into a false smoke stack, added for this purpose, allowing FDR to raise and lower himself between decks. He sometimes surprised unsuspecting first-time guests when he emerged in his wheelchair from the fake smokestack on the upper boat deck.

The president spent a significant amount of time onboard, at least prior to the US entry into the World War II. Part of the time was spent relaxing by playing poker, fishing, or sorting his stamp collection. At other times, FDR worked aboard his presidential yacht, meeting with congressional leaders as well as his civilian and military advisers for strategy sessions. On the *Potomac*, he had them alone, with no interruptions. On March 29, 1941, he made one of his famed "fireside chat" radio broadcasts to the nation from the *Potomac*.

The *Potomac* also played a critical role in a very important meeting that occurred in August 1941, just a few months before Japan bombed Pearl Harbor. Although the actual meeting took place aboard the *USS Augusta*, the *Potomac* secretly transported FDR from his "staged" fishing trip to Martha's Vineyard to the *Augusta*, which then steamed to the coast of Newfoundland. There, FDR had his first meeting with Great Britain's Prime Minister Winston Churchill. After the beginning of World War II, FDR had little time for leisure and spent much less time aboard the *Potomac*. Plus, security was an issue due to German submarines cruising off the coast of the eastern US.

Following FDR's death in April 1945, the *USS Potomac* was sold, and after disappearing from its historical role, it reappeared in 1980. Unfortunately, it was used for drug smuggling and was seized in San Francisco Bay. US Customs sold the aging relic, which had been sunk for a short time and then re-floated, for

Franklin Roosevelt's World War II-era presidential yacht, *USS Potomac*

$15,000 to the Port of Oakland. Work from many organizations and individuals, plus $5 million, has finally restored the vessel.

Today, the *Potomac* is open for dockside tours and even offers opportunities to sail on two-hour cruises into San Francisco Bay. The docent-led tours take you through most of the ship, including the radio room where FDR made his only public radio address aboard ship, the engine room, the pilot house, and the president's stateroom. Unfortunately, the original presidential furnishings are no longer around, but the restoration has closely approximated the yacht's original look and feel.

Tours take approximately 45 minutes, and there is a 15-minute film in the visitor center that shows FDR in action aboard the presidential yacht, focusing on the historical activities aboard the *Potomac*.

**HOURS:** Wednesday, 10:30 AM to 2:30 PM; Friday and Sunday, noon to 3:30 PM; 2-hour history cruises on alternating Thursdays and Saturdays from May through September, departing at 11 AM (check website for dates and cruise fees).

**COST:** Dockside tour: 13–59, $7; 60 and over, $5; 12 and under, free.

**LOCATION:** 540 Water Street, Jack London Square, Oakland

**PHONE:** 510-627-1215

**WEBSITE:** www.usspotomac.org

# 16 USS Hornet Museum

**WHAT'S HERE:** Historic aircraft, an opportunity to sit in the ship captain's chair, and a short history film

**DON'T MISS THIS:** The aircraft, including the last HUP-1 Retriever, which is a 1950s-era search-and-rescue helicopter

Size is something that always attracts attention, so this museum—which is an aircraft carrier moored beside numerous military cargo ships—definitely stands out. Yet when you stand on the deck or up in the primary flight-control center on the "island" and imagine aircraft landing and taking off, the deck suddenly seems very, very small.

The *USS Hornet* (CV-12), a World War II-era carrier, is now retired at the old Alameda Naval Air Station near Oakland. Over the past couple of centuries, the Navy has attached the name *USS Hornet* to eight different ships, the first back in the Revolutionary War against Great Britain. The first aircraft carrier to be named *Hornet* (not the one here, which was the seventh *Hornet*) carried the designation CV-8 and fought at the Battle of Midway in World War II. That ship's most remembered action was loading Jimmy Doolittle's Army

B-25 bombers here at Alameda early in the war, and then steaming across the Pacific and launching the future general's famous raid on Tokyo.

The Japanese sank the *USS Hornet* CV-8 at the Battle of Santa Cruz in October 1942, but her successor was already under construction, although initially a different name was planned for her. Built in just 16 months, with a construction crew that was 25 percent women, the ship's name was changed to *USS Hornet* before she launched and headed into war. The new *Hornet*, designated CV-12, was attacked by the Japanese 59 times before war's end, but the Japanese never hit her with a bomb, a torpedo, or a kamikaze aircraft. Nonetheless, more than 250 of the *Hornet's* pilots and crew were killed.

While many pilots were lost, they inflicted significantly more damage on the Japanese, shooting down a record 62 enemy aircraft in one day and 255 in a single month. The *Hornet* also launched the first air attacks against Tokyo since her predecessor had launched the Doolittle Raid two years earlier.

With a bit of imagination, you can stand on the deck and envision being in the mid-Pacific back in 1969, watching firsthand what the world was watching on television. This *USS Hornet* made world news when her crew recovered the *Apollo 11* space capsule and the first astronauts to walk on the moon. The Navy retired the *Hornet* (CV-12) from service soon after that, and in 1991, she was named a National Historic Landmark.

Touring the *USS Hornet* today is a great adventure, and after wandering through some of the inner portions of the second deck, it's easy to understand how new sailors could get lost on this nearly 900-foot-long floating city. Fortunately, all tours begin on the main hangar deck, where numerous aircraft, ranging from a World War II TBM Avenger torpedo-bomber to an A-4 Skyhawk used during the Vietnam War, are located. For aircraft history buffs, probably the last remaining HUP-1 Retriever—a 1950s-era search-and-rescue helicopter—sits at one end of the hangar deck. And because the *Hornet* picked up *Apollo 11* (and *Apollo 12* just four months later), there is an *Apollo* capsule on display, although it's one of the practice capsules, not one that traveled to the moon. There are opportunities to see other aircraft, including an F-14 Tomcat, which never actually flew off the *Hornet* because it requires a larger deck in order to be launched.

While the second deck is a self-guided tour, getting into the "island," (the ship's operational center), requires a docent guide, and there are usually several available. You'll be climbing narrow and steep ladders to get out on the main deck. The deck actually was redesigned partway through the ship's career, going from the original straight design to the angled landing deck. With the angled deck, if a landing plane missed its arresting cable, it simply went over the edge and into the ocean, rather than crashing

Flight-control center on the *USS Hornet*

into aircraft positioned at the take-off end of the deck. It made life much safer for those working on the flight deck, although it didn't do much for unlucky pilots.

Once up in the island's primary flight-control center—five levels above the deck—you'll have a perfect view of the entire deck. This is where the air boss controlled every aircraft being launched or recovered. Nobody, including the ship's captain (or the admiral in the case of the *Hornet* because it was a flagship), messed with the flight boss and his operations.

Other parts of the docent-led island tour include the navigation bridge, the chart room where the ship's location was constantly plotted, and the pilot house where control of the ship's speed and direction were maintained. If you're lucky, you might be able to sit in the captain's chair.

Back on the main hangar deck, take time to view the short movie about part of the ship's history, or browse through the gift shop. The adventurous can take a ride in a flight simulator for an extra fee.

> **HOURS:** Daily, 10 AM to 4 PM. Closed Thanksgiving, Christmas, and New Year's Day.
> **COST:** Adults, $14; seniors and military, $12; 5–17, $6.
> **LOCATION:** Pier 3 at the Alameda Port in the old Alameda Naval Air Station, Alameda
> **PHONE:** 510-521-8448
> **WEBSITE:** www.uss-hornet.org

# 17 Winchester Mystery House

**WHAT'S HERE:** A mansion with 160 rooms, most finished, but many not

**DON'T MISS THIS:** The number 13 theme throughout the expansive home

If this San Jose mansion weren't a California registered historic landmark and on the National Register of Historic Places, it could easily be confused with a Disneyland funhouse. Yet the history of the home and of Sarah Winchester, heiress to the Winchester Firearms fortune, is too bizarre to be anything but a true California tale.

Sarah Lockwood Pardee married William Wirt Winchester, son of the Winchester firearms company founder, in 1862. Living in New Haven, Connecticut, they were wealthy and happy, but everything changed when their infant daughter died in 1866. Sarah Winchester was obviously distraught and became chronically depressed. When her husband died 15 years later, she apparently sought a spiritualist for answers to her questions and her depression. With the help of the spiritualist, she came to believe that she was being haunted by the spirits of Indians and soldiers killed by Winchester rifles—and she believed these spirits had caused the deaths of her husband and her daughter. The only cure was for Sarah Winchester to move out West and begin building (and building and building) a house. The new rooms would keep the spirits confused and Sarah Winchester safe from the same fates that befell her child and husband.

Money was not an issue. Sarah Winchester had received several million dollars following her husband's death. She ultimately received nearly 50 percent of the Winchester Repeating Arms Company stock, providing her with an income of $1000 per day—and with no income taxes to pay. The money allowed her to be both eccentric and a recluse.

Winchester moved to San Jose in 1884, purchasing an unfinished eight-room farmhouse just outside of town. Besides a crew of servants, she hired a team of carpenters and instructed them to begin building, adding room after room, 24 hours a day. Winchester often changed designs and the rooms midstream, sometimes leaving rooms unfinished and abandoned. Some of the rooms wrapped around earlier rooms, some had doorways that led nowhere, and some contained windows that opened only to reveal an earlier wall. Some rooms were never completed and some never survived, being removed and remodeled before the plaster was even dry. Many of the later stairs were built with a short, 2-inch rise instead of the normal 5 inches, forcing them into tiny back-and-forth spaces squeezed into the earlier normal stairwells as they led from floor to floor. Apparently, the short rise in the steps was needed to accommodate Winchester's arthritis-ridden legs.

She paid her servants and other help very well, usually twice the wages they could get elsewhere for the same work. Winchester also paid them in cash, sometimes in gold coin, and almost always at the end of each day. She demanded complete dedication and fired anyone she heard talking about her weird ways. She kept her carpenters busy day after day, year after year, and she spared no expense in construction. The grand ballroom cost $9000 to build, in the days when an entire home could be built for $1000—and it was never used, because Winchester didn't invite guests into her home. Even today, Tiffany glass, exotic woods, and expensive wall coverings that never made it into any of the rooms are stacked in other rooms.

Between 1884, when she started building, and 1922, when she died in her sleep, Winchester spent about $5.5 million, constantly adding to her bizarre but beautiful mansion. The day she was found dead in one of her many bedrooms, her carpenters dropped their tools and immediately quit, knowing that their paychecks had died with her. In the end, the original eight-room house contained 160 rooms, most of them finished, but many not. Others had been

Many of the Winchester mansion's doors lead to nowhere.

boarded up following damage from the 1906 earthquake that had trapped Winchester in her bedroom.

The one-hour tours through the mansion are led by guides, and you will be climbing several sets of tiny stairs. It's a fun tour with lots of stories about Winchester's idiosyncrasies—be sure to watch for the recurring "13 things" theme throughout the house, from 13 panes in myriad stained-glass pieces, to 13 cupolas on the greenhouse, to 13 windows in the 13th bathroom. Obviously, Winchester was a bit superstitious.

The home also features a small museum that houses a large collection of firearms, most of them made by Winchester Repeating Arms Company. At one end of the large gift shop is an exhibit featuring many of the non-firearm products that Winchester manufactured over the years—sporting goods such as fishing rods and reels and baseball equipment, numerous hand tools, and even a push lawn mower.

Kids love to tour the house, with all the secret passages, dead-end doors, and windows that open into other rooms, and the tour is short enough that most shouldn't get too bored.

---

**HOURS:** There are three different tours, all with different prices and times. The house opens for tours beginning at 9 AM, with varying ending times. The best thing to do is to call or check the website, as hours and tours can change. Open daily, except Christmas.

**COST:** Mansion tour: Adults, $19.95; 65 and older, $16.95; 6–12, $13.95. There are additional fees for the Grand Estate Tour (includes Mansion and Behind-the-Scenes tours), or the Behind-the-Scenes tour.

**LOCATION:** 525 South Winchester Blvd., San Jose

**PHONE:** 408-247-2000

**WEBSITE:** www.winchestermysteryhouse.com

---

# 18 Filoli

**WHAT'S HERE:** Historic mansion of a California gold mine owner

**DON'T MISS THIS:** The many acres of beautiful gardens

The strange name for this amazing home, located in Woodside, just 30 miles south of San Francisco, is tied directly to its owner's approach to life: Fight for a just cause. Love your fellow man. Live a good life. William Bowers Bourn, owner of the Empire Mine (see Empire Mine State Historic Park, page 159), began construction of this country manor home in 1915. Two years later, he and his wife, Agnes Moody Bourn, moved in; it was then that the Bourns started designing the acres of formal gardens for which the home has become world-renowned.

In designing his Georgian-style home, Bourn intended for it to outlive him and provide a lasting legacy that could be enjoyed by all for centuries to come. While its architecture may be thought of as primarily Georgian, it has that special addition of personality often described as California eclectic—it includes French doors, a roof of Spanish tile, and the exterior features a brick pattern known as Flemish bond. The home's U-shaped floor plan is reverse from Spanish homes, which have courtyards in the back; Bourn placed a large central courtyard at his main entryway to the front of the home.

When visiting, it's difficult to decide whether to walk the gardens first or tour the home. Fortunately, while guided tours of the house are available each day, you can simply walk in the front door and tour the home at your leisure. Docents, stationed in most of the main rooms, are available to answer questions. Only the main floor is open for tours, and all of the rooms are furnished, although most of the furniture is not original.

After both Bourns died in 1936, the home was sold to William and Lurline Roth, owners of Matson Navigation Company. They maintained the home and gardens until 1975, when Lurline Roth donated the house and 125 of its original 654 acres to the National Trust for Historic Preservation. While the furniture was sold, in subsequent years, some of the original pieces have made their way back to Filoli. Many of the rooms include photographs taken around 1925 that show how the rooms once appeared, so it is easy to compare them with their furnishings today.

The home's 36,000 square feet include 43 rooms and 17 fireplaces. The primary rooms have 17-foot-high ceilings, while the ballroom, which comprises the majority of one of the "leg" wings, has 22.5-foot ceilings. The 70-foot long ballroom features oak parquet floors and an appropriately sized baroque marble fireplace. The walls were originally painted a solid color. Following the onset of Bourn's poor health, brought on by several strokes, he could no longer travel to their daughter's home in Ireland, so his wife, Agnes Moody Bourn, had huge murals painted on the ballroom walls. The murals depict scenes of their daughter's Irish countryside home. The Bourns had given the 11,000-acre Irish estate as a wedding gift to their daughter, Maud, and her new husband.

The more curious things in the home are the safes—full-sized, walk-in wall safes. One in the butler's pantry keeps the fancy silver; another, in what was originally William Bourn's office, held the millions of dollars in gold bars that

Entry to a small portion of Filoli's expansive gardens

were transported from his Empire Mine before being shipped to the US Mint in San Francisco.

Most people come here to see the 16 acres of formal gardens. The gardens, found behind the home, are surrounded by undeveloped areas that provide an informal woodland extension to the formal terraces, lawns, reflecting pools, and ornamental paths. The gardens are extremely well manicured, keeping 14 horticulturists, numerous student interns, and more than 100 volunteers very busy. If you visit the gardens, be aware that many of the thousands of flowering plants have yet to bloom when the home first reopens in mid-February each year, although the grounds, hedges, and early-blooming flowers are well worth seeing.

When the Bourns started their extensive gardens in 1918, they planted an orchard with 1000 trees, with the intention of supplying themselves and their many guests with fresh fruit. Today, only 150 of those original trees remain and are being preserved, along with newly planted trees. The orchard is usually closed to the public, but you can return here during the annual Autumn Festival in early October for special orchard tours and fruit samplings.

Much of the gardens' lasting beauty can be attributed to Isabella Worn, who supervised the original plantings and continued to work for the Bourns. When the Roths acquired the property, Worn was kept on staff to continue her award-winning work creating these amazing gardens. Her influence is still seen today, not only with the design and species selections for the annual plantings in the garden "rooms," but also in the trees and shrubs that are approaching a century of age.

The walkway that leads to the garden's southern end is lined with more than 200 Irish yews. They were grown from cuttings taken from the yews at Muchross House in Ireland, first transplanted to the Bourn's country home at Empire Mine, and from there to Filoli. The far end of the walkway leads to the top of a small hill, offering a wonderful view and great opportunity for a photo of the gardens and home.

A visitor center is adjacent to the parking lot; the center features a short video about the home's history and is a wonderful introduction prior to visiting the home and gardens.

**HOURS:** Mid-February to late October, daily, 10 AM to 3 PM. Closed the remainder of the year.

**COST:** Adults, $12; 5-17, $5.

**LOCATION:** 86 Cañada Road, Woodside

**PHONE:** 650-364-8300

**WEBSITE:** www.filoli.org

# San Francisco and Greater Bay Area Tours

## Family/Kids Transportation Tour

**ESTIMATED DAYS:** 1–2

**ESTIMATED DRIVING MILES:** 5

San Francisco features myriad historical transportation offerings for the whole family. First stop: the **San Francisco Cable Car Museum** (page 89), at 1201 Mason Street (at Washington Street), which is also a cable car stop. Don't forget to go downstairs and see the underground cables that propel the cable cars throughout the city.

San Francisco is known for the great earthquake of 1906 and the resulting fire that destroyed much of the city. At 655 Presidio Ave., about 2.5 miles away, is the **San Francisco Fire Museum** (page 96). Some of the old water pumpers that were active in the 1906 fire are on display here, along with many other fire-fighting artifacts. The museum occupies a couple of the bays of an operating fire station, so things can sometimes get very realistic with sirens blaring.

Maritime transportation is another aspect of San Francisco's transportation history, and another 2.5 miles away, down on the waterfront near Fort Mason and the Hyde Street Pier, is the **San Francisco Maritime Museum** (page 85). The museum comes in two parts; the first is the big, white, boat-shaped building that houses two floors of historic maritime exhibits, and a couple of blocks away, several historic ships are berthed at the Hyde Street Pier, including the 256-foot-long, three-masted *Balclutha*. A few more blocks away, at Fisherman's Wharf Pier 45, the *SS Jeremiah O'Brien* (page 87), one of only two remaining World War II Liberty Ships, is open for tours. The restored ship periodically offers special short voyages for the public.

If you can, try to make it to San Francisco during the annual **October Fleet Week** (650-599-5057; www.fleet week.us/fleetweek), when you'll get a

Outside the San Francisco Cable Car Museum

chance to see hundreds of ships and boats. The Golden Gate Bridge is the backdrop as historic ships, active US Navy vessels, and swarms of big and small sailboats fill the bay, with a spectacular air show highlighting the festivities.

# Island-Hopping Tour

ESTIMATED DAYS: 1

ESTIMATED DRIVING MILES: 0

Part of the fun of San Francisco is the opportunity to ride on boats, and what better places to visit but islands filled with history? Start at San Francisco's Pier 41, where you can board a **Blue & Gold Fleet ferry** (415-705-5555; www.blueandgoldfleet.com) to **Alcatraz Island** (page 79) and see the notorious prison that housed many of the country's worst criminals. After wandering through the old cell blocks and the exercise yard, if you've signed up for the "Island Hop Tour," you can board another ferry that will take you farther across the bay to **Angel Island State Historic Park** (page 81). Once here, jump on one of the **tram tours** (415-897-0715) around the island, or, if you brought bicycles with you on the ferry (yes, they are allowed, but bring helmets), you can bike around the island on a relatively level and paved road. Just don't miss the last ferry back to San Francisco.

# Romantic Tour

ESTIMATED DAYS: 1–2

ESTIMATED DRIVING MILES: 5

San Francisco is one of the most romantic cities in the US, with more to do than you can imagine. Head over to **Golden Gate Park** (San Francisco Parks and Recreation Department: 415-831-2700), where you can spend the day wandering through the fabulous **de Young Museum** (page 94), which is filled with exotic (some even erotic) art and collections, especially from the South Pacific. There are great views of the city from the museum's new tower. Adjacent to the de Young is the wonderfully calming and relaxing **Japanese Tea Garden** (San Francisco Parks and Recreation Department: 415-831-2700), where you can spend an hour or more walking hand in hand. Then stroll across Dr. Martin Luther King Jr. Drive and enjoy the **Strybing Arboretum and Botanical Gardens** (www.sfbotanicalgarden.org).

To end your day, drive down to the wharf for a dinner at any one of the dozens of great restaurants, or try dinner and dancing while cruising the bay on one of the **Hornblower tour boats** (800-467-6256; www.hornblower.com).

# San Francisco and Greater Bay Area Travel Information Centers

California Welcome Center (San Francisco)
www.sfvisitor.org
415-956-3493

Redwood Empire Association/Northern California Visitor's Bureau
www.redwoodempire.com
415-292-5527 or 800-619-2125

San Francisco CVB Visitor Information Center
www.sfvisitor.org
415-391-2000

Oakland Convention & Visitors Bureau
www.oaklandcvb.com
510-839-9000

San Jose Visitor Information Center
www.sanjoseca.gov/visitors.html
888-847-4875

Great Valley

Klamath National Forest

Redding **1**

44

Lassen National Forest

395

Six Rivers National Forest

5

Lassen Volcanic National Park

Red Bluff

89

36

101

Mendocino National Forest

99

Chico

**2**

Quincy

Plumas National Forest

395

99

Oroville

Truckee National Forest

89

Truckee

101

20

Clear Lake

20

Grass Valley

Lake Tahoe

Ukiah

Yuba City

Marysville

89

Clearlake

5

99

Auburn

Placerville

Eldorado National Forest

29

Woodland

Folsom

**12** **13**

50

Davis

Sacramento

Santa Rosa

**3** **4** **5**

49

Sierra National Forest

395

1

101

**6** **7** **8**

Mono Lake

**9** **10** **11**

5

99

San Rafael

Stockton

Yosemite National Park

Inyo National Forest

San Francisco

Oakland

Tracy

120

880

580

Oakdale

120

Modesto

49

280

San Jose

Mariposa

Sequoia National Forest

Kings Canyon National Park

5

Atwater

101

Merced

Santa Cruz

1

Gilroy

**14**

Los Banos

152

41

Monterey

Salinas

99

Madera

Fresno

180

Carmel

101

23

**15** **16**

Sequoia National Park

1

Hanford

Visalia

PACIFIC OCEAN

Lemoore

199

199

Big Sur

Los Padres National Forest

Coalinga

Allensworth

**17**

99

1

Delano

46

Wasco

Cambria

Paso Robles

5

101

Bakersfield

58

114

# Great Valley

California's Great Valley lies between the bottom of the Cascade Range to the north and the base of the Tehachapi Mountains to the south. To the east, it bumps into the Sierra Nevada foothills, and to the west, the Coastal Range. In the middle is the rich and fertile valley itself, and the Sacramento and San Joaquin valleys, waiting to share the wealth of their mansions and museums.

For thousands of years, much of the Great Valley flooded each winter, creating ideal winter habitat for millions of ducks and geese. Elk and grizzlies wandered the grass-covered lands, while salmon filled the main rivers and their many tributaries. Naturalist John Muir wrote to a friend: "This valley of the San Joaquin is the floweriest piece of level I have ever walked, one vast level, even flower bed. A sheet of flowers, a smooth sea ruffled a little by the tree fringing of the river and here and there of smaller cross streams from the mountains."

The pedestrian-only Sundial Bridge crosses the Sacramento River at Turtle Bay Exploration Park.

This wild valley remained essentially intact until the California Gold Rush brought thousands of people, some of whom realized the potential that such land offered to farmers. Over the years, a plethora of dikes and dams and canals were built to harness the wild waters, and the plow replaced the wildflowers with orchards, cotton fields, and vineyards. Major highways dissected the Great Valley into tiny pieces punctuated by ever-growing towns and cities.

Located near the Great Valley's geographic center and long before Sacramento became the Golden State's capital, the Sacramento Valley was a primary access route to the gold mines, to wood for fueling stoves, and to wild game for food. What began as Sutter's Fort and following the discovery of gold was transformed into the growing city of Sacramento became the beginning, or ending point, depending on one's perspective, of the famed Pony Express and the transcontinental railroad.

In Sacramento, and in many other cities within the Great Valley, there are numerous mansions, from the Governor's Mansion and Crocker Art Museum—both mansion and museum—along with museums that house the state's history. The California Railroad Museum, with its huge collection and operating historic railroad equipment, celebrates the technology that changed the country, while The California Museum for History, Women, and the Arts celebrates the Californians who changed the country—and the world. The State Capitol serves as both historic museum and the Golden State's operating seat of government. Farther south in the Great Valley, the homes of those who did well financially in this new land are open to the public. A Merced doctor left us the Meux Home, while the Kearney Mansion in Fresno was the home of the California raisin king, Martin Kearney. And for those who chose the wrong side of the law in an attempt to make their fortunes, there's the Folsom Prison Museum that looks at a darker part of California's history.

# TRIVIA

1 Where can you see the doll that belonged to Patty Reed, one of the ill-fated Donner Party survivors?

2 Which 1860s home featured indoor plumbing and a bathroom with a flush toilet, all rarities at the time?

3 What future Supreme Court justice lived in the Governor's Mansion as governor from 1943 to 1953?

4 Where can you ride in historic railcars along the bank of the Sacramento River?

5 About which site did legendary musician Johnny Cash write a song?

6 Where can you find the very first Pony Car (Mustang) manufactured by Ford?

7 Name the oldest art museum in the West.

8 What is California's only town ever founded, financed, governed, and lived in only by African Americans?

*For trivia answers, see page 326.*

# 1  Turtle Bay Exploration Park

**WHAT'S HERE:** Exhibits on natural and cultural history, hands-on experiments, and gardens

**DON'T MISS THIS:** A stroll across the Sacramento River on the Sundial Bridge

Turtle Bay, located in Redding, is a challenge to describe, since there is so much here—part visitor center and part nature center, with an anchor museum that effectively ties everything together. The beautiful Sundial Bridge, whose design is iconic of Turtle Bay and this area, stretches across the Sacramento River where its waters meander past the museum. Without a doubt, this is one educational experience that is sure to please the entire family, and the kids won't have any idea that they're actually visiting a museum!

Turtle Bay's 300 acres of opportunities for fun and learning focuses on the natural and cultural history that surrounds the adjacent Sacramento River, and the special relationships between them. Inside the main Turtle Bay Museum, which is the perfect place to start, a leafless tree stands not far from the entrance. Beneath the tree's base, clear floor tiles provide a view of the root system, which looks remarkably similar to the tree's upper branches. Nearby, a cedar bark lodge, its shape similar to a Plains Indian tepee, was the type of shelters that the local Wintu used.

Accessed from the first floor, visitors can walk down into a replica limestone cave, something found in several of California's mountainous areas. The manufactured cave is realistic, right down to its colorful stalactites and stalagmites, but it's great for anyone too claustrophobic to explore the real thing. Two large galleries adjacent to the main museum feature special exhibits such as art shows, science exhibitions, and more on a regular basis.

The Sacramento River has always been known as a great fishing river, especially when the salmon and steelhead make their annual trips back to the gravel beds and hatcheries to start a new generation of their species. While the big fish can sometimes be seen in the river's clear waters below the Sundial Bridge, the museum's underwater fish viewing station offers an easier alternative. Here is an opportunity to see steelhead, salmon, striped bass, and even sturgeon up close.

For those who have a bit more scientific curiosity, the museum offers a hands-on science area—an all-time favorite for kids young and old. There are various scientific instruments available for use, such as microscopes, all prepped for viewing of everything from leaves to butterfly wings. Other kid-favored stations include a hands-on demonstration area that allows the use of 19th century tools, such as butter molds. And for the Gold Rush prospector days, there is a shelf full of supplies including tea, nails, blankets, corn meal, and more to play with. One challenge is to see how many days of supplies you can stuff into a set of saddlebags for a pretend extended trip searching for that big gold nugget!

Leave the museum and take the short walk to Paul Bunyon's Forest Camp. Here is an opportunity to learn about what's going on in California's forests, while running through the major playground built to resemble a forest, an awesome tree ring maze to navigate, and several water table activities. There is a logging exhibit that, among other things, shows the tools used by today's firefighters. There are periodic live chats with firefighters who demonstrate how the tools are used in putting out the 8000 or so wildfires that usually burn more than 300,000 acres of forest, chaparral, and grassland in California each year. There are also some wilderness creatures, all very much alive, including king snakes and gopher snakes, burrowing owls, and more. Outside, in a large demonstration area, there is an opportunity to learn about California's water cycle, from rain to streams to dams to irrigation systems.

If it's not one of those 100-plus degree summer days that the northern Sacramento Valley is noted for, strolling through the McConnell Arboretum and Gardens is a relaxing way to spend time at Turtle Bay. Mediterranean and Pacific Rim plants are clustered across the 20-acre garden site. And for those who enjoy butterflies, there is even an enclosed butterfly garden that offers a look at the plants best suited for attracting the showy creatures to home gardens.

One of the biggest changes in this part of California, besides the towns and freeways, was the construction of Shasta Dam, and the museum includes a very interesting exhibit on the dam's construction. Outside the museum is the last remnant of the huge concrete structures that were part of the dam's construction. Referred to as the "Monolith," it is part of the old Kutras Aggregate Plant's gravel-processing facility, which provided much of the gravel needed for the 6.5 million cubic yards of concrete that went into Shasta Dam. The plant closed in 1945, the same year the dam was completed.

There is still more to see at Turtle Bay, so plan on spending a good part of a day there, especially if you bring children. And if you get hungry, there is a small café with an outside seating area that overlooks the Sundial Bridge and the Sacramento River.

**HOURS:** March through October, daily, 9 AM to 5 PM; same hours November through February, except the museum is closed on Monday.

**COST:** Adults, $11; 65 and older, $9; 15 and under, $6.

**LOCATION:** 840 Auditorium Drive, Redding

**PHONE:** 530-243-8850

**WEBSITE:** www.turtlebay.org

Turtle Bay's main museum features a look at an entire tree, from the limbs above and the root structure below the see-through "ground."

# 2  Bidwell Mansion State Historic Park

**WHAT'S HERE:** Historic furnished mansion and visitor center

**DON'T MISS THIS:** The portrait hanging in the main entry hall

John Bidwell had come to California seven years before the Gold Rush, spending part of that time managing John Sutter's ranch, which he called Hock Farm (see Sutter's Fort State Historic Park, page 123). That job ended when he joined the initial rush to the gold fields in 1848. Bidwell headed to the Feather River, where he discovered gold and hired Indians to do most of his heavy digging. It's unknown how much gold he found, but after a short time, he left his mining claim and the trading post he had established, disposed of the property from his original Mexican land grant, and purchased 28,000 acres near Chico Creek. Here, he established a large and diversified ranching and farming business, which proved very successful.

In 1849, Bidwell was elected one of California's first state senators. He headed to Washington, DC, where he helped lobby successfully for California statehood. In 1864, following President Lincoln's election, Bidwell was elected to Congress and returned to Washington, DC, where he met Annie Ellicott Kennedy, and, 18 months after his term ended, he convinced her to become his wife.

Annie Bidwell arrived in California to a partially completed, 26-room mansion that her husband was building for her. The three-story home, with its exterior plaster walls, featured modern conveniences not found in most homes in the 1860s, including indoor plumbing and water systems, a bathroom with a toilet, and gas lighting. Annie caused more than a few changes in her husband's life. She strongly disapproved of alcohol, so her husband ordered that all his vineyards be destroyed. John Bidwell's foreman ignored the order and instead dried the wine grapes, creating California's first commercial raisin business.

In 1875, Bidwell ran for governor under the Independent Party's banner. He was opposed to business monopolies, pushed for election reform, and supported prohibition, among many other stands that he and Annie had taken over the years. A mudslinging campaign, paid for by the railroads and other monopoly interests opposed to his election, portrayed Bidwell as excessively moralistic and an anti-alcohol fanatic. Bidwell was defeated in the end, but 15 years later, the Prohibition Party nominated him for governor again. He had no chance of winning—and he didn't.

In 1900, Bidwell died while cutting firewood. Annie Bidwell lived in the

Bidwell Mansion

mansion for 18 more years, initially gifting 1900 acres of their property (and later 301 acres) to the city of Chico for use as a public park. She gave her home to the College Board of the National Presbyterian Church, which, in 1923, sold it to Chico Normal School. The mansion became a state historic park in 1964.

Today, the Italian Villa-style home is open for tours. Most of the rooms have been restored and furnished with period pieces to resemble how they appeared in photos taken while Annie Bidwell lived here. About 20 percent of the home's furniture belonged to the Bidwells, including the parlor's grand piano, which was shipped "express" around the Horn in 1868. It took just six months for the piano to be delivered, rather than the more typical 18 months. Just outside the parlor on the hallway wall is a life-sized painting of John Bidwell. Alice Reading painted the portrait in 1903, and it features the illusion of his body turning and following you as you walk by. Apparently, it wasn't appropriate for women to be artists then, at least in Annie Bidwell's eyes, so Alice Reading was only allowed to affix her initials on the painting, not her entire name.

The second floor features several of the home's 12 bedrooms. That was not a good location for bedrooms in a town where summer temperatures reach 100 degrees, and upstairs rooms become even hotter. Possibly, the plantation windows served as summer escapes to cooler sleeping arrangements on the outside balcony. The indoor toilets that Bidwell included were thought strange by his neighbors and visitors. Many believed that having to perform such bodily tasks inside a house, rather than in an outhouse, was unsanitary.

Even though there is a nursery on the second floor, the Bidwells never had children, although they were quite fond of them. Annie's sewing room is also on the second floor. She often gave sewing classes to the local Mechoopda Maidu Indians, whom her husband had protected for decades from the often fatal consequences of the Gold Rush.

In addition to more bedrooms on the third floor, there is a large, open room that in most homes of this stature and time period would have served as a ballroom. It did not become such in the Bidwell home, although that may have been John Bidwell's original intention. Annie was also opposed to smoking and dancing, so he never had the opportunity to host such a party.

**HOURS:** Wednesday through Friday, noon to 5 PM; weekends, 10 AM to 5 PM; closed Monday and Tuesday. Tours leave on the hour, with the last leaving at 4 PM.

**COST:** 17 and older, $2; all others, free.

**LOCATION:** 525 The Esplanade, Chico

**PHONE:** 530-895-6144

**WEBSITE:** www.parks.ca.gov/parksindex

# 3 The California Museum for History, Women, and the Arts

**WHAT'S HERE:** California Hall of Fame and exhibits celebrating the history and remarkable women of California

**DON'T MISS THIS:** The Japanese-American internment camp exhibit

This museum is located in the midst of the hustle and bustle of thousands of state workers in downtown Sacramento, just two blocks from the State Capitol (see page 125) in the State Archives building. The museum's mission is to showcase California's remarkable history, yet it is unique in that it is the first to dedicate a permanent major gallery to the accomplishments of women in California.

Nothing in California is static, and this museum is no exception. In late 2006, it was revamped to include numerous high-tech interactive exhibits. There is always a temporary exhibit in the main lobby of the multistory State Archives building, just outside the museum's first-floor gallery. This exhibit generally focuses on California, be it the aviation industry, water, the people, or historical events such as the World War II internment of Japanese-Americans.

The internment camp exhibit did so well focusing public interest on California's role in such an important national historical event that it has now become a more permanent exhibit in the first-floor gallery. It features a reconstructed portion of one of the primitive wooden barracks that became home for thousands of Japanese-Americans. Inside, it has been furnished to look as it did in 1943, with the old military-style bunks, a hot plate for cooking, women's clothes hanging out to dry, and more.

The remainder of the first-floor gallery looks at the beginning of California and includes a host of historic documents that date from the state's Constitutional Convention at Colton Hall (see page 198) in Monterey. It also includes a copy of the congressional act that made California a state in 1850.

In an earlier life, the museum was known as the California State History Museum, but in 2004, California First Lady Maria Shriver saw the need for an exhibit that focused on the contributions of California's women. She spearheaded the development of the "California's Remarkable Women" exhibit, which included a look at California women,

The Japanese-American internment camp exhibit is in the first-floor gallery.

121

ranging from space pioneer Sally Ride to the co-founder of the United Farm Workers, Dolores Huerta.

The second floor's original California's Remarkable Women exhibit has become permanent, featuring well-known women as well as those who have never made the history books. One of the more prominent women here is Minerva, the state's symbol. She was the Roman goddess who sprang full-grown from the head of Jupiter—a fitting symbol for California, which became a state without going through the normally long process. Minerva is also the patron of intellect and the arts, symbolizing excellence in creativity and education, and she represents much of what makes California great, from the state's commerce to her natural bounties.

A panel on Amelia Earhart unfortunately contains no personal items belonging to the famed pilot, but it does feature graphics and a summary of her life. Earhart earned her pilot's license in Long Beach in 1922 and went on to set women's altitude, distance, and speed records in flight. She disappeared in the Pacific in 1937 during her second around-the-world attempt. Also featured is Sally Ride, who earned her doctorate at Stanford University and in 1983 became the first American woman to orbit Earth on the shuttle *Challenger*.

Other women featured here have more eclectic claims to fame—such as Ruth Handler. After watching her daughter Barbara dress up her dolls, Ruth defied skeptics by developing the now popular doll Barbie in 1959. Barbie has since become the largest selling fashion doll in history.

In the entertainment field, there are hundreds of women with California ties. Elizabeth Taylor is one of those who succeeded as an actress, business woman, and activist. You can also learn about southern California's master French chef Julia Child and Joan Kroc, the philanthropist who funded homeless shelters and the famous Ronald McDonald House Charities. Kroc also funded the arts in San Diego, giving National Public Radio $200 million and presenting the Salvation Army with $1.5 billion for their community centers.

The museum provides a great overview of California's history, and because it is tied to the State Archives, it frequently features "new" old treasures that have been pulled from the vaults. It also has become the home of California's newly created Hall of Fame, which inducts and features prominent Californians such as Ronald Reagan, Cesar Chavez, Walt Disney, Amelia Earhart, Sally Ride, and the Hearst and Packard families.

Check the website for upcoming exhibits and special events. This is a state building, so security is tight. Backpacks and other such containers are generally searched.

**HOURS:** Tuesday through Saturday, 10 AM to 5 PM; Sunday, noon to 5 PM. Closed on major holidays and at 1 PM on December 24 and December 31.

**COST:** Adults, $7.50; seniors (55 and over), $6; ages 6-13, $5.

**LOCATION:** 1020 O Street, Sacramento, in the State Archives building

**PHONE:** 916-653-7524

**WEBSITE:** www.californiamuseum.org

# 4 Sutter's Fort State Historic Park

**WHAT'S HERE:** Restored historic pre-Gold Rush fort that includes an audio tour
**DON'T MISS THIS:** Living history days when docents are in costume

Swiss native Johann "John" Augustus Sutter played an instrumental, albeit accidental role in California's history. It was his sawmill, located on the South Fork of the American River, where his employee James Marshall discovered gold in 1848, triggering the great Gold Rush. And just the winter before, Sutter had sent rescuers to search for members of the ill-fated Donner Party, who spent much of the winter trapped, starving, and freezing near the crest of the Sierra Nevada (see Donner Memorial State Historic Park, page 165).

Sutter was born in Germany in 1803, but he was a Swiss citizen. He traveled a very circuitous route to his new California home. In 1834, at the age of 31, Sutter left his wife and five children and sailed from Europe to New York. He settled in Missouri for a while before heading to Santa Fe and then moving to Kansas in 1837. By 1838, his businesses, which included a hotel, were not successful, so he packed his belongings and went to work for the American Fur Co., ending up at the Hudson's Bay Co. headquarters in Fort Vancouver (today's Washington state). From there, he sailed to Hawaii, and after being stuck in the Sandwich Islands longer than he had planned, sailed for Sitka, Alaska, before being directed to land at the official port of entry at Monterey instead of his destination, Yerba Buena (San Francisco). Finally, in 1839, Sutter and his eight Hawaiian workers made it up the Sacramento River in smaller boats and landed near what one day would be 28th and C streets in Sacramento.

In 1840, Sutter became a Mexican citizen, which was required in order to own land, and Mexican Governor Juan Bautista Alvarado granted him 48,000 acres. While Sutter's vision for the settlement he called New Helvetia (Sacramento) was set high and likely achievable, events that changed the history of California, coupled with his own business ineptitude, caused him to lose everything. Sutter employed local Indians to help build his adobe fort and the interior buildings, including his own headquarters in the central building (which can be toured today). In addition to quarters for many of his workers, he constructed a grist mill to grind the wheat he was growing on part of his farming operations,

a bakery, a blacksmith shop, and a carpenter shop that included the equipment needed to make wooden barrels and wagon wheels.

As more settlers arrived, additional businesses were added, including a gunsmith to maintain his fort's arsenal of rifles and cannons, and weavers who

Sutter's Fort features many of the items used by California's settlers during the 1840s.

made blankets, among many other needed cloth items. Today, all of these shops can be found in the fort. Some are used during Pioneer Demonstration Days and Living History Days, while others are filled with historic artifacts from the Gold Rush period.

Things began going badly for Sutter with the advent of the Bear Flag Revolt in 1846, when the Mexican flag that Sutter flew over the fort was replaced by the Lone Star flag, which was quickly replaced by the Stars and Stripes. Sutter's fort was initially taken from him, but soon returned. Then, in 1847, Sutter contracted with James Marshall to build a sawmill on the South Fork of the American River. He required a steady supply of lumber for his growing fort and related businesses. When Marshall shared with Sutter that he had discovered gold, Sutter wanted it kept secret. Fat chance! Within weeks, much of Sutter's empire was crumbling as a never-ending horde of miners swarmed over his lands.

As the Gold Rush continued, men well-schooled in the art of business trickery swindled Sutter out of much of his land and other holdings, sending him toward bankruptcy. Sutter's eldest son attempted to help, but Sutter ultimately was forced to sell the fort for just $7000 in 1849. With his wife and children, who had finally joined him in 1850, Sutter moved to his ranch, Hock Farm, near Marysville. When his house and most of his belongings burned in 1865, Sutter headed for Washington, DC, in an unsuccessful attempt to convince Congress to pay him for his valuable assistance in California's transition from a Mexican state to the 31st state of the Union. Sutter died in 1880, just two days after Congress adjourned, failing to act on his request.

Today, Sutter's Fort, partially restored and partially reconstructed, serves as a living museum of California's early pioneers. Even though the fort is located just a few blocks from the freeway in midtown Sacramento, once you enter the fort's gates, city sites vanish and an entirely different world awaits. There remain a few technological links to the "new world," such as the electronic sensors located in the exhibit areas and in most of the shops and other buildings. They click on an audio tour information tape explaining the exhibits and other historical aspects of the fort.

Sutter's Fort is a great place for kids, especially during the monthly Pioneer Demonstration Days and the periodic Living History Days. On these special days, volunteers dress in period clothing and do everything the early settlers would have done, including working in the blacksmith shop, making candles, baking bread, weaving cloth, and more. These fun days are filled with opportunities to see how Sutter and his settlers worked and lived here more than 150 years ago. There are also numerous exhibits throughout the fort that deal with everything from Indians to Sutter to the Gold Rush. One of the smallest exhibits—and one of the most interesting—is the tiny doll that belonged to 8-year-old Patty Reed, one of the Donner Party survivors.

**HOURS:** Daily, 10 AM to 5 PM. Closed Thanksgiving, Christmas, and New Year's Day.

**COST:** Adults, $4; 6–16, $2; on Pioneer Demonstration Days and Living History Days, fees are $6 for those 17 and over, and $3 for those 6–16.

**LOCATION:** 2701 L Street, Sacramento

**PHONE:** 916-445-4422

**WEBSITE:** www.parks.ca.gov/parkindex

# 5  State Capitol Museum

**WHAT'S HERE:** Restored historic offices, 40-acre park and gardens, and a Vietnam War memorial

**DON'T MISS THIS:** The rotunda as seen from inside the capitol

California has enjoyed a tumultuous history, and that turbulence is no more evident than with the state's regal capitol building, located in the state capital city of Sacramento. Aside from the never-ending disagreements that have gone on inside the senate and assembly chambers since it was opened for business in 1869, the arguments began even before California gained statehood in 1850. The state's constitution was written and passed in Monterey, the Mexican-era capital. In 1849, the delegates voted to make San Jose the first state capital, at least temporarily, under the Stars and Stripes. It was soon moved to Vallejo, then to Sacramento, before returning to Vallejo, and then to Benicia (see Benicia Capitol State Historic Park, page 77). It finally landed in Sacramento for the last time in 1854. In subsequent years, Oakland, San Jose, and Berkeley attempted to "steal" the title of capital, and Monterey made the last failed bid in 1941.

Enter the capitol through the main west entrance, where the giant state seal is imbedded in the walkway, and you'll encounter the rotunda of this Italian Renaissance Revival building. What most people don't notice is that the beautifully painted interior rotunda actually is nestled inside the much larger and taller exterior rotunda, which is visible from the capitol grounds. Out of view is a rickety spiral stairway that rises between the top of the interior rotunda and allows access to the capitol's cupola, that tiny perch at the very top of the building. Unfortunately, the cupola is off limits to the public, although there is a view from the tiny perch available on the capitol's website.

The restored historic portions of the capitol are situated across the west end on the main floor. While most of these offices remain relatively static, other exhibits are changed to reflect different aspects of California's history. You can view the historic offices through their doorways from the main hall, but it is best to join one of the free tours, which will take you inside the offices, where you can hear stories about what happened in them at different times in history. For example, the governor's office revisits the days after the 1906 San Francisco earthquake; stacked on

California State Capitol

Governor George Pardee's desk are telegrams and newspaper accounts of the disaster (see Pardee Home Mansion, page 101).

There are two historic state treasurer's offices, one from 1906 and the other from 1933. The biggest difference, at least for those working there, was that in 1905 the safe held the state government's entire account of $8 million in gold and silver coin. A few years later, the legislature changed the law, allowing the treasurer to move the state's funds to banks and other investments. In 1933, the office safe held only $23,000 in cash, and the remainder was in bonds and securities.

This museum is unique in that it is a working museum. Upstairs, today's assembly and senate are at work making laws, and, usually, the public is allowed to watch. Obviously, more exciting is a look at the present-day governor's office, which is found on the first floor in the non-historic part of the capitol; a quick peek inside the reception area is allowed. You may get lucky and catch a glimpse of the governor walking through to the office or to the "horseshoe" offices where much of the governor's staff take care of the day-to-day business with the legislature and the public.

There is much more to see both inside and outside the capitol building. Walk through much of the annex (built in 1951) near the present-day governor's office, and there are displays from each of California's 58 counties. In the basement beneath the rotunda is a series of murals, originally painted around the main floor rotunda in 1913 by San Francisco husband and wife artists Arthur F. and Lucia Kleinhans Mathews. The panels were removed from the main rotunda during the capitol's 1976 restoration and moved to the basement in order to restore the rotunda to its original state.

The capitol is situated near the west end of a 40-acre park, originally designed as a Victorian garden. It has changed since those early days, now offering many monuments and memorials. One of the more impressive and moving ones is the Vietnam War Memorial. For those interested in trees and flowers, Capitol Park features exotic plants from around the world, a trout pond, and a large rose garden.

**HOURS:** Daily tours from 9 AM to 4 PM; building is open daily, 8 AM to 5 PM. Closed Thanksgiving, Christmas, and New Year's Day.

**COST:** Free

**LOCATION:** Capital Ave. at 9th Street, Sacramento; the museum tour office is in the capitol building basement, room B-27.

**PHONE:** 916-324-0333

**WEBSITE:** www.capitolmusuem.ca.gov

An interior view of the capitol dome

# 6  California State Railroad Museum

**WHAT'S HERE:** Historic steam locomotives and cars from the beginning of California's earliest railroads

**DON'T MISS THIS:** The *St. Hyacinthe*, a 1920s sleeper car that rocks

Proclaimed by many to be the finest railroad museum in the world, the California State Railroad Museum, from a historical perspective, is well situated in Old Sacramento. Prior to 1850, the railroads in the US were nearly all located along the Atlantic Coast, and they were relatively short, independent lines. When the "Big Four,"—Collis P. Huntington, Charles Crocker, Leland Stanford, and Mark Hopkins—formed the Central Pacific Railroad, they were acting in response to the 1862 Pacific Railway Act, which allowed the Central Pacific to begin building the western leg of the first transcontinental railroad. On January 8, 1863, the Big Four broke ground for their new railroad at Front and K streets in Sacramento, just two blocks from today's railroad museum.

The Big Four became quite wealthy from their enterprise, although California and the Union also benefited. With the Civil War raging since 1861, California was guaranteed to remain part of the Union and not join the Confederate States. When the transcontinental railroad was completed in 1869, and the Civil War ended, California's wealth, from gold and silver to its bountiful agricultural products, could be shipped to new markets in the East quickly and inexpensively.

Even for visitors with no interest in railroads or in railroading history, the museum offers visual delights that also happen to tell much about the industry's history in California and in the US. Those delights begin as soon as the introductory film ends (worth the few minutes it takes to view) and the huge screen opens, revealing the full-sized diorama of a railroad construction site high in the Sierra. This is where the workers, mostly Chinese laborers, used up to 500 kegs of black powder each day, as they attempted to blast train tunnels through the Sierra's solid granite.

Walk through the Sierra scene, and you enter the main gallery, where more of the museum's steam locomotives, dating from 1862 to 1944, are displayed. With its brightly painted steel and highly polished brass trim, the beautiful but diminutive Southern Pacific No. 1, the *C.P. Huntington*, does not look like a locomotive that ever saw much service—but it did. On the opposite end of the size-spectrum is the million-pound behemoth, Southern Pacific's articulated cab-forward No. 4249. Unlike regular steam locomotives, with their smokestacks in front, the cab on the No. 4249 was placed at the front, so when traveling through the Sierra tunnels and snow sheds, the sparks and smoke would be released behind the engineer and not in front of his face.

Next to the big cab-forward is another of the locomotives that appears more like a piece of fine steel artwork than a hardworking machine. The Virginia & Truckee Railroad No. 13, *Empire*, has been beautifully restored and surrounded by mirrors so the brightly polished brass, new oak, and repainted steel can be better viewed and appreciated.

The museum's numerous exhibits include rolling stock such as a mail car that once was the mainstay of the US Postal Service's pick-up and delivery system across the country. Rather primitive but effective catch devices allowed the train to pick up mail at every small station without stopping. Arriving mail was simply tossed off in canvas mail bags as the train passed by. Docents demonstrate where and how mail was sorted, delivered, and picked up on the train's trips back and forth across the country.

Another favorite railcar takes many older visitors back to their youth, when trains were the main form of long-distance transportation in the US. The *St. Hyacinthe* is a Canadian sleeper car built in the late 1920s. You can board the all-steel, Pullman-style car and walk past the tiny, curtain-covered upper and lower sleeping berths that line the aisle. The sleeper car re-enacts its night travels as it gently rocks back and forth; the methodical sounds of the clicking rails and the harshness of the passing signal bells can be heard as the train "speeds" toward its destination.

There is much more to see here, including additional steam locomotives, modern diesel-electric locomotives, a private luxury railcar, and a refrigerated freight car. One exhibit allows you to walk beneath an old locomotive. There is also a second level, much of which looks down onto the museum's main floor. Among the many exhibits on the second floor are numerous model train layouts.

Outside and across the open quad from the main museum is the Central Pacific Passenger Station. The re-created 1860s depot also has its share of old trains. From April through September, this is where (for an additional fee) you can board one of the museum's trains for a ride along the Sacramento River. The museum also hosts various exhibits, periodic rail fairs, and other special events.

> **HOURS:** Daily, 10 AM to 5 PM; last entry is at 4:30 PM. Closed Thanksgiving, Christmas, and New Year's Day.
>
> **COST:** Adults, $8; 6–17, $3.
>
> **LOCATION:** Corner of 2nd and I streets, Old Sacramento
>
> **PHONE:** 916-445-7378
>
> **WEBSITE:** www.parks.ca.gov/parkindex

The California State Railroad Museum's locomotive logo is the historic *C.P. Huntington*, which can be seen inside.

# 7 Leland Stanford Mansion State Historic Park

**WHAT'S HERE:** Restored mansion of one of the Big Four members of the Central Pacific Railroad

**DON'T MISS THIS:** The locomotive motif designed into several pieces of furniture

It may be little difficult to envision how this 19th century mansion appeared when it was first constructed in Sacramento in 1857. At that time, the surroundings were much more rural, with mostly open land and only a few scattered homes nearby. Today, more recently constructed state office buildings dwarf this four-story, 19,000-square-foot former home of railroad developer and California Governor Leland Stanford.

The mansion was originally built by Sacramento merchant Shelton Fogus, who constructed a much smaller, Renaissance Revival-style home. Leland Stanford, one of the Central Pacific Railroad's "Big Four," purchased the home in 1861, and over the next few years, he quadrupled the size of the house and significantly altered its exterior appearance. One of those remodels included elevating the house about 12 feet so the main living quarters would no longer be susceptible to the periodic flooding from the nearby Sacramento and American rivers.

Stanford came to California in 1852 to join his two brothers, already successful businessmen in Sacramento. With a partner, Stanford started his own business, which soon proved very successful. Additional business successes followed, putting him in the company of other well-to-do businessmen and into the middle of California's developing politics. As one of the founders of the California Republican Party, Stanford felt his many political ties would guarantee his election to the highest state office, and thus, he began the final major expansion of his mansion. He wanted to ensure that it would be suitable as a home and office for California's governor. Stanford's prediction came true, and in January 1862, he was sworn in as governor of California.

In 1868, Leland Stanford, Jr., was born to his proud—and very rich—parents. They traveled extensively with their son, introducing him to museums and historical sites throughout the world. Unfortunately, while traveling in Florence, Italy, with his parents, Leland Jr. died of typhoid fever at age 16. His heartbroken parents decided that the "children of California" would become their children. They significantly expanded their already generous giving by founding and endowing the Leland Stanford Jr. University in Palo Alto, known today as Stanford University.

Stanford became a US senator following his time as governor, but he died in that office in 1893, leaving the future of his estate in question. Later, his wife, Jane, sold their San Francisco home—much bigger than their Sacramento mansion—and gave the funds to the young and struggling Stanford University to ensure its financial survival.

Jane Stanford also donated their Sacramento home and all of its furnishings to the Catholic Church for use by the Sisters of Mercy as an orphanage. The same order had cared for her son during his fatal illness in Italy. In later years, it became a residence for dependent high school girls. One of the upstairs bedrooms has been restored to reflect this period of the home's history. The state of California acquired the property in 1978, but the Sisters remained here until 1987.

One of the first things the Sisters of Mercy did when they turned the mansion into an orphanage was to remove all the Stanford's furniture, art, chandeliers, and the gold-leaf-framed mirrors. Today, all of those original items have been returned to the home, so most of what is in the rooms was here when the Stanfords lived in the home. On the tours, old photos show how closely the rooms appear to their original status, from paintings and pianos to carpets and drapes. Stanford incorporated a theme from his most successful business, the Central Pacific Railroad, into some of his furniture, especially in the dining room, where the locomotive motif can be seen in many of the pieces.

During its history, the home also served as the "gubernatorial mansion" for three governors, Leland Stanford, Frederic Low, and Henry Haight. Today, it once again serves as a ceremonial office for California's governor, and tour groups are allowed to peak in on the office, although the governor rarely makes appearances here. The mansion is also reserved for important gatherings of the governor, some state agencies, and the legislative leadership, including the speaker and the president pro tempore. The visitor center next to the Stanford Mansion features a short introduction film on the lives of Leland and Jane Stanford. The visitor center also houses several exhibits reflecting the family history.

**HOURS:** Daily, 10 AM to 5 p.m; tours are on the hour, with the last beginning at 4 PM. Closed Thanksgiving, Christmas, and New Year's Day. Although the mansion is open for public tours at least 75 percent of the time, call ahead and confirm that it hasn't been reserved for use by the governor or others.

**COST:** Adults, $8; 6–17, $3.

**LOCATION:** 800 N Street, Sacramento

**PHONE:** 916-324-0575

**WEBSITE:** www.parks.ca.gov/parkindex

The restored mansion that once served as Leland Stanford's official governor's residence is once again being used by California governors for their official events.

# 8 Governor's Mansion State Historic Park

**WHAT'S HERE:** Furniture, clothing, and more from past governors and their families

**DON'T MISS THIS:** The beds that Ronald and Nancy Reagan used for the short time they lived here as California's governor and first lady

California has never had a home that was built exclusively as a governor's mansion. Even the historic Governor's Mansion began as a private residence for Albert Gallatin, a partner in Sacramento's Huntington & Hopkins Hardware Store. He had the 30-room Victorian home constructed in 1877, both as a place to live and as a showcase for his wealth and success. Ten years later, Gallatin sold the home to Joseph Steffens, the father of famed journalist and author Lincoln Steffens.

The state of California was searching for an executive home conveniently located near the state capitol and elegant enough to impress foreign and other dignitaries. In 1903, Steffens sold his home to the state of California for just $32,500, and for the next 64 years it was used by 13 governors as their official executive mansion.

George Pardee, governor from 1903 to 1907, was the first to reside here (see Pardee Home Mansion, page 101). For all of the governors, it was just a short ride or walk to the state capitol. When Pardee was in office, he spent a lot of time dealing with the aftermath of the great San Francisco earthquake in 1906. The names of many of the governors who lived here, such as James Norris Gillett (served from 1907 to 1911), James Rolph, Jr. (served from 1931 until his death in 1934), and Culbert Olson (served from 1939 to 1943), are now unfamiliar. Other governors became better known in the years that followed their stays at the downtown mansion. Earl Warren (governor from 1943 to 1953) became chief justice of the US Supreme Court. Ronald Reagan (governor from 1967 to 1975) became the 40th president of the US. He and wife, Nancy, lived in the old mansion for only a short time; they moved out because they feared the house was a firetrap. They lived most of Reagan's two terms as governor in a private residence located in midtown Sacramento, a short distance away.

Little has been done to change the appearance of the Governor's Mansion since the Reagans moved out. It became part of the California State Park System and has been maintained much the way it was left. Each governor was allotted a

Thirteen governors made this 1877 Victorian their official residence.

131

budget to make whatever changes were necessary in the home to better fit that governor's lifestyle. Any additions, including furnishings, became state property and had to remain after they left office. For most, changes included painting the interior rooms, and for one, it included layering a coat of paint over the marble fireplace in the dining room. A subsequent governor had the paint removed. Pardee added the 1902 Steinway piano in the front parlor, and Hiram Johnson purchased the room's velvet sofa and chairs. Even the mansion's very first 1950s black-and-white television is still in one of the rooms.

The dining room features one of several sets of china and crystal that various governors purchased over the years. It obviously was a very different time when the governors lived here, as indicated by the small glass holders at each end of the table filled with cigarettes for after-dinner inhalation.

No one ever thought to have an elevator added to the home, so at the many social events during the early years, anyone needing to use a bathroom had to climb the winding stairway to the second floor. There are nine bathrooms in the mansion, yet only one is located downstairs, and it wasn't added until the 1930s. One other needed improvement never completed was the addition of central air conditioning. Summer heat could send the home's interior temperatures to 100 degrees. Some of the rooms finally received window air conditioners, which helped somewhat.

Upstairs, the bedrooms look much as they would have during different governors' stays. Several of the governors had kids, and that is apparent in one of the bedrooms with the 45-rpm record, dolls, and other items on display. Also, most governors and their spouses apparently slept in separate bedrooms, often blamed on the long and late hours they were forced to keep, not to mention the middle-of-the-night and early-morning phone calls that would have continually disturbed their spouses' sleep. For the short time the Reagans lived here, they broke with tradition and slept in the same bedroom, although their separate twin beds are still here.

The docent-led tours also visit the kitchen, which is straight out of the 1950s, with the double electric stove. An old waffle iron, something most kids may never have seen, sits on one of the counters, next to where a hot plate of some sort burned its design into a wooden shelf. Maybe the Reagans were right in their assessment of the mansion as a firetrap.

Outside the mansion, you can enjoy the gardens and even take a look over a fence and see Governor Pat Brown's swimming pool. Brown enjoyed walking home from the capitol each day, and during Sacramento's hot summers, he often headed across the street from the mansion and used the hotel pool to cool off. His friends had the mansion pool added so he could enjoy swimming closer to home.

**HOURS:** Daily, 10 AM to 5 PM; tours are on the hour, and the last tour is at 4 PM. Closed Thanksgiving, Christmas, and New Year's Day.

**COST:** Adults, $4; 6–16, $2.

**LOCATION:** 1526 H Street, corner of 16th and H streets, Sacramento

**PHONE:** 916-323-3047

**WEBSITE:** www.parks.ca.gov/parkindex

# 9 Crocker Art Museum

**WHAT'S HERE:** Paintings from many California and European masters
**DON'T MISS THIS:** Famous *Sunday Morning in the Mines* painting by Charles Nahl

One of Sacramento's venerable 19th century mansions also has the distinction of being the longest continually operating art museum in the West. The Crocker Art Museum began when Judge Edwin B. Crocker and his wife, Margaret Eleanor Rhodes Crocker, purchased what was originally a much smaller home in 1868. Crocker then commissioned an architect to redesign the home into something much more representative of his place in society. A large part of his vision included adding an entire new wing to the Italianate mansion. The new structure included a bowling alley, skating rink, and a billiards room on the ground floor; a library and natural history museum on the main floor; and gallery space for the Crockers' growing art collection on the upper floor. Today, if you enter the museum through the oversized front doors, it is immediately obvious that the Crockers spared no expense, combining the finest hardwoods and tiles with impeccable workmanship.

Although initially trained as a civil engineer, Crocker also studied law and ultimately made his money after he and his second wife came to California in 1852. Here, he renewed the law practice he had in Indiana and became involved in Republican politics. Following Lincoln's election as US president and Leland Stanford's election as California's governor, both in 1861, Crocker was appointed as a justice to the California Supreme Court in 1863. The following year, he became the legal counsel for the Central Pacific Railroad Company, organized in part by his brother Charles Crocker, one of the railroad's "Big Four," along with Stanford, Mark Hopkins, and Collis P. Huntington.

Crocker suffered a stroke in 1869, and afterward he retired from the railroad. It was then that he began renovating his newly acquired home—or at least hired the architect to handle it for him. While the work was being done, Crocker and his family left for Europe and didn't come back until 1871. They returned with hundreds of pieces of art acquired during their extended European vacation and moved into their newly renovated home, complete with its own private art gallery. The initial Crocker collection included 700 paintings and 1300 Old Master drawings, which, today, is one of the finest collections anywhere. At the time, Crocker's art collection was one of the largest privately held collections in the country.

Unfortunately, Crocker died just three years after moving into his new home, and in 1885, Margaret Crocker

The Crocker Art Museum was originally a private home.

133

gave the Crocker Art Gallery and most of its collection to the city of Sacramento and the California Association of Museums. Margaret spent her remaining years shuttling between homes in Sacramento, San Francisco, Lake Tahoe, Los Angeles, and New York. She died in 1901.

Something that makes the museum especially important to California is its collection of works by early California artists. One of the best known, if not by name, certainly by his work, is Charles Christian Nahl and his painting, *Sunday Morning in the Mines*. The 9-by-6-foot oil painting hangs above the grand staircase to the upper floor and depicts the two "idyllic" sides of life in the California gold mines—that of dedicated gold miners spending their Sunday reading, doing laundry, and writing letters home, contrasted with the carousing, drunken, fighting madness of the other side. At the opposite end of the gallery is Thomas Hill's even larger and more glorious painting, *Great Canyon of the Sierra, Yosemite*. In the surrounding gallery are dozens of paintings by Dutch, Flemish, German, and other European artists.

Over the years, the museum has added additional wings, and it continues to grow, with another 100,000-square-foot expansion planned for 2008. The museum's growing collection of art, not only its paintings and drawings, but its collection of international ceramics, is a wonderful complement to an incredibly beautiful 19th century home.

> **HOURS:** Tuesday through Sunday, 10 AM to 5 PM (open until 9 PM on Thursday). Closed Monday, Thanksgiving, Christmas, and New Year's Day.
>
> **COST:** Adults, $6; 65 and older, $4; students (with ID), $3; under 6, free.
>
> **LOCATION:** 216 O Street, Sacramento
>
> **PHONE:** 916-264-5423
>
> **WEBSITE:** www.crockerartmuseum.org

## 10 The Sacramento Museum of History, Science, Space, and Technology

**WHAT'S HERE:** A walk through Sacramento's history, including the local newspaper, the canning industry, and gold from California's mines

**DON'T MISS THIS:** The gold nugget exhibit

The Sacramento Museum of History, Science, Space, and Technology is broken down into two separate facilities; history and technology are concentrated at the Old Town Sacramento destination, while science and space are found at another location across town. For the purposes of this book, the following listing focuses solely on the Old Town museum and the historical aspects it presents of the Sacramento area.

Sacramento is known as a pivotal point in the great Gold Rush, and many people visiting this very attractive museum will likely be struck with a slight case of gold fever while viewing the displays of real gold in its many forms, from nuggets and veins in quartz to its loose form found in rivers. In addition to showing the real stuff, the museum's exhibits cover the types of mining done in California, from placer and hydraulic mining to the deep hard rock mines. It also explains the early prolific use of hazardous chemicals, such as mercury, commonly used to extract gold from its ancient hiding places.

Beyond the gold, this museum begins a timeline of exhibits that start with crossing the Great Plains and some of the more common items those hearty adventurers brought with them. River transportation was an important part of Sacramento's early days, and kids will enjoy the replica of the wheelhouse of the *Eclipse*, a paddle-wheeler that plied the river between Sacramento and San Francisco. There are costumes inside the wheelhouse for kids to play dress-up—an opportunity for parents to take some memorable photographs of their museum visit.

The 1850s timeline includes fire engines and photographs of the fires that burned parts of the city. There's also an old syringe that belonged to Dr. Frederick Hatch, who survived a shipwreck near San Francisco before making it to Sacramento to begin his practice. The one thing noticeably different from today's syringes is their size—they used some really *big* needles in those early days.

One of the more fascinating exhibits is beneath your feet—the floor itself. A large section is constructed of clear glass, and while walking on it is a strange sensation, it allows you to see below ground level, where an exhibit features many of the artifacts, especially pieces of china, unearthed by archeological digs throughout Sacramento.

Take the escalator to the second level and enter the world of "Gold Rush Gulch," during Gold Rush California. Partly designed for the younger set, there is a child-size miner's cabin with everything from a stove and pans for kids to use while exercising their imaginations. Other exhibits include gold-mining tools and clothes and alternative homes such as the boarding houses, where, during the cold winter months, a miner could live for $3 a week.

In many of California's history museums there is usually a mention of the Chinese who settled throughout the state. This museum has a wonderful collection of 19th century Chinese dolls of every description. There is also additional information about the Chinese and their lives in early California.

As the years progress, the exhibits include more of the common things that

The museum offers several hands-on activities for kids.

were part of the lives of the people living in and around Sacramento. And they aren't any different from those found in any large city's history museum, from Kodak cameras to musical instruments. Exhibits move through the two World Wars and into a 1950s dining room setup with those yellow vinyl chairs.

Sacramento has always been an agricultural town, and a large exhibit back on the first floor, but visible from the second floor, illustrates the history of the many large canneries here. The myriad colorful company labels on the wooden packing crates illustrate the diversity of crops, from tomatoes to pears. One of the area's biggest crops is almonds, and there's an early almond huller that managed to take much of the hand labor out of packaging shelled nuts.

**HOURS:** Labor Day through Memorial Day, Tuesday through Sunday (and Monday holidays), 10 AM to 5 PM; Memorial Day through Labor Day, daily, 10 AM to 5 PM. Closed Thanksgiving, Christmas, and New Year's Day.

**COST:** Adults, $5; 60 and older, $4; 13–17, $4; 4–12, $3; under 3, free.

**LOCATION:** 101 I Street, Old Sacramento

**PHONE:** 916-264-7057

**WEBSITE:** www.thediscovery.org

# 11 Towe Auto Museum

**WHAT'S HERE:** Cars and a few trucks from nearly every era of automotive history

**DON'T MISS THIS:** Henry Ford's very first "car"

It took a little luck, some coincidental timing, and a lot of hard work to merge several significant car collections into a single 72,000-square-foot museum near the Sacramento River in the capital city. When Nevada casino magnate Bill Harrah passed away in 1978, questions arose about the future of his huge personal automobile collection. Plans to bring the collection from Reno to Sacramento via the newly formed California Vehicle Foundation, the brainchild of two Sacramento car enthusiasts, didn't materialize. Another collector, Edward Towe of Montana, inquired about the Sacramento group's interest in obtaining his collection of more than 240 Fords. Towe was looking for a new home for his cars. In September 1986, less than a year after he sent a letter of interest to the California Vehicle Foundation, the cars arrived in Sacramento, cementing the real beginning of the Towe Auto Museum.

The cavernous museum is divided into several exhibit themes that range from "Dream of Mobility" and "Dream of Luxury" to "Dream of Cool" and "Dream of Speed." While the museum possesses an extensive collection of vehicles dating from 1880 through the 1980s, numerous private owners allow their vehicles to be exhibited.

One of the most historically significant vehicles in the collection is Henry Ford's very first "car." For several years, Ford, an engineer at the Edison Illuminating Co., spent his spare time inside a rented shed tinkering on various projects. In 1896, one of the things Ford tinkered into existence was his first gasoline-engine-powered vehicle, dubbed the Quadracycle. It looks more like a carriage with bicycle wheels powered by a strange little motor than a car. While one might question Ford's early planning abilities (he had to take a sledge hammer to the shed's narrow wood and stone doorway in order to get his "car" out for its first test drive), no one can question his ultimate achievement. He successfully fired up the Quadracycle and later that summer sold it for $200, making it the very first Ford sold.

While the automobile became as ubiquitous in the US as horses and buggies had once been, what grabbed most people's attention was the need for speed, style, and luxury—and the auto industry has always been there to meet that need, or to help create the need through their marketing efforts.

It wasn't long before the "muscle car" era arrived, with vehicles like the museum's 1970 Dodge Charger RT, which sold new for $3266, or the 1969 Ford Mustang, Boss 302, with its 290 horsepower V-8 and a $3588 price tag. Long before Detroit introduced its hot rods, car enthusiasts were making mechanical and styling changes to their older cars to make them faster and fancier. The bright red 1932 Ford Coupe is a perfect example of what hot rod enthusiasts where doing (and what they continue to do) to assembly line cars originally designed as basic work or family transportation.

The need for speed is represented by numerous cars designed for the track and those designed for the street—or a little of both. In 1909, a well-publicized New York to Seattle auto race was held, and that winning Ford Model T Racer is in the museum's collection. The winner took 23 days to travel the 4000 miles, which, considering the absence of roads and maps, wasn't a bad time. A white convertible Ford Mustang sits quietly on the museum floor, but back on April 9, 1964, this particular Mustang was the very first to roll off the assembly line. That first "Pony Car" introduced a whole new era of automobile styling. Only eight days later, a Ford dealer in Ft. Lauderdale, Florida, sold that same vehicle as very first Mustang. One of the most popular street and track racers in the museum is the 1966 Shelby 427 Cobra. The Cobra's 425 horsepower engine pushed the 2350-pound, aluminum-bodied car from zero to 100 mph in 13 seconds, and through the quarter mile in 13.8 seconds at 106 miles per hour.

The museum has added several other exhibits to its large collection of cars, including an old repair garage and a 1950s-era ice-cream parlor. The Yosemite

A re-created garage scene at the Towe Auto Museum

display highlights the ability of cars to allow more people to explore and become aware of our world. These early luxury cars with enough stamina and power took people to some of the most beautiful places in the Sierra.

From luxury cars to bizarre creations on wheels, there is something here for anyone with even the slightest interest in the invention that changed California and an entire nation.

> **HOURS:** Daily, 10 AM to 6 PM. Closed Christmas Eve; call to confirm.
>
> **COST:** Adults, $7; seniors, $6; high school students, $3; grade school students, $2.
>
> **LOCATION:** 2200 Front Street, Sacramento
>
> **PHONE:** 916-442-6802
>
> **WEBSITE:** www.toweautomuseum.org

# 12 Folsom Prison Museum

**WHAT'S HERE:** Hangman's noose, guns, uniforms, and other items related to Folsom Prison's long history

**DON'T MISS THIS:** The "talking" inmate in his cell

Infamous Folsom Prison has endured its well-deserved notoriety for well over a century. The state of California had not originally planned a prison for Folsom, but Horatio G. Livermore, a local developer, needed cheap labor. In the early 1860s, Livermore acquired control of the Natoma Water and Mining Company with the intention of floating logs down the American River to his mill. Since he needed to build a dam and canal, Livermore convinced the state that Folsom would be a great place for a prison—and he offered to donate the land in exchange for prison labor. The state agreed to the deal.

The site was perfect for other reasons, too. It was close to the American River and its "free" hydroelectric power, and there was a nearby source of granite that the convicts could quarry in order to build their own prison. They began construction in 1878, and the first prisoners arrived to the partially completed prison in July 1880. Chong Hing, an immigrant from Canton, China, had the dubious honor of being the first official prisoner when he and 43 of his fellow inmates were transferred from San Quentin to Folsom. There was plenty of room for them, since 324 of the 8-by-4-foot cells had been completed. Unlike most of today's jails, the walls were granite, and the cell doors were solid steel with a small peek hole, not the steel bars seen in later years.

Folsom Prison was designed to hold prisoners who were serving the longest terms, essentially the worst of the worst habitual criminals. In the early years, the guards were permitted to punish prisoners pretty much as they pleased: to tie them up by their thumbs, whack them with clubs, or simply place them in straitjackets. The prisoners retaliated with riots and escape attempts, most of which were unsuccessful, although many turned deadly either for the prisoners or the guards. One of the bloodiest escape attempts occurred in 1937, when several convicts took Warden Clarence Larkin hostage, ultimately stabbing and nearly decapitating him during their unsuccessful try for freedom. The warden's killers paid the ultimate price for his murder and were the first to be executed in San Quentin's gas chamber.

While you may experience some trepidation walking into an operating prison to visit its small museum, there is little to worry about. The museum is actually just outside the formidable granite prison walls. There's also a new Folsom Prison (officially called California State Prison, Sacramento), and its turnoff is just a half mile before the dead-end road leading into old Folsom Prison. You'll see a visitors' parking lot to the left before the dead-end. From there, it's a short walk to the museum.

The small museum is an eye opener for anyone contemplating becoming a correctional officer. Some of the exhibits include actual weapons made by convicts; there's every kind of stabbing instrument you could think of, and many you couldn't, and even firearms, or at least some really good fakes. And for all those who succumbed to the hangman's noose, there's a hangman's rope and a description of the technique, such as the 6-foot, 6-inch drop before the rope stopped, snapping the condemned prisoner's neck.

Numerous historic photos and newspaper articles (several about the deadly attempted escape that killed Warden Larkin), crafts created by past prisoners, and a look at uniforms and other prison-related ephemera fill the museum. There are several weapons used by guards, including a 10-barreled, .45-.70-caliber Gatling gun.

Outside the museum, one of the original guard towers has been set up, giving a prisoner's view of where guards were always stationed—with their loaded, high-power rifles—just waiting and watching. On the walk back to the parking lot, stop by the small visitor gift shop, but don't be startled by the trustee inmate who works at the shop (trustees are clothed in blue jeans and blue chambray shirts). The gift shop is filled with various prisoner-made craft items that are for sale. Two quick bits of prison trivia: Singer Johnny Cash, whose song *Folsom Prison Blues* is told from the perspective of an inmate, performed at

Folsom Prison, across the street from the museum

Folsom Prison, but never served time here, and Folsom Prison makes all of California's vehicle license plates.

**HOURS:** Daily, 10 AM to 4 PM. Closed Thanksgiving, Christmas, and New Year's Day, and occasionally if docents aren't available; call to confirm.

**COST:** 12 and older, $2.

**LOCATION:** 300 Prison Road, off of Natoma Street in Folsom. Watch for the Folsom State Prison sign, and be sure to follow all posted warnings, policies, and procedures.

**PHONE:** 916-985-2561 ext. 4589

**WEBSITE:** www.cdcr.ca.gov/Visitors/fac_prison_FSP.html (There is no official website for the museum, but this official prison site offers directions and additional information.)

# 13 Folsom Powerhouse Museum

**WHAT'S HERE:** The original turbines and generators and exhibits about the hydroplant

**DON'T MISS THIS:** Walk up to the top of the forebay structure to see where the water entered the power plant's penstocks

Except during power outages, few people think much about electricity when they turn on a light. But back in the late 19th century, many thought it impossible to transmit high-voltage electricity over long-distance lines, and some insisted that power must travel in a straight line. All of these tales were put to rest when the Folsom Powerhouse, the first plant anywhere to transmit electricity over a long distance, went online in July 1895.

The story begins with one of this Gold Rush town's early developers, Horatio G. Livermore. He gave up looking for gold and decided that purchasing water rights was a more profitable business. He was instrumental in the construction of nearby Folsom Prison (see page 138), eventually using convict labor to build the dam and canal he required to divert a consistent water source from the American River into his hydroelectric power plant. He was planning to operate a sawmill with electric power, but, as it turned out, the American River was not good for floating logs through its maze of big boulders.

Livermore didn't give up. Instead, he built what today is one of the oldest hydroelectric plants in the world, and sent its power over 22 miles of high-voltage lines to Sacramento. Sacramento celebrated this spectacular fete on Admission Day, September 9, 1895, with a night-time "Great Electric Carnival" that drew thousands of people from around the state. More than 30,000 came from San Francisco alone to witness this new technological achievement as electric lights outlined the state capitol and others illuminated the night sky, all visible from 50 miles away.

The old powerhouse ultimately was sold to Pacific Gas and Electric, which operated the plant until 1952. Although the generators were still working in 1952, the construction of Folsom Dam required that the small dam providing water to the powerhouse's penstocks be removed. Several years later, PG&E donated the powerhouse to California's State Parks, and it has since been placed on the National Register of Historic Places.

The two-story brick powerhouse is open for self-guided tours and occasionally for guided tours, usually when an extra docent is available. There's an opportunity to walk on top of the forebay structure and peer down on the small forebays that stored water; these forebays allowed rocks, sand, and other sediment to drop out before the water was sent flowing down to the penstocks, which are the large pipes that directed the water's forceful 55-foot drop to turn the turbines below. The 250 gallons of water per second that passed through the turbines and into the generator shafts caused them to spin at 300 revolutions per minute, generating 800 volts of electricity. You can see the generators inside the powerhouse, as well as control panels that sent the relatively low voltage to the outside transformers that boosted the 800 volts to 11,000 volts that was, in turn, transmitted to Sacramento. Once the turbines used the water's force, the water was directed down a tailrace and returned to the American River.

The grounds also include a blacksmith shop. Down near the water's edge (once the American River, but now Lake Natoma, formed by Nimbus Dam and serving as Folsom Dam's afterbay), there are several bedrock mortars used by the Native Americans who once lived here.

| | |
|---|---|
| **HOURS:** | Wednesday through Sunday, noon to 4 PM. |
| **COST:** | Free |
| **LOCATION:** | Across the street from the intersection of Riley and Scott streets, Old Town Folsom |
| **PHONE:** | 916-988-0205 |
| **WEBSITE:** | www.parks.ca.gov/parkindex |

Folsom Powerhouse provided power to Sacramento from 1895 until 1952.

# 14 Castle Air Museum

**WHAT'S HERE:** Extensive collection of World War II and Vietnam War-era military aircraft

**DON'T MISS THIS:** The B-52 cockpit with all of its gauges and controls

Castle Air Museum, located in the town of Atwater, is visually deceptive. Perched in front of the museum's parking lot is an SR-71 Blackbird, the famous US Cold War spy plane capable of exceeding speeds of 2100 mph. There are also a few World War II birds within view, but little else can be seen out front. That's because this museum features endless pathways that wind through acres of park-like setting, with benches for visitors to rest under the shade of the planes' giant wings.

The museum is located at what was once officially Castle Air Force Base, a victim of the nationwide base closure program in 1995. The old runways and many of the buildings are now part of the local commercial airport. Since the museum's opening in 1981 while the base was still active, its collection has grown to more than 40 aircraft, making it one of the largest air museums west of the Rocky Mountains. The museum welcomes additional planes every year, and the collection continues to grow.

The old airbase and its museum are named after medal of honor winner General Frederick W. Castle. General Castle was killed on Christmas Eve in 1944, when three Messerschmitt Me-109 fighters attacked and shot down his B17 while he was on his 30th bombing mission over Germany. The general managed to get most of his crew out before his aircraft lost a wing and went into a fatal spin with him still aboard.

The indoor portion of the museum holds a collection of aircraft engines, uniforms from as early as World War I, old photos, and a couple hundred military unit shoulder patches. One unique exhibit is the cockpit of a real Vietnam War-era B-52 bomber that is attached to one end of the museum building. Although you can't sit in the pilot's seat, it offers a great look at all the switches, dials, and knobs the pilot and co-pilot had to know in their sleep in order to fly the big, black machines.

The bulk of the exhibits are located outside. The collection starts with the major World War II workhorses, a B-17 Flying Fortress and a B-24 Liberator. More Liberators were built than any other aircraft in history—18,841. There is also the smaller B-25, the same kind of twin-engine, medium bomber that Colonel Jimmy Doolittle and his raiders flew off the deck of the *USS Hornet* for their famous one-way raid on Tokyo during

Colorful artwork was a feature on the noses of most World War II bombers.

the early days of World War II (see USS Hornet Museum, page 104). War tends to spur technology, and the Boeing B-29 was one result. Used primarily in the Pacific Theater, it was the first bomber with a pressurized crew compartment. The B-29 displayed at the museum is a composite of parts from three different B-29s used as targets at the China Lake Naval Weapons Center in California's eastern desert (see US Naval Museum of Armament and Technology, page 312).

Other military aircraft displayed, at least those with creative nicknames, include the Douglas C-47 "Gooney Bird" and the Navy's SA-16 "Albatross." The museum grounds also hold a large number of fighter jets, ranging from an F-84F Thunderstreak to an F-86 Sabre to a Canadian-built CF-100 Mk V Canuck, one of the largest fighters ever built. It was eclipsed by the US Air Force's F-105 Thunderchief, lovingly called the "Thud" and "Lead Sled" by its Vietnam War-era pilots, and not because it was light and nimble. The F-105 was the heaviest single-seat fighter ever built.

One of the largest and most unusual aircraft is the RB-36H Peacemaker. This Cold War dinosaur was North America's strategic defense against a potential Russian attack. The big reconnaissance bombers were built in the 1950s with a design twist—its six huge engines and their propellers were mounted on the front wings, facing backward. Also here is what became the backbone of the Strategic Air Command's air attack during the 1950s was the Boeing B-47 Stratojet. By 1957, the US military had more than 2000 of the world's first swept-wing bombers in use.

Thousands of Vietnam War-era veterans became familiar with one of the workhorses of that war, the C-123. The twin-engine, propeller-driven aircraft hauled up to 15,000 pounds of supplies or quickly converted to handle up to 61 soldiers. During the Vietnam War era, it was one of the favorite planes flown by Air America, the CIA's secret operations arm in Southeast Asia.

The museum has a small gift shop and a restaurant that specializes in "Bomber Burgers." Considering that many of the café's customers are Air Force veterans, the burgers must be a hit.

---

**HOURS:** April through September, daily, 9 AM to 5 PM; October through March, daily, 10 AM to 4 PM. Closed Easter, Thanksgiving, December 24 and 25, and New Year's Day.

**COST:** Adults, $8; 60 and older and 6–17, $6; active military, free.

**LOCATION:** 5050 Santa Fe Drive, Atwater

**PHONE:** 209-723-2178 or 209-723-2182

**WEBSITE:** www.elite.net/castle-air

# 15 The Meux Home

**WHAT'S HERE:**   Historic home of an early and prominent Fresno physician
**DON'T MISS THIS:**   The 17th century Staffordshire tea service

Thomas Meux graduated from medical school at the age of 22 and then gained a lifetime of experience in just four years as an assistant surgeon in the Confederate Army. In 1887, driven by his wife's poor health, Meux moved her and their three children to California, settling in the newly incorporated town of Fresno. Here, he established a medical practice and also built his family a home. It was completed in 1889 and cost $12,000, making it one of the most expensive and fanciest homes in Fresno.

Meux lived in the home until his death in 1929, at age 91. Anne, one of his daughters, remained unmarried her entire life and lived in the home for 81 years. She died in 1970 at age 85, and the city of Fresno purchased the home in 1973, with the intention of restoring the grand Victorian.

The home's exterior is comprised of converging roof lines, punctuated by several chimneys and a five-sided tower. Different treatments have been used on the walls to enhance its Victorian-era charm. Some are horizontal clapboard, while the upper portion of the tower is covered with fancier fish scale and variegated shingles.

The home's interior has been beautifully restored and is fully furnished with pieces that, for the most part, are not original to the family, but would have been found in homes during that period. The parlor was often the main room, where most guests spent their time while visiting. In keeping with the Victorian-era hospitality, the room was very formal, and the sliding doors could close it off from the remainder of the house when needed. Some of the home and its furnishings appear to have been ordered from catalogs or purchased from stores that carried quantities of manufactured goods, rather than being custom-made. The fireplace mantel is most likely machine made. The mantel holds many small art objects, including English vases and a soapstone statue of a girl and her dog.

The parlor is where, in 1907, the middle child, Mary Meux, wed her husband, Henry Barbour, who had recently arrived from New York. Thomas Meux was having a home built nearby as a wedding gift

The Meux Home was constructed in 1889.

for the newlyweds, but Mary became pregnant and was due before it could be completed. She gave birth to her son in the family home, in her pink and green bedroom.

A 17th century Staffordshire tea service sits on a table and reflects one of the apparent habits of people during the late 1800s—the accompanying sugar bowl is quite large compared with the remainder of the service. Music was a part of the family's life, as witnessed by the Edison cylinder phonograph that sits on the mahogany table.

The dining room, where the family enjoyed many formal and informal meals, still retains its original wallpaper, extraordinary considering its age. It is thought that decades of fireplace, gas fixtures, and kerosene lamp smoke has darkened the once bright, floral design paper. The beautiful mahogany sideboard is thought to be 14th century English, and the oak dining table is set, ready for the evening meal.

Meux's wife, Mary, likely spent much time in the master bedroom, as her health was poor, and, in her later years, she became deaf and blind. But when still able to see, she enjoyed the unobstructed winter views of the snow-capped Sierra in the distance. The bedroom's fireplace mantel is stained walnut, and like the home's other five fireplaces, it is designed to burn coal rather than wood.

| | |
|---|---|
| **HOURS:** | Friday through Sunday, noon to 3:30 PM; last tour is 3 PM. Closed Easter, Memorial Day, July 4, Thanksgiving, Christmas, and New Year's Day. |
| **COST:** | Adults, $5; ages 13–17, $4; ages 5–12, $3. |
| **LOCATION:** | 1007 R Street (corner of Tulare and R streets), Fresno |
| **PHONE:** | 559-233-8007 |
| **WEBSITE:** | www.meux.mus.ca.us |

# 16 Kearney Mansion

| | |
|---|---|
| **WHAT'S HERE:** | Both original and non-original furnishings, including Kearney's personal office, with his plans for his never-completed five-level chateau |
| **DON'T MISS THIS:** | A close look at what are really adobe walls covered with plaster and topped with peaked dormers |

Martin Theodore Kearney—the Fresno County raisin baron—constructed this gorgeous mansion as his temporary residence, while his much larger mansion—the Chateau Fresno—was being built. Unfortunately, Kearney died in 1906, shortly after ground was broken for his chateau, so construction was halted on the home and never resumed.

Kearney was born in 1842 in England to Irish parents. At the age of 12, he traveled with his working class parents to the US, where they settled in Massachusetts. When he turned 18, Kearney headed for Boston and quickly worked his way from salesman to manager of a trunk business. During those five years, Kearney focused on learning the "ways of a gentleman," studying foreign languages, dancing, and more.

In 1869, Kearney was ready for California, and he arrived looking and acting every part the gentleman he had worked so hard to become. He also arrived with money and promptly purchased 8640 acres in Fresno County, paying just $2.50 per acre. Kearney had made the purchase, sight unseen, from the land's owner while on board the ship that carried him from the East Coast to San Francisco.

That same owner, Dr. Edward B. Perrin, convinced Kearney that with the introduction of irrigation, the land would produce rich harvests. Kearney thus envisioned the creation of an agricultural development where he would install the needed irrigation canals, roads, and other infrastructure across his newly acquired land. He would then sell 20-acre parcels to investor-farmers who would grow a variety of crops, which ultimately included grapes that could be dried into raisins. Successfully enlisting the help of several financial backers, Kearney became the key promoter and the manager of the first successful "farm colony" in the Central Valley. Kearney and his associates, along with various financial supporters, purchased additional lands and went about developing and selling nearly 200 parcels.

In March 1883, Kearney purchased another 6800 acres near Fresno and called it his Fruit Vale Estate. It was here that he planned to expand what was turning out to be a very profitable business, growing grapes and drying raisins. He tried to convince other growers in the area that working together would benefit everyone. In 1898, Kearney founded the California Raisin Growers' Association, designed to both improve the quality of raisins and also to better market raisins to the rest of the country and to the world. Kearney was successful in convincing many growers to join forces, but the eight years that his association existed were described as stormy, as the very independent growers vied for support of their own points of view and interests. Following Kearney's death in 1906, many of those same growers founded a new organization, adapting the majority of Kearney's original policies and procedures. Their new cooperative evolved into today's Sun Maid Growers of California.

Prior to his death, Kearney had made arrangements that upon his death, 5400 acres of raisin vineyards—his Fruit Vale Estate, valued at $1.5 million—were to be given to the University of California. Today, the 225 acres surrounding the mansion are a county park. The Kearney Mansion and the park are on the National Register of Historic Places, and are open to the public. The Fresno County Historical Society manages the home's public tour program.

The Kearney Mansion is one of California's largest adobe homes.

The Kearney Mansion is actually two separate buildings, both rectangular and built with unseen 2-foot-thick adobe brick walls. An elaborate French Renaissance design covers the adobe walls with a layer of painted plaster, topped with high, peaked roofs and dormers. The entry has both original and non-original furnishings; the carved chairs and bench are originals from Germany, while the carpeting is a reproduction.

One of the more interesting rooms is Kearney's personal office. It includes plans for his five-level Chateau Fresno, along with numerous photographs and other documents the land and raisin baron used when he sat in this very room more than 100 years ago. On the second floor, Kearney's large bedroom and private bathroom contain many features original to the home, including his brass bed and maple furnishings.

**HOURS:** Friday, Saturday, and Sunday, hourly, 1 PM to 3 PM. Closed on legal holidays that fall on Friday, Saturday, or Sunday.

**COST:** Adults, $5; seniors and students, $4; 12 and under, $3.

**LOCATION:** 7160 West Kearney Blvd., Fresno

**PHONE:** 559-441-0862

**WEBSITE:** historicfresno.org/nrhp/kearney.htm

# 17 Colonel Allensworth State Historic Park

**WHAT'S HERE:** Colonel Allensworth's restored home, the old schoolhouse, and numerous reconstructed buildings

**DON'T MISS THIS:** The five annual events (February, May, June, and October) that bring this quiet town back to life

While there are no mansions here, this entire town is a museum. Located 7 miles west of Earlimart off County Road J22 and south on Rural Route 43, the ghost town of Allensworth is the only California town to be established, financed, and governed by African Americans. Colonel Allen Allensworth came here in 1908 and founded what he hoped would be an all black farming community.

Allensworth was born into slavery in 1842 and served with the Union forces during the Civil War. He later married and returned to civilian life, earning his doctorate in theology. In 1886, he again entered military service as a chaplain in an African American regiment, becoming the first black person to reach the rank of lieutenant colonel. He retired in 1906 and headed for California. Two years later, he and a partner created the California Colonization and Home Promotion Association, purchased 800 acres along the Santa Fe

Railroad line, and began to build his colony. From the beginning, it was designed to give blacks an opportunity to live in their own community, free of discrimination. People from across the country bought into his new town, which he named Allensworth.

The town was situated at a railroad stop, which provided a significant economic benefit to the community's businesses and farm operations. With the town growing rapidly, the small school was replaced by a newer, larger schoolhouse, soon resulting in the creation of California's first black school district. As more businesses added new buildings to the several blocks of streets that had been laid out, the town continued to prosper.

An unforeseen problem—one that still plagues farmers today—proved to be the beginning of the end for Allensworth. The water table began to drop, and because the town lacked funds to drill new and deeper wells, the water shortage reached a critical stage by 1914. That same year, the Santa Fe Railroad moved its stop to another town, and Colonel Allensworth was killed in an accident while in southern California. World War I followed, along with a general economic slump, thus forcing many of Allensworth's citizens to give up their dreams and leave for greener pastures. In the 1960s, arsenic was discovered in the meager water supply, ending the town for good.

What remained of Allensworth's few buildings were scheduled for demolition in the early 1970s when several dedicated people helped the old town become a California State Historic Park in 1976. Today, the colonel's home and the old schoolhouse have been restored, and many of the town's homes and business buildings have been reconstructed on their original sites. The barbershop is one of the latest buildings to be reconstructed and furnished. It looks as if it could be open for business today. A small visitor center near the schoolhouse regularly features a movie about the town's history.

There are seldom many visitors in the town. In fact, the first impression many get after crossing the railroad tracks and driving down into Allensworth is that this is an abandoned ghost town. And that is often true, except when school groups fill the town's dirt streets and also during five major celebrations held each year. The Black History month celebrations are in February, Old Time Jubilee is held in May, the Juneteenth Celebration is in June, and the Rededication is in October. All of the events bring hundreds of supporters, history buffs, and families to town for a day of living history programs, tours of the colonel's home, plenty of great food, and lots of old-time fun. Dates change, so it is best to contact the park for specific information.

**HOURS:** Daily, 8 AM to 6 PM. Closed Thanksgiving, Christmas, and New Year's Day.

**COST:** Day-use vehicle fee, $4 (self-pay at entrance).

**LOCATION:** Seven miles west off Earlimart on County Road J22 and south on Rural Route 43

**PHONE:** 661-849-3433

**WEBSITE:** www.parks.ca.gov/parkindex or www.friendsofallensworth.com

# Great Valley Tours

## Sacramento History Tour

**ESTIMATED DAYS:** 1–2

**ESTIMATED DRIVING MILES:** 5

Sacramento is full of history, and a great place to start is at one of the earliest historic sites, **Sutter's Fort State Historic Park** (page 123). This is a fun place for kids, especially on days when docents are dressed in period costumes. The **State Indian Museum** (916-324-0971) lies just outside the fort's walls, offering an even earlier look at California. From the 1840s at Sutter's Fort, it's a short 2.5-mile trip to **Old Sacramento**, at 2nd and I streets, the city's premier destination. One of the best parts of Old Sacramento is the **California State Railroad Museum** (page 127) that will take you on a trip back through time to the construction of the transcontinental railroad and its steam locomotive era, all the way to today's modern diesel-electric locomotives. Here you can even ride one of the old trains, departing from the adjacent historic Central Pacific passenger station for a ride along the Sacramento River.

After Old Sacramento, it's time to backtrack about nine blocks east on Capitol Ave. to the **State Capitol** (page 125), where not only are legislative bills passed and laws made, but a portion of the capitol has been restored to reflect its 1906 character. That 1906 theme coincides with the 1906 San Francisco earthquake, so you can view Governor George Pardee's office and many other offices as they appeared a century ago. You can also stroll through the many acres of Capitol Park's gardens, trees, and numerous memorials.

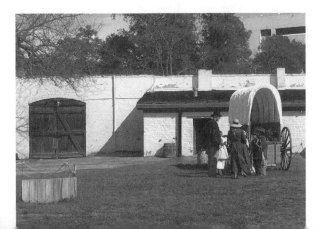

Sutter's Fort often features living-history days.

# Family/Kids Day Tour

ESTIMATED DAYS:  1

ESTIMATED DRIVING MILES:  2

The Gold Rush town of Folsom is located about 28 miles east of downtown Sacramento, although it's probably better known for its notorious prison than its place in Gold Rush history. Located just outside the walls of California's second oldest prison (after San Quentin), the **Folsom Prison Museum** (page 138) is open for a close look—or about as close as most people want to get—to life and death in this old fortress. Just a couple of miles away by road, but closer if you could go directly along the American River, is the historic **Folsom Powerhouse Museum** (page 140). The first powerhouse to transmit electricity over long distance lines, the generator turbines and the old electrical controls are still here. And **Lake Natoma** (Folsom Lake State Recreation Area: 916-988-0205), actually the American River flowing between Folsom Dam upstream and Nimbus Dam downstream, is available and easily accessible for a little fishing. Just up the hill one block are the shops and restaurants of the historic part of **Folsom** (www.visitfolsom.com), where you can find everything from antiques and jewelry to chocolate and Chinese food.

# Romantic Tour

ESTIMATED DAYS:  1–2

ESTIMATED DRIVING MILES:  2

Sacramento was the supply point for most of the Gold Rush miners, the original starting point for the Central Pacific Railroad, and after several years of statehood, California's capital. As such, it attracted the rich and powerful, who built homes and businesses. One of the fanciest mansions, and the West's oldest art museum, is the **Crocker Art Museum** (page 133), built around 1868, and located four blocks southeast from Old Sacramento. It's a great place to start a romantic tour that focuses on elegance and charm.

Several blocks away from the Crocker Art Museum, Leland Stanford, one of the "Big Four" founders of the Central Pacific Railroad, built his home, now **Leland Stanford Mansion State Historic Park** (page 129). While Stanford's home served as a temporary governor's mansion, your next stop should be the permanent **Governor's Mansion** (page 131), a little over a mile away, that was purchased in 1903. The new home served 13 governors, the last of whom was Ronald Reagan, who moved out after a short time, calling it a firetrap. It's been restored and now offers an inside look at the privileged lives of some of California's earlier governors. If you get to Sacramento during the December holiday season, the mansion is decked out in its Christmas finery.

# Great Valley Travel Information Centers

Sacramento Convention and Visitor's Bureau
www.discovergold.org
916-808-7777

Central Valley Tourism Association
www.visitcentralvalley.com
800-514-5539

Folsom Chamber of Commerce
www.folsomchamber.com
916-985-2698

Fresno Convention & Visitors Bureau
www.fresnocvb.org
800-788-0836

Bakersfield (Greater) Convention & Visitors Bureau
661-325-5051

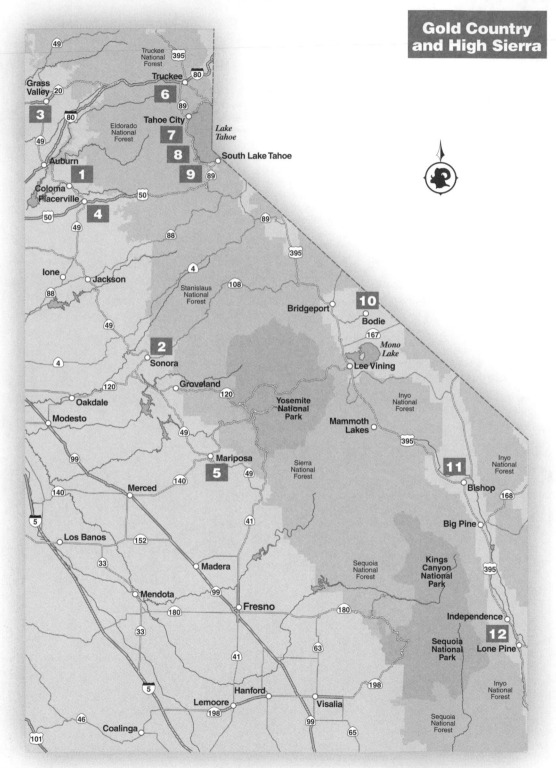

**Gold Country and High Sierra**

# Gold Country
# and High Sierra

In the early 1850s, thousands of easterners saw the Sierra Nevada as an obstacle to their future riches. Viewing the distant mountains from San Francisco in 1776, the Spanish missionary Pedro Font referred to the range as "Sierra Nevada," or "jagged range that is snowed upon." That is something the ill-fated Donner Party discovered firsthand in 1846–47.

Nineteenth century naturalist John Muir called these mountains the "range of light." In the late 1800s, it was California's rich who first began using the Sierra's Lake Tahoe as a summer playground. Today, the 400-mile-long Sierra is a four-season recreation mecca drawing millions of people each year. Hundreds of lakes, lush forests, and tumbling

This cottage served as William Bourn's mountain home when he visited his Empire Mine operations.

153

streams bring campers and fishermen during the relatively short summer months and skiers and snowmobilers during winter. Lake Tahoe's deep blue waters as well as the glacier-carved granite spires and cascading waterfalls of Yosemite Valley to the south are world renowned.

The majority of High Sierra visitors come from the Great Valley, the San Francisco Bay Area, and Los Angeles. As they drive eastward to escape smoggy, 100-degree days, most cross Hwy. 49, California Gold Country's thoroughfare. Along Hwy. 49, which travels the length of this thin, north-south band of gold-rich rivers and hills, many Gold Rush-era towns thrived for a few months or several years, then died and vanished. Others survived but dwindled in size and population as gold mines shut down throughout the 19th and 20th centuries. Today, many of these surviving towns, such as Sonora, Jackson, Placerville, and Auburn, are growing as California's population increases and people discover the serene beauty and rich history of the Sierra foothills.

The story of the Gold Country and High Sierra's history is today told in dozens of small museums run by local history buffs and a handful of larger museums and early mansions operated by the state and federal governments. Visiting Columbia State Historic Park or Marshall Gold Discovery State Historic Park can give you a glimpse back to the days of the state's early explorers and the gold seekers' drudgery. Head east over the crest to Lake Tahoe, and the opulent living enjoyed by California's rich and sometimes famous remains evident today at mansions such as Vikingsholm or the Pope Estate.

# TRIVIA

1 Which mansion is a replica of a 17th century Viking castle?

2 Who discovered gold on the American River and kicked off the California Gold Rush?

3 Which Lake Tahoe historic site features two homes built by the founders of banks?

4 Where can you see a wheelbarrow built by the future "horseless carriage" magnate?

5 Which town was commonly known as one of the most notorious of California's Gold Rush towns?

6 Where can you find the largest gold nugget to have survived California's 19th century mining operations?

7 Which Paramount Studios movie features the visitor center at the Laws Railroad Museum and Historical Site?

8 Around which Gold Rush town did miners take more than $150 million (at $30 per ounce) in gold during its first 50 years of existence?

*For trivia answers, see page 327.*

# 1 Marshall Gold Discovery State Historic Park

**WHAT'S HERE:** Museum on the Gold Rush and several historic buildings, including a Chinese store

**DON'T MISS THIS:** The full-sized replica of Sutter's sawmill, where James Marshall discovered gold

"**B**oys, I believe I've found a gold mine!" Those are the words sawmill boss James Marshall exclaimed to his Mormon workers after discovering gold nuggets in the tailrace of the sawmill he had constructed on the American River at Coloma. It was January 24, 1848, and what soon followed was the biggest migration the country had ever witnessed.

Prior to his historic discovery, Marshall led a relatively unremarkable life. In 1834, he began his slow journey West, stopping in Missouri to try his hand at farming, among other things. In 1845, he joined a wagon train heading over the Oregon Trail, and the following year, he landed in Sutter's Fort, near the juncture of the American and Sacramento rivers (see Sutter's Fort State Historic Park, page 123). He found employment immediately as a carpenter and wheelwright making wheels, carts, wagons, spinning looms, and furniture. In 1846, he joined the California Volunteers, and helped the Americans in their successful war against Mexico.

Following the war, Marshall returned to what would someday become Sacramento and went to work for John Sutter, who owned significant land in the area and had built Sutter's Fort. Sutter hired Marshall to construct and manage a sawmill in order to supply the fort with much-needed lumber. Marshall headed east along the American River looking for a spot near an ample supply of timber for Sutter's new sawmill. The local Maidu and Nisenan Indians called the small valley where Marshall chose to build the mill, "Culluma." It became known on maps as Coloma.

After Marshall's discovery, he and Sutter attempted to keep the gold a secret, hoping to make the sawmill operation a success. But word leaked out quickly, and soon the mill workers were off searching for their own gold mines. Ironically, Marshall gained nothing from his discovery. Within a couple of years, the mill was abandoned and, with it, Marshall's hope for the future. He lived later around Coloma, running a small blacksmith shop, and he died a poor man.

This Mother Lode museum is relatively small, considering the magnitude of Marshall's gold discovery to the history of California and the world. The main museum's exhibits explore not only Marshall's life, but those of the local Indians and the settlers and miners who followed gold to Coloma. Marshall's Pennsylvania long rifle, with its double-set trigger, is on display. Marshall purchased the .36-caliber muzzle-loader as a young man and carried it with him across the Oregon Trail to California. Other exhibits include everything from the tools needed for gold mining, such as pans and rockers and sluice boxes, to the scales used to measure the precious metal and the pouches used to carry it.

In 1947, an excavation uncovered several heavy timbers from the original sawmill, but most of the original mill had been stolen or was washed downriver in the flood of 1862. In 1967, a replica mill, located across Hwy. 49 from the museum, was reconstructed just a few dozen yards from the original discovery site, which is marked by a stone monument along the river. The replica was built on higher ground above the river to protect it from periodic high water. Unlike the original mill, which used water power, this one has a hidden electric motor so that staff can provide lumber-cutting demonstrations.

Elsewhere around the park, outdoor exhibits continue the story of gold's impact on California. Two 1850s-era stone buildings are located a short walk from the main museum. Originally, they were leased to members of the local Chinese community. Today, the Wah Hop and Man Lee stores are filled with exhibits; one is a Chinese store with everything from medicines to food that would have likely been for sale here, and the other features exhibits on gold-mining technology, from the early placer mining to the development of hard-rock mining. A portion of one room tells the story of the huge, self-contained dredges that worked the ancient river bottoms on and near the Feather, Yuba, Sacramento, and American rivers.

Marshall Gold Discovery State Historic Park also contains a historic cemetery about a half mile from the museum. It's filled with men, women, children, prostitutes, murderers, and unknowns, and is just fun to walk through. And at the top of the tall, tree-covered hill that sits behind the museum, there is a monument to James Marshall. A trail winds up the hillside from behind the museum to the monument, or you can drive around the side of the park about a quarter mile and turn onto Hwy. 153, apparently California's shortest highway. It's less than a half mile long and ends at the picnic area where the Marshall monument is located. Ask for directions to both places at the museum.

**HOURS:** Daily, 10 AM to 3 PM, sometimes later if staffing is available. Closed Thanksgiving, Christmas, and New Year's Day.

**COST:** $5 per vehicle.

**LOCATION:** Marshall Gold Discovery State Historic Park is on both sides of Hwy. 49, in the center of Coloma, about 9 miles northwest of Placerville.

**PHONE:** 530-622-3470

**WEBSITE:** www.parks.ca.gov/parkindex

Reconstructed water-powered sawmill where James Marshall discovered gold on the American River in 1848

# Columbia State Historic Park

**WHAT'S HERE:** Museum, exhibits in historic buildings, shops, and stagecoach rides

**DON'T MISS THIS:** A chance to pan for real gold

Columbia State Historic Park, an open-air, working, hands-on museum near Sonora, is about as close as you can get to a real, living Gold Rush town—which makes it a great destination for the entire family.

The candy store and the various gift shops are a bit touristy, but the other exhibits, such as the wooden trough where kids and adults can pan for gold—and find it!—and the original stagecoach, add an authentic touch to learning about history. The park's main museum is filled with everything from rock samples and gold dust to old books, pistols, and other treasures.

Columbia's original name was Hildreth's Diggins, after two brothers who first discovered gold in the area in 1850. Within weeks of their discovery, thousands of miners had set up tents and shanties, and the town's name was changed to American Camp, and then to Columbia, a more permanent-sounding name.

Since water was scarce, Columbia was considered a "dry diggins." Initially, gold panning could be done only during the wet winter months when seasonal streams flowed. The gold proved to be plentiful enough for longer-term investment, so investors formed the Tuolumne County Water Company to bring water to the mines. But their water's high price inspired the miners to create their own Columbia and Stanislaus River Water Company in 1854. The miners completed a 60-mile-long aqueduct in 1858 that moved water to where it was needed most. With the water-supply issue solved, hydraulic mining—washing away hillsides with streams of water directed through high-pressure nozzles or monitors—became the preferred technique for moving large quantities of soil in search of gold. During the town's first 50 years, at least $150 million in gold was taken from the ground, and that was when gold sold for $30 an ounce, less than one tenth of today's value.

With all this development and the large quantities of gold being taken, the town of Columbia began to acquire permanency. Unfortunately, most of it was constructed of wood. As happened to most 19th century mining towns in California, Columbia (or at least the entire six city blocks in the central business district) burned to the ground in 1854. The only structure to survive was a single brick building, which stands at the corner of Main and Washington streets. New buildings, made of brick with the addition of iron shutters to further protect against fire, were reconstructed on the old sites. The town also established a fire department, along with several cisterns designed to hold enough water to fight fires anywhere in the city.

In 1857, fire struck again, this time destroying all the wooden buildings in a larger, 13-block area around the central business district. Most of the brick buildings survived. This time, the town acquired a hand-pumper fire engine and, later, a second, larger hand-pumper. The pumpers can be seen in the town's old firehouse, and each year at the annual firemen's muster, they are brought out and put to use in demonstrations.

In the end, what fire couldn't destroy, the passing of the Gold Rush did. By the 1870s, most of the people were gone, and miners who were still trying to make a living in the area tore down the vacated buildings in order to mine the undisturbed ground beneath them.

In 1945, Columbia's main business district was still evident, albeit derelict, and the town was designated a California State Historic Park. Park staff began a restoration program that continues today; numerous mini-museums and exhibits, such as the 19th century dental office, a Chinese store, and the Wells Fargo building, are spread throughout the town. Saloons serve up sarsaparilla for the kids and spirits for the adults, and many restaurants and cafes provide a variety of food and goodies to please any hungry visitor. And for those wanting a little more of the Gold Rush experience, trips to real gold mines are available for a fee, as are stagecoach rides through town and the park's "back hills," replete with bandits.

Two hotels also have been restored. The Fallon Hotel is a great place to spend the night with the family; kids are typically shocked when they realize there are no televisions, telephones, electrical outlets, or toilet facilities in the rooms (most of the rooms use a shared bathroom), but they are placated when they find the old-fashioned ice-cream parlor downstairs. The City Hotel is much more formal and also has a very nice restaurant on the premises.

Staff and docents hold living-history programs regularly, and the Columbia Gold Rush Days, during the first week of June, offer even more fun and exciting hands-on activities. Contact the park for schedules.

**HOURS:** Museum is open daily from 10 AM to 4 PM; most town shops are open daily, 10 AM to 5 PM (restaurants, hotels, and the theater usually remain open later). Park museums and exhibits are closed Thanksgiving, Christmas, and New Year's Day.

**COST:** Free

**LOCATION:** From Hwy. 49, approximately 2 miles north of Sonora, turn north onto Parrotts Ferry Road and drive about 2 miles to Columbia State Historic Park.

**PHONE:** 209-588-9128

**WEBSITE:** www.parks.ca.gov/parkindex

Columbia's historic main street

# 3  Empire Mine State Historic Park

**WHAT'S HERE:** The original hard-rock mine's building and the main shaft tunnel that once took miners 5000 feet below the earth's surface

**DON'T MISS THIS:** The room-size 3-D model of the mine's miles of shafts and tunnels

For the first couple of years following James Marshall's discovery of gold in 1848, miners spent their time and energy chasing the easy gold found loose in river gravels. In June 1850, local miner George McKnight discovered gold imbedded in a surface quartz vein about a mile away in what is now Grass Valley. A few months later, lumberman George Roberts discovered gold in a rock outcropping where the park's main parking lot is now located. Word quickly spread, and another stampede of hopeful miners soon arrived. But they ran into unexpected troubles when they attempted to dig and separate gold from solid rock. Within a year, with hundreds of 30-by-40-foot mining claims scattered throughout the area, the land was pock-marked with "coyote holes" that looked like water wells between 20 and 40 feet deep. Many miners were injured or died when these holes caved in during attempts to pry, blast, and dig out the gold-bearing quartz.

As occurred in other parts of the Mother Lode in later years, disappointed claim owners sold their plots of land to speculators and developers who hoped to consolidate the claims into larger gold operations. Originally called Ophir Hill Mine, the Empire Quartz Hill Company acquired and changed the mine's name in 1852. It changed hands several more times until 1869, when financier William Bourn purchased a controlling interest. Bourn died just five years later, and his son, William Jr., took over mining operations at the age of 22.

The young Bourn pushed the mine shafts deeper than anyone thought possible, finally making the company profitable in 1884. Much of that success was attributed to Bourn's cousin, George Starr, who, when hired, started at the bottom of the company and very quickly became the mine superintendent. Starr was always introducing new technologies to make operations more efficient. Prior to World War I, he brought mules into the mines to pull loaded ore cars along the drifts (side shafts) to the main line, where the huge, powered cables could quickly bring the loaded carts to the surface. The mules were well cared for, but most lived their entire working lives underground, brought up only when they became too old to continue working.

The mine's success was further advanced when Cornish miners entered the picture. Experienced hard-rock miners from Cornwall, England, they brought the needed skills, willingness, and a few pieces of equipment such as the "Cornish pump," which surpassed other devices in removing large amounts of water from the deep shafts, allowing them to be made deeper than ever before.

Under Starr's management, the Empire's owner became very rich—so much so that Bourn didn't spend much of his time in his rustic cottage at the mine, but instead lived at the 43-room mansion he called Filoli (see Filoli, page 108), located on 600 acres 30 miles south of San Francisco.

Failing health forced Bourn to sell his interest in the mine in 1929 to Newmont Mining Corporation, which also bought control of the nearby North Star Mine. The combined operations meant Grass Valley essentially missed the Great Depression, as employment opportunities and wages continued flowing to the community.

The Empire-Star Mine was closed during World War II because it was considered nonessential to the war effort, but the mine reopened in 1945. Since the US government fixed the price of gold at $35 per ounce, the mine's profits plummeted, and by the late 1950s, the mine was finally closed for good. During its lifetime, the Empire Mine had produced 6 million ounces of gold, worth more than $2 billion at today's prices.

While some of the equipment was sold at auction, much still remains, including the main buildings. Entry into the Empire Mine grounds is through a small museum that does a great job telling the mining story, including that of the Cornish miners who were so instrumental to the company's success. Two things in the museum are of special interest: The first is the gold display that includes several fist-sized chunks of quartz that contain anywhere from 3 to 7 ounces of gold. The second is the bedroom-sized 3D model of the Empire Mine that shows its numerous main shafts and drifts that took miners 5000 feet below the earth's surface.

The park consists of two very different areas. The first is the manicured lawns and gardens of the handsome Empire Cottage, William Jr.'s "cabin," where he stayed while visiting the mine. The cottage, which is open for tours, is designed as an English manor home. The outside is constructed of local rock, and much of the interior is paneled with redwood. This is a great area to spend a warm summer day wandering along the waterways, fountains, and gardens, and beneath the giant pines and firs.

The other side of the park is the mine operations and equipment area, where the main shaft, machine shop, blacksmith shop, welding shop, mine office, and more are located. The two-story mine office was originally constructed in 1898, and today it has been restored and serves as a walk-through museum. In the same building is the refinery room where the amalgam—a mercury and gold mixture from the stamp mill—was heated until the highly toxic mercury evaporated and was captured for reuse. The remaining gold "sponge" was melted and cast into 89-pound gold bars and shipped first to Bourn's Filoli home, then to the San Francisco Mint. After 1910, a more efficient cyanide process was implemented that could recover both gold and silver.

The main mine shaft entry has a viewing area several feet below the surface, where the sleds were loaded with workers and shot down the steeply

Visitors can climb a short distance
down the mine's main shaft.

inclined shaft at 600 feet per minute to their work areas. The mined ore was moved up at 1200 feet per minute, all accomplished by steel cables that workers controlled from the hoist house located behind the head-frame (which no longer exists) and the mine entrance. Most of the buildings still have much of their equipment in place, from giant lathes powered by overhead pulleys to the tool-sharpening shop where hundreds of rock drills were re-sharpened daily.

**HOURS:** Daily, 10 AM to 5 PM. Closed Thanksgiving, Christmas, and New Year's Day.

**COST:** Adults, $3; 6–16, $1.

**LOCATION:** 10791 E. Empire Street, Grass Valley

**PHONE:** 530-272-8522

**WEBSITE:** www.parks.ca.gov/parkindex

## 4  El Dorado County Historical Museum

**WHAT'S HERE:** Gold Rush-era mining equipment and other 19th century exhibits, including the Pony Express and a wheelbarrow made locally by John Studebaker

**DON'T MISS THIS:** A pair of 9-foot-long, 25-pound skis that John "Snowshoe" Thompson used to deliver mail over the Sierra Nevada for 20 years

Gold is certainly the main theme of El Dorado County's history, but this museum covers so much more, both before and following the Gold Rush. The museum sits at the edge of one of the few Gold Rush-era towns that survived, Placerville—better known as Hangtown during its heyday. The Pony Express, logging, a small but integral piece of the Studebaker automobile history, and a unique winter mail-delivery system are very much a part of the county's history.

John "Snowshoe" Thompson responded to an 1856 advertisement for someone willing to haul mail from Placerville, California, to Genoa in Utah Territory (now Nevada) during the winter months. Thompson had left his native Norway as a 10-year-old child in 1837, and he landed in California as a young man in 1851 in search of that elusive golden fortune. Having missed out on the gold, he decided to take the job, remembering his childhood days in Norway when "snowshoes"—actually 9- to 10-foot-long wooden skis—were a major mode of winter transportation. With his 25-pound skis attached to his feet with leather straps, Snowshoe made regular treks across the Sierra each winter for 20 years,

161

until his death in 1876. He skied between 25 and 40 miles each day, and in the original true spirit of the post office, neither rain nor sleet nor blizzards nor freezing temperatures kept him from his appointed rounds. A pair of Thompson's big wooden skis is part of the exhibit.

The Pony Express also enjoys a small exhibit inside the museum. For its very short-lived history, from April 1860 to October 1861, it is nonetheless one of the most popular pieces of American history and folklore. The exhibit includes one of the company's employment advertisements soliciting potential riders: "young fellows not over 18, willing to risk their lives daily—orphans preferred." Wages were $25 per week, a significant amount considering most families then made only $300 to $500 per year.

The museum includes several wagons sporting the name Studebaker, and for good reason. John Studebaker, one of the younger brothers of the Southbend, Indiana-based Studebaker wagon company, came to California in 1853, with the expectation of striking it rich. During his stage ride West, gamblers fleeced him of all but $50. Too broke to purchase gold-mining supplies, he went to work making strong, quality wheelbarrows of wood, reinforced with iron. He sold them to the hundreds of local miners for $10 each, and demand was such that within a few years, he had saved between $6000 and $8000. In 1858, he took his money, having already learned something about the dangers of gambling, and headed back East where he bought out one of his brothers in the family wagon-building business.

John Studebaker had made connections in high places and was able to secure government contracts for his company's wagons during the Civil War. Ultimately, his wagon company was one of the few to make the transition successfully from building and selling horse-drawn vehicles to manufacturing and selling horseless automobiles. He returned to Placerville in 1912 and posed for a photo in front of the blacksmith shop where he got his start. The photo is in the museum's exhibit, along with one of his 1850s-era wheelbarrows. The museum's collections also include several restored Studebaker wagons.

The surrounding pine and fir forests provided another livelihood for Placerville and other Sierra foothill towns. Lumber mills sprang up to supply the need for wood products in the growing valley cities. Because roads were few in those early years, one lumber company devised an ingenious way to get its logged and milled timber across the deep and steep American River gorge to its drying facilities in Camino. It "simply" transported railcars stacked with freshly cut lumber across the canyon on a cable tramway, one car at a time. Exhibit photos document a steam locomotive backing each loaded railcar onto a tram suspended by steel cables, which was then pulled across the canyon, high above the river. At the other side, the railcars were moved off the tram, which

A 19th century general store is part of the museum.

returned for another load. Although the old cable tramway no longer exists, the museum's diorama and photos show the mill and the cable system in operation.

Other exhibits and hundreds of artifacts inside and outside the museum provide a little more insight into the lives of these early adventurers, both those who succeeded and those who perished. One such notable is Charlie Parker, who drove a stage for many years, yet upon his death "he" was discovered to have been a woman living in a man's clothing, in a man's world—and doing a fine job!

**HOURS:** Wednesday through Saturday, 10 AM to 4 PM; Sunday, noon to 4 PM; Tuesday open for research only, by prior appointment. Closed Thanksgiving, Christmas Eve, Christmas, and New Year's Day.

**COST:** Free

**LOCATION:** 104 Placerville Drive, next to the El Dorado County Fairgrounds, about one block from Hwy. 50, Placerville

**PHONE:** 530-621-5865

**WEBSITE:** www.co.el-dorado.ca.us/museum

# 5  California State Mining and Mineral Museum

**WHAT'S HERE:** Vast mineral collection and the largest gold nugget to survive from the Gold Rush

**DON'T MISS THIS:** The 13.8-pound crystalline gold nugget

Many museums in the Mother Lode region include a few gold specimens in their collections of Gold Rush history artifacts. The California State Mining and Mineral Museum, located in Mariposa, part of the gold country's "Southern Mines," has one of the best collections anywhere. The museum's mineral collection was started in 1880 and was originally exhibited in San Francisco's Ferry Building. Today, the collection includes more than 13,000 objects, from mining tools to rare minerals and gemstones. Unfortunately, as large as the museum is, only a small portion of the collection can be exhibited at any one time, but what is shown is quite impressive.

Most visitors are looking to see gold—after all, this is gold country—and the museum doesn't disappoint. In its vault exhibit, among other gold samples, is a single 13.8-pound mass of crystalline gold, the largest such specimen to have survived from California's 19th century mining operations. Known as the "Fricot Nugget," William Davis discovered the piece on the American River in 1865. He sold it for $3500 to Jules Fricot, who sent it to the 1878 Paris Exposition. When the gold was returned to Fricot following the exhibition's closure, he apparently put it in his safe-deposit box in an Angels Camp bank. There it remained until 1943, when a state Division of Mines employee trying to track down the nugget contacted Marie Burton, who was related to Fricot. They went to the safe-deposit box, which she had apparently been paying for all those years, but never opened. Inside was the 13.8-pound specimen. She donated the piece to the museum.

The museum also has an operational scale model of a gold mill, from the stamps to the gold-separation process. The model is more than 100 years old. The museum features its own assay office with a look at, among other things, the process used to determine from a small ore sample how much gold might be found in every ton of ore that was mined in a particular vein. For a different firsthand look at hard-rock mining, a mine tunnel starts inside the museum and actually goes back into the hillside behind the museum. Inside are exhibits showing how gold was taken from deep inside the mountains of California during the 19th and early 20th centuries.

While the focus for many may be gold, the museum includes exhibits of many different minerals from around the world, and from California, too. Benitoite, the state's official gem, is one of those minerals; a relatively soft and beautiful sapphire-like blue stone, the only place in the world where this very rare gem is found in crystals large enough to be seen by the naked eye is in California's San Benito County. Included in the museum's galleries is a fluorescent mineral display. Minerals that appear very different when viewed under ultraviolet light are shown in both regular light and under an ultraviolet lamp, providing a look at their unique glow-in-the-dark properties.

There is something here for anyone interested in either minerals or in California's gold history. The museum features an annual gem show held in mid-April and other special events throughout the year.

HOURS: Contact the museum, as hours are subject to change: October 1 through April 30, daily (closed Tuesday), 10 AM to 4 PM; May 1 through September 30, daily, 10 AM to 6 PM. Closed Thanksgiving, Christmas, and New Year's Day.

COST: Adults, $3; 16 and under, free.

LOCATION: Mariposa County Fairgrounds, 1.8 miles south of Mariposa on Hwy. 49

PHONE: 209-742-7625

WEBSITE: www.parks.ca.gov/parkindex

California State Mining and Mineral Museum

**Donner Memorial State Park Museum**

**WHAT'S HERE:** Exhibits about early pioneers and building the transcontinental railroad

**DON'T MISS THIS:** The actual campsite locations of different Donner Party families

This state park, the nearby Sierra pass, and the adjacent lake all carry the name Donner, after the ill-fated immigrant party that became trapped in the mountains when snow arrived early during the winter of 1846–47. The museum, located on the outskirts of Truckee near Donner Lake, looks at the history of the Donner Lake area, from the Washoe Indians to the Donner Party to the construction of the transcontinental railroad.

A new museum, designed to replace the park's existing Emigrant Trail Museum that has been here since 1962, is being designed and should be completed by winter 2008. The new High Sierra Crossings Museum, located on an adjacent site, will provide an expanded look at the themes found in the current museum.

The Donner Party's ordeal drew national attention to the dangers of attempting to cross the Sierra summit late in the year. Unfortunately, the Donner Party, led by prosperous Illinois farmers George and Jacob Donner, were not aware of the perils of crossing the Sierra Nevada during fall and early winter. Their first mistake was listening to travel directions from Lansford Hastings, who advised that his "shortcut," which he'd never actually traveled, was much faster. By the time they reached Truckee Meadows (near Reno, Nevada) it was late October, and early Sierra snows had already fallen. After a few failed attempts the cross the summit, the different families—not all were Donners—separated into several smaller camps in the area.

Running out of the food and provisions they had brought with them, the travelers were dependent on hunting and fishing, two skills that most of the camp's men lacked. The museum's exhibits include a Hawken rifle that Donner Party member William Eddy borrowed from one of the other members and used to kill an 800-pound grizzly bear with a very lucky shot that surprised Eddy and his fellow camp members. In December, a few starving members attempted to escape through the deep snows. Stories came out later that some of those who survived that

The Donner Party monument's 22-foot-high stone base marks the snow depth in the winter of 1846–47.

GOLD COUNTRY & HIGH SIERRA

escape attempt did so by eating the flesh of those who had died. Rescue was slow in coming once word reached Sutter's Fort. The last survivors weren't rescued until April, and during that wait, reports of additional cannibalism were revealed. Only 49 survived of the original 91 members of the party who had left Illinois a full year earlier.

The museum is located within a few hundred feet of some of the camp sites, and inside it houses a few tiny remnants of the Donner Party's encampments. Buttons, gun flints, and other small artifacts are included in the exhibits. The museum also includes a film depicting the Donner Party history. Outside is a monument that was completed in 1918 and is dedicated to all the pioneers who came through here during the 1840s. The large bronze statue stands on a stone base that rises 22 feet above the ground—the depth of the snow during the winter of 1846-47, when members of the Donner Party were trapped here.

The museum also celebrates and documents the surveying and construction of the transcontinental railroad, as the Big Four—Leland Stanford, Charles Crocker, Collis P. Huntington, and Mark Hopkins—pushed their workers hard to cross the Sierra. The exhibit includes a look at one of the engineering marvels of the day; required to drill a 1659-foot-long tunnel through solid granite, they blasted a vertical shaft near where the tunnel's center would be. From there, workers were able to blast east and west lateral tunnels through the solid granite and meet with other workers chipping through the rock from the east and west entrances toward the center shaft. With just black powder and hand tools to remove the solid granite, gaining just 7 inches of tunnel each day was considered great progress. Often, the powder charges simply shot out of the hand-drilled holes like a gun, failing to crack the rock.

The museum also looks at the history of Truckee, a town that began as Coburn's Station, a stage stop tied closely with the High Sierra crossings. From its role as a stopover for both supply wagons heading to the Virginia City silver mines and for the logging industry, which provided not only timbers to support the hundreds of miles of mine shafts, but lumber for homes and businesses, Truckee has been the linchpin for the area's settlement. It was also a very wild town in its earlier years, with bars and brothels and trains and train robbers.

HOURS: Daily, 9 AM to 4 PM. Closed Thanksgiving, Christmas, and New Year's Day.

COST: $6 fee per vehicle for parking; the museum is free.

LOCATION: 12593 Donner Pass Road, at the east end of Donner Lake, Truckee

PHONE: 530-582-7892

WEBSITE: www.parks.ca.gov/parkindex

## 7  Ehrman Mansion

**WHAT'S HERE:**  Early 1900s Craftsman-style home and open forest lawn on the shore of Lake Tahoe

**DON'T MISS THIS:**  General William Phipp's historic log cabin

San Francisco banker and businessman Isaias W. Hellman built his family a summer home on the western shore of Lake Tahoe in 1903, on what eventually would become a nearly 2000-acre estate. Known by any of several names today—Ehrman Mansion, Hellman-Ehrman Mansion, or Pine Lodge—the three-story stone and wood structure sits on a hillside providing expansive views of Lake Tahoe. The grounds, a state park since 1965, include many of the original support buildings, such as the pump house, caretaker's home (staff office), the children's house (staff housing), ice house, the carriage house/garage, two boathouses (with historic boats inside), and the ever-popular tennis court that is open for public use.

Winter recreation—skiing and snowboarding—did not exist around Tahoe in any commercial form during the early 1900s, thus the 11,000-square-foot Craftsman-style home was used only during the summer. Each summer, the Hellmans would bring with them up to 27 paid staff, including cooks, servants, and nannies for the children. Hellman worked in San Francisco and generally spent only weekends at his Tahoe estate. When his wife died in 1908, his youngest daughter, Florence, took over management of the summer home and responsibility for entertaining a constant procession of guests. Following her father's death, Florence inherited the home. She and her husband, Sidney Ehrman, a San Francisco attorney, continued the summer traditions of opening Pine Lodge for friends and family.

When California State Parks acquired the property in 1965, the initial plans included demolishing the home and returning the hillside to a more natural state. Fortunately, the home was saved, along with its many outbuildings, although the family furniture had been removed. The furniture inside the home today is primarily either period pieces or reproductions and is based on photographs and interviews with those who lived in or visited the estate during the Ehrman years.

Because this was always a summer home, there is no heating system. The only heat available is from fireplaces located in the dining room and living room. Original pieces still in the house include the fireplace tiles, custom made in Holland, and the Spanish-made chandelier hanging just inside the front door. The mission furniture and bear rug in the

The Ehrmans' Pine Lodge at Lake Tahoe

living room look remarkably similar to furnishings in the home when the Ehrmans vacationed here. A luxury in 1903, the home had electricity and indoor plumbing. A steam generator kept the lights on until 11 PM and the plumbing was fed via water redirected from General Creek, located down the hill directly behind the home, and pumped up to fill the water tank.

The dining room walls are unique, made of slender strips of woven redwood, while the upper walls are covered with woven grasses. The dining room is where every guest was expected to be each evening, dressed in their best clothes and ready for the evening meal. Otherwise, they were free to spend the day hiking to a now long-abandoned and overgrown picnic area up General Creek, swimming in the frigid lake, fishing from the pier, cruising the lake in one of the Ehrmans' power boats, playing tennis, or simply relaxing and reading.

The large kitchen features a commercial stove, refrigerator, and modern kitchenware, all used by the staff to keep the Ehrmans and their guests well fed. Prior to 1945, it had been more work for the staff, as there was only an ice box (kept cold by ice hauled up from the ice house located down near the creek) and a wood stove for cooking. The woodhouse was just out the back door. After all these years, the original linoleum floor remains relatively intact.

Up the circular staircase there are eight bedrooms on the second floor, including two round bedrooms at each end of the house. Florence Ehrman added the elevator that rises through the center of the staircase when her health no longer allowed her to walk the stairs. Brass beds, feather mattresses, Navajo rugs, and several bathrooms awaited guests. Sidney Ehrman maintained an office in his bedroom for those days he chose to stay at the lake rather than commute back to San Francisco. The third floor is closed for tours. Its storage closets, four bedrooms, and one bath were for staff and were very plainly decorated and furnished.

The front porch, with the two round rooms at each end, served as a place where guests could relax on the wicker furniture or play billiards, if they chose. During summer, the gardens in front of the porch are filled with brightly colored flowers. From the front porch, it's a steep walk down to the pier and boathouses, but it's worth the stroll. The boathouses contain historic boats from the period. Two miles of beach and several miles of trails also can be explored.

The small log cabin near the north boathouse belonged to General William Phipps, a self-proclaimed general, who settled here in 1860. Phipps became the first full-time, non-Indian resident of Sugar Pine Point, the name given to both the park and to the land jutting into Lake Tahoe. When Phipps first claimed his homestead, there were significant stands

The dining room features a woven redwood wall covering.

of old-growth timber. In fact, much of the Tahoe Basin was once covered by vast stands of old-growth sugar pines, cedars, and firs. Nearly all of the trees were harvested, turned into heavy beams, transported over the eastern mountains, and used to support the construction of the hundreds of miles of mine shafts in Virginia City's silver mines.

**HOURS:** The grounds are open all year. Mansion tours are offered daily, usually from June through September, depending on snow levels. Tours are from 11 AM to 4 PM through Labor Day and during October only on weekends, or until freezing weather or snow force the home to be closed.

**COST:** Day-use vehicle fee to enter the park: $6; house-tour fee: adults, $5; 6–17, $3.

**LOCATION:** In Ed Z'Berg-Sugar Pine Point State Park, on Hwy. 89, about 10 miles south of Tahoe City and 1 mile south of Tahoma, along the west shore of Lake Tahoe. Look for the wooden sign on the lakeside of the highway.

**PHONE:** 530-525-7982 or 530-525-7232

**WEBSITE:** www.parks.ca.gov/parkindex

## 8  Vikingsholm

**WHAT'S HERE:** Early 20th century stone and timber home built and furnished to resemble a 17th century Norse chieftain's home

**DON'T MISS THIS:** The upstairs bedrooms with locks on the outside of the doors

Often those with money entertain a whimsical sense of need. Such was the case with Lora J. Knight, who was born in 1864 as Lora Josephine Small in Galena, Illinois. At the age of 64, she built a Scandinavian castle on Lake Tahoe's Emerald Bay, one of California's most spectacular and most photographed sites. Knight certainly had the wealth to live wherever she wanted; she and her sister married the two young Moore brothers who were partners in her father's law firm. Their husbands managed to gain controlling interests in companies such as National Biscuit, Diamond Match, Union Pacific, and Rock Island Railroad. Lora and James Moore's only son married Helen Fargo, whose family was associated with Wells Fargo.

As the wealthy often did, the Moores traveled extensively, purchasing a home they seldom used in Montecito, near Santa Barbara, in 1916. They also owned property at Lake Tahoe's north shore, an area that today is known as Dollar Point. James died soon after their Montecito purchase, and in 1920, Lora married Harry Knight, a St. Louis stockbroker. That marriage didn't last long, ending in divorce.

In 1928, Lora Knight, desiring a summer home at Lake Tahoe and having sold her north shore property, purchased 239 acres at the head of Emerald Bay, which included Fanette Island. It cost just $250,000. Infatuated with the Nordic architecture she'd seen during her many travels, she hired a Swedish architect to design Vikingsholm. To ensure authenticity, she and her architect traveled throughout Scandinavia during the summer of 1928, photographing historic buildings, collecting antiques such as the home's 17th century chieftain's table, and copying patterns of antique furniture and other features to be included in the home.

Just before the early snows fell in 1928, foundation work began. The following summer, 400 workers completed the home, including quarrying granite from the cliffs behind Vikingsholm and hand-hewing the huge wooden beams throughout the three-story home. Everything used in the construction, except the leaded glass windows brought back from Sweden, was found in the Tahoe area. While the rock work and the fitting of the many timbers—often without the necessity of nails, bolts, or other fasteners—is intriguing, one of the most notable accents was the sod roof. Meant to provide both insulation and grazing for animals when used in Scandinavia, at Lake Tahoe it provided insulation, and with no goats to graze it, a colorful array of wildflowers during the region's relatively short summer.

The decorative floral paintings on the walls and ceilings in the library and morning room are reminiscent of those found in peasant homes, while the living room's intricately carved and painted dragon ceiling beams were similar to those used in Viking castles. In their original state, the dragons represented areas of the home where only the chieftain and special guests could congregate. Although some of the home has been restored and repaired (a tree once crashed through one part), little or nothing has been done in other areas. For instance, the very wide wood paneling in some of the rooms—originally stained and sealed with banana oil, and then protected with a final coat of wax—show little wear and tear since the day they were finished.

This was a summer home for Knight. During the 1930s, access around Emerald Bay was at best a dirt road and became completely impassable during the winter. The majority of guests arrived by automobile rather than by boat, and Knight exhibited her hospitality upon their arrival. Their vehicles were washed, serviced, and their gas tanks filled. Her guests enjoyed very leisurely visits, swimming, boating, or hiking up to Eagle Falls. Breakfast was served at 8 AM, lunch at 12:30 PM, and dinner at 6:30 PM, and all guests were expected to be in the dining room promptly for each meal. Knight served tea every afternoon, and occasionally would entertain her guests in the small tea house she had constructed on Emerald Bay's Fanette Island. The schedule helped the 15 people Knight commonly employed at Vikingsholm keep everything running smoothly.

The granite for Vikingsholm's walls was quarried nearby.

Knight died in 1945 at age 82. Vikingsholm and its 239 acres were sold, ultimately passing to Harvey West, a Placerville lumberman. In 1953, he sold the home and the property to California State Parks for half its value, donating the remainder. Today, Vikingsholm is part of Emerald Bay State Park.

The public has access to Vikingsholm all year, but tours through the home are held only during summer. During winter, the home is a popular destination for snowshoers and cross-country skiers. On summer weekends, the parking lot is often full, as tens of thousands of people each year stop for the spectacular views of Emerald Bay and Lake Tahoe from the overlook. It's a 1-mile walk down the dirt access road to Vikingsholm, and, for many, it feels like a 2-mile walk back up.

**HOURS:** Tours through Vikingsholm are offered daily mid-June to Labor Day (and some weekends afterward, weather and staffing permitted), 10 AM to 4 PM, every half hour.

**COST:** Vikingsholm tour fee: adults, $5; ages 6–17, $3.

**LOCATION:** At Lake Tahoe, along Hwy. 89 at the northwest side of Emerald Bay, about 22 miles south of Tahoe City. The parking lot is well-marked.

**PHONE:** 530-541-3030

**WEBSITE:** www.parks.ca.gov/parkindex

# 9 Tallac Historic Site

**WHAT'S HERE:** Three summer homes and their support buildings located on the shore of Lake Tahoe

**DON'T MISS THIS:** The garden and pond at the Pope Estate

Along Lake Tahoe's South Shore, near Camp Richardson, is the now historic site of what its original owner, Elias J. "Lucky" Baldwin, dubbed the "grandest resort in the world" when he opened it in 1880. These sentiments may have been hyperbole created by an entrepreneur catering to San Francisco, Virginia City, and Sacramento's rich, but the Tallac Resort certainly was one of the grandest resorts at Lake Tahoe. It included two hotels and a huge casino that boasted a ballroom, a ladies' billiard and pool room, bowling alleys, a stage for theatricals, 500 electric lights, and $10,000 worth of French plate mirrors.

Today, all that remains of the resort is the preserved site, but many of those same rich and occasionally famous people who visited the Tallac Resort fell in love with Lake Tahoe and decided to build their own summer homes here. Three of those homes, the Baldwin, Pope, and Heller estates—certainly mansions during their time—have been restored and are open for public tours during the late spring, after the snow has melted, and through the summer. They are within easy walking distance, perhaps 5 to 10 minutes from each other on well-marked and relatively level, firm-surfaced trails.

## Baldwin Estate

"Lucky" Baldwin died in 1909, leaving his vast real-estate holdings around Lake Tahoe to his daughter, Anita, who, in turn, gave her daughter, Dextra, 6 acres along the lakeshore. Looking for a quiet retreat away from her life in San Francisco and Los Angeles, Dextra used the site's small cabins from 1915 until 1920. The cabin here today is one of two thought to have been moved to their current site near the main house from the Tallac Resort before it was razed. In 1920, Dextra ordered a new home built and instructed the architect to "spare no expense." Those words resulted in a 4000-square-foot, Scandinavian-style, hand-hewn log cabin, which allowed Dextra to live and entertain in

the manner and luxury in which she was accustomed. Her small log cabins then became family and guest cottages.

Today, the main home is the Baldwin Museum, which features numerous exhibits on the family's life and the local Washoe Indians. The U-shaped house museum is open to the public and features a short video that provides a good overview of the area's history.

Dextra Baldwin's 4000-square-foot log cabin

## Pope Estate

George P. Tallant, the son of the founder of Crocker Bank, built this home in 1894. Five years later, Lloyd Tevis, founder and director of Wells Fargo, acquired the property and added most of the additional buildings and amenities found today, including ponds, rock gardens, and the rustic bridges. It wasn't until the 1920s that George A. Pope, a shipping

and lumber magnate, acquired the home. The family apparently required as many as 12 gardeners to maintain their extensive gardens, but the main attraction is the home. It is both the oldest and the largest of the three mansions at the Tallac Historic Site.

The Pope mansion's windows provide beautiful views of Lake Tahoe.

An imposing stone fireplace and a floor-to-ceiling redwood bookcase highlight the living room. It was here that family and guests spent many evenings reading, playing cards, watching silent movies, or playing the piano. The home includes four bedrooms, 14 closets, a smaller fireplace in the dining room, and an office. Several of the rooms have been refurnished based on historical photos.

Outside, a breezeway connects to the main kitchen, not particularly convenient for the cooks and servants, but an important safety feature when wood-fired stoves where used for cooking. Even if you miss the tour, strolling through the estate, peering through some of the windows, and wandering around the many outbuildings—the kitchen, servants' dining room, larder, gardeners' bathroom, and more—is an enjoyable way to spend some time.

During summer, docents lead tours of the home, and there are numerous living history and children's programs and special events. If walking from the Baldwin Estate, you will likely enter along a pathway the leads through the home's garden and past the private pond, stocked with very large trout. Surrounding the trout pond and its small waterfall is an extensive collection of trees and shrubs, not all of them native to Lake Tahoe.

## Heller Estate

The owners of several sites around Lake Tahoe have used "Valhalla" to describe their estates, and Heller was one of them. The term Valhalla is Norse, meaning "hall of the slain," but it also refers to a Norse mythical figure, Odin—the god of art, culture, war, and the dead—who receives and feasts with the souls of heroes who had fallen bravely in battle.

Growing up in the early 20th century, Walter Heller, who eventually went on to become president of Wells Fargo Bank, had accompanied his family to Lake Tahoe and stayed at the Tallac Resort. At age 27, he acquired property near the site of the old Tallac Resort that had closed in 1916, and he began construction of a summer home in 1923. It was completed the following year and included a heavily timbered, Nordic-style grand hall with a massive stone fireplace. The same year he built his Valhalla, Heller gave up his advertising business and founded an investment-counseling company that proved very successful. He also became a director of Wells Fargo Bank, in addition to continuing as the president and senior partner of this brokerage house.

During the years they used the home, the Hellers traveled to Tahoe with their household staff, including the boatman, valet, maids, cook, chauffeur, and governess. Heller and his wife, Claire, divorced in 1936, and Claire took title to the Tahoe home. She and her ex-husband

The Hellers continued using this Lake Tahoe mansion even after their divorce.

continued using the home—on alternating weekends—for 20 years, until his death in 1956.

Today, the Tahoe Tallac Association manages the Heller Estate for the Forest Service, using it as a community events center. The home and its boathouse have been restored (the boathouse is a community theater); the estate is open to the public for tours, and it is also used for weddings, art exhibits, and meetings.

> **HOURS:** Dates and times change, so call to confirm. Opens Memorial Day weekend and subsequent weekends until early June, then daily through mid-September, 10 AM to 4 PM. The grounds are open from dawn to dusk. Tours of the Pope Mansion are offered at 11 AM, 1 PM, and 2:30 PM.
>
> **COST:** Access to the grounds is free; Pope House tours, $5.
>
> **LOCATION:** Just off Hwy. 89, north of South Lake Tahoe; take the second right turn north of the Camp Richardson Resort. The roadway is well-signed.
>
> **PHONE:** Forest Service: 530-543-2600; Tahoe Heritage Foundation: 530-544-7383; Baldwin Estate: 530-541-5227.
>
> **WEBSITE:** www.tahoeheritage.org or www.fs.fed.us/r5/ltbmu/recreation/tallac

# 10 **Bodie State Historic Park**

**WHAT'S HERE:** Original historic wooden homes and business buildings that are kept in a state of arrested decay

**DON'T MISS THIS:** A walk through the historic hillside cemetery overlooking the town

On the eastern side of the Sierra, a miner named Waterman S. Body (sometimes spelled Bodey) discovered gold in 1859. Following that, thousands of hopeful miners trudged to the fledging community at just over 8000 feet above sea level, suffering through incredibly harsh winters and deadly mine cave-ins just to make a dollar. Sadly, their dreams of becoming rich were seldom realized.

The town was named after Waterman Body, but the spelling was changed to "Bodie" because of concern that people would mispronounce the name as "body." As the town grew, so did the problems. Many hopeful miners were killed before they ever had a chance to become rich, as the rate of murder reached almost one per day during the town's heyday. With 65 saloons and little else to do in this town of 10,000, wild gunfights, robberies, and street fights provided much of the entertainment. Every time the church bells rang, they tolled the ages of those killed, and the bells rang often. In 1881, several churches were established in Bodie, yet the Reverend R.M. Warrington witnessed only "a sea of sin, lashed by the tempests of lust and passion."

Today, the streets are quiet except for the wind that nearly always rustles through the old buildings. What is left of the town is significant, considering that 95 percent of the town is now gone, much of it destroyed by fires. If you wander among the dozens of dry wooden buildings maintained in a state of arrested decay, it's obvious why fire has always been and continues to be the town's number one enemy.

A small museum holds many examples of mining tools and the simple things needed in day-to-day life during the late 19th and early 20th centuries. More interesting are the dozens of buildings, from stores to homes to the one remaining church. It's been said that ghosts wander through some of the old buildings, and it's easy to understand why. Many remain in their original states—people simply got up and left them, never to return. Store shelves, although quite dusty, are still stocked, old pool tables remain, and tattered curtains frame the windows of abandoned and empty homes. Inside the morgue, caskets attest to the harsh realities of living in Bodie, especially the child-sized boxes. Children fared little better than adults, as a walk through Bodie's cemetery will prove.

At one time, 30 mines operated around Bodie, providing plenty of low-paid employment for hundreds of workers and riches for a few of the more successful mine owners and their stockholders. J.S. Cain was one of those successes. He owned the Midnight Mine, which happened to be located adjacent to the Standard Mine. The Standard had begun small and changed hands a couple of times, before becoming a very productive gold mine for its new owners. After gaining control in 1877, and until 1915, those owners took millions of dollars from the mine's deep shafts, but, unfortunately, much of it came via their deliberate trespass into Cain's Midnight Mine property. Cain won in court and took over the Standard mining operations. Two homes belonging to the Cain family survive near the middle of town. Much of the Standard Mine's mill remains on the hillside, overlooking the town where it operated until 1938. It's dangerous to go wandering in the buildings, so portions of the mill are off limits.

The Bodie Mining District produced nearly $100 million in gold and silver from 1860 to 1941, at a time when gold sold for between $20 and $35 per ounce and silver went for just $0.70 to $1 per ounce. Cain's Standard Mine captured more gold than any of the other mines that ever operated in Bodie.

Visiting California's best-preserved gold mining ghost town is truly a walk back in time. But it is important to be prepared for rough roads and quickly changing weather before visiting. Bodie can be reached only by driving over dirt

Even lawless Bodie had churches.

roads, the shortest of which is about 3 miles long. There are no services of any kind in Bodie, and the nearest town is Bridgeport, about 20 miles away. During winter, the 10 miles of paved road from Hwy. 395 and the final 3 miles of dirt road into Bodie are not cleared of snow, so while the town is open all year, getting there in winter will generally require a snowmobile ride from Hwy. 395. Most of the thousands of people who visit each year come during the late spring (once the snow is gone), summer, and early fall.

**HOURS:** The park and museum are open Memorial Day through Labor Day, daily, 8 AM to 7 PM; the remainder of the year, they are open 9 AM to 4 PM. Once the road is closed because of snow, the museum generally is not open.

**COST:** Adults, $3; 6–12 $1.

**LOCATION:** From Hwy. 395, approximately 7 miles south of Bridgeport, take Bodie Road 13 miles east into the park. The last 3 miles are unpaved and can get quite rough, although they are generally passable by all vehicles (except during winter snow and early spring mud).

**PHONE:** 760-647-6445

**WEBSITE:** www.parks.ca.gov/parkindex

# 11 Laws Railroad Museum and Historical Site

**WHAT'S HERE:** Historic railroad depot, trains, historic buildings, and a taxidermied one-headed, two-bodied lamb

**DON'T MISS THIS:** The shed where docents and staff restore locomotives and railcars

Darius Mills described the railroad that he, William Sharon, and Henry Yerington constructed in the early 1880s as "the railroad that was built 300 miles too long or 300 years too soon." Considering that the line extended only 300 miles from near Carson City in the north to Keeler in the south, some believe that what was called the C&C Railroad (Carson River to Colorado River) was a bust from the very beginning. Still, the line operated from 1883 until its final run in April 1960.

Many things came together to cause the railroad to cease operations. Its narrow gauge tracks (3 feet between tracks compared with the standard gauge of 4 feet, 8.5 inches) didn't allow for the direct switching of railcars, thus requiring freight to be unloaded and reloaded onto Southern Pacific's cars, which rode the wider, standard gauge tracks. With potential passengers and freight using cheaper trucks, buses, and cars, combined with the closure of mines along the right-of-way, the railroad was doomed to financial failure. Yet the original founders managed to get out in 1900, selling their line to Southern Pacific for $2.75 million.

When the last train passed through the small railroad town of Laws, located just northeast of Bishop, many of the town's old buildings were dismantled for use elsewhere. Two general stores, homes, pool halls and dance halls, barns, the post office, and many warehouses disappeared. The railroad's old depot, the agent's house, the turntable, and the oil and water tanks were still standing in 1965 when a group of railroad buffs decided to save the remnants of Laws.

This is not your typical big city museum; it's something of a cross between a revived ghost town and a collection of railroad equipment. It's also one of those really fun places to spend a couple of hours exploring. Kids, especially, will have a ball here because there are no staff telling them to stop having fun—within reason, of course. With the exception of the rail depot structures, Laws' remaining buildings have all been moved to this site, which does little to detract from their place in local history. In fact, what's been created resembles an old western town with a close look at how people lived more than 100 years ago.

The visitor center was originally built by Paramount Studios in 1966 for part of the set for the movie *Nevada Smith*, starring Steve McQueen. Cowboy aficionados should wander down the wooden walkway to what was originally a local rancher's chicken coop that was moved here. It holds collections of saddles, horseshoes, several dozen different branding irons, an old stage, and a hearse with a casket in the back. For kids who like weird stuff, there's a taxidermied lamb, but it's not just your normal lamb; it's a Siamese lamb, with one head and two bodies.

This is a little hidden jewel of a museum. In all, there are about 30 historic buildings here, paralleling both sides of the railroad tracks that run through the center of "town," past the depot. They range from the post office with its 1905 mailboxes, to a miner's shack, wagon barn, print shop, schoolhouse, tractor garage, and blacksmith shop. Each is filled with its related historical items, ranging from pianos and cars to tools and clothes. There are collections of pot-bellied stoves and printing presses and 19th century bottles and rifles.

The central attraction here is the old depot, which has been restored, and the train. Locomotive Number 9 sits on its narrow gauge tracks, the same tracks it operated on for nearly a century. There's usually a docent or two wandering around who can answer any of your questions about the railroading days in Laws.

The Laws train depot appears as it might have in 1900.

**HOURS:** Daily, 10 AM to 4 PM. Call regarding holiday closures.

**COST:** Donation requested.

**LOCATION:** From Hwy. 395 just north of Bishop, take Hwy. 6 east about 4.5 miles to Silver Canyon Road, and follow the signs; the museum is on the right.

**PHONE:** 760-873-5950

**WEBSITE:** www.thesierraweb.com/bishop/laws

# 12 Manzanar National Historic Site

**WHAT'S HERE:** A museum, remnant buildings, and ruins from the World War II Japanese internment camp

**DON'T MISS THIS:** The cemetery and a walk among the remnant garden areas created by the Japanese internees

Manzanar is located on the eastern side of the Sierra, in the Owens Valley north of Lone Pine. Its desert-like land was home to miners and ranchers, who began using the Owens Valley in the early 1860s, forcing the Paiute Indians off lands they had inhabited for 1500 years. Manzanar (Spanish for "apple orchard") began as a settlement in 1910, with farmers raising apples, peaches, pears, potatoes, and alfalfa on the surrounding lands. The Los Angeles Department of Water and Power began acquiring land and water rights in 1905. By 1929, the department owned all of Manzanar's land and water rights. As the Department of Water and Power transported the water out of the Owens Valley to meet the needs of a growing metropolis, Owens Valley agriculture began to die, turning much of the valley into a desolate landscape.

Just months following the Japanese attack on Pearl Harbor on December 7, 1941, President Franklin D. Roosevelt signed an executive order that resulted in 120,000 Japanese-Americans being taken from their homes and businesses in California, Oregon, Washington, and parts of Arizona. They were moved to 10 relocation camps primarily because of reactions based on fear and a prevalent anti-Asian prejudice that existed on the West Coast. There was never evidence that any of these people had ever been a threat to national security.

In March 1942, the first of what would be 10,000 Japanese-Americans—men, women, and children—were forcibly moved to this desolate land. According to one prisoner at Manzanar, William Hori: "We had about one week to dispose of what we owned, except what we could pack and carry for our departure by bus…for Manzanar."

The Japanese-Americans lived in barracks arranged in "city blocks." They had little privacy in their living quarters, forced to squeeze eight people into each 20-by-25-foot room. Up to 400 people in each block shared the men's and women's showers and toilets. Their barracks provided little comfort in the desert's summer heat, which often soared above 100 degrees, or during winter, when temperatures dropped to below freezing. The desert winds constantly blew sand and dust through the cracks and holes in wooden walls, covering everything they owned. Directly across the valley, the Sierra's eastern escarpment rose abruptly several thousand feet.

Haruko Niwa, who was interned at Manzanar from 1942 until 1945, described her first impression of her new home: "The first morning in Manzanar when I woke up and saw what Manzanar looked like, I just cried. And then I saw the high Sierra mountain, just like my native country's mountain, and I just cried, that's all."

There were freedoms allowed within the sprawling 6600-acre complex. Many of the internees worked in the types of jobs they had been forced to leave. They were paid, although wages were low. Still, their resourcefulness resulted in gardens of fruits and vegetables; they raised livestock, printed their own newspaper, operated a general store, created a bank, and operated schools. The high school graduated classes in 1943, '44, and '45.

Many of the internees would spend most of three years here. Some were allowed to leave Manzanar early in order to join the US military, others to attend college, or to take jobs in the Midwest or the East. The last few hundred departed the camp in November 1945.

While most of the buildings at the encampment are now gone, much still remains, especially in the aging memories of those who endured Manzanar. Today, Manzanar is the most complete of the 10 relocation camps, and the National Park Service has constructed a new visitor center and museum that serves to document the stories of the more than 10,000 Japanese-Americans who were forced to spend up to three and a half years here.

The museum's numerous exhibits tell the story of these interned families. Exhibits are mostly photographs of the camp and of the people who lived here. With the war going on, an internment camp was not high on the priority list for supplies. Much of the furniture was constructed of discarded wooden shipping crates, and some of those pieces are on exhibit. A wooden guard tower, with barbed wire at its base, sits near the center of the exhibit gallery, a reminder that the people here were indeed in prison. The museum also features a moving 22-minute movie, *Remembering Manzanar*, shown every half hour.

You can also pick up a map here that will guide you on a 3.2-mile driving tour of the camp. Even with frequent stops to wander through some of the old gardens, ruins, and the cemetery, the tour takes less than an hour. One of the few buildings remaining is the gymnasium. The internees constructed the building in 1944, and they used it to stage plays, conduct school graduation ceremonies, and hold other social events. Most of the

Entrance to Manzanar National Historic Site

auto tour takes you past signs that indicate where buildings once stood, such as the high school site. A dozen yards or so off the road at the Block 34 Mess Hall site, there are remnants from the most extensive of the many Japanese gardens. The plants have long since died, but the rock and concrete waterways and waterfalls, absent the water, remain.

The cemetery is one of the most dramatic of the remaining sites. The monument's backdrop is the snow-clad Sierra that appears to rise straight up from the valley floor to the west. As many as 80 people were once buried here, although only six graves remain. Each April, the cemetery is the site of an annual Manzanar pilgrimage of those Japanese-Americans who once lived here and of those who wish to remember the injustice.

**HOURS:** April 1 through October 31, daily, 9 AM to 5:30 PM; November 1 through March 31, daily, 9 AM to 4:30 PM. Closed Christmas.

**COST:** Free

**LOCATION:** 5001 Hwy. 395, 6 miles south of Independence and 9 miles north of Lone Pine

**PHONE:** 760-878-2194 ext. 10

**WEBSITE:** www.nps.gov/manz

Manzanar cemetery monument, looking toward the east side of the Sierra

# Gold Country and High Sierra Tours

## Gold History Tour

**ESTIMATED DAYS:** 2–3
**ESTIMATED DRIVING MILES:** 124

While it would be nice to follow this tour based on each destination's time and place in California's history, such an itinerary would require some backtracking. Instead, begin in the north at **Empire Mine State Historic Park** (page 159) in historic Grass Valley. The museum offers a close look at the challenges of mining gold ore from deep beneath the earth, and the walk down to the opening of the main mine shaft can send shivers up your spine. Traveling from the last days of hard-rock mining to one of the earliest forms of mining, we head south for about 42 twisting miles along Hwy. 49 to the town of Coloma. Here, set beside the American River is **Marshall Gold Discovery State Historic Park** (page 155), where the entire California Gold Rush began. The park features a museum and the restored sawmill where those first gold nuggets were found.

**Columbia State Historic Park** (page 157) is the next destination, and it's one where you can easily spend the better part of a full day. Here, you can spend the night in one of the Columbia's **historic hotels** (800-532-1479; www.cityhotel.com) and see a play at the historic **Fallon House Theatre** (209-532-4644; www.sierrarep.org) if you plan far enough ahead. Columbia is about 82 miles south of Coloma on Hwy. 49, just a few miles outside Sonora. This restored Gold Rush town and its museum offer a look at how the early '49ers mined most of the gold—they simply moved tons of dirt, washing it through various devices

The Columbia blacksmith shop operates regularly.

that separated the gold from the river gravels. And there are fun things for kids and adults to try, from riding on an old stage to panning for real gold. A great time to visit is during the annual June **Columbia Diggins** 1852 event (www.columbiacalifornia.com/ events.html).

# Romantic Tour

**ESTIMATED DAYS:** 1–2
**ESTIMATED DRIVING MILES:** 15

There are few more romantic and beautiful places to visit in California than Lake Tahoe. That isn't a recent revelation; San Francisco's rich and famous discovered Lake Tahoe in the late 1800s and began building summer homes, several of which are now open to the public. Begin at South Shores' **Tallac Historic Site** (page 171), located near Camp Richardson on Hwy. 89. Some of the earliest luxury hotels (most burned) and homes were located along the lake's south shore, including the **Baldwin Estate** (page 172). The owners of this 4000-square-foot Scandinavian-style log cabin spared no expense when they built it in 1920 on the site of an early hotel. Within a short walking distance is the **Pope Estate** (page 172), originally constructed in 1894 by George Tallant, the son of the founder of Crocker Bank. Its extensive gardens and the trout pond were developed by a later owner, George Pope, a shipping and lumber magnate. Another short stroll will bring you to the **Heller Estate** (page 173), known as Lake Tahoe's Valhalla, a Norse term referring to the myth of Odin.

If you leave the Tallac sites and drive north about 6 miles along Hwy. 89, Emerald Bay will come into view. At the north side of the bay is a large parking lot and a trail that leads down to **Vikingsholm** (page 169), a replica of a Scandinavian castle that Lora Knight built at the head of Emerald Bay in 1926. This is a great place for a picnic lunch and casual stroll along the bay's shoreline. Hike the mile back to the parking lot, then drive another 8.5 miles north along Hwy. 89 to the **Ehrman Mansion** (page 167), part of **Ed Z'Berg Sugar Pine Point State Park**. Sometimes referred to as Pine Lodge, the expansive mansion

The dining room at Vikingsholm overlooks Emerald Bay.

was built on the 2000-acre estate in 1903. Its incredible views of Lake Tahoe make this a great place to spend an evening walking out on the pier and watching a full moon rise over Lake Tahoe—if you time it right.

# Family/Kids Extended History Tour

**ESTIMATED DAYS:** 2–3

**ESTIMATED DRIVING MILES:** 160

There's nothing like a good ghost town in the high desert to ignite a child's imagination, and **Bodie State Historic Park** (page 174) is the best California has to offer. About 7 miles south of Bridgeport on Hwy. 395 is the turnoff to Bodie, which is located 13 desolate miles east down a narrow road, the last 3 miles of which are dirt (the Bodie road is closed during winter until the snow melts in late spring). After two or three hours wandering around Bodie's old buildings and the cemetery, it's probably best to go back the way you came to Hwy. 395, although if you have a good map, an alternative mostly dirt road to the southeast (Cottonwood Canyon) will put you near Mono Lake a few miles quicker. Either way, you'll pass by **Mono Lake Tufa State Reserve** (760-647-6331; www.parks. ca.gov/parkindex) on Hwy. 395 as you continue south. Take time to stop here for a look at the strange and beautiful tufa formations down along the south edge of the lake. They look similar to the stalagmites you find in some caves.

From Mono Lake it's about 78 miles on Hwy. 395 south to **Laws Railroad Museum and Historical Site** (page 176). About 5 miles before reaching **Bishop** (a good place to find a hotel for the night; www.bishopvisitor.com) on Hwy. 395, take the Hwy. 6 turnoff east and follow the signs (about 4.5 miles) to the historic town site. This is a great place for kids to run and see some really cool things, from steam locomotives to old tools, all related to how Californians have lived for the past 150 years.

In the morning, leave Bishop and drive south another 52 miles on Hwy. 395 to the World War II-era Japanese-American interment camp at **Manzanar**

Steam locomotive at the Laws Railroad Museum and Historical Site

**National Historic Site** (page 178). The museum here tells the story and the ruins and cemetery mark the tragedy of that war's unfounded paranoia. Don't miss the driving tour through the old camp's ruins, and be sure to stop at the cemetery monument and leave a few coins as a small offering.

Remnants of elaborate gardens and pools built by interned Japanese-Americans can still be seen on a drive through Manzanar's expansive grounds.

# Gold Country and High Sierra Travel Information Centers

Sacramento Convention and Visitor's Bureau
www.discovergold.org
916-808-7777

California Welcome Center, Merced
www.yosemite-gateway.org
209-384-2791

Gold Country Visitors Association
www.calgold.org
800-225-3764

El Dorado County Chamber of Commerce & Visitors Authority
www.visit-eldorado.com
530-621-5885 or 800-457-6279

Lake Tahoe Visitors Authority
www.bluelaketahoe.com
800-288-2463

Mono County Tourism & Film Commission
www.monocounty.org
800-845-7922

Bishop Area Chamber of Commerce & Visitors Bureau
www.bishopweb.com
760-873-8405

**Central Coast**

Tracy

580

680

Modesto

49

Yosemite National Park

Inyo National Forest

395

San Jose

Mariposa

17

101

140

Merced

Santa Cruz

152

152

Los Banos

152

99

41

Sequoia National Forest

Kings Canyon National Park

**1**

156

Hollister

33

Mendota

Madera

Fresno

180

**3** **4** **5**

San Juan Bautista

**6** **7**

Salinas

**8**

180

**2**

Monterey

Carmel

68

101

25

33

5

145

Soledad

Pinnacles National Monument

Hanford

Visalia

198

Sequoia National Park

Greenfield

**9**

Lemoore

198

Tulare

Sequoia National Forest

Big Sur

Los Padres National Forest

King City

Coalinga

198

41

**10**

G14

San Lucas

43

99

Lucia

Jolon

G18

Delano

Fort Hunter Liggett

G14

**11**

Cholame

Paso Robles

Shandon

46

Wasco

Cambria

46

Morro Bay

Atascadero

101

58

Taft

5

Bakersfield

San Luis Obispo

**12**

58

99

Pismo Beach

166

*PACIFIC OCEAN*

Guadalupe

Santa Maria

166

Cayuma

166

Vandenberg Air Force Base

1

101

Los Padres National Forest

33

Angeles National Forest

Gorman

5

Lompoc

Santa Ynez

**13**

Solvang

**14**

Santa Barbara

Ojai

Santa Paula

Simi Valley

Goleta

**15**

101

118

Ventura

Oxnard

101

**16**

Thousand Oaks

1

Channel Islands National Park

# Central Coast

The Central Coast stretches from near Santa Cruz on the coast and San Jose inland south to the Ventura County line. The region holds its own important niche in California's history and in the Golden State's modern agricultural empire. Its coast, from the surfing waves at Santa Cruz to the spectacular scenery of Big Sur, along with its missions, mansions, and museums, attract millions of visitors every year.

The area's human history goes back untold thousands of years, with its numerous Native American villages reaping the benefit of the ocean's plentiful food supply. Unlike the Native Americans, the Spanish missionaries avoided the rugged mountains and cliffs of Big Sur. Along this part of California, they turned inland, establishing several of their

Mission San Antonio de Padua

missions well east of the rugged coastal mountains, along a crude trail that gained the name El Camino Real, or the King's Highway. Today, portions of the original El Camino Real are incorporated into US 101, with side roads that lead to several of the best missions in California—San Juan Bautista, Carmel, La Purisima, and Santa Barbara.

Historically, Monterey quickly became the center of California's Spanish and subsequent Mexican governments. After the Americans gained control of California under the 1848 Treaty of Guadalupe de Hidalgo, representatives from throughout California gathered at Monterey's Colton Hall. Here they wrote the state's new constitution, embracing the coming of US statehood.

Today's agriculture and wine industries have transformed most of the inland hills and valleys that once ran wild with bear, elk, waterfowl, and deer into some of the world's most productive agricultural lands. The fertile valleys that the missionaries settled along the King's Highway now are covered with vineyards and fields of lettuce, artichokes, and brussels sprouts.

Historical tourism has become one of the region's most popular attractions, and a big part of that attraction is visiting the many unique missions, mansions, and museums this part of California has to offer. One of California's grandest mansions, Hearst Castle, sits on a coastal hilltop from where its owner, William Randolph Hearst, could survey the Pacific Coast and his thousands of acres of ranch land. Old Monterey is a gold mine of historic treasures, including California's first Custom House and several of the earliest and most elaborate adobe homes built by the region's first successful business and political leaders, such as Thomas Larkin and John Cooper. Salinas has created a beautiful museum dedicated to its homegrown Pulitzer Prize-winning author John Steinbeck, while the Presidential Library and Museum of former Hollywood star and White House resident Ronald Reagan is tucked into Simi Valley in the southern part of this section of California.

# TRIVIA

1 Which Pulitzer Prize-winning novelist lived much of his life in the small agricultural town of Salinas?

2 Which mission is located on the San Andreas fault?

3 Which museum best represents the farming history of the Central Coast?

4 Where did a young career soldier named William Tecumseh Sherman live while assigned to Monterey as a lieutenant?

5 How many rooms were in the main house when Hearst was finally forced to stop building his castle?

6 Which museum features an official presidential jet?

7 At which mission is California's Spanish mission system founder Father Junipero Serra buried?

8 Where was California's constitution debated, written, and signed?

9 Near which future mission did Gaspar de Portola's expedition first encounter 8-foot grizzly bears, which nearly killed some of the expedition's pack mules?

*For trivia answers, see page 328.*

# 1  Mission San Juan Bautista

**WHAT'S HERE:** Active mission church and museum exhibits on mission life

**DON'T MISS THIS:** The adjacent San Juan Bautista State Historic Park

Like most of the missions in California, Mission San Juan Bautista is owned by the Catholic Church, but unlike at most others, the plaza and historic buildings around the mission church and museum are a part of San Juan Bautista State Historic Park. This site offers an opportunity to see a mission that has had a continuous succession of pastors since its founding on June 24, 1797, as well as a chance to see how some of the 19th century townspeople lived.

Construction of today's mission church didn't begin until 1803, and it was finally dedicated in 1812. Its walls, which are 40 feet high, are the tallest of all the California missions. It's likely that if Father Fermin de Lasuen, the founding padre, had known that the location he chose for the mission sat directly on top of the San Andreas fault, he would have chosen another site. Several years after the mission was constructed, Thomas Doak, a seaman apparently disenchanted with life at sea, deserted his ship *Albatross* anchored in Monterey Bay and escaped to San Juan Bautista. He earned his room and board at the mission by painting the altar and altarpiece (reredos). His choice of gold and green with red accents remains bright even today. In 1817, the workers finally added floor tiles, some of which had acquired animal footprints as the clay lay drying in the sun.

Because the mission sat directly on the San Andres fault, needless to say, it was partially destroyed by the great 1906 earthquake that decimated San Francisco. The damaged walls were repaired and reinforcing steel was added to prevent any recurrence should another quake strike. The famed fault line is just a few yards east of the church; ask one of the staff or a docent to point it out for you.

Today, much of the original mission is still standing, and part of it is used to house museum exhibits, while the church remains a very active and popular parish within the

local community. The padre's living quarters and also the rooms where Indian converts once worked now serve as museum exhibit space. The exhibits feature priest vestments, beautifully hand-illustrated choir books, and furniture from the mission's late 18th and early 19th centuries. Outside, a portion of the garden remains, although it was once surrounded by an additional wing of mission rooms. One curious, albeit useful architectural addition is the hole made

Mission San Juan Bautista

near the bottom of the side entry door into the Guadalupe Chapel. The round hole allowed cats to enter and catch the mice that flourished throughout the mission during the 19th century, consuming large quantities of grain and other foods meant for the padres and the Indians.

At the mission's peak in 1805, each day, 1200 Indians worked the fields and at other mission businesses, especially in the profitable hide and tallow trade. As many as 4500 Native Americans are buried in the cemetery on the side of the church, although only a small number of marked graves remain. Next to the cemetery's stone wall is a remnant of the original El Camino Real, the "King's Highway" that connected all of the missions.

Across the large grass quad is the state historic park. Several of the restored buildings are significant to the town's early history. The Castro-Breen Adobe became the home of Patrick and Margaret Breen, who, with their seven children, were survivors of the ill-fated Donner Party during the winter of 1846–47. They arrived with no money, but in early 1848, following the announcement about the discovery of gold in Northern California, their 16-year-old son headed for the goldfields. He soon returned with $10,000 in gold, which allowed the family to purchase the home originally built in 1838–41 for Jose Antonio Castro, Alta California's northern district prefect. Breen family ancestors lived in the home until 1933. It is now a museum with a wonderfully large garden in the backyard.

In 1858, local businessman and restaurant owner Angelo Zanetta built the Plaza Hotel, located next door to the Castro-Breen Adobe. It has been restored to its 1860 appearance, when it served as a hotel featuring one of the best restaurants in town, making it a favorite stage stop. Nearby, also facing the large grass plaza, is the Plaza Stable. It served the needs of the numerous stage companies that once operated through town before the railroad was constructed elsewhere and the town's economy lost much of its vitality. Today, the stable is part of the historic park and is home to numerous wagons and carriages, along with the tools and other assorted equipment used by wagonwrights.

Adjacent to the stables is a two-story adobe and wooden structure that served many purposes. In 1868, Zanetta and a business partner transformed what was originally a one-story building that likely housed cavalrymen (and before that, unmarried Indian women) into a two-story building they envisioned as the county courthouse. Unfortunately for them, nearby Hollister was made the county seat, and it gained the honor of being home to the courthouse. Instead, Zannetta and his partner turned their building into a hotel and, later, Zanetta made it his family's home. The upstairs is a large, open room that often was used as a community meeting place. Its floor is supported by 30-foot-long redwood beams that provided a bit of spring, which made it very popular for dances. Over the years, it saw its share of grand balls, political rallies, and temperance meetings.

---

**HOURS:** The mission is open daily, 9:30 AM to 4:45 PM. Closed major holidays. The State Historic Park is open daily, 10 AM to 4:30 PM. Closed Thanksgiving, Christmas, and New Year's Day.

**COST:** Ages 12 and older, $3; 4–11, $1.

**LOCATION:** Corner of Second and Mariposa streets, San Juan Bautista

**PHONE:** Mission: 831-623-4528; San Juan Bautista State Historic Park: 831-623-4526

**WEBSITE:** www.oldmissionsjb.org

# 2 Carmel Mission

**WHAT'S HERE:** Exhibits on mission life and beautiful summer flowers

**DON'T MISS THIS:** Father Junipero Serra's original unearthed casket

Father Junipero Serra landed in Monterey Bay by ship and founded Mission San Carlos Borromeo in 1770. The following year, Father Serra moved the mission's location from near Monterey's presidio to its present location in Carmel, building temporary wood structures. This was only the second mission to be founded in California, and with supply ships from Mexico and Spain almost nonexistent, life was difficult. It would be several years before the Carmel Mission would see the crude wooden buildings replaced with the more permanent adobe structures that are associated with today's missions.

As soon as the padres were able to convert Indians and bring them into the mission in larger numbers, construction of the adobe structures began. Indian labor was also necessary for the agricultural production that provided food for the padres and their "neophyte" converts. From 1770 to 1836, the Carmel missionaries baptized more than 4000 Indians.

Father Serra founded eight other missions, but by 1784, he was 71 years old and in poor health. His lifelong friend and fellow padre, Juan Crespi, had died just over two years before and had been buried before the Carmel Mission's altar. Serra returned to the Carmel Mission and died here on August 28, 1784. He was interred next to Father Crespi. Displayed near the altar is Father Serra's original casket, which the mission carpenter made of wood. In the 1882, there was some disagreement about whether Serra was really buried at the Carmel Mission, so his body was exhumed. When it was discovered that, in fact, it was Serra, he was reburied in a more modern casket.

In the year following Serra's death, Father Fermin Lasuen was elected mission president, and under his leadership, nine missions were added to those previously founded by Father Serra. By 1794, Father Lasuen had nearly 1000 Indians working for the mission and raising crops and livestock. The Carmel Mission was one of the most popular with the father-presidents. It had been their headquarters until Father Lasuen's death in 1803, when the headquarters was moved to Mission Santa Barbara. In 1834, the mission was secularized, and its lands

Father Junipero Serra's remains are buried near the altar, not here in this nearby monument casket that was completed in 1924.

CENTRAL COAST

were transferred to local Mexican landowners, even though they were to have been divided, at least in part, among the Indians. Padre Jose Real, who had taken over the mission the year before, moved his residence from the mission to Monterey, seldom returning to conduct church services in Carmel. The mission was abandoned and fell into disrepair.

Some minor restoration work—mostly putting on a temporary roof—was begun as early as 1884. In 1931, a concerted effort began to restore the mission to its original condition. In 1961, Pope John XXIII designated the Carmel Mission as a Minor Basilica.

Today, the church is one of the most visited sites on the Monterey Peninsula. A wall surrounds the garden in the front of the church and its two towers. Inside, the high, arched ceiling is strikingly different from the other missions.

The museum that occupies the old mission rooms in front of the church entrance includes a kitchen and dining area that had a "hot-water heater." Water was heated in a stone basin built into the wall and then allowed to pass through an opening in the wall between the kitchen and the dining area. The Carmel Mission claimed California's first library, with an extensive collection of books. A re-creation of part of the library fills one of the restored rooms. Near the end of the hallway is the room where Father Serra was said to have died; in it is a simple cot and little else.

In the mission's front court, near the entrance to the cemetery, the diminutive Harry Downie Museum offers a look at the mission's restoration process. Downie became involved in the restoration of several missions, and his work at Carmel is documented in this small stone building with a collection of tools, artifacts from archeological digs (including a cracked bell), and some of Downie's drawings and photographs. An audio message provides a quick overview of Downie's efforts.

**HOURS:** Weekdays, 9:30 AM to 4:30 PM; weekends, 10:30 AM to 4:30 PM. Closed Good Friday at 1 PM, Easter Day and the Monday following, Thanksgiving and the Friday following, Christmas Eve at 1 PM, Christmas Day and day following, New Year's Eve at 1 PM, and New Year's Day and day following; also closed on some Monday national holidays, but it changes annually, so call to confirm.

**COST:** Adults, $5; seniors, $4; ages 7 and up, $1.

**LOCATION:** 3080 Rio Road, Carmel

**PHONE:** 831-624-1271

**WEBSITE:** www.carmelmission.org

Carmel Mission's inner courtyard

# 3 Custom House and Pacific House Museums

**WHAT'S HERE:** Museum of early California history in the Pacific House and the restored Custom House filled with typical trade products

**DON'T MISS THIS:** Sebastian the talking parrot

Located just a few yards from Monterey's famed Fisherman's Wharf, the Custom House and the adjacent Pacific House together tell the story of this vital 18th and 19th century California seaport and historic capital of Mexican California.

The Custom House began operation in 1822 and served the growing town as both a place of government business and community gathering. During its early years, the Custom House's primary role was as the government inspection station for the cargos of every ship that wanted to trade in Mexican-controlled California. Ship captains were required to submit to inspection and then to pay taxes based on the value of their cargos.

As California's hide and tallow industry boomed to serve the needs of the burgeoning Industrial Revolution, so, too, did Monterey's port, her merchants, and her ranchers. There seemed to be an insatiable need for leather in the East for the giant belts that powered the factories' steam-driven machines. Monterey also served as a halfway point for spices, silks, and other goods en route from the Far East and the eastern US.

The Custom House features a small exhibit on one of the more notable sailors who happened into Monterey, Richard Henry Dana. In 1835, Dana wrote: "Our cargo was an assorted one, that is, it consisted of everything under the sun. We had, in fact, everything that can be imagined. From Chinese fireworks to English cart wheels… ." Dana, a well-to-do Harvard student (later a graduate, author, and lawyer), signed on as a common sailor and sailed around Cape Horn to California in 1834. He later published *Two Years Before the Mast* (1840), a narrative that describes the hardships of a sailor's life aboard a vessel that travels round trip from Boston to California between 1834 and 1836.

Inside the Custom House, a cornucopia of goods representing what would have passed through customs during the 1830s fills the museum. While there is everything from clothes to dishes to wooden barrels of flour to a real parrot named Sebastian—and several items likely not recognizable in today's world—some of the more interesting items are the "California banknotes," also known as cowhides. Dried hard and flat, the cowhides proved to be a much more popular trading commodity than the limited amount of coin and currency in circulation at the time. These same hides were shipped by the thousands each year to the East Cost. They were generally valued at about $1 for local trading purposes, hence their nickname.

Monterey's Spanish-era Custom House includes an upstairs residence.

Also downstairs is a small area with exhibits about the Custom House and some of its early history; upstairs is where the custom agents and soldiers once lived. A small portion at one end has been restored, allowing views over the port. Outside, the Custom House's flagpole is in the same location where US Naval Commodore John Drake Sloat first raised the American flag over what he was claiming as part of the US in 1846.

The Pacific House sits just across the plaza from the Custom House and has served many purposes since Thomas Oliver Larkin (see Larkin House, page 197 constructed the building in 1847 for use by the US Army Quartermaster Corps. The large walled area behind the building, which today is a beautiful garden spot that hosts many weddings and other events, was originally the corral for the army's horses. The building also served as a court room and government office space before the completion of Colton Hall (see Colton Hall, page 198), where California's state constitution was written in 1849. In 1850, it had turned into a tavern, and in July of that year, it hosted the farewell dinner for California's last military governor, General Bennett Riley.

Today, the building is part of Monterey State Historic Park, and it is a great place to begin any walking tour of historic Monterey. The museum includes a look at Native Americans and works through the various groups, from the Californios to the US military, who have called Monterey their home. It includes exhibits on some of the archeological findings over the years, as well as a small exhibit on the plein air art movement.

Upstairs, the museum features the Holman collection of Native American artifacts, from baskets and projectile points to clothing and beadwork. It is one of the most extensive collections exhibited in this part of California.

HOURS: Daily, 10 AM to 3 PM. Closed Thanksgiving, Christmas, and New Year's Day.

COST: Free

LOCATION: 20 Custom House Plaza, near Fisherman's Wharf, at the end of Alvarado Street in Old Monterey

PHONE: 831-649-7118

WEBSITE: www.parks.ca.gov/parkindex

Pacific House Museum

# 4  Cooper-Molera Adobe

**WHAT'S HERE:** Historic Mexican-era home of one of Monterey's early leading citizens

**DON'T MISS THIS:** The outside gardens and farm animals

When it was constructed in 1830, the adobe home that Captain John Rogers Cooper built reflected his business success and his associated wealth, as well as his standing in the small community. Cooper first sailed from New England and into Monterey Bay aboard his merchant ship *Rover* in 1823. Being captain and part owner in the ship, Cooper decided to sell it to Mexican Governor Luis Arguello and settle in Monterey. Before finally settling down in Monterey, he undertook two voyages to China for the Mexican government.

In 1827, Cooper became a Mexican citizen and changed his name to Juan Bautista Cooper; he also began a very profitable business trading in merchandise and commodities, including cowhides, tallow, and sea otter pelts. He married 18-year-old Encarnacion Vallejo, the sister of the very powerful General Mariano Guadalupe Vallejo (see Lachryma Montis, page 36). Cooper built the home for his family and furnished it with pieces acquired from throughout the world.

Over the years, Cooper enlarged his original home as his businesses thrived and his family grew to include six children. When his businesses took a major downturn, he sold the western half of his adobe home. A portion of his home's land was subdivided as well, which is why the Spear Warehouse is located on what was originally Cooper's property. In 1845, Nathan Spear sold his portion of the property to Manuel Diaz, who constructed a small commercial building on the corner that is now the Cooper Museum Store. During one of Cooper's remodels, he was forced to buy back a 5-foot-wide piece of his original property so he had room to add the interior stairway to his second floor. The Spear Warehouse sits directly behind the Cooper Museum Store, inside the walled complex and includes several exhibits open to the public.

The Cooper family moved to San Francisco in 1865, and following Cooper's death in 1872, Doña Encarnacion (his wife's sister) and her children inherited the home. In later years, Frances Molera, Cooper's granddaughter, acquired the entire parcel and its adobes. Upon her death in 1968, the property was donated to the National Trust for Historic Preservation and it became part of Monterey State Historic Park.

Cooper-Molera Adobe

One benefit of having had the home remain in the extended family through several generations is that most of the luxurious furnishings that Cooper purchased for his wife remain in the home today. Cooper showcased his affluence in part by adding a second floor to his adobe home, and he included not only the interior staircase (during this period, if there was a second floor, the stairway was almost always located outside), but two adjacent parlors–one for the women and another for the men. Some of the Cooper family's original furnishings include a beautiful Steinway piano—one of two pianos in the home—and numerous tables, chairs, and other furniture that fills each of the rooms.

The National Trust worked closely with California State Parks during an extensive restoration and earthquake retrofitting project. Some of the details that went into the restoration and the retrofitting reinforcement can be seen on the tours. A small portion of the original adobe walls, the floor, and an old foundation have been left open for viewing. And on the second floor, pieces of the original wallpaper have been kept and can be compared with the nearly exact replica made during the restoration efforts.

Whether you go on a guided tour of the home or just walk by, be sure to stop in the museum store and then slip out the back door. Besides the horno oven and the barn, staff and volunteers maintain the historic gardens, which include representative plants from the Spanish and Mexican periods, such as lavender, jasmine, and poinsettias. The wisteria that grows along the porch posts was introduced in 1858. Fruit trees in the small orchard are representative of what the Coopers would have had in their garden. And there are usually a couple of sheep and several chickens wandering around to keep the kids entertained.

**HOURS:** Cooper Museum Store and the Gardens: Monday through Friday, 10 AM to 4 PM; Sunday, 1 PM to 4 PM. Adobe home tours: Monday, Wednesday, Friday, Saturday, and Sunday, 3 PM. Tour space is limited, so sign up at the Cooper Museum Store in advance, especially during the summer and on weekends, and call to confirm tours.

**COST:** Free

**LOCATION:** Corner of the intersection of Polk, Munras, and Alvarado streets, Monterey

**PHONE:** 831-649-7111

**WEBSITE:** www.parks.ca.gov/parkindex

The Cooper-Molera Adobe garden includes fruit trees and vegetables, along with sheep and chickens.

# 5  Larkin House

**WHAT'S HERE:** Furnishings from both the original owners and additional period pieces in one of California's first two-story adobe homes

**DON'T MISS THIS:** The tiny adobe house where famed Civil War General William Tecumseh Sherman lived while assigned to Monterey as a lieutenant in 1847

Thomas Oliver Larkin came to Monterey from Massachusetts in 1832, and quickly became an extremely successful merchant. He came initially to assist his half-brother, Captain John Rogers Cooper, with his many business operations. As the leading procurer of highly sought-after sea otter pelts and as the head of a large cattle operation, Cooper was already one of the most important men in Monterey.

Larkin married an East Coast woman he met during his trip to California. Rachel Hobson Holmes had come to Monterey attempting to catch up with her sailor husband. But he had left on another ship just a short time before his new bride arrived and was soon killed near Lima, Peru. Holmes, already friends with Thomas Larkin, soon married him and then found out that she had inherited $4000, a princely sum of money in those days.

Larkin worked for Cooper only long enough to save $500; he then set off to start the first of many businesses. Over the years, Larkin did everything from being a merchant to participating in the construction of both the first Monterey wharf and the first wharf in San Francisco. He ran his first store from rooms that were part of the adobe home that he started building during the 1830s. As his business operations and family grew, he continued to add rooms to his house in stages. What is the dining room today was likely part of his original mercantile; the trap door in the ceiling allowed him to more easily move valuable merchandise, such as guns, from the store to his living quarters above, affording significantly more security from potential robbers.

The home he built was one of the first two-story adobe homes in California, and one of the most luxurious. He successfully combined the traditional Mexican adobe style with features found on New England homes, such as the hip roof and the milled wood trim found throughout the interior. He included an interior staircase to the second floor, something not found in these early traditional Mexican-era California homes. And he had multiple fireplaces inside his home, which only the richest homeowners could afford.

Eventually, the home passed out of the Larkin family. In 1919, Alice Larkin Toulmin, Thomas Larkin's granddaughter, discovered the home and purchased it, moving in a few years later. She was determined that her grandfather would be remembered for all that he did during

Thomas Larkin constructed one of Monterey's grandest adobe homes.

his life, not the least of which was to serve as the first and only US consul to Alta California while the future state of California was still under Mexican rule.

Larkin Toulmin was the daughter of a very well-to-do East Coast shipping magnate and spent much of her life traveling the world. During her travels, she collected many of the 19th century antiques that fill the home today, such as the opium bed in one of the bedrooms. With the exception of a desk that Thomas Larkin purchased and had shipped around the Horn, very little of her grandfather's property remains in the home.

In the courtyard garden is a small, one-room adobe building. During part of 1847, it served as quarters for Lieutenant William Tecumseh Sherman, while he was assigned to duty in California, a time and place he very much disliked. Sherman later became one of the Civil War's most important generals.

> **HOURS:** Garden is open daily, 10 AM to 4 PM; guided tours are offered on Wednesday, Saturday, and Sunday at 2 PM. Tour space is limited, so sign up prior to the tour at the home, especially during summer and on weekends. Call to confirm tour times.
>
> **COST:** Free
>
> **LOCATION:** 510 Calle Principal, Monterey
>
> **PHONE:** Automated tour information: 831-657-6348; general information: 831-649-7118
>
> **WEBSITE:** www.parks.ca.gov/parkindex

# 6 Colton Hall

**WHAT'S HERE:** Re-created meeting place that hosted California's Constitutional Convention

**DON'T MISS THIS:** The small stone jail, used between 1854 and 1954, located behind Colton Hall

Today, the museum at Colton Hall—the first US government building in California—is quite modest, but what occurred here in 1849 was pivotal in California's transformation from Mexican rule to California statehood. The building is named for Navy Chaplain Walter Colton, who arrived with the US fleet when Commodore John D. Sloat first raised the US flag over what had been part of Mexico. Colton was appointed Monterey's first American alcalde, a position of governing power that established him as both mayor and judge.

In 1848, Colton ordered the construction of an important new building in Monterey. With financial assistance not forthcoming from any higher government office, Colton financed the construction through the sale of town lots and through fines on liquor shops.

He tossed in the fines charged to gamblers and added free labor from convicts in the town's jail. The building, completed in 1849, was aptly named Colton Hall.

Soon after its completion, Colton Hall was chosen as the convention site for the creation of the California Constitution. Even before the US Congress had officially approved the admission of California to the Union, 48 delegates elected from California's 10 districts arrived in Monterey. They met daily from September 13 to October 3, 1849, working out acceptable language. Issues included whether women could own property, if California should be a slave state or free state, who could vote, and even where the state boundaries would be located to the east, either at the Sierra Nevada or the Rocky Mountains. As portions of the constitution's text were completed, they were translated into Spanish for the benefit of the eight delegates who did not speak English. The constitution was ratified on October 13, 1949, and on September 9, 1850, California became the 31st state of the Union.

Although Monterey served as the capital of both Spanish and Mexican California, the delegation chose San Jose as the first capital under the Stars and Stripes. San Jose is where the first California legislature convened. The capital was moved several times (see Benicia Capitol State Historic Park, page 77, and State Capitol Museum, page 125).

Colton Hall has served as an official government building since it was constructed. Even though it lost out to another building in San Jose as the first state capitol, it served as the Monterey County seat until 1873. From 1873 to 1896, Colton Hall was a public school, before becoming city offices, police courts, a hospital, and the rationing office during World War II.

Today, the downstairs remains a cluster of city offices, while upstairs has been restored to look as it did when the delegates were working on California's constitution. Assorted papers and quill pens cover the delegates' desks. A small exhibit space is also tucked into part of the upstairs.

Outside and around back is the city's original jail, built in 1854. Though small, the jail was used until 1956, and had a perfect record of no escapes. The small jail is open to the public during the same hours as Colton Hall.

**HOURS:** Daily, 10 AM to 4 PM. Closed Thanksgiving, Christmas, and New Year's Day.
**COST:** Free
**LOCATION:** Pacific Street, between Jefferson and Madison, Monterey
**PHONE:** 831-646-5640
**WEBSITE:** www.monterey.org/parkindex

Behind historic Colton Hall is the old stone jail that was used for more than 100 years.

# 7 Monterey Maritime Museum and History Center (Stanton Center)

**WHAT'S HERE:** Monterey's maritime history, from whaling to sardines

**DON'T MISS THIS:** The *USS Macon* exhibit—the last of the US Navy's dirigibles

Overlooking Monterey's Fisherman's Wharf and the harbor, the Monterey Maritime Museum possesses a few things not found in most other maritime museums. The first and most obvious upon entering the museum—or even standing outside, especially at night—is the 8-foot-tall, first-order Fresnel lens that came from the Point Sur light station, located about 20 miles south along the Big Sur coast. Part of the exhibit for this 4330-pound collection of glass prisms includes a look at how they amplify and beam such a small point of light such great distances. The light cast by a lens this size and placed at the height of Point Sur was visible for 23 nautical miles.

Much of the museum's collections came from one man's efforts. In 1918, at the age of 17, Allen Knight, who spent much of his life living in San Francisco and nearby Carmel, signed onto a four-masted sailing ship as an able-bodied seaman. Inspired by his youthful adventure, he developed a lifelong love for collecting everything nautical. By 1960, he had acquired 9000 photographs, 250 ships' logbooks, and 30 ship models, among many other items. His collection became the basis for Monterey's first maritime museum.

Near the museum's Fresnel lens is another piece of the area's history. On February 12, 1935, two lighthouse keepers at Point Sur witnessed the rigid airship *USS Macon* crash just offshore. All but two of the helium-filled dirigible's crew survived the crash into the ocean. The craft belonged to the US Navy and the big balloon actually used a special trapeze mechanism to launch and recover airplanes while in flight. As long as three Boeing 747s, the *Macon* carried four Sparrowhawk F-9 C-2 airplanes. The crash marked the end of the Navy's dirigible program. In 1990, an effort was made to photograph the sunken *Macon*, which rested 1450 feet beneath the ocean's surface. Several parts of the airship and its Sparrowhawks were recovered, and some of those pieces are exhibited in the museum. Other pieces are at the historic light station at Point Sur State Historic Park.

In addition to numerous models of historic ships, the museum houses a real ship of sorts. The Monterey Bay Aquarium Research Institute has donated one of its underwater research vessels, which is displayed along with information about its deep diving work in Monterey Bay, one of the deepest bays in the world.

The museum features a 19th century sailing vessel's reconstructed captain's cabin.

Throughout the museum are pieces of maritime history, from early navigational equipment and small cannons to pieces of 19th century naval uniforms. Tucked into one corner upstairs is the captain's quarters that was part of a ship purchased by Douglas Fairbanks and used in his 1926 movie *The Black Pirate*. He had the ship dismantled and then reconstructed on a Hollywood sound stage.

A small exhibit features a doctor's medicine chest, or at least what passed for medicine in a much earlier age—with some of these concoctions still used today. Numerous glass vials are labeled for witch hazel, soda mint tablets, syrup of ipecac, and more.

Whaling was a major industry during the latter half of the 19th century. The museum examines the industry and some of its early tools, from different harpoons to the block and tackle needed to move the massive mammals onto shore and move their blubber into the rendering pots. On the opposite end of the size scale, sardines and Monterey became synonymous during the early 20th century, as millions of tons of the small fish were netted, processed, packed, and shipped all over the world. The exhibit includes photos and samples of the sardine cans and some of the many colorful labels that helped identify the different packing companies and their products.

**HOURS:** Daily, 10 AM to 5 PM. Closed Wednesdays, Thanksgiving, Christmas, and New Year's Day.

**COST:** Adults, $8; seniors, 60 and over, $5; 13–18, $5; under 12, free.

**LOCATION:** 5 Custom House Plaza, Monterey

**PHONE:** 831-372-2608

**WEBSITE:** www.montereyhistory.org or www.montereyhistory.org/maritime_museum.htm

# 8  National Steinbeck Center

**WHAT'S HERE:** Exhibits depicting Steinbeck's life and his writing career

**DON'T MISS THIS:** The GMC truck and camper that Steinbeck and his dog traveled in while gathering material for his book *Travels with Charley in Search of America*

This premier museum, in the small agricultural town of Salinas, is dedicated to one of America's best loved and most successful authors. Salinas also happens to be the place where John Steinbeck was born (in 1902) and spent much of his life, and it is the backdrop for some of his novels, including *East of Eden*. Clips from the film version of this book are shown in the first gallery, where the screen is, appropriately, set in the side of a railway box car—the kind used to ship Salinas Valley produce across the country.

The museum's numerous distinctive galleries serve as a timeline of Steinbeck's life and his writings. There is a quick look at his early life, but most of the exhibits focus on his writing career, which really began with his first published work in 1924, when *Adventures in Academy* appeared in the *Stanford Spectator*. He had enrolled at Stanford following his high school graduation but left in 1925 without graduating. Like most students, Steinbeck spent his summers taking various jobs, from ranch hand to chemist assistant for the Spreckels Sugar Company, where he tested the sugar content of sugar beets.

*Tortilla Flat*, published in 1935, wasn't his first novel, but it was his first commercially successful book. It was followed in 1937 by *Of Mice and Men*, a hugely successful work that was also made into a Broadway play and movie. While Steinbeck obviously enjoyed the financial success, he abhorred publicity. He enjoyed people, but always on his own terms. He once returned from a trip to San Francisco, angry and sickened that people had actually recognized and approached him.

Having been raised in an agricultural town, Steinbeck discovered the plight of farm workers, and from that experience, he penned *The Grapes of Wrath* in 1939. As the museum's exhibits and films depict, he was no longer welcomed in his own hometown, due to this book and other articles he had written on the subject. His accurate portrayal of the lives of transient farm workers and their families brought down the wrath of the rich growers and their bankers. Although it was not his first work on this subject, *The Grapes of Wrath* became his most famous and earned Steinbeck the 1940 Pulitzer Prize for fiction. It also brought about book bans and book burnings.

Steinbeck had a knack for taking his own life's adventures and turning them into wonderful, entertaining stories. His family owned a small cabin in nearby Pacific Grove, so Steinbeck spent much of his early life near Monterey's canneries, meeting interesting characters doing interesting things. One of his best friends was Ed Ricketts, the owner of Pacific Biological Laboratories. Ricketts collected sea-life samples for shipment to universities and other science labs throughout the country. In the museum, a small slice of Cannery Row is reproduced, as is a representative part of Doc Ricketts' lab, including samples of his collecting work, such as a giant acorn barnacle and a purple sea urchin stored in bottles of preservative.

Another exhibit area focuses on the films that were made from Steinbeck's novels. Some of these are shown in continuously rolling clips and include *The Grapes of Wrath*, *Life Boat* (directed by Alfred Hitchcock), *A Medal for Benny*, and *East of Eden*, among others. Soon after *Life Boat* was released in 1944, Steinbeck bought a house in Monterey, but he became as unwelcome there as in his hometown. He moved to New York the following year.

John Steinbeck's truck and camper from his 1960 cross-country trip

In 1961, Steinbeck published *The Winter of Our Discontent*. Disillusioned with writing fiction, it was to be his last novel. The following year, he was awarded the Nobel Prize for literature. In the years that followed, Steinbeck continued to write, but his focus was non-fiction.

In 1960, at the age of 58, in what some considered an effort to prove he was still physically capable of taking on such an adventure, Steinbeck took his wife's poodle, Charley, and drove his green GMC pickup and white camper over 10,000 miles. They traveled across 34 states as they went around the perimeter of the country, talking with people and collecting stories that would become his 1962 book, *Travels with Charley in Search of America*. Along with a large map depicting the duo's travels, the museum has Steinbeck's pickup truck and the camper he named *Rocinante*, after Don Quixote's horse. In the back of the camper is a typewriter—and assorted bottles of alcohol. John Steinbeck died on December 20, 1968, in New York, following a heart attack and stroke.

The museum is fun to wander through, exploring a part of our country's past as depicted in Steinbeck's many novels. In days when cell phones, emails, and computers didn't exist, it's nice to see copies of original typed manuscripts and portions of the thousands of letters he wrote.

**HOURS:** Daily, 10 AM to 5 PM. Closed Easter, Thanksgiving, Christmas, and New Year's Day.

**COST:** Adults, $10.95; 62 and up, students with ID, and military with ID, $8.95; 13–17, $7.95; 6–12, $5.95.

**LOCATION:** One Main Street, Salinas

**PHONE:** 831-775-4721

**WEBSITE:** www.steinbeck.org

# 9 Monterey County Agricultural & Rural Life Museum

**WHAT'S HERE:** Early and mid-20th century farm equipment and an exhibit barn featuring the agricultural riches of Monterey County

**DON'T MISS THIS:** An example of the small houses that Spreckels Sugar provided to some of its employees

While most people likely think of the ocean when talking about Monterey County, most of the county lies inland, where farming has been its biggest claim to fame—and fortune. Produce such as lettuce, artichokes, and strawberries cover fields through the northern part of the county around Salinas, while vineyards have taken over vast stretches of the hillsides and valleys farther south. Celebrating that agricultural bonanza is the focus of the Agricultural & Rural Life Museum in King City.

The museum is a sprawling complex inside San Lorenzo Park and is comprised of six different buildings. The huge exhibit barn, with its oversized ventilation fan slowly turning in the ceiling, is a great place to start, as its numerous exhibits provide a look at the history and diversity of farming in the county. Also inside the barn is the Monterey County Tourist Information Center, should you need additional information about things to see and do in the area.

Outside the barn is a vast collection of farm equipment that covers the period from the late 1800s until World War II. There are dozens of tractors of all makes representing the 1920s and '30s, from a 1927 Farmall Regular, the first "all-purpose" tractor made by International Harvester, to hay balers, bean planters, and hay rakes. There's a 1929 grain harvester that was designed specifically as a side-hill combine harvester to work on the county's many hilly farms. Before the widespread use of chemical weed killers, farmers ran cultivators between the rows to remove weeds from the furrows. Different styles were made—disc or spring tooth—depending on the types of and heights of the crops being tilled and the width of the furrows. Most of the equipment is labeled, and there are a few interpretive signs scattered throughout the expansive exhibit area.

One of the unique aspects of rural farm life was the houses provided by the farm owners for their employees. Spreckels Sugar, for instance, constructed four types of houses for its employees, and one of those 24-by-26-foot houses has been moved to the park. Its interior walls were covered with cloth and paper and it originally sat on a mud sill foundation.

Because the railroad was so critical to the success of local farmers–it essentially opened up the entire country as a market for their produce–it's only appropriate that such a major form of transportation be represented at the museum. In 1884, a millionaire lumberman named Charles King purchased 13,000 acres in order to grow wheat. Most people thought he was crazy because there was no water, and the only transportation for moving farm produce was mule wagons. King, who was friends with Collis P. Huntington, one of the Big Four of the Central Pacific Railroad, convinced the railroad magnate to extend his Southern Pacific line down the valley from Soledad. Huntington agreed, and in 1886, the first train destined to haul King's grain arrived.

King partnered with J. Ernst Steinbeck, father of famed novelist John Steinbeck (see National Steinbeck Center, page 201), and they built a grain warehouse. Over the next few years, more

The restored rail depot is the centerpiece for an extensive collection of antique farm equipment.

buildings were added to the growing town, including a train depot in 1903. The depot operated into the 1980s, when Southern Pacific finally abandoned it. The depot was moved to the museum complex where it resides today, open to the public.

The museum has other historic buildings, including a blacksmith shop and the La Gloria School that was built in the late 1880s. Until it was closed in the early 1960s, the school had served hundreds of students and also the community as a gathering place for dinners, entertainment, and other local events.

**HOURS:** The Exhibit Barn is open daily, 10 AM to 4 PM. The Spreckels House and the school-house are open April through October, Friday through Sunday, 12:30 PM to 3:30 PM. All are closed Thanksgiving Day and the Friday after; December 23, 24, 31; and New Year's Day.

**COST:** Park entrance, Monday through Friday, $4 per vehicle; weekends, $5 per vehicle; walk-ins, free; the museum is free.

**LOCATION:** In King City at San Lorenzo Park

**PHONE:** 831-385-8020

**WEBSITE:** www.mcarlm.org

# 10 Mission San Antonio de Padua

**WHAT'S HERE:** The very first mission bell cast in California

**DON'T MISS THIS:** An original mission grapevine that still produces grapes

In 1771, San Antonio de Padua became the third Spanish mission that Father Junipero Serra founded in California. It remains one of the most rustic, with no paved parking lots or walkways, but with numerous ruins in the surrounding fields to explore. The mission church still stands, and if you stand back and gaze at the entrance, it's obvious that there is an "added-on" front entry section—called a companario—that stands about 12 feet out from the main church. It is constructed of fired brick, unusual for the missions that almost always used sun-dried adobe blocks. Its three arches and the square bell porticos on each end add an interesting and attractive architectural twist to an otherwise plain church. More important to the mission is that residing in the center bell niche is the very first mission bell made in California. The 24-inch-diameter bell weighs 500 pounds and was made specifically for San Antonio.

Father Junipero Serra founded this mission in a valley that Spanish explorer Gaspar de Portola had discovered two years earlier. Serra was apparently surprised on the first day as a local "pagan" Indian watched the founding ceremony. He offered the Indian gifts, and the man soon returned with many more of his people. By the early 1800s, the mission boasted more than 1200 neophytes converted and working to further the goals of the church.

In 1773, the mission site was moved farther up Los Robles Valley, in order to assure a more reliable water source. Father Buenaventura Sitjar, during his 23 years at San Antonio, designed and constructed an elaborate system of dams and small canals that not only irrigated the wheat fields and provided water to the mission, but also turned the waterwheel-powered gristmill added in 1806 that ground the mission's abundant grain harvest. One piece of historic trivia: The very first marriage in California performed by the Catholic Church occurred here on May 16, 1773.

In 1810, work was finished on what, by then, was the third try at completing a permanent church that could survive earthquakes. The workers floated large timbers from the mountains down the San Antonio River; they were needed to span the 200-foot-long and 40-foot-wide structure, and the 6-foot-thick walls had no trouble supporting the big beams.

The same church, although once again reconstructed, stands at the mission today. While the mission is approximately 20 miles east of US 101, near the small town of Jolon, it is worth the drive. But be warned—the mission itself is located on Fort Hunter Ligget, an active base and the nation's largest US Army Reserve command post. There are strict entry requirements, so be sure to read the information at the end of this listing before making the trip.

The mission was abandoned in the mid-1850s, but in 1903, the Native Sons of the Golden West began its restoration. They encountered a setback when much of their work was damaged in the 1906 San Francisco earthquake. Although they began restoration again the following year, it wasn't until 1948 that the effort really got underway; the William Randolph Hearst Foundation donated most of the funding required for this reconstruction. Hearst once owned most of the land between here and his Hearst Castle home on the coast at San Simeon (see Hearst San Simeon State Historical Monument, page 207).

The mission museum features an exhibit on chocolate with an explanation about its popularity as a beverage in Spain after being introduced from Mexico in the 16th century. A common process was for the drink to begin as a paste of powdered chocolate, cinnamon, and sugar that was formed into large tablets. The tablets were melted into hot milk and then whipped to a froth. Among the many other exhibits are pottery chards, a silver-and-black beaded woman's purse or reticule from the 19th

Mission San Antonio's church altar

century, various English wares, period guns, and church-related artifacts such as very large prayer books. There is an old wine storage and processing area in the cellar.

Outside the mission's exhibit rooms and the church, two areas should not to be missed. The first is the garden area inside the mission walls. Of particular interest is the old grapevine near the well. It's an original vine from the mission, and it still produces grapes. The other area that beckons exploration is the outside grounds. As you walk around, a tour map will direct you to numerous sites of the original mission, from the 1810 cemetery and ruins of the majordomo's home, to the watermill and remnants of the mill-race.

As mentioned earlier, the mission is located inside Fort Hunter Liggett, near the community of Jolon. You must gain entry through a guarded gate, and the following documents are required: a valid driver's license or identification for each adult, valid vehicle registration, and proof of current auto insurance. There are no exceptions made, so be sure you have the required documentation. Also, it's a good idea to call the mission prior to your arrival to make sure the base isn't on alert and closed to the public.

**HOURS:** Memorial Day weekend through Labor Day, daily, 8 AM to 6 PM; the rest of the year, daily, 8 AM to 5 PM. Closed Easter, Thanksgiving, and Christmas.

**COST:** $2 donation is requested.

**LOCATION:** On Fort Hunter Liggett, approximately 18 miles south of King City on Jolon Road, and then 5 miles northwest to the end of Mission Creek Road. There are very strict entry requirements—please see information above.

**PHONE:** 831-385-4478

**WEBSITE:** www.sanantoniomission.org

# 11 Hearst San Simeon State Historical Monument

**WHAT'S HERE:** Art treasures collected from around the world, from tapestries to silver pieces to parts from old European churches to Chinese vases

**DON'T MISS THIS:** The two swimming pools, the 104-foot-long Neptune pool outside and the 81-foot-long T-shaped indoor pool

In 1919, media tycoon William Randolph Hearst delivered a simple request to renowned architect Julia Morgan: "Miss Morgan, we are tired of camping out in the open at the ranch in San Simeon and I would like to build a little something... ." With that understatement, Hearst embarked on three decades of work with Morgan as they planned and built La Cuesta Encantada, "the Enchanted Hill." Although construction was never officially finished, the complex includes the 115-room main house, guest houses, two magnificent swimming pools (one indoors), and 8 acres of gardens. The main house and each of the guest houses are elaborately furnished and decorated with European antiquities and art. Today, this "little something" is better known as Hearst Castle or Hearst San Simeon State Historical Monument.

Hearst had the benefit of a large inheritance. His father, George Hearst, had become a multimillionaire, primarily through silver and copper mining companies that he owned in Nevada. When George Hearst died in 1891, he left $18 million to his wife, Phoebe, who was 22 years younger than her husband. When Phoebe died in 1919 at age 76, she left most of her $11 million estate to their son, William, who was by now 55 years old and had already developed a fortune of his own through his publishing empire.

After Hearst inherited this money, he decided to develop his estate where he and his family had camped for many years—on a hilltop 1600 feet above the Pacific Ocean. Hearst owned the surrounding 250,000 acres and 50 miles of shoreline. His ranch was about half the size of the state of Rhode Island. By the time Hearst began building his new home, he was one of the richest men in the US, and he spared no expense on his new project.

From rough sketches, his dream began to appear on the hilltop estate. Much of the design for the rooms in each of four "casas" or houses was determined by the art collections Hearst had decided would be exhibited. Hearst had a warehouse full of antiques collected over his lifetime, and his castle was also going to be his personal art museum. Rooms designated to hold the huge tapestries or the fireplaces or the wooden ceilings taken from ancient castles or monasteries had to be large enough to properly showcase the treasures. Outside, the gardens were filled with mature plants and trees, brought in and planted at a time when modern heavy construction equipment didn't exist.

Hearst and his architect continued adding to the main house, La Casa Grande, until it reached 115 rooms. He also had three guest houses built, the largest of which is the 14-room Casa del Mar. It sits on the edge of a hill and its backside is nearly five stories high. It was the first to be completed, and the house in which Hearst stayed while La Casa Grande was being completed. The guest houses were meant as opulent sleeping quarters and thus contained no eating or cooking facilities. Those activities were saved for the main house.

The main house was designed and constructed in pieces, with little forethought given to how each of the differing architectural themes could be integrated. That seemed to be more of a problem for Julia Morgan than for Hearst. While Morgan was thinking country villa, Hearst's persuasive control created twin towers that, when coupled with the other features, made La Casa Grande more cathedral than anything else. Inside, some of the impressive rooms are filled with architectural pieces such as Spanish choir stalls, which impart a sense of almost religious awe.

In practical effect, every aspect of the home, even the old mustard and catsup bottles that grace the dining room table (perhaps a quirk left over from his camping days), is more museum than house. Ancient art objects are everywhere, from a Roman mosaic floor to an 1826 Gregorian chant book, from Carrara marble statues to 1000-year-old Greek pottery, from the late 15th or early 16th century French tapestry in the billiard room to the silver and enamel Tiffany & Co. lamp that likely belonged to his mother.

Hearst kept his guests well entertained. They would go horseback riding, hiking, or simply sit and relax. His many guests include leaders of state such as President Calvin Coolidge and Great Britain's Winston Churchill, as well as the famous, such as Charles Lindbergh, Charlie Chaplin, George Bernard Shaw, and many more. It's likely that on warm summer days, many of his guests lounged around the Neptune swimming pool. The 104-foot-long pool is surrounded by colonnades reminiscent of an ancient Roman temple. From the pool on clear days, there are great views of the ocean. There's also an 81-foot-long, T-shaped indoor pool of gold and blue tile with a cantilevered diving balcony for those cool days when the ocean fog rolled in.

There is so much to see here that several tours, each featuring a different aspect of Hearst Castle, are offered numerous times each day. Reservations, especially during summer and on holiday weekends, are always recommended. Check the website or call for specific tour times and date availabilities. All tours require a bus ride from the visitor center up the twisting, narrow road to the hilltop estate. Every tour requires a significant number of steps. Those with special needs should contact Hearst Castle in advance of arrival.

**HOURS:** Daily, first tours begin at 8:20 AM and last tour departs at 3:20 PM; there are also seasonal evening tours. Closed Thanksgiving, Christmas, and New Year's Day.

**COST:** Adults, $24 peak season (May 15 through September 15) or $20 off season (September 16 through May 14); ages 6–17, $12 peak season or $10 off season; additional cost for evening tours.

**LOCATION:** Hearst San Simeon State Historical Monument, 750 Hearst Castle Road, San Simeon

**PHONE:** Tour information, 800-444-4445; accessibly designed tour information, 866-712-2286; recorded information, 805-927-2020

**WEBSITE:** www.parks.ca.gov/parkindex

# 12 Mission San Luis Obispo

**WHAT'S HERE:** Restored mission and a small museum

**DON'T MISS THIS:** The outside gardens

This mission is no longer the remote outpost it was when Father Junipero Serra founded it in 1772. Three years before, Gaspar de Portola and his expedition had come through the area as they headed back to rediscover Monterey Bay. The expedition's members encountered bears, which they hoped could be added to their food supply. Unfortunately for his soldiers, these were grizzly bears, and the 8-foot-tall beasts did not die easily, nearly killing a couple of the pack mules. Portola's diarist, Padre Juan Crespi, recorded the name (depending on the translation) as La Cañada de los Osos, the Valley of the Bears. In 1772, when nearby Mission San Antonio had nearly run out of food, a hunting party was sent back to the Valley of the Bears. They had better luck the second time, bringing back 9000 pounds of salted and dried bear meat, in addition to seed grain that they had obtained from the local Indians in exchange for bear meat.

After the successful hunting party returned, Father Serra decided that the valley would be an ideal location for his fifth mission. He traveled to the site and celebrated Mass, then he gave Father Jose Cavaller, five solders, and two neophytes (Indians) the monumental task of building the mission, converting the local Chumash Indians to Christianity, and developing the cattle and agricultural enterprises needed for the mission to survive.

Perched on a small hill near the middle of town, the mission church and support buildings were originally made of adobe with thatched roofs. But these buildings burned down, in part due to accidental fires and in part as the result of the local Indians who occasionally became upset with the Spaniards and shot fire arrows onto the tinder-dry roofs. Following the third time that fire ravaged the small outpost, the padres decided that clay tile roofs, similar to those found back in Spain, would solve their problems.

In pits filled with clay, Father Cavaller and the Indian workers led horses that tromped through the clay. When adequately pliable, the clay was removed and pressed over the half-cylindrical tile forms. After drying in the sun, the green tiles were then fired in an oven, which baked them hard, making them both fire- and waterproof. The tile-making was so successful that the idea spread to the other missions, ending leaky roofs and Indian fire arrow attacks.

Following secularization in 1834, when Mexico took over the mission lands, the mission fell into disrepair. Fortunately, within several years, the surrounding town began to prosper, and sometime later, members of the local community decided to repair the mission. In 1868, they began removing the tile shingles, and they added a New England-style bell tower, wooden clapboard siding, a false wooden ceiling, and a wooden floor placed over the mission's original clay tiles. A fire in 1920 revealed the original mission's structure, and by 1934, it had been more accurately restored.

The mission's museum is housed in one of the wings, with numerous exhibits depicting life during the 18th and 19th centuries. In addition to Indian artifacts, the mission-era furniture provides a look at how the later missionary fathers lived. Outside, gardens surround the mission, which is situated next to a small city park. A fountain and statue of Father

Mission San Luis Obispo

Serra are located near the front of the mission, while in back, paved walkways wind through flower gardens and beneath wooden archways covered with grapevines.

HOURS: Daily, 9 AM to 4 PM. Closed major holidays.
COST: Donations welcome.
LOCATION: 751 Palm Street, San Luis Obispo
PHONE: 805-543-6850
WEBSITE: www.missionsanluisobispo.org

# 13 La Purisima Mission State Historic Park

WHAT'S HERE: **Best restored mission in a rural setting with living-history programs**

DON'T MISS THIS: **The animal corrals and a walk through the gardens**

The Spanish missionaries founded Mision la Purisima Concepcion de Maria Santisima in 1787. Today, La Purisima, a California state historic park located near Lompoc, is the most completely restored of California's 21 Spanish missions and an inspiring place to visit, especially with children. What makes La Purisima even more special is its isolation from modern homes, businesses, and busy streets. The canyon and hillsides appear much as they would have more than two centuries ago. It is not difficult to stroll from the parking lot, along the dirt path, to the mission and a 19th century world. Docents even dress in costume for the many school tours and for periodic weekend living-history programs.

The original mission was constructed several miles from its present location, and the padres worked hard to build a successful mission and to convert the local Chumash Indians to Christianity. The Chumash, or "neophytes" as they were called by the missionaries, were the mission's primary labor source for construction, farming, raising cattle, and the day-to-day operational needs of the mission.

By 1804, there were more than 1500 neophytes working and living at the mission; however, during the next three years, 500 died from diseases for which

The church altar at La Purisima Mission

CENTRAL COAST

211

they had no natural immunity. The mission struggled during this time, in part because of the reduced number of Indian workers available.

Father Mariano Payeras, who had come to the mission in 1804, requested permission from the Catholic Church to move the mission to a new site several miles away that had better access to El Camino Real, the King's Highway, which connected all of the missions. The new location in La Cañada de los Berros (the Canyon of the Watercress) also was more suitable for agriculture. Father Payeras and his neophytes constructed a new mission in a linear design rather than the more traditional quadrangle, which is evident as you explore the mission's buildings. Speculation is that the padre was planning a design that would allow mission inhabitants to escape the buildings in the next big earthquake.

The new mission was much more prosperous. By 1820, the mission counted 9500 cattle 12,600 sheep, 1305 horses, 288 mules, and 86 swine, along with assorted ducks, geese, and chickens. By 1824, the death of Father Payeras, coupled with the diminishing numbers of Indian workers available, caused the mission's prosperity to fade.

Ultimately, it was the Indians who lost the most. Under the original secularization program, the mission's neophytes were supposed to receive land, cattle, and farming implements in order to work for themselves. That never occurred at La Purisima. Instead, in 1834, Mexican Governor Jose Figueroa officially secularized the missions and appointed a mayordomo to oversee the mission. Soon, the land was sold, and none of it went to the Chumash, who had worked there for so many years. The padres moved to nearby Mission Santa Ines.

In 1845, the mission was sold at auction for $1100 and subsequently was owned by several different people. For 90 years, the mission's adobe buildings were left to dissolve back into the earth. Then in 1934, through a series of donations and land purchases, the old California Division of Beaches and Parks acquired the mission, and soon afterward, crews of President Roosevelt's Civilian Conservation Corps began arriving.

The CCC crews became amateur archeologists, locating the mission's ruins and foundations, including the church. Once the restoration plan was in place, they reconstructed most of the mission's buildings using essentially the same techniques the padres and their Chumash workers had used more than a century earlier. They made, dried, and stacked thousands of adobe bricks, and topped the new buildings with tiles made from locally dug clay. California State Parks has provided more restoration work over the years, adding equipment and furnishings that would have been found in the original mission.

Today, besides the military clothing and arms, the collection includes mission bells, and there are horses, pigs, and cattle wandering in the surrounding corrals. In the gardens grow many of the same agricultural products found here in the early 20th century, adding to the mission's authenticity and ambiance.

The restored mission soldiers' barrack

There is a new visitor center located adjacent to the parking lot that provides information about the mission. Docents in costume are often working around the grounds, engaged in many of the activities that would have been commonly seen during the mission's heyday. There are daily guided tours, but call for times, as they change.

**HOURS:** Daily, 9 AM to 5 PM. Closed Thanksgiving, Christmas, and New Year's Day.
**COST:** $4 parking fee.
**LOCATION:** 2295 Purisima Road, Lompoc
**PHONE:** 805-733-1303 or 805-733-3713
**WEBSITE:** www.lapurisimamission.org or www.parks.ca.gov/parkindex

# 14 Mission Santa Ines

**WHAT'S HERE:** Audio tour of the museum exhibits that include some of Father Junipero Serra's vestments

**DON'T MISS THIS:** The old paintings inside the church

On September 17, 1804, Father Estevan Tapis founded Mission Santa Ines, a long day's travel of 30 miles from Mission Santa Barbara. He named the mission after the 4th century Christian martyr and saint who was beheaded by the Romans. The English translation of her Spanish name is "Saint Agnes." To confuse matters, the nearby town was named Santa Ynez (now known as Solvang), which is the Americanized version of the same Spanish name.

This was one of several inland missions designed to reach the estimated 1000 Chumash Indians who lived in the surrounding mountains and valleys. By the time the padres arrived to establish Mission Santa Ines, 200 local Indians were ready for them, having already been introduced to missionary beliefs from other converted Indians. Upon setting up a temporary altar, the fathers baptized 20 Indian children on the founding day.

Like its neighboring missions, Mission Santa Ines was severely damaged by the 1812 earthquake. It was also the center of a relatively large Indian uprising in 1824. The Spanish guards, who were mostly uneducated and paid meager wages, took out their unhappiness on the

Mission Santa Ines

213

neophytes (converted Indians) who worked for the mission. Following what the Indians considered unnecessary cruelty when a Santa Ines soldier flogged one of the neophytes, the Indians revolted, burning several buildings, but not the church. The Indians fled, but the soldiers caught them, killing several and later executing some of the leaders and sending others to jail.

Once Mexico gained its independence from Spain and passed its secularization laws in 1834, the mission system was doomed to collapse. The lands were sold to private individuals and the Chumash left the missions, removing the labor force needed to run the cattle and other profitable operations. Mexican Governor Manuel Micheltorena transferred 35,000 acres of mission land in 1843 to Alta California's first bishop, Francisco Garcia Diego y Moreno, who established a seminary, California's first institute of higher learning. A year later, the seminary moved, and in 1846, Mexican California's last governor, Pio de Jesus Pico, illegally sold the mission for $7000 (see Pio Pico State Historic Park, page 263). Three weeks later, the US took military control of Alta California. In 1862, President Lincoln transferred the mission back to the church.

Today, the mission has been restored, and it is an active parish for about 1000 families. Within the mission buildings are collections from throughout the mission period, including vestments worn by Father Junipero Serra at another mission. Some of the more elaborate and colorful priest vestments were actually made from women's ball gowns donated for the purpose. The wonderful collection of mission bells provides an opportunity to see them up close rather than only at the top of bell towers.

Tools such as branding irons, ropes, and candle molds from the early 19th century are displayed, and there are audio stations along the tour route that provide additional information about the artifacts. The audio program describes everything from the musical instruments to the polychrome wood carvings and crosses from various mission periods. Inside the church, numerous paintings have been restored and hung for viewing. Nearly all of the paintings were collected from other missions, yet they are quite interesting and beautiful. In the mission church, one painting of particular interest shows Jesus wearing a hat, something not seen elsewhere.

The mission's gardens are worth spending time exploring, even though they are only about one third their original size. Across the parking lot from the church are benches beneath trees that overlook a steep drop-off, providing a view of the outlying valley and hills. It's a nice place to take a break and enjoy the pastoral beauty while envisioning a time when the mission Indians harvested 3400 bushels of wheat, 3000 bushels of corn, along with beans and peas from the fields before you. The mission also had 7000 cattle, 5000 sheep, 100 goats, 100 pigs, 120 mules, and 600 horses. This was a very busy place.

---

**HOURS:** Daily, 9 AM to 5:30 PM. Closed at 3 PM on Good Friday, Easter, Thanksgiving, Christmas, and New Year's Day.

**COST:** Adults, $3; seniors, $2.50; children, free.

**LOCATION:** 1760 Mission Drive, Solvang

**PHONE:** 805-688-4815

**WEBSITE:** www.missionsantaines.org

# 15 Mission Santa Barbara

**WHAT'S HERE:** Beautiful church featuring twin bell towers and a Roman temple facade

**DON'T MISS THIS:** The Moorish fountain and lavanderia where mission Indians washed clothes

Founded in 1786, Mission Santa Barbara—the "Queen of the Missions"—is one of the most recognizable of California's 21 missions. Its twin bell towers, the curious but beautiful Roman temple facade, and a large expanse of grass in front where the mud huts of Indians once sat make it one of the most strikingly attractive missions. The Roman influence came from the 27 BC renderings of Vitruvius Pollio; the mission's namesake is the Christian Roman virgin whose head her less-than-understanding pagan father lopped off.

Father Junipero Serra initially founded the mission, or attempted to, in the spring of 1782, but the Spanish governor refused to allow the needed work to be done that would actually establish a new mission. It wasn't until two years after Serra's death, on the Feast of Saint Barbara in December 1786, that Father Fermin Francisco de Lasuen actually raised the cross that allowed the mission to become official. He placed Father Antonio Paterna in charge of Santa Barbara, and Paterna began the real work of constructing the needed buildings.

Perhaps that rough start was an omen of what was to come, at least during the early years. Three adobe churches were built, each larger than its predecessor, until the last was destroyed in the 1812 earthquake. Following the earthquake, work was begun on the church that exists today, but it wasn't completed until 1820. Other construction was added over the years as the mission prospered and grew. The friary was originally one story, but a second floor was added, and the mission finally was completed in 1870. The fountain in front of the mission predates most of the present-day structures; it was completed in 1808.

In the early 1800s, the mission and its agricultural operations thrived. At different times during that period, there were more than 5200 head of cattle, more than

Mission Santa Barbara

11,000 sheep, along with other animals, and the Indians were growing wheat, corn, beans, peas, oranges, olives, and wine grapes. While the mission's work of converting the Indians to Christianity continued, the population, and thus the number of laborers, increased until about 1830. After that, there were no Indians left to convert and the number of those living and working on the mission grounds decreased.

As with all the missions, following Spain's loss of Alta California to Mexico in 1822, and then Mexico's secularization of the missions in 1834, the mission's operations began to quickly decline. Unlike the other missions, the padres at Santa Barbara were allowed to continue conducting church services, and when California became part of the Union, President Lincoln gave the missions back to the Franciscans. Thus, Santa Barbara has been an active mission since its founding.

Outside the mission, near the side of the church's cemetery and also across the street, are remnants of the original aqueduct that brought water from a small reservoir that the padres built about 2 miles away. Below the Moorish fountain, constructed in 1808, is the lavanderia where Indian women washed clothes.

The mission's museum, in the rooms that once served as the padres' homes and rooms for guests, is a well-preserved collection of mission-era artifacts. The exhibits include Chumash baskets, tools, hymn books, priest vestments, several restored rooms such as the kitchen, and more. The mission Indians raised livestock as well as various grains and other foods. It was important for the mission's well-being that they be taught the skills needed to not only harvest, but to turn these items into more valuable trade goods. In addition to leather from cowhides and cloth from wool, Indians learned to make wooden furniture, pottery, and ironwork. A sampling of those products is included in the exhibits. The kitchen has been reconstructed and appears to have been used very recently—and for a very long time.

Santa Barbara hosted the first bishop of the Californias, and some of his personal belongings are part of the collection. With such important church leaders attached to Santa Barbara, the mission also became the archive for important Franciscan documents, including those created by Father Junipero Serra. Other church-related items include music books, priest vestments, and musical instruments. Near the end of the museum tour is the Chapel Room where a video is shown that illustrates the long history of the mission.

Inside the main church, numerous paintings hang, depicting various religious scenes. Most were brought from Mexico and South America, and a couple are more than 200 years old. The image of a skull and crossbones is carved above the church's other side door, indicating the way to the cemetery. Here, more than 4000 Indians were buried, along with some of Santa Barbara's early settlers and others who had relationships with the mission.

**HOURS:** Daily, 9 AM to 5 PM. Closed major holidays.

**COST:** Ages 12 and over, $4; 6–11, $1.

**LOCATION:** 2201 Laguna Street, Santa Barbara

**PHONE:** 805-682-4149

**WEBSITE:** www.sbmission.org

# 16 Ronald Reagan Presidential Library and Museum

**WHAT'S HERE:** A walk through exhibits of Ronald Reagan's life, from high school to Hollywood to politics

**DON'T MISS THIS:** Tour of a retired *Air Force One*

Ronald Reagan was born in Illinois in 1911 to parents who struggled to make ends meet. As a young man, he got into radio broadcasting, and then he moved into the film industry, securing a contract with Warner Bros. Studios. By 1941, he had appeared in 50 motion pictures. He became a member of the US Army Air Force's motion picture unit during World War II. Following the war, his movie career was slow to revive, but television brought Reagan both fame and fortune when he became host of the *General Electric Theater*, a weekly television program that ran from 1953 to 1962 and featured top Hollywood and Broadway stars.

Reagan was a registered Democrat during most of his early years, but his strong business philosophy wasn't supported by Democratic Party candidates, so, in 1962, he switched sides. Thus began his rapid ascent up the ranks of Republicans, passing through the governorship of California from 1967 to 1975 before ending up in Washington, DC, in 1980 as the 40th US president. During his eight years in the White House, Reagan oversaw a major rebound of the US economy, the collapse of the Communist Soviet Union, and the fall of the Berlin Wall. He also survived an assassin's bullet.

This president's library and museum sits atop a hill with expansive views of the local mountains, Simi Valley, and the Pacific Ocean. The museum is a visual trip through Reagan's life, from his birth certificate and early years with his merchant father and his mother who, typical of the time, was a housewife. There are photos of his years in high school and as a lifeguard. Like many successful people, Reagan credits his parents for some of his success in life: "I learned from my father the value of hard work and ambition and maybe a little something about telling a story. From my mother I learned the value of prayer, how to have dreams and believe I could make them come true."

The exhibits continue their walk through Reagan's life. He was fascinated as a kid by the movies that featured the US Cavalry coming to the rescue of pioneers, so he headed to Hollywood to follow one of his dreams of becoming an actor. He played opposite Betty Davis, Humphrey Bogart, and other big-time Hollywood stars. Perhaps his most famous role was George "the Gipper"

*Air Force One* was used from 1973 to 2001.

217

Gipp in the 1940 film *Knute Rockne All American*. The museum features a small theater showing clips from many of Reagan's films.

Following the war, Reagan spent time traveling throughout the US, but he never forgot about a girl named Nancy waiting back home. The museum showcases some of the many love letters he sent the future first lady, and it even has the red leather restaurant booth where he proposed to her. The museum continues through his life with a brief stop at the California's governor's office and then onto his candidacy and election to the presidency.

The museum holds a reproduction of the Reagan White House Situation Room; unlike today's many "prime-time TV" presidents, his situation table seated only 10 people. Another exhibit recounts the arms treaty in 1987 that required the US and the Soviet Union militaries to deactivate many of their nuclear missiles. One of the US Pershing II missiles caught in that treaty is on exhibition—minus its nuclear warhead, of course. The former president's high-back, brown leather chair is here, as well as a full-sized reproduction of the Oval Office, with his desk and the ever-present jar of Jelly Belly jelly beans. A sign on his desk reads: "It Can Be Done."

The museum offers a very small taste of what it's like to attend a formal White House state dinner (Reagan held 56 state dinners during his eight years in the White House). The dinners required a staff of 100, including 36 waiters, and two months of preparation. Reagan was fond of more basic cuisine than was served at the state dinners, where his preference for meat loaf, macaroni and cheese, and monkey bread would have likely been ridiculed by the other heads of state. Tex-Mex meals, also a favorite of both Reagan and Vice President George Bush, were served during their weekly private lunches.

The Reagans enjoyed their California homes; the first was their place above Malibu and later Rancho del Cielo, situated in the Santa Inez Mountains above Santa Barbara. There is a model and short video of Rancho del Cielo, along with some of Reagan's personal items, such as his saddle and his old aluminum canoe. The Reagans were popular with heads of state from around the world who sent them hundreds of gifts during their time in the White House. A few of those gifts are exhibited, including jewelry and clothing.

One of the most spectacular attractions is the actual *Air Force One* parked in a glass-walled addition to the main museum. President Reagan and six other presidents used the "Flying White House" from 1973 to 2001. There is also a small presidential motorcade that features Reagan's 1984 limousine and a few other cars.

Outside the museum, looking toward the Pacific Ocean, is a replica of the White House south lawn. Ronald Reagan's final resting place is also here.

**HOURS:** Daily, 10 AM to 5 PM. Closed Thanksgiving, Christmas, and New Year's Day.

**COST:** 18–61, $12; 62 and over, $9; 11–17, $3; under 11, free.

**LOCATION:** 40 Presidential Drive, Simi Valley

**PHONE:** 800-410-8354

**WEBSITE:** www.reaganfoundation.org or www.reaganlibrary.net

# Central Coast Tours

**T**

## Mission Tour

ESTIMATED DAYS:  3–5
ESTIMATED DRIVING MILES:  250

You should plan a week or more to visit six of the Central Coast's best missions. Much of that time you will likely spend exploring some of California's most popular vacation spots, which just happen to be right next to several of the missions. Begin in the north at **Mission San Juan Bautista** (page 189) and the quaint historic town (and state historic park of the same name). The mission church sits just a few feet away from the San Andreas earthquake fault. From here, head over to US 101, then south to Hwy. 156, which, after about 40 miles, will bring you to the Monterey Peninsula and the **Carmel Mission** (page 191).

Carmel (www.carmelcalifornia.org) and the **Monterey** (www.monterey.org) area are great places to spend the night before driving back to US 101 (through Salinas is shorter), where you'll head south once again. About 92 miles later, following a turnoff or two at King City, you'll find yourself at the gate into Fort Hunter Liggett. This is where you will find **Mission San Antonio de Padua** (page 205; be sure to read the requirements for entering the military base). This is one of the most isolated missions, making your experience here different than at those missions sitting in the middle of modern-day towns and cities.

From Mission San Antonio, it's once again back to Hwy. 101 and south another 60 miles to the first of several turns onto country roads (check your map) to what we consider California's best and most authentic mission—**La Purisima Mission State Historic Park** (page 211).

Ornate door at Mission Santa Ines

This is a great place for kids of all ages because of the farm and ranch animals, the docent demonstrations, and special events. Even more so than Mission San Antonio, La Purisima comes the closest to re-creating the look, sense, and feel of mission life.

From La Purisima Mission, it's only about 20 miles to the Danish town of **Solvang** (www.solvangusa.com), where you may want to spend some extra time exploring. Out near the end of town on Mission Drive is **Mission Santa Ines** (page 218), named after a 4th century Christian who was beheaded, becoming both a martyr and a saint. There are a couple of different routes to our last mission in Santa Barbara, about 34 miles away. **Mission Santa Barbara** (page 215), known as the "Queen of the Missions," truly has one of the most magnificent churches, and the grounds are beautiful. And when you're missioned-out, **Santa Barbara** (www.santabarbaraca.com) has a great beach, pier, and lots of restaurants just a few blocks away.

# Family/Kids Tour

**ESTIMATED DAYS:** 1–2

**ESTIMATED DRIVING MILES:** 8

The Monterey Peninsula offers a thousand things for families to do, but to add a tiny history lesson and a lot of fun, start your day by heading over to the **Carmel Mission** (page 191). It's a chance to wander the grounds and see the museum exhibits that depict California's early days under the Spanish and Mexican flags. Afterward, an 8-mile drive north on Hwy. 1 from Carmel to Old Monterey will open more doors for exploration. Just steps away from Fisherman's Wharf are the **Custom House and Pacific House Museums** (page 193), both part of Monterey State Historic Park. The Custom House, built in 1822, also served under the Spanish and Mexican flags before the Stars and Stripes was run up its flag pole in 1846. Inside the Custom House is an assortment of goods that would have been found here in 1822. Nowhere nearly that old, Sebastian the parrot adds his squawking voice to this historic government building. The Pacific House Museum is a short stroll away, and it offers a look Monterey's history through numerous exhibits.

Afterward, wander down to **Fisherman's Wharf** (www.montereywharf. com), where you can rent a bike for a ride along miles of bike trail, go for a kayak ride on the bay, or visit the famed **Monterey Bay Aquarium** (www. mbayaq.org), about 10 minutes away.

Carmel Mission

# Central Coast
# Travel Information Centers

Monterey County Convention & Visitors Bureau
www.montereyinfo.org
831-657-6400 or 888-221-1010

San Luis Obispo County Visitors & Conference Bureau
www.sanluisobispocounty.com
805-541-8000 or 800-634-1414

Santa Barbara Conference & Visitors Bureau
www.santabarbaraca.com
805-966-9222 or 800-549-5133

Ventura Visitors & Convention Bureau
www.ventura-usa.com
805-648-2075 or 800-483-6217

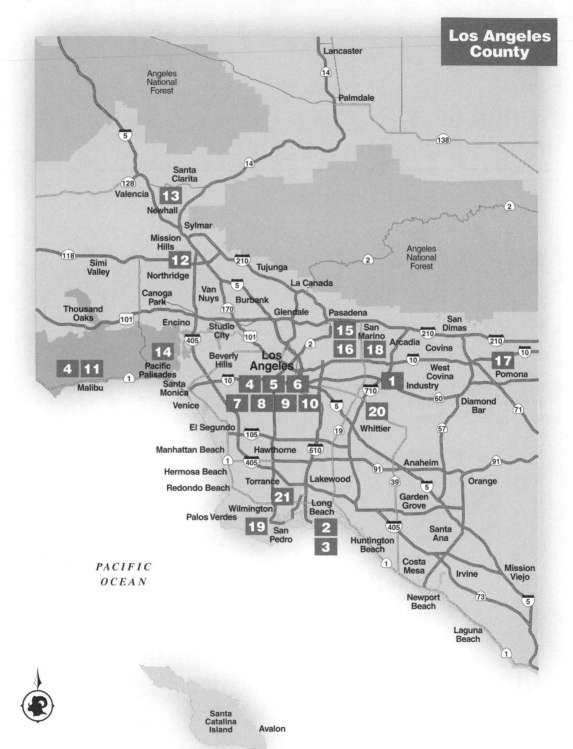

Los Angeles County

Lancaster

Palmdale

Angeles
National
Forest

Santa
Clarita

Valencia

**13**

Newhall

Sylmar

Mission
Hills

**12**

Simi
Valley

Northridge

Tujunga

La Canada

Angeles
National
Forest

Canoga
Park

Van
Nuys

Burbank

Thousand
Oaks

Encino

Glendale

Pasadena

San
Dimas

Studio
City

Los
Angeles

San
Marino

Arcadia

Covina

**14**

Beverly
Hills

**15**

**18**

West
Covina

**17**

Pacific
Palisades

**16**

Industry

Pomona

**4** **11**

Santa
Monica

**4** **5** **6**

**1**

Diamond
Bar

Malibu

Venice

**7** **8** **9** **10**

**20**

El Segundo

Whittier

Manhattan Beach

Hawthorne

Anaheim

Hermosa Beach

Lakewood

Redondo Beach

Torrance

Orange

Garden
Grove

Wilmington

**21**

Long
Beach

Santa
Ana

Palos Verdes

**19**

San
Pedro

**2**

Huntington
Beach

**3**

Costa
Mesa

Irvine

Mission
Viejo

Newport
Beach

PACIFIC
OCEAN

Laguna
Beach

Santa
Catalina
Island

Avalon

# Los Angeles County

**LA.** These two letters evoke some of the most powerful, persistent, and peculiar visions for people throughout the world, even for those who have never visited this sprawling megalopolis. Today's Los Angeles—with its maze of freeways and millions of people, its beaches and movie stars, and its museums and mansions—had very humble beginnings a little more than 225 years ago.

Spain was the first European power to populate what was originally named El Pueblo de Nuestra Senora la Reyna de Los Angeles de Porcuincula. That mouthful was a carry-over from the name Gaspar de Portola gave to the LA River in 1769, Rio de Nuestra Senora la Reyna de Los Angeles de Porcuincula.

During its early years of Spanish and Mexican control, the greater Los Angeles area was a relatively sleepy community, and the primary activities revolved around the missions. But things began to change after California escaped Mexican control in 1848. Enterprising business people such as Phineas Banning entered the picture. In 1850, he built LA Harbor in order to serve his own passenger and freight needs. New businesses soon followed, as did the mansion Banning built for himself in Wilmington.

Nonetheless, Los Angeles was not all that attractive during those early years. It lacked many essentials, such as major transportation links with the eastern US, until the advent

Page Museum at La Brea Tar Pits

of railroads. It also lacked adequate water supplies to support widespread development, until a few creative minds were able to secure large quantities from the eastern Sierra Nevada, a couple of hundred miles away.

The advent of World War II brought tens of thousands of workers from across the country to work in southern California's aircraft, ship-building, and other war-manufacturing centers. Many of them stayed; they liked the idea of perpetual summer on the beaches and the glamour of its movie industry. And they loved the idea that in California, with a little hard work and a bit of luck, anyone could be successful.

By the early 20th century, the film industry began to bloom, in part because of the area's moderate weather. The homes of some early Hollywood stars of both the silent movies and the talkies are now house museums. They include silent western film star William S. Hart's home and the ranch of Will Rogers, the highest-paid Hollywood star in the early 1930s. You can also get a closer look at the lives of the rich and famous of years past at historic mansions, including the Adamson House in Malibu, and the Fenyes Mansion and Gamble House (of Proctor and Gamble) in Pasadena.

Perhaps also due to the good weather—and to the lifestyles of the rich and famous—cool cars and LA have become synonymous. The Petersen Automotive Museum takes you for a ride through the history of the automobile, including a look at cars that have been owned by stars and cars that have starred in their own movies. The Wally Parks NHRA Motorsports Museum, located in Pomona, exemplifies the phrase "the need for speed," with its collection of garage-built hot rods and high-performance race cars.

There is so much to see and experience in Los Angeles County that a week of mission, mansion, and museum hopping will only touch the surface. Plan on several return visits to gather it all in, with a break now and then to hit those fabulous beaches.

# TRIVIA

1 In which mansion can you find tiled floors designed to look like Persian rugs?

2 The owner of which mansion raised shire horses like those used by England's knights?

3 Which museum features the original white Herbie #53 Volkswagen from the 1969 Disney film?

4 Name the second oldest museum in Los Angeles, which attracts thousands of kids each year.

5 Which mansion was built following a young son's discovery of oil in a field on their property?

6 Name the two museums in the Los Angeles area that were created by a private foundation established by one man's wealth.

7 Where can you watch scientists working in an active archeological pit?

8 Which famous "singing cowboy" created the Museum of the American West?

9 Where is Bob Hope buried?

10 Which mansion was used as an occasional set for the television hit *The West Wing*?

*For trivia answers, see page 329.*

# 1 Workman and Temple Family Homestead

**WHAT'S HERE:** Two homes: The earlier Workman home was built with adobe walls made to look like stone, and the newer Temple mansion is a Spanish Colonial Revival-style home.

**DON'T MISS THIS:** The exquisite use of stained glass throughout the Temple home

This historic homestead, established in the 1840s, dates from California's colorful Mexican era and consists of three separate historic sites: William and Nicolasa Workman's house, built in the 1870s, which enlarged an existing 1840s-era adobe; the 1920s Spanish Colonial Revival mansion built by Walter and Laura Temple; and the two families' nearby El Campo Santo, one of the area's oldest private cemeteries. The Workman and Temple families were closely tied, both in business and by marriage.

In 1841, at the age of 19, F.P.F. Temple left Massachusetts, sailed around the Horn, and joined his half-brother, Jonathan Temple, who had been in Los Angeles since 1827. Jonathan was well-placed in the small community, owning the first American-style store. He later became involved in extensive cattle operations in the area (see Los Cerritos Ranch House, page 229).

William Workman had arrived in California from Taos, New Mexico, in 1841, having previously been a merchant, trapper, and outfitter. Soon afterward, he aided the rebellious Alta California's Mexican Governor Pio Pico (see Pio Pico State Historic Park, page 263) in a conflict against the Mexico City-based Governor Manuel Micheltorena. A few months later, Workman received a nearly 49,000-acre land grant, possibly as payment for his services. (His allotment was reduced to 18,000 acres after California became a US state).

At some time during this period, Workman and the younger F.P.F. Temple became acquainted and entered into various business arrangements. By 1845, F.P.F. had met and married Antonia Margarita, Workman's daughter. Following the discovery of gold at Coloma in 1848, Workman and his new son-in-law moved cattle north to the gold fields, where the demand for beef made them rich. They acquired additional ranchos and expanded their beef businesses to include butcher shops, meat markets, and other commercial buildings in booming Gold Rush towns such as Columbia and Sonora. Temple also became involved in Los Angeles politics, and he was elected to the first Los Angeles County Board of Supervisors; he also was one of the founders of the Los Angeles Water Works Company.

Ultimately, Temple suffered a financial downfall that began in 1875 as the result of his banking enterprise. Workman and Temple had joined their financial forces with the well-to-do San Francisco banker Isaias W. Hellman (see Ehrman Mansion, page 167) and began Los Angeles's second bank, Hellman, Temple, and Company, with Workman as a silent partner. In 1871, Hellman bought them out, starting his own Farmers and Merchants Bank, while Temple and his former partners started their own bank.

In 1875, both banks closed because of a panic spurred by the collapse of some very speculative Virginia City silver-mining businesses. Rancher, capitalist, and Nevada silver-mine speculator Elias J. "Lucky" Baldwin (see Baldwin Estate, page 172) loaned Temple and his partners money, secured by their many properties, to keep their bank afloat. The bank ultimately failed, and Baldwin foreclosed on Temple and Workman, acquiring much of their property, except the house, in a series of bank foreclosures and court actions between 1876 and 1879. Workman committed suicide in 1876, and Temple died in 1880 at the age of 58.

Financial hardships forced the surviving family to sell the homestead in 1912. F.P.F.'s son Walter began to turn the family fortune around when, in 1914, his own 9-year-old son, Thomas, discovered oil bubbling up in a field on their property. The rights were leased to Standard Oil, and the Temples received 12.5 percent of the oil income. The first wells began producing in 1916, and by 1926, 16 wells, some "gushers," had significantly replenished the Temple family fortune. Walter Temple repurchased the homestead in 1917.

There are two homes on the property. The oldest belonged to William Workman, who built his country home in the early 1870s around an existing three-room adobe that had been on the site for 30 years. He added a second floor, along with decorative details such as an exterior painted to look like granite and brick. Unfortunately, today, while the exterior of the home has been restored to appear as it did in the 1870s, the home remains closed to the public, awaiting seismic retrofitting and interior restoration. You can still enjoy the outside gardens and just a few steps away join one of the tours of the fully restored Temple Home, which was built in 1927, after the family had reacquired the property.

Following his repurchase of the homestead, Walter Temple began planning for the remodel of the original Workman home and cemetery, and he began building his own Spanish Colonial Revival-style home, which the family called La Casa Nueva. That home was completed in 1927, following five years of construction.

A guided tour of Temple's La Casa Nueva is a must. The white adobe walls, dark-colored woods, wrought-iron work, and the Spanish-style tiles on the stairway to the second floor exemplify the home's Spanish links. It's likely that day-labor workers, albeit very good craftsmen, hand carved the many doors and beams found throughout the home.

There is much to see inside, and although most of the furnishings did not belong to the Temple family, they are still exquisite period pieces. Recently, a family member donated the Temple's original 19th century Chickering piano, which is in exceptional condition.

Each room in the home has a unique stained-glass window. Over the entry stairway is the largest piece of stained glass, a mural of a mythical California. In other rooms, subjects for the glass work

Gateway to the Temple home

include oil wells, flowers, and, in the music room, portraits of famous composers. One set of glass doors has exquisite stained-glass portraits of what appear to be Spanish-era Temple ancestors but are actually the two oldest Temple children. The images were copied from photographs taken about 1920.

The boys' bedrooms, including Walter Temple Jr.'s room, is decorated as though the boys are not home, but are away attending their private school. Walter Jr. died in 1998 and provided much of the information about the home's furnishings and history before his passing. Walter, Jr.'s older brother, Thomas, was a Harvard-educated lawyer, but to his father's disappointment, he never practiced law. Instead, Thomas became a "lowly" historian and genealogist, but he was much respected for the work he did. Thomas conducted much research and wrote extensively about the San Gabriel Mission, one of his favorite subjects.

There is much more to see on the tour, including the dining room, other bedrooms, and the outside courtyard. Be sure to look up at the outside beams in the courtyard, where you'll see carved faces of the family's many pets. The historic family cemetery is located on the same grounds, about a five-minute walk from the homes.

**HOURS:** Wednesday through Sunday, tours hourly from 1 PM to 4 PM. Closed major holidays.

**COST:** Free

**LOCATION:** 15415 East Don Julian Road, City of Industry

**PHONE:** 626-968-8492

**WEBSITE:** www.homesteadmuseum.org

## *Long Beach*

## 2 Rancho Los Alamitos

**WHAT'S HERE:** A Monterey colonial ranch house with western furnishings and huge shire horses in the barn and corral

**DON'T MISS THIS:** The expansive cactus garden

What began as a small, early 19th century adobe that served as the center of a cattle ranch has changed significantly over the past 200 years. Through those two centuries, the adobe was owned by numerous people, including Mexican Governor Jose Figuero (from 1834 to 1835), American Abel Stearns (from 1842 to 1865), who was the first mayor or alcalde of Los Angeles while still under Mexican control, and, finally, by members of the local Bixby family (from 1881 to 1967).

The history of Rancho Los Alamitos began in 1790, when Spain awarded Manuel Nieto, a soldier in Gaspar de Portola's expedition into Alta California, a 300,000-acre land grant, which had been split into six ranchos by 1834. One was Rancho Los Alamitos (Little Cottonwoods Ranch), comprised of only 3600 acres. John and Susan Bixby moved to the ranch in 1878 and created the beginning of a successful ranch and dairy farm. In 1881, John W. Bixby & Partners purchased a controlling interest in the business.

In 1911, the Bixby's son, Fred, assumed ownership of the ranch, and since he needed a larger ranch to run all of his cattle, Bixby converted Rancho Alamitos into a feed-lot operation and brought cattle from his other ranches here to fatten them for market.

Bixby enjoyed his gentleman's ranch, much of which was constructed by his father; however, his wife, Florence, found it a little too rustic for her tastes, even though the Monterey Colonial-style ranch house was a significant improvement over the ranch's original adobe house. Several of the owners, including Abel Stearns, and especially the Bixbys, made improvements over the years, adding the gabled roof, wooden floors, and additional rooms around the original adobe. The U-shaped house surrounds a small garden area—a traditional Mexican hacienda plan—and is enclosed on the fourth side by an adobe wall. The foundations consist of red brick that was originally brought around the Horn from New England.

Things changed somewhat for the Bixby family in 1921 when oil was discovered on property they owned at Signal Hill and again in 1926 at Seal Beach. The additional oil wealth allowed Bixby to add a second wing to the original home and likely increased his ability to purchase such treasures as the Persian and Navajo rugs in his home. About 90 percent of the furniture, art pieces, and other items in the home today are from the Bixby family.

The home is quite masculine in its decor, and includes such things as a giant set of steer horns that grace an entry hallway. But it also included features more suited to Florence Bixby's tastes, such as a large collection of pressed glass that she received over the years from the many visitors who arrived with pieces as gifts. Fred, meanwhile, purchased a pool table as a gift for the local YMCA. Those in charge at the YMCA thought that such a gift was inappropriate for young minds, so Fred kept the table, turning his home's music room into a pool room.

There is much to see and learn on the docent-led interior tours. Curiosities such as the family's two kitchen stoves

The front of the main home overlooks extensive gardens.

usually bring questions from visitors. The family's cook refused to use the new electric stove when it was installed, instead clinging to what she knew best, the old wood cook stove. She continued to use the wood stove until the woodcutter left and she could no longer get wood.

There are also exhibits in the outside barns, including information about the local Native Americans and about the huge shire horses that Bixby raised. England's knights also used shire horses, which were bred for their size and power. There are usually a couple of the beautiful animals wandering in the corral.

On the grounds that surround the home, Florence hired well-known landscape architects to help her design her garden masterpieces. Today, pathways meander throughout those same gardens that still are maintained around the home. Unfortunately, the ranch has been reduced to just over 7 acres and it is surrounded by homes, although Florence's gardens do an excellent job of buffering and blocking the modern intrusions from view. Be sure to wander through the cactus garden—the size and variety of plants are amazing.

To reach the home, you will have to enter through a private residential security gate at the intersection of Anaheim Road and Palo Verde Ave. Simply tell the guard you are visiting Rancho Los Alamitos, and you will be directed to drive to the top of the hill. From there, turn left, and the entrance to the home is almost immediately on your right.

**HOURS:** Wednesday through Sunday, 1 PM to 5 PM, with tours every half hour (the last one begins at 4 PM). Closed Memorial Day, Labor Day, Thanksgiving and the Friday following, Christmas, and New Year's Day.

**COST:** Tours are free

**LOCATION:** 6400 Bixby Hill Road, Long Beach

**PHONE:** 562-431-3541

**WEBSITE:** www.rancholosalamitos.com

# 3 Los Cerritos Ranch House

**WHAT'S HERE:** Restored and furnished adobe home that dates from 1844 and a small museum

**DON'T MISS THIS:** The huge Moreton Bay fig tree that has been here since 1880

In 1784, Spanish soldier Manuel Nieto was granted 300,000 acres of land, which was later reduced to 167,000 acres following a disagreement with the nearby mission. Nieto settled near today's Whittier and raised cattle and horses. Following his death in 1804, his children inherited his land, which was later split into six ranchos. His daughter, Manuela

Cota, received the 27,000-acre Rancho Los Cerritos (Ranch of the Little Hills). Besides raising cattle, she and her husband reared 12 children, but when Manuela died in 1837, her heirs sold the rancho six years later to John Temple.

Temple was a cattleman and ran up to 15,000 head on his ranch, using the very profitable hide and tallow business to supplement his Los Angeles mercantile business. Temple built the two-story adobe here in 1844 as a headquarters for his expansive cattle operations, although he spent most of his time living in Los Angeles. The beautiful gardens were added during the late 1840s. In 1866, Temple sold Rancho Los Cerritos to Flint, Bixby & Company, owned by brothers Thomas and Benjamin Flint and their cousin Lewellyn Bixby. Bixby was from the same family that would come to own another early Long Beach adobe at Rancho Los Alamitos (see page 227). The selling price? A mere $20,000.

The history gets a bit confusing as Lewellyn Bixby brought in his brother, Jotham, to manage the newly acquired ranch. Three years later, Jotham bought a half interest in the property and lived in the home until 1881. Life in the adobe was anything but tranquil. Jotham Bixby and his wife raised seven children here, and provided a home, both temporary and permanent, for a number of cousins, aunts, and uncles.

Jotham moved away from raising cattle and ran as many as 30,000 sheep on his ranch, but even that business proved to have its economic downturns. Jotham turned to leasing and selling parts of the original ranch, and by 1884, the budding new town of Long Beach occupied the rancho's southwest corner. Other towns soon followed, and soon the old Cerritos adobe home, which had been converted to a rental, was well into a state of disrepair. The old Rancho Los Cerritos had ceased to exist, as was evidenced by the many nearby private homes and the Virginia Country Club (golf course) that was developed just behind the adobe.

In 1930, Llewellyn Bixby Sr., Lewellyn Bixby's son, purchased back control of the adobe and remodeled it for his family. (The family's use of different first name spellings and the addition of "senior" can be confusing: Lewellyn Bixby was the father of Llewellyn Bixby Sr.; Llewellyn, Jr. was Llewellyn, Sr.'s son.) This is when indoor plumbing, electricity, and telephone service was brought into the home.

Today, the house museum features numerous exhibits, including the foreman's "room and office" that has been restored to appear as it likely did in the 1850s. The foreman was lucky enough to get his own room and a bed. Some of the artifacts are original; some are reproductions. Other exhibits along the one wing of rooms include the 1870s food storeroom, where the family kept their food supplies, which they bought in bulk, such as the 50-pound barrels of flour.

Interior courtyard entrance of
Los Cerritos Ranch House

Several of the rooms in the main house have been restored. The dining room is similar to the same room in the Llewellyn Bixby, Jr. era. The major difference is the oak floor, which wasn't added until Bixby's 1930 restoration and remodeling of the house. Prior to that, the floor had been redwood. The parlor was where the families did most of their socializing, whether after dinner or when guests were visiting. It also was the only room that had a heat source, for those relatively cold Southern California winter nights.

The Bixby's bedroom was upstairs in the main adobe. They kept their baby in the master bedroom with them. There are several other rooms, some with views of the garden that is located behind the adobe.

The backyard gardens were replanted during the 1930s and showcase a dozen of the trees from the Temple era, including the huge Moreton Bay fig that has been here since the 1880s. So visitors could more easily find his home, Temple planted the large Italian cypress trees (there once were more) as landmarks visible from great distances.

**HOURS:** Wednesday through Sunday, 1 PM to 5 PM. Closed Easter, July 4, Thanksgiving and the Friday following, Christmas, and New Year's Day.

**COST:** Free

**LOCATION:** 4600 Virginia Road, Long Beach

**PHONE:** 562-570-1755

**WEBSITE:** www.rancholoscerritos.org

## Los Angeles

## 4  The Getty Center and The Getty Villa

**WHAT'S HERE:** Hundreds of art pieces from as early as 1300 AD at the Getty Center, and one of the most extensive collections of antiquities at the Villa

**DON'T MISS THIS:** The spectacular views of Los Angeles and the Pacific Ocean from the Getty Center patio

J. Paul Getty, born in 1892, was one of America's most successful early 20th century entrepreneurs. He inherited his father's oil company, which he reorganized into Getty Oil Co., and became the director and principle owner. Getty controlled almost 200 different businesses worth $3 billion at the time of his death in 1976. A true philanthropist, he shared his tremendous financial success with the rest of the world through his endowments of the arts. Getty enjoyed art and collected European paintings, Greek and Roman antiquities, and 18th century French decorative arts throughout his life. His endowment has allowed the museum to significantly expand its collections of antiquities, paintings, illuminated manuscripts, sculptures, and photographs.

There are two separate facilities, the oldest and recently refurbished Villa in Malibu and the newer Getty Center in Los Angeles. The bulk of the Getty collection is housed and exhibited at the Getty Center, which sits high in the Santa Monica Mountains and on clear days provides a spectacular view of Los Angeles, Long Beach, and the Pacific Ocean. Aside from the view, the center's architectural design is an adventure in itself. You move through multilevel galleries to a beautifully designed garden area that includes a cascading creek and both plant and metal sculptures.

The art collection includes some 450 European paintings from as far back as 1300 AD. The individual mini-galleries divide the paintings by eras and styles. Inside the galleries, the period rooms are decorated in styles appropriate to their selection of paintings, a complete departure from the soaring lines of the exterior architecture. From Vincent van Gogh's *Irises* (1889) to Pierre-Auguste Renoir's *La Promenade* (1870) and dozens of other painters' works, the collection provides a comprehensive journey through the history of painting as an art form.

The Getty's collection includes many more art forms. Drawings, whether they are the "finished" piece or merely the prelude to a completed painting or sculpture, often tell much more about an artist's creativeness than what has been written. This is especially true of 15th and 16th century artists, about whom little is known. As an example, the Getty possesses Desiderio da Settignano's only drawing known to exist, *Studies of the Virgin and Child*. He was one of the most important Florentine sculptors of the Renaissance.

Decorative arts from the mid-17th to mid-19th centuries were a focus of Getty's early collecting, especially those from Paris. The museum has since substantially added to those early personal collections, expanding to furniture, glass, ceramics, silver, and more. The museum's focus for the past quarter century has been on Renaissance and 17th century bronzes and neoclassical sculptures from French and British artisans, along with 18th and 19th century terra-cotta and marble sculptures.

If your tastes run to contemporary art, your only choice at the Getty is the photographic collection. It is primarily from British and American photographers, and for anyone familiar with the history of photography and its many masters, most of these names will be familiar: Alfred Stieglitz, Walker Evans, Man Ray, Edward Weston, Julia Margaret Cameron, Paul Strand, and the list goes on.

If, however, you'd prefer to study the oldest collections, it's possible to travel back well over 1000 years with the Ottonian, Byzantine, Romanesque, Gothic, and Renaissance manuscripts held in the museum's collection. Some of the oldest include an illuminated copy of the Koran, an 11th century Ottonian benedictional, and a 12th century German gospel book.

In art, there is little that isn't represented at the Getty. The antiquity collection, the marble sculptures, Greek vases, and such are now displayed at the refurbished Getty Villa in Malibu. The Villa is dedicated to education through the studies of ancient Greek,

Roman, and Etrurian cultures and art. The home houses more than 44,000 pieces of art, although only a small fraction of the total collection can be exhibited at any one time.

Both locations continually rotate portions of their extensive collections, so returning to either museum will allow opportunities to view different aspects of the collections. The Getty's website provides an extensive listing of its collections, changing exhibitions, and new educational programs. While the Getty Center is generally open, the Villa requires reservations, which are free and can be obtained online, but check well in advance as they are extremely popular and sometimes difficult to get.

**HOURS:** The Getty Center: Tuesday through Thursday and Sunday, 10 AM to 6 PM; Friday and Saturday, 10 AM to 9 PM. Closed Monday. The Villa: Thursday through Monday, 10 AM to 5 PM. Closed Tuesday and Wednesday. Both museums are closed on January 1, July 4, Thanksgiving, and Christmas Day.

**COST:** Both museums are free, but there is a $7 (cash only) parking fee. The Villa at Malibu: Advance, free tickets are required to enter, and groups of nine or more must make reservations. Tickets are available online or by calling 310-440-7300.

**LOCATION:** The Getty Center is at 1200 Getty Center Drive, Los Angeles, about 12 miles northeast of downtown Los Angeles. The only way to reach the museum is by tram from the parking structure. While the tram is free, on some days the boarding line can be quite long, so it's wise to take whatever items you need with you. The Villa at Malibu is at 17985 Pacific Coast Hwy., Pacific Palisades, 1 mile north of Sunset Blvd.

**PHONE:** 310-440-7300

**WEBSITE:** www.getty.edu

# 5 California African American Museum

**WHAT'S HERE:** Exhibits on African religion, slavery in the South, and the movement West brought about by the two World Wars

**DON'T MISS THIS:** The controversial Topsy-Turvy doll, with its black doll's head on one side and a white doll's head on the other

This museum's permanent collections and changing exhibits reflect the African American movement West, beginning in Africa, with a look at their cultural development from slavery to freedom and beyond. The museum also places an emphasis on African American migration and contribution in settling the West, especially California.

Part of that story actually predates the advent of the famed Buffalo Soldiers of the 1860s and '70s Indian Wars and even mountain man and explorer James Beckwourth's life among the Crow and Blackfoot Indians. In fact, in 1781, African Americans made up more than half of the non-Indian population of the pueblo known as Los Angeles. They also sailed the oceans and came to California during the Gold Rush to take their places among the thousands of other gold seekers from around the world.

The museum includes several galleries, beginning with Western Africa cultures. Much of the permanent collection is made up of art and ceremonial artifacts; many are representative 20th century pieces, because such artifacts from earlier centuries are extremely rare. Just inside the main gallery entrance is a carved warrior, the *Verandah Post*, which once stood on courtyard verandas where various celebrations were held. Other carvings and ceremonial face masks come from Nigeria, Democratic Republic of Congo, and the Ivory Coast.

One particularly distinctive piece in the collection is the portrait of an Oba, which is both a mortal ruler and a living god. It comes from Benin-Nigeria's 20th century Edo culture and is cast in brass. The use of brass is significant; its permanence represents a kinship destined to last forever.

Within the same main gallery is a simple document that represents the unfortunate reality of the slave trade: a bill of sale from the H.R. Irbin, state of Arkansas, Jefferson County, received from Robert M. Scaff, for the sum of $1500 as full payment for "Selah, a 34-year-old Negro woman," and for Charles, her 4-year-old son. The document further warranted that the two slaves were "of sound body and mind." It is dated October 1860.

At the end of the 18th century and well into the 1860s, cotton was the crop of choice in the South, creating a huge demand for inexpensive slave labor to plant and harvest the white bonanza during this non-mechanized era. With slavery legal in the US, hundreds of ships sought to capture cargoes of very profitable slaves from along Africa's west coast. At the end of the Civil War and legal slavery in this country, 91 percent of America's 5 million African Americans were living in the Deep South.

Few historical or cultural artifacts have survived from the days of slavery, but from documents and stories passed down through generations, historians have created a reasonably accurate look at the lives of these early African Americans. From the foods they ate, the celebrations they enjoyed, and the folk art they created, much can be learned about their joys and tragedies. The Topsy-Turvy doll was one such piece of folk art that became a popular child's toy at the time. The museum's collection includes a Topsy-Eva doll that represented characters in Harriet Beecher Stowe's 1852 anti-slavery novel, *Uncle Tom's Cabin*. The name for these controversial dolls came about because they featured a black doll, often with a headscarf on one end, and a white doll in an antebellum-style dress on the other end. When turned over, the doll's dress would cover the opposite torso and face. Experts tend to disagree on whether the dolls were designed for slave children so that when the "master" came around they could show only the white face, or perhaps they were given to white children as "maid dolls."

Following the Civil War, the exodus of African Americans from the South

California African American Museum

began slowly, but political and economic opportunities pulled many both North and West. In the 1880s, during the great land rush giveaways, African Americans began moving to Oklahoma Territory. World War I created a demand for factory workers, and between 1915 and 1920, 500,000 African Americans moved to northern cities seeking employment. The buildup to World War II brought about the migration of even more African Americans. By 1940, 23 percent of African Americans were living in the urban North and West.

Additional exhibits examine the discrimination against African Americans, with one particular look at the PGA's efforts to keep African Americans from playing in professional golf events. The focus is on the efforts of Bill Spiller, who attempted to gain access to PGA tournaments in part by declaring war on the tactics and laws that prohibited African Americans from participating.

The museum also looks at the significant contributions that African Americans have made to the world's music. One exhibit case features singer Ella Fitzgerald's gold lamé gown, along with several photos of her performances. Other African America figures of prominence, such as Los Angeles Mayor Tom Bradley, are also included in several of the exhibits.

Much of the museum is dedicated to temporary exhibits related to African American culture and history. It's best to check the website for current exhibits.

**HOURS:** Wednesday through Saturday, 10 AM to 4 PM; the first Sunday of each month, 11 AM to 5 PM. Closed Thanksgiving, Christmas, and New Year's Day.

**COST:** Free

**LOCATION:** 600 State Drive, Exposition Park, Los Angeles. Paid parking is available at the 39th Street and Figueroa Street parking lot.

**PHONE:** 213-744-7432

**WEBSITE:** www.caamuseum.org

# 6  Page Museum at La Brea Tar Pits

**WHAT'S HERE:** The fossilized remains of thousands of animals from 40,000 years ago, including saber-toothed cats, 3500-pound ground sloths, and more

**DON'T MISS THIS:** The viewing platforms overlooking active excavations in Pit 91

When someone mentions Los Angeles, people don't usually think about Ice Age animals such as dire wolves, saber-toothed cats, and 12-foot-tall Columbian mammoths. Unless, of course, your destination is the La Brea Tar Pits. For more than 40,000 years, the famous fossil site has been the unintended burial ground for millions of plants and animals. The sticky, black "tar" that oozes to the earth's surface from what 100,000 years ago was the ocean floor, is really asphalt. Over the years, it bubbled up through narrow fissures and formed pools that attracted and captured unwary animals. As they struggled to escape, they attracted bigger predators, such as saber-toothed cats. Seeing an easy meal, they, too, became permanently stuck in the black goo.

Unlike most fossil deposits that are usually found as pieces in layers of broken and washed-away sedimentary rock, La Brea's fossils are well-preserved. And they are much younger than the fossils of dinosaurs that became extinct 65 million years ago. La Brea has preserved entire Ice Age ecosystems, from plants and diatoms to small and large mammals and reptiles. Today, the La Brea Tar Pits have become a rich mine of information for researchers. With so many recovered skulls of saber-toothed cats, for instance, scientists can determine how quickly their teeth were worn or broken as they became older.

The museum is divided into three parts. The most obvious is the large pits or ponds filled with the actual bubbling asphalt. A family of mammoths (replicas, obviously) stand at one end. An adult mammoth is caught up to its belly and struggling in the frightful asphalt, while its mate and youngster look on. A pathway meanders around the main tar pit and throughout the grounds.

The Page Museum offers a close-up look at a sampling of the animals that have died at La Brea over the past 40,000 years. Several of the vanished species are represented, or at least their bones are here. There are hundreds of skulls and other fossils exhibited as well. It's probably good that some of these creatures no longer wander through Los Angeles; the cute little tree sloth found in South American jungles once had relatives that moved to the ground to make their homes. Over millions of years, they evolved to become much larger; the extinct Harlan's ground sloth, a species found in abundance at La Brea, stood over 6 feet tall and weighed close to 3500 pounds.

One of the main attractions inside the museum is the working laboratory. Visitors can view scientists working on newly recovered fossils, carefully cleaning the asphalt from the ancient bones and reconstructing skeletal remains. A semicircular glass window surrounds the lab, offering views of the action, as slow and meticulous as it is.

Outside and behind the museum, a walkway leads to Pit 91. This active excavation area is continuing the legacy of humans using the tar pits. Native Americans were the first to use the sticky asphalt to seal their boats and waterproof baskets. When the Spanish arrived in the 18th century, they named the area Rancho La Brea, or the "Tar Ranch." The early Spanish and Mexican ranchers discovered bones in the tar pits but likely assumed they were unlucky cows.

Fossils on display in the Page Museum

During the early 1900s, the University of California, Berkeley, and the predecessor of the Los Angeles County Natural History Museum, began large-scale excavations. From 1913 to 1915, paleontologists and the workers they hired to dig deep into the 96 quarries recovered more than a million fossilized bones. On a much smaller scale, that same work continues today in Pit 91. From viewing platforms, you can see workers carefully removing fossils from the 6-inch-deep, 3-foot-square grids laid out in the bottom of the pit. The work moves so slowly that only about four grid areas can be completed during the two-month excavation season each year. But that small area may reveal more than 1000 bones, along with insects, shells, and the remains of plants.

**HOURS:** Monday through Friday, 9:30 AM to 5 PM; Saturday, Sunday, and holidays, 10 AM to 5 PM. Closed July 4, Thanksgiving, Christmas, and New Year's Day.

**COST:** Adults, $7; 62 and over and students, $4.50; 5–12, $2; under 5, free.

**LOCATION:** 5801 Wilshire Blvd., Los Angeles

**PHONE:** 323-934-7243

**WEBSITE:** www.tarpits.org

# 7 Petersen Automotive Museum

**WHAT'S HERE:** Historic cars that were owned by stars or that starred in their own films

**DON'T MISS THIS:** The original Herbie and the Batmobile

Southern California is the epitome of the automotive lifestyle, so what better place to find one of the world's best automotive museums than in Los Angeles?

The Petersen Automotive Museum's massive 300,000-square-foot building is divided among four floors. The museum is on the first three floors, and there is a glass-walled penthouse conference room for special events on the top floor. In addition to its hundreds of automobiles, motorcycles, trucks, and a vehicle or two of indeterminate nomenclature, the museum has some amazing exhibits. Here, you can wander through full-sized exhibits and dioramas representing different eras and aspects of the history of Southern California's love affair with the car.

The Streetscape Tour winds through more than 30 exhibits that will make you feel as if you've stepped back in time to a 1901 blacksmith shop, where one of Southern California's first cars was built. Farther down is a 1960s-era home garage, with two cars inside and the basketball hoop attached to the roof above the driveway. There's also a classic auto repair shop, a gas station, and a custom car shop. For Baby Boomers, there is a 1950s diner with a 1959 Cadillac convertible and a 1931 Ford hot rod parked outside. And watch out for the life-size motorcycle cop hiding behind the billboard, waiting to catch speeders!

Located on Wilshire Blvd. near the movie capital of the world—Hollywood—the museum features numerous vehicles of motion-picture fame. The white 1963 Volkswagen known as Herbie from the original *Love Bug* movie is prominently displayed. You will also find Batmobiles from two different eras of the famed superhero; there's the Batmobile from the 1989 movie *Batman* starring Michael Keaton, as well as the 1966 version seen in the television series starring Adam West. For sci-fi fans, the taxi from the 1982 movie *Blade Runner* is on display, as well as Professor Fate's Hannibal 8 rocket car from the 1965 comedy-adventure movie *The Great Race*.

Cars once owned by some of Hollywood's best-loved actors also can be seen here. One car displayed was owned by Leo Carrillo (see Leo Carrillo Ranch Historic Park, page 284), better known as "Pancho" on television's long-running *Cisco Kid*. It is custom built and painted the color of Carrillo's favorite palomino, "Loco," and a long-horned bull's head with eyes that light up is attached to the front. There is also a 1934 Ford hot rod that once was the property of film star Nicolas Cage, and a somewhat more conventional vehicle, a 1956 Jaguar XKSS that actor Steve McQueen owned.

The museum displays numerous luxury cars, including Jean Harlow's 1932 Packard Phaeton and the French-built, super-luxurious and "modern" streamlined Delehaye from three different years, 1937, 1939, and 1948. There are automobiles from other foreign car makers, such as a 1932 Duesenberg convertible coupe and American classics such as Chryslers, Cadillacs, and Packards from the 1920s and 1930s. Trucks and motorcycles round out the museum's exhibits.

The museum's third floor Discovery Center offers kids and adults a chance to learn about the history of the automobile, as well as how technology from gears to batteries to gasoline engines actually work. Kids can sit on a police motorcycle and start the siren in one exhibit that demonstrates how sound waves travel. And as a souvenir of your visit, the entire family can dress in old-time coats, scarves, and goggles and sit in a 1910 Model T for a family self-portrait.

As with most auto museums, some of the vehicles on display may belong to private individuals who have loaned them to the museum for exhibit purposes, and occasionally the museum will

Petersen Automotive Museum

loan vehicles from its private collection to other museums for temporary exhibits. At other times, special traveling exhibits are featured here. Because of this, you may see a favorite car in the museum during one visit only to find that it is no longer displayed in the gallery when you return with friends a month or two later. But the return trip is worth the cost of admission.

> **HOURS:** Tuesday through Sunday, 10 AM to 6 PM; the Discovery Center closes at 4 PM weekdays and 5 PM on weekends. The museum is closed Monday, but open the Monday of Memorial Day and Labor Day weekends. It is closed Thanksgiving, Christmas, and New Year's Day.
>
> **COST:** Adults, $10; 62 and over, $5; 5–12, $3.
>
> **LOCATION:** 6060 Wilshire Blvd., Los Angeles
>
> **PHONE:** 323-930-2277
>
> **WEBSITE:** www.petersen.org

# 8 Natural History Museum of Los Angeles County

**WHAT'S HERE:** A look at the wildlife and their habitats, along with Native American cultures and more

**DON'T MISS THIS:** For adults, the gem exhibits; for kids, the Discovery Center

Built in 1913, this museum is the second oldest cultural institution in Los Angeles—and one of the best. With more than 33 million specimens in its collection, most everyone first entering the museum will be captivated by two battling dinosaurs—full-size skeleton replicas of a tyrannosaurus rex and a triceratops. From the dueling dinosaurs in the grand foyer, the museum opens into several permanent halls, including two world-famous habitat halls that showcase numerous full-size dioramas of African and North American mammals in their natural environments.

For bird lovers, the collection ranges from the smallest of hummingbirds to

Natural History Museum of Los Angeles County

the great Indian hornbill, from endangered species such as marbled murrelets and snowy plovers to eagles and condors. There is a wonderful exhibit that shows kids and their parents what makes a bird a bird, such as their specialized bones and feathers. The condor cliffs and walkway through the tropical rainforest give you a bird's-eye view of two seldom-seen bird habitats.

At one end of the museum, besides a changing exhibit area, there is an amazing gem and mineral collection. You can wander through the specially darkened exhibit and view some 2000 specimens, ranging from 300-plus pounds of gold to sapphires, emeralds, and star rubies.

On the opposite side of the museum is the Discovery Center and Insect Zoo, a place that attracts kids like fly paper. In addition to the numerous glass cases full of real bugs such as rhinoceros beetles, tarantulas, and scorpions, there are oversized models of a bee and a mosquito to help visitors understand how bugs live and work.

While you might be tempted to think that a Megamouth is a scientific name for an overly vocal kid, it's actually the world's rarest shark, and the museum houses a male that is nearly 15 feet long. Since the first Megamouth was discovered in 1976, only 17 have ever been caught. The museum's Megamouth specimen is kept sealed in a glass-topped, coffin-like vat filled with a liquid preservative.

For a break from the wildlife, there are a couple of cultural exhibits. The Times Mirror Hall of Native American Cultures holds more than 800 Native American artifacts. The exhibit includes a replica of a two-story pueblo cliff dwelling and many cases filled with a wide selection of textiles, baskets, pottery, jewelry, and beadwork from numerous tribes.

**HOURS:** Monday through Friday, 9:30am to 5 PM; Saturday, Sunday, and holidays, 10 AM to 5 PM. Closed July 4, Thanksgiving, Christmas, and New Year's Day.

**COST:** Adults, $9; students 18 and over with ID, $6.50; 13–17, $6.50; 5–12, $2; under 5, free.

**LOCATION:** 900 Exposition Blvd., across from the University of Southern California, Los Angeles

**PHONE:** 213-763-3466

**WEBSITE:** www.nhm.org

Inside the Natural History Museum
of Los Angeles County

# 9  Museum of the American West

**WHAT'S HERE:** Extensive collection from the American West, from authentic cowboy duds and guns to the Hollywood versions

**DON'T MISS THIS:** The re-creation of the famous gunfight at the OK Corral

America's "favorite singing cowboy," Gene Autry, is the only person on the Hollywood Walk of Fame who has five stars—one each for radio, records, film, television, and live theatrical performance. To give something back to his fans and to the community, he founded the Autry Museum of Western Heritage in 1988, which has since merged with the Southwest Museum of the American Indian (page 243), thus becoming the Autry National Center. For a relatively new museum, its collections are remarkable in their breadth and quality, providing a well-documented look at the American West's history, cultures, and mythologies. Ironically, many of those mythologies were either invented or perpetuated by television and Hollywood films, two of Gene Autry's many claims to fame.

The museum, located in the Griffith Park area, is divided into numerous galleries on two levels. The main floor provides a large area reserved for changing exhibits that, in the past, have ranged from the films of Sergio Leone (some of Clint Eastwood's early "spaghetti" westerns) to George Catlin and his Indian paintings. These are large, comprehensive, and beautifully designed temporary exhibits and always worth seeing.

For Western movie buffs, the museum contains extensive exhibits on Hollywood and television, including one on Gene Autry's distinguished career in the entertainment business that spanned some 60 years. Popular westerns, whether on television or at the movies, spawned a multimillion-dollar side business selling cowboy products ranging from play gunfighter sets to kids' lunch boxes. Here's an opportunity to see some of the old master cowboys, at least the Hollywood kind and in Hollywood fashion, from Tom Mix to John Wayne. The television heroes such as the Lone Ranger and the Cartwrights of *Bonanza* are here, too.

The numerous permanent exhibits throughout much of the remainder of the museum, especially the second-floor galleries, look at how the West really was. The museum loosely follows a timeline covering the opportunities that drew thousands of people out West during the 1840s and 1850s. Numerous artifacts from what became either cattle trade or major migration trails, the Santa Fe Trail and the Overland Trail, have a home in the museum's exhibit cases.

The Autry National Center includes the Museum of the American West

241

A very large painted diorama provides a look at the representative changes in the West. It begins with Native Americans and wild beasts and moves on to trappers, the US Cavalry, settlers, cowboys and cattle country, and, of course, Hollywood's version of the West, featuring Tom Mix, Gene Autry, and Clint Eastwood. Wandering farther into the exhibit galleries reveals numerous Cavalry weapons, including an 1890 model .45-caliber Gatling gun. Dr. Richard Gatling patented the six-barreled gun in 1861. It used paper cartridges and could fire 200 rounds per minute. The museum's more modern version used brass cartridges and fired 1015 rounds per minute.

Clothing was obviously important to the 19th century soldiers fighting in the West, whether it was against Mexico or the Indians. This collection includes many pieces, such as a buckskin shirt that a soldier wore while fighting in the southwest campaigns in 1874. And for those soldiers who found themselves on the Great Plains during winter, there is the heavy fur coat worn by a 22nd Infantry soldier during the 1870s Indian Wars. General George Armstrong Custer usually comes to mind when talking about the Plains Indian War, so the museum has a pair of binoculars and a pair of Smith and Wesson .32-caliber, Tiffany & Company-etched revolvers presented to him in 1869.

The Community Gallery looks at a variety of groups in the West: the American Indians; the African Americans, who used the railroads to escape the tyranny of slavery by traveling to El Paso, Denver, Oakland, and Los Angeles; and the Chinese, who, in largest numbers, made California their home. The museum explores the conflicts and the new laws, both good and bad, which resulted from the appearance of these often very unwelcome newcomers. Many immigrants, including the Irish, Germans, and other Europeans, were often unwelcome.

The Earps and Doc Holiday have their reputations reviewed with a look at the realities and myths of the infamous gunfight at the OK Corral. And, since gambling was a pastime for so many in the old West, the museum has its own saloon bar with all the various tools of the gambler.

Both lawmen and outlaws are celebrated, or at least remembered. Collections include the Western lawmen's tools, including badges, guns, and shackles. For the bad guys, photos of their dead bodies—something that those in the early West seemed to enjoy taking—seems recognition enough. There is even the story of how Sheriff Pat Garrett

Gene Autry, America's singing cowboy, at work

tracked down Billy the Kid and, on July 14, 1881, shot the young outlaw when he entered a darkened bedroom.

Among the numerous other collections found throughout the many galleries are Colt firearms in one of the most complete collections anywhere, ranging from early Colt revolvers to the modern AR-15 and M-16 automatic rifles. The extensive saddle exhibit includes dozens of saddles from early vaquero to modern parade models. The collection also does a great job of tracking the history of the American cowboy saddle.

Outside, behind the museum's galleries, is a re-creation of the many "western" backdrops seen in movies. The Trails West exhibit includes deserts and mountains from the Sierra Madre to the Sierra Nevada. There's even a Gold Rush site where kids can try panning for the bright metal that forever changed California's history.

There is so much to see here that you can easily spend half a day or more wandering through the history of the West. There is also an upscale but reasonable, cafeteria-style restaurant and large gift store at the museum, and the Los Angeles Zoo is just across the parking lot.

> **HOURS:** Tuesday through Sunday, 10 AM to 5 PM. Closed on Mondays except Martin Luther King Day, President's Day, Memorial Day, and Labor Day. Closed Thanksgiving and Christmas.
>
> **COST:** Adults, $7.50; seniors (over 60) and students, $5; 2–12, $3; free to all on the second Tuesday of each month.
>
> **LOCATION:** 4700 Western Heritage Way, Griffith Park, Los Angeles
>
> **PHONE:** 323-667-2000
>
> **WEBSITE:** www.autrynationalcenter.org

# 10 Southwest Museum of the American Indian

**WHAT'S HERE:** Extensive collections of pottery from throughout the Americas and other Native American artifacts

**DON'T MISS THIS:** The ethnobotanical garden

The oldest public museum in the city of Los Angeles is perched high atop Mt. Washington, overlooking the skyscrapers of downtown. The museum's name is somewhat misleading because its collections today are more geographically diverse than its name indicates. Its founders, including journalist, photographer, historian, and amateur anthropologist Charles Lummis, and the members of his Southwest Society (the western branch of the Archeological Institute of America), named the original museum in 1907 based on their primary geographic interest. Yet among the museum's original exhibits were Asian and European art. Today, the museum's focus is on Native American artifacts and history.

In 2003, the Museum of the American West (page 241) and the Southwest Museum of the American Indian merged to become the Autry National Center. With the cooperation and involvement of Native Americans, the museum's goal is to advance knowledge, understanding, and appreciation of diverse indigenous peoples.

Today, the museum's collection numbers over 350,000 artifacts. While the basket collection alone includes 13,000 pieces, there is no attempt nor need to display the museum's entire collection. The curatorial staff has done an excellent job dividing the museum into appropriate galleries and selecting artifacts that best tell each story—and there are hundreds of stories here.

The museum's four permanent galleries explore the native cultures of California, the Northwest Coast, the Great Plains, and the Southwest. Exhibits of artifacts compare and contrast these groups' cultures and social practices, their food gathering, their social and political organizations, their recreation (which includes centuries-old gambling games), their approaches to religious beliefs, and their art, especially through basketry and pottery. For anyone familiar with the tribal names—Piute, Maidu, Lakota, Cheyenne—the museum offers a refreshing look at those and many other tribes. Some of the differences are obvious, such as the clothing worn by the desert Indians and the coastal tribes, while others are not so obvious, such as the often subtle changes in basketry patterns. The Great Plains exhibit features a striking red, blue, and yellow tepee that Darrel Norman, a Blackfoot Indian, created and raised for the museum.

The museum also includes many rare and beautiful pieces of pottery. While there are some pieces that go back 2000 years, much of the museum's focus is on more recent 19th and 20th century pottery making. There are many pieces from the Southwest's Zuni and Hopi Indians, along with pots from many other tribes. The changing technologies and techniques are highlighted, from carved designs to the red-slipped vessels painted with several different mineral colors. The pieces range from plain painted pots to polychrome bowls to figurative ceramics. The exhibits include some of the best pottery that was created by either women or "men-women," referred to as the "berdache." These were men who at an early age adopted women's clothing and their roles in the communities; they were simply accepted for who they were.

The museum features temporary exhibits on a regular basis, including art pieces that are exhibited near the center stairway, next to the gift shop. Outside,

An example of Zia polychrome pottery

amid striking views of Los Angeles from the museum's Mt. Washington perch, there is an ethnobotanical garden, a fancy word that refers to a garden with many plants used by Native Americans for food, basketry, and daily living.

**HOURS:** Tuesday through Sunday, 10 AM to 5 PM. Closed on Mondays except Martin Luther King Day, President's Day, Memorial Day, and Labor Day. Also closed Thanksgiving and Christmas.

**COST:** Adults, $7.50; students and seniors, $5; 2–12, $3; free to all on the second Tuesday of each month.

**LOCATION:** 234 Museum Drive, off Ave. 43 from the Pasadena 110 Freeway, near the top of Mt. Washington, Los Angeles

**PHONE:** 323-221-2164

**WEBSITE:** www.autrynationalcenter.org

## *Malibu*

# 11 Adamson House

**WHAT'S HERE:** Malibu mansion that features extensive use of custom tile

**DON'T MISS THIS:** The view of the beach from the swimming pool and a look inside Rhoda Adamson's closet

This location—on a small piece of pristine beach that juts into the Pacific Ocean between Malibu Lagoon and the beach leading to Malibu Pier—is as spectacular as the home that occupies it. Although the home wasn't constructed until 1929–30, the history of this family—which includes the development of a local railway, ranching operations, and interests in oil, insurance, and an electric company—goes back much further. Merritt Adamson, the man responsible for building the Adamson House, worked for Fredrick Rindge on Rindge's expansive Malibu ranch, and he eventually married Rindge's daughter, Rhoda Agatha Rindge.

Originally from Massachusetts, Fredrick Rindge grew up accustomed to his family's East Coast affluence, but upon inheriting $2 million, he moved to California in 1887. In 1892, Rindge purchased this Malibu property for about $10 per acre and soon added much more, including a huge home up Malibu Canyon in 1895. He built a railroad along the coast (today's Pacific Coast Hwy.) simply to keep Southern Pacific from doing the same on *his* property.

Before working for Rindge, Merritt Adamson grew up on his family's 40,000-acre sheep ranch in Arizona. He came to California after selling the ranch following his father's death. While attending law school at the University of California, Adamson met and married Rhoda Rindge, and he soon became superintendent of her family's huge Malibu ranch. The couple decided they would create their own dairy empire, so, in 1916, on 600 acres near today's Ventura Blvd. in the San Fernando Valley, they started Adohr Stock Farms. (Adohr was Rhoda spelled backwards.) With a great advertising slogan that included a photo of their "Adohr-able" baby (born on Valentines Day 1917), they proceeded to develop one of the most advanced and successful dairy businesses in the world. Although Adamson died in 1949, his son, Merritt Jr., continued living in the famed Malibu beach house and managing the dairy business.

In 1968, the state of California purchased the property, making it part of the Malibu Lagoon State Beach. The home has been restored and is a treat to visit, especially because much of the family's original items are still in the house, including Rhoda Adamson's clothes, hanging neatly in her closet.

The home's Spanish Colonial Revival architecture fits in well with southern California's Spanish and Mexican heritages. The most prominent architectural feature is the tile. While most Spanish-style houses use tile, few incorporated as many custom-designed tiles as the Adamson House. It was helpful that Rhoda's father had founded Malibu Potteries and had hired some of the best tile designers in the country for what became a very desirable product. The brilliantly colored ceramic tiles are used throughout the home, on walls and floors as accent to the Mediterranean influences that include Italian, Persian, and Moorish design features. This is no more noticeable or elegant than in the loggia, just past the entrance hall and approaching the living room. Realistic Persian rugs, including their end fringe, have been designed into the floor tiles.

Mahogany beams support the ceiling in the living room, which provides views of the ocean. At the end of the room is a "donkey window," a pointed, arched window that brings a touch of Moroccan influence into the home. The entire floor is of tile, featuring a tan basket weave pattern. The room's furniture belonged to the Adamson family during the 1920s and 1930s and has not been restored.

One thing missing from this home that is found in so many other "mansions" is an abundance of paintings adorning the walls. Apparently, Rhoda Adamson felt that there were enough design and color features in her home already, so the only painting is a still life found over the mantel in the dining room. The upstairs bedrooms and bathrooms are as elegant as the downstairs.

Adamson House living room

Although the bedroom walls are somewhat less decorated, the bathrooms are filled with colorful tile designs that would make most people today a bit dizzy.

Outside, expansive lawn and gardens surround the home, its patios, and the swimming pool, all recipients of custom-designed tile. There is a large, star-shaped, brightly colored tile fountain near the center of the lawn. The Malibu Lagoon Museum is also found on the property and contains a collection of items and rare photographs highlighting the history of the Malibu area, from the early Chumash Indians through Spanish California.

**HOURS:** Grounds are open daily from 8 AM to sunset; house tours are available and the museum is open Wednesday through Saturday, 11 AM to 3 PM (last tour leaves at 2 PM). Closed July 4, Christmas, and New Year's Day, and during heavy rain.

**COST:** 17 and over, $5; 6–16, $2.

**LOCATION:** 23200 Pacific Coast Hwy., Malibu. Entrance for parking and the nature area is at Cross Creek Road, adjacent to the Malibu Creek bridge. Walk east across the bridge and follow the dirt lane to the Adamson House. A county parking lot (fee) is located directly in front of the Adamson House. Parking inside the home's gates is available only to vehicles with disabled plates or placards and is strictly enforced.

**PHONE:** 310-456-8432 or 818-880-0350

**WEBSITE:** www.adamsonhouse.org

## *Mission Hills*

## 12 San Fernando Mission

**WHAT'S HERE:** Significantly restored mission that includes many of the early workrooms used by weavers, carpenters, and more

**DON'T MISS THIS:** Bob Hope's burial place, located on the mission grounds just outside the church

The Spanish founded San Fernando Rey de Espana in 1797, the 17th of their 21 missions, near several springs in the area that is now known as Mission Hills. The springs guaranteed a continuous supply of water in the parched climate, thus allowing for a very large operation. At its peak in 1819, the mission padres and the nearly 1000 Indians who worked here managed more than 13,000 head of cattle, supplying a large trade in tallow, hides, and finished leather. The padres also grazed 8000 sheep and 2300 horses, the mission system's third largest operation.

During Mexico's secularization of the missions during the mid-1820s, the new Mexican governor ran into some issues with the mission's Father Francisco Gonsalas de Ibarra. The good padre was partial to his Spanish ancestry and refused to declare his allegiance to the upstart Mexican government. Nobody forced the issue with Father Ibarra, who didn't leave until 1835. By that time, most of the Indians were also gone, so maintaining the mission and finding replacement workers was impossible.

In 1842, excitement came by way of a mini-gold rush, six years before James Marshall started the big rush with his gold find in Northern California. A local ranch foreman discovered gold while pulling onions for his dinner. Word of his discovery spread, but the seemingly inevitable gold fever failed to spread much beyond the locals, which was good because the gold played out within a few months. Even so, prospectors managed to destroy not only much of the remaining mission's lands, but parts of the mission itself.

Like most of the California missions, San Fernando was abandoned. After 1847, its tiles and any other useful materials were stolen, and most of its adobe walls were left to melt back into the earth. But San Fernando Mission once again became a church in 1923, and a restoration program was begun that continues today, with a few major bumps in the road such as earthquakes that have caused extensive damage along the way.

As you walk the grounds and wander through the various support buildings, you will soon realize this is one of the larger mission restorations. About the time you think you've seen all there is to see, including artifacts either from the original mission or from the same time period, you round a corner and find another wing of restored and furnished rooms.

One of those is an entire wing where many of the rooms were used as a hotel during the mission's heyday. The mission's location, just a day's horseback ride from Los Angeles, made it a popular overnight destination. This wing serves as the centerpiece of the mission's restoration efforts. The rooms are filled with everything from pottery and Indian baskets to paintings and books. There are items used by Pope John Paul II during his 1987 tour of the US, including the vestments that he wore at his Dodger Stadium services.

Today, with the mission so close to Hollywood, and with a large cemetery just across the street, many notable film stars have found their final resting places within view of the mission. Bob Hope was buried just outside the church, in the mission's cemetery. The site includes a beautiful garden and a wall commemorating the famous comedian. The story goes that when Hope's wife, Dolores, asked him where he wanted to be buried, Bob answered, "Surprise me." She did.

Courtyard fountain at San Fernando Mission

**HOURS:** Daily, 9 AM to 4:30 PM. Closed Thanksgiving and Christmas.

**COST:** Adults, $4; 7–15, $3; 6 and under, free.

**LOCATION:** 15151 San Fernando Mission Blvd., Mission Hills

**PHONE:** 818-361-0186

**WEBSITE:** www.missionsofcalifornia.org/missions/mission17.html

## *Newhall*

## 13 William S. Hart Mansion

**WHAT'S HERE:** Elaborate Western furnishings, including authentic art and movie props from Hart's silent films

**DON'T MISS THIS:** Hart's original tiny ranch house (located near the parking lot), which once was used as a movie set and is now a museum

William Hart was Hollywood's first cowboy film star, beginning his career as an actor and director during the silent-film era. His Spanish Colonial Revival home was a very popular architectural style among successful film stars of the day. Inside, though, it's all cowboy.

Hart wasn't born a cowboy. He started life in 1864 in New York and worked for a time in that state as a Shakespearean actor. Although he began his stage-acting career in his 20s, the film bug didn't strike him until he was 49; it was 1913, and the film industry was still quite new.

Hart struck it rich in Hollywood, making more than 65 silent films by the time he was 60 years old. He worked with his horse, Fritz, which created some consternation with directors and film crews. Hart was 6'2" and Fritz was a pony, so when mounted, Hart always appeared overly large—or his horse much too small. Other than his choice of horses, Hart's films were story-driven and especially realistic, a somewhat unusual combination for the time. Yet the films made him a favorite among moviegoers who loved films such as *Tumbleweeds* (1925), his last movie and probably his best known. He began to lose out to the newcomers once the "talkies" emerged. Given his stage experience, Hart could have continued making movies, but he wasn't ready to forfeit his realism for the razzle-dazzle action the audiences were becoming accustomed to from the likes of cowboy Tom Mix.

In 1921, just four years before he retired from acting, Hart purchased 230 acres in the hills outside Los Angeles and named his new spread Horseshoe Ranch. There was a small, old ranch house at the bottom of the hill that served him as a film set, its walls constructed so that they could be easily removed for film crews. Hart had stayed at the ranch house during his periodic visits to the property, but he wanted something more comfortable and befitting a movie star of his stature. Besides, it wasn't nearly large enough to house his growing collection of cowboy memorabilia and Native American artifacts.

In 1927, Hart moved into his new 10,000-square-foot, 22-room house situated at the top of a hill overlooking much of his ranch. Most of what remains in the house in the way of furniture and art was present when Hart lived here. Apparently, he made few changes during the nearly 20 years he lived in the home. There are numerous paintings and sculptures, some by such notables as Charles Russell, Joe De Young, Charles Christadoro, and Frederic Remington.

A collector of Western items, Hart covered much of his home's floors with Navajo rugs that he purchased between the 1880s and the 1930s. During his time, they were walked on by himself and his guests; today, most are stored with a representative sampling set out for viewing. It's difficult to differentiate between what are authentic Western artifacts or Hollywood film props. There are Indian pots, blankets, and baskets (authentic). And there is a full-length buffalo fur coat that weighs about 35 pounds (movie prop), a silver-studded saddle (he used only for public appearances), and a Roman shield (stage prop).

Unlike most people today, Hart had two kitchens in his home. The large main kitchen was downstairs, and a smaller kitchen was upstairs. Apparently, the upstairs kitchen worked well for Hart's sister, who lived in the house with him. She had injured her back in an auto accident during a trip out to see him on a movie set in the desert, and being able to prepare meals upstairs saved her the pain of using the stairs. The downstairs kitchen is typical of most 1920s kitchens, including the old ice box that required regular deliveries of ice from town.

Hart seemed to know just about everyone who was anyone during his life, and some he met in peculiar ways. One day, a plane buzzed his house several times, and when an irritated Hart tracked down the plane's owner via its tail number, he met Amelia Earhart. Add famed lawman Wyatt Earp (Hart served as a pallbearer at Earp's funeral) and all the Hollywood film stars of his time, and it's obvious he kept a very busy social calendar. One of those Hollywood notables gave Hart a gift that draws the attention of most visitors today, especially the kids. In the "multipurpose" room, a giant Alaskan Kodiak bear rug covers part of the floor. It was a gift from Will Rogers (see Will Rogers State Historic Park, page 251), but since neither Rogers nor Hart were hunters, nobody is quite sure who shot the bear.

William S. Hart Mansion dining room

Hart died in 1946 and left his home and property to Los Angeles County to be used by the public for free. Touring the "old" ranch house that is located adjacent to the park's lower parking lot can be done at any time during open hours.

**HOURS:** Mid-June through Labor Day, tours are Wednesday through Sunday, 11 AM to 3:30 PM; the remainder of the year, tours are Wednesday through Friday, 10 AM to 12:20 PM, and Saturday and Sunday, 11 AM to 3:30 PM. Closed July 4, Thanksgiving, Christmas, and New Year's Day.

**COST:** Free

**LOCATION:** William S. Hart Park at 24151 San Fernando Road, Newhall. There is a small building and mini-museum at the base of the hill, and the house is at the top of the hill. It's about a quarter-mile hike on a dirt path to the top of the hill. While not extraordinarily steep, it may take away your breath if you have not been walking much lately and are hurrying to make a scheduled tour. If you are unable to walk and have a disabled placard for your car, contact the office near the main parking lot or call them in advance for directions to the upper parking area.

**PHONE:** 661-254-4584

**WEBSITE:** www.hartmuseum.org

## *Pacific Palisades*

# 14 Will Rogers State Historic Park

**WHAT'S HERE:** Home filled with the belongings and lifetime mementos of Will Rogers, the 1920s and '30s star of radio and film

**DON'T MISS THIS:** The weekend polo matches in front of the ranch house

In 1932, Will Rogers was Hollywood's most popular and highest-paid star. But in his heart, he was simply a Cherokee Indian and a cowboy from Oklahoma, where he was born in 1879. Rogers never graduated from high school, opting instead to join a cattle drive. He may have lacked a formal education, but Rogers spent his entire life making up for it through his prolific reading and his unique ability to communicate with anyone using his homespun outlook on life, politics, and the human condition. Rogers enjoyed a worldwide following. His humor connected with everyone, from kings and presidents to the common man. One of his oft-repeated sayings, "I never met a man I didn't like," was something that truly fit Will Rogers.

Rogers began his theatrical career in vaudeville, often featuring his amazing roping tricks and philosophical humor. As his Hollywood film career was taking off during the 1920s, Rogers began acquiring property near Santa Monica. He eventually purchased more than 300 acres in what is today Pacific Palisades. He expanded his small cabin to many times its original size and continued construction of other facilities on his surrounding ranch over the next several years.

Even as a movie star with 71 movies to his credit, a radio broadcaster, and a syndicated newspaper columnist, Rogers continued to live his cowboy life. He had no need for the fancy mansions of other successful movie stars; he insisted that his ranch house have a simple board- and batten-clad wood exterior, and that the interior finishes be equally rustic. Inside the home, the rooms and furniture are comfortable. There are plenty of Indian rugs, a steer's head for roping practice, and more than a few mementos from his life as a cowboy. The long, covered front porch offered Rogers and his many guests beautiful views of the surrounding mountains. From his second-floor bedroom, Rogers could see one of his favorite places on the ranch, his expansive riding stable. One of the first things that he did after returning from almost any trip away was to head to the stable and saddle one of his horses. With 300 acres of his own and easy access to much of the rugged Santa Monica Mountains, there were plenty of places for Rogers and his friends to ride.

In addition to the 31-room main ranch house and the expansive stable, the ranch included corrals, a riding ring, cow-roping arena, and a golf course. Rogers also had a polo field in the large open space in front of his house. The polo field remains today and is used for weekend polo matches. It's not uncommon to see some of the local Hollywood stars riding in friendly competitions.

The house has been restored and is open for tours that offer an inside look at where Will Rogers lived until his untimely death in 1935. He and his good friend Wiley Post died in an airplane crash near Barrow, Alaska. Following Rogers' death, his wife, Betty, made very few changes to the home, finally turning it over to become a California State Historic Park in 1944.

For those who are unfamiliar with this entertainment giant, the visitor center features numerous exhibits, including short films featuring Will Rogers in both silent movies and "talkies." Docent and staff tours are available, as well as self-guided audio tours. There are miles of trails for hiking, biking, and horseback riding, and picnic tables for enjoying a leisurely meal.

**HOURS:** Daily, 8 AM to sunset; guided walking tours are available Tuesday through Saturday, 11 AM, 1 PM, and 2 PM; call for the ranch house tour schedule.

**COST:** $7 per vehicle.

**LOCATION:** 1501 Will Rogers Park Road, Pacific Palisades

**PHONE:** 310-454-8212

**WEBSITE:** www.parks.ca.gov/parkindex

## 15 Fenyes Mansion

**WHAT'S HERE:** Fully furnished home including the "art" room that Eva Fenyes used as the center for many meetings of Pasadena's creative minds

**DON'T MISS THIS:** The Finnish Folk Museum, originally the owner's private sauna

The Fenyes home is one of the few remaining mansions that once graced Pasadena's Millionaire's Row, the most popular neighborhood for millionaires to build their expansive homes during the late 19th and early 20th centuries. It is also one of the very few Pasadena mansions open to the public. Eva Fenyes and her second husband, Dr. Adalbert Fenyes, arrived in Pasadena from New York in 1895. This was about 20 years after the original two dozen or so Indiana, Michigan, and Illinois families arrived here, purchased land at $6 per acre with the intention of growing oranges, and, in 1875, named their community Pasadena. The new town quickly became a key stop for the Atchison, Topeka, and Santa Fe Railway that moved thousands of tons of oranges to the East Coast each year, originally in cars cooled by ice.

Eva and Adalbert likely left the harsh winters of the East for California's mild climate. Eva had been a businesswoman in New York, owning rental properties, among other enterprises. Her New York family had money, unlike her husband, whom she had met in Europe.

Eva sold their first home in Pasadena and purchased this 5-acre parcel, which was unusual for a woman to do at the beginning of the 20th century. Eva worked closely with noted architect Robert D. Farquhar on both the exterior architecture and the interior furnishings, designed to match the elegance of the East Coast's upper-crust homes. Her Beaux Arts home was completed in 1906. Like many of us today, Eva found that more room was needed, so she added a solarium, an entomology laboratory, and a study to the original 10,000-square-foot home.

Fenyes Mansion tours include a walk through the main door and into the front yard garden.

253

The Fenyes were certainly a mainstay of the Pasadena society elite. Besides being a landowner, Eva Fenyes was also an artist of some note. She made her home the meeting place for the area's creative minds—writers, artists, and business leaders.

The home also served as the Finnish Consulate from 1947 to 1964. Y.A. "George" Paloheimo, the husband of Eva Fenyes' granddaughter Leonora, served as the Finnish consul in southern California, New Mexico, and Arizona. The office he used during his 17 years at the post has been re-created. It even includes the private hotline to the consul general's servant, who, among other tasks, was responsible for preparing Paloheimo's private sauna. The sauna, which has been converted to the Finnish Folk Art Museum, is tucked neatly behind the mansion among the gardens. The tour of the mansion includes a walk through this small but very interesting museum.

Because it is so close to Hollywood and the film industry, the mansion has served as the backdrop for several television shows and movies, including films shot as early as 1912 by the legendary D.W. Griffith. Somewhat more recently, Peter Sellers' *Being There* (1979) was shot at the Fenyes, and with a little bit of Hollywood magic, the mansion has doubled as the White House for *Eleanor and Franklin: The White House Years* (1977) and myriad footage for the NBC drama *The West Wing*.

Besides the beauty of the century-old home, what makes this mansion different from so many others is that it stayed in the family until it was donated to the Pasadena Museum of History in 1970. With only a few minor exceptions, all of the furnishings are original to the home.

Docents lead tours of the home, and they are full of information about the home's history and its furnishings. As with many such mansions that depended on servants, there is an obvious dichotomy between elegance and utility within the home's 18 rooms. Those rooms where the family lived and where callers visited are filled with fine furniture and art. Their walls are covered with beautifully finished hardwoods and silk. But move into the servants' areas and "plain" is what best describes their world. Even the servant side of interior doors that lead to "public" rooms such as the dining room and main foyer, are plain painted or stained soft woods, while the family side are done in expensive hardwoods.

Interior of the Finnish Folk Art Museum

**HOURS:** Docent-led tours (the only way to tour the interior) are offered Wednesday through Sunday, 1:30 PM and 3 PM; reservations are generally needed during summer.

**COST:** House tour only: Adults, $4; 12 and under, free.

**LOCATION:** 470 West Walnut Street, at the corner of West Walnut and Orange Grove Blvd., Pasadena

**PHONE:** 626-577-1660

**WEBSITE:** www.pasadenahistory.org

# 16 The Gamble House

**WHAT'S HERE:** A home, its Craftsman architecture, and nearly all of its furnishings personally designed by famed architects and brothers Charles and Henry Greene

**DON'T MISS THIS:** Guest bathroom that has never required repainting since it was built in 1908

When architecture is discussed, the names Greene and Greene are always mentioned among the prominent leaders of the Arts and Crafts movement. Brothers Charles and Henry Greene's early 20th century blending of function and beauty with the natural environment is most evident in the home that they designed and built in 1908 for David and Mary Gamble of the Procter and Gamble Company. They designed not only the home but the lighting fixtures, much of the furniture, and the decorative hardware as well.

David Gamble was not the founder, but a second-generation member of Procter and Gamble. Following his retirement in 1895, his wife enjoyed spending winters in Pasadena, rather than in their home in Cincinnati. Tired of hotels, in 1907, the couple decided to build a retirement home in Pasadena. Rather than choosing to live along Pasadena's famous Millionaire's Row, the Gambles purchased a lot just a short distance away. It's unknown why they chose Greene and Greene, but the quality of other homes in an area designed by the well-known architects may have been a significant consideration.

Considering the overwhelming amount of detailed handcraftsmanship that was required, it's amazing to think that from the March 1908 groundbreaking, only 10 months passed before the home was completed. Although it would take another two years before all of the custom-designed and built furniture would be completed, David and Mary Gamble and their two younger sons (oldest son, Cecil, was already on his own), along with Mary's unmarried sister, Julia Huggins, moved into the home in 1909. The family made only a few small design modifications to the home, such as exchanging the clear glass windows for windows with a cut glass rosebush design so that their neighbor's kitchen workers couldn't see into the Gambles' dining room.

The kitchen is relatively plain, as was common in such homes, even though by today's standards the solid maple kitchen floor appears fancy. The maple was actually the room's sub-flooring. Linoleum originally covered the maple, because in 1908 linoleum was considered a must-have for anyone of wealth. Rather than tile or stainless steel, the Gambles used sugar pine for the kitchen counters because it helped muffle the kitchen sounds of banging pots and pans.

The family had a guest bedroom and a family guest bedroom, the difference being the location within the home and who was allowed to sleep where. The downstairs guest bedroom was for those who weren't related to the Gambles—their subtle way of telling guests where they stood on the "importance" hierarchy. The upstairs guest bedroom, on the same level as the family's bedrooms, was generally reserved for visiting relatives and very close friends. But even the beds in the guest bedrooms received the same design treatment as the remainder of the home; the nickel-plated beds included rose buds carved into the footboard and headboards of the bed, with sterling silver inlayed features on some of the furniture pieces.

The extraordinary craftsmanship at this National Historical Landmark is evident throughout the home, with fine examples of mortise, tenon, and scarf joints used extensively in the exquisite woodwork. Another example of the extra effort that went into creating the home is evidenced in the guest bathroom. Considering the amount of moisture created in bathrooms and the fact that the guest bathroom has not been repainted since the home's construction in 1908, it remains in relatively good condition. Much of its longevity can be attributed to the original eight coats of white paint that workers applied to the walls following its construction.

The Gambles—and their architects—wanted to make the upstairs bedrooms feel more comfortable and less formal than the downstairs rooms. As such, the upstairs ceilings are 2 inches lower than those downstairs, to make the rooms seem more cozy. Oregon pine is used on the walls, as opposed to the dark Burma teak found downstairs, thus allowing for more color and less formality.

One of the home's only anomalies was Aunt Julia's bedroom. During the late 19th century, it was not uncommon for a woman, if still unmarried by her late 20s, to be considered a spinster. And a spinster often went to live with the sibling best able to care for her. In the case of the Gambles, Mary Gamble's younger sister, Julia Huggins, came to live with them and functioned as part of the family. As was the custom, it was only right that Huggins have her own bedroom, but that created a problem. She had never been to California and refused to believe that California winters did not get as cold as the Midwest winters she had grown up in. She insisted that a Franklin stove replace the fireplace the architects designed into her bedroom. Apparently, she arrived before the stove was installed and discovered that her family was right about the weather. Unable to admit she was wrong, Huggins refused to allow workers to complete the originally planned fireplace, so the unfinished space for the stove remains. She also insisted on bringing her own bed, which didn't match the Greene and Greene home and furniture design, much to their consternation.

David Gamble died in 1923, and Mary passed away in 1929, leaving the home to Cecil, their oldest son. Cecil and his wife, Louise, allowed Aunt Julia to continue living in the home until her death in 1943. In 1945, Cecil put the house on the market, asking $35,000. It didn't sell, so the couple made it their full-time home in 1946. In 1954, Cecil and Louise invited an architecture student from the University of Southern California to photograph the home as one of the premier examples of Greene and Greene's Arts and Craft architecture. This kind gesture began a relationship with the university that continues today; the city of Pasadena now owns the property, while the University of Southern California operates the home.

**HOURS:** Guided one-hour tours, Thursday through Sunday, noon to 3 PM; tours often fill quickly on weekends. Tickets go on sale at 10 AM Thursday through Saturday, and at 11:30 AM on Sunday in the visitor center next to the home.

**COST:** Adults, $8; seniors (65 and over) and students with ID, $5; 12 and under, free, but must be with an adult.

**LOCATION:** 4 Westmoreland Place (parallels the 300 block of North Orange Grove), Pasadena. Limited parking is available directly in front of the home.

**PHONE:** 626-793-3334

**WEBSITE:** www.gamblehouse.org

## *Pomona*

## 17 Wally Parks NHRA Motorsports Museum

**WHAT'S HERE:** Custom cars, drag racers, hot rods, and numerous exhibits filled with the drivers' equipment and promotional posters

**DON'T MISS THIS:** The chance to test your reaction time at the "Christmas tree" start lights

Exemplifying the phrase "the need for speed," the museum, presented by the Automobile Club of Southern California, focuses much of its attention on the West Coast's contributions to custom cars, hot rods, and drag racing. The 28,500-square-foot museum offers abundant space for exhibiting its 80 to 90 vehicles, from garage-built hot rods to drag-racing monsters. For anyone who has ever thought of building a custom rod, this is the museum to visit for ideas.

Like most automotive museums, many of the cars here are on loan and may not be present at any given time. Many owners temporarily remove their pride and joys for auto shows and periodic runs to different parts of the country, such as "Hot August Nights," held in Reno each year. The museum has several cars that exemplify the 1950s craze for what became known as "Frenched" headlights and taillights and other radical design changes. A late 1940s Ford or Chevy is chopped, lowered, and many of its parts, from the engine to its taillights and hubcaps, are often taken from other car manufacturers if they better match whatever the owner has envisioned for his ride.

Drag racing is one of those pastimes that began in the 1940s when young men, eager to go fast enough to keep up with their pulsating testosterone, began modifying those early six and eight-cylinder Ford and Chevy engines. They headed out to lightly used country roads and held their own impromptu races. Things began to change in 1950, when C.J. "Pappy" Hart, the father of modern drag-racing, opened the first commercial drag strip in the country in Orange County. His drag strip closed in 1959, ultimately becoming today's John Wayne International Airport. During his career, Hart ran other drag-racing enterprises, and following his "retirement," he went to work for the National Hot Rod Association's Safety Safari, which traveled to different races, emphasizing the need for safety in racing. He was given a special golf cart for his race track duties, and that cart is part of the museum's collection—not fast, but cute.

The museum features many of those early drag-racing cars, but also has lots of the big-guy drag racers—cars owned and raced by some of the biggest names in drag racing. One of those is the black beauty owned by Don "The Snake" Prudhomme. His 1968, 398-cubic-inch, super-charged Chrysler motor pushed this dragster to over 196 miles per hour down the traditional quarter-mile strip of asphalt raceway.

Nearly every wall in the museum, including a center divider wall, features exhibit cases. The exhibits contain just about everything one could think of related to racing, from racing posters, tickets, and buttons, to racing team jackets and race car drivers' helmets and uniforms. There are engines and engine parts, all from the racing world. And if you feel as though a static exhibit needs a bit of action, there's a big-screen television that shows various drag races from around the country.

For those wanting to test their reaction skills, the museum has a "Christmas tree," the sequential starting lights used at all drag races. Visitors can try their hands—or feet—to see how fast they can

Wally Parks NHRA Motorsports Museum

punch the gas pedal when the green light flashes on. Stomp the gas pedal too early and you get disqualified. There's a timer that will tell you just how fast your reactions are.

The museum also includes a few very quick motorcycles like the 1997, 1500 c.c. Suzuki that managed to run the quarter-mile strip at 189.27 miles per hour in 7.245 seconds. There are a few vehicles that ran on the Bonneville salt flats, designed strictly for attaining maximum speeds. One of the earliest is from 1951, the roadster powered by a Ford flathead that ran at 146.8 miles per hour. A few years later, another car in the museum's collection hit 313 miles per hour, and the speeds only went up from there. The museum tells the entire story.

**HOURS:** Wednesday through Sunday, 10 AM to 5 PM. Closed Easter, Thanksgiving, and Christmas.

**COST:** Adults, $5; seniors (60 and older) and ages 6–15, $3.

**LOCATION:** Los Angeles County Fairgrounds, Gate 1, 1101 W. McKinley Ave., Pomona

**PHONE:** 909-622-2133

**WEBSITE:** museum.nhra.com

## San Marino

# 18 Huntington Museum

**WHAT'S HERE:** Impressive art collection, including some by European and American masters, along with rare manuscripts such as an original Gutenberg Bible

**DON'T MISS THIS:** A walk through the expansive "gardens of the world"

There aren't many museums in the world that can surpass the Huntington Museum's elegant historic buildings and the art treasures they hold. Henry Edwards Huntington—the man partially responsible for gathering much of the vast collections held at what was once his home—was born in 1850. At age 22, he went to work for his uncle, Collis P. Huntington, one of the "Big Four" owners of the Central Pacific Railroad. Twenty years later, Henry moved to San Francisco to help manage the Southern Pacific Railroad. On his way there, he stopped in San Marino to visit the estate of J. DeBarth Shorb, which he later purchased. That estate would eventually become his home and museum.

In 1902, Huntington moved his operations to Los Angeles, where, among other business enterprises, he expanded the city's electric railway, a move that further prompted population growth. This growth only accelerated his profits, derived from the water and power businesses, as well as the land he owned and developed. So pervasive and in demand was he in the business world, Huntington at one time served simultaneously on 60 corporate boards.

When Huntington reached age 60, he retired and dedicated his life to collecting art and landscaping his 600-acre ranch. He sold about half the acreage shortly after his retirement, and in 1910, workers completed his new home, the Beaux Arts mansion that is now the Huntington Gallery. In retirement, Huntington decided to wed. In 1913, he married Arabella Duval Huntington. Although she was his uncle Collis Huntington's widow, Arabella was also Henry's age.

Arabella Huntington also enjoyed collecting, and her interest was art. With the money inherited from her late husband, joined with the fortune that her new husband had accumulated, she was free to purchase just about anything that caught her fancy. And purchase she did. Arabella was the person most responsible for collecting much of the best art pieces that the museum owns today. Henry's primary interest was in collecting rare books and manuscripts. His collection had grown so extensively that in 1920 he built a separate library on the grounds to house the collection.

In 1919, the Huntingtons transferred their San Marino property and the collections to a nonprofit educational trust. This marked the beginning of the Huntington Library, Art Collections, and Botanical Gardens. Arabella died in 1924, and Henry followed in 1927. Both are buried on the property in a mausoleum designed by John Russell Pope, who also helped design the Jefferson Memorial in Washington, DC.

It is very easy to spend several hours here, just wandering in the expansive gardens that cover 150 acres on the west and south sides of the property. The Asian-themed gardens include a Chinese garden, Japanese house and garden, and a wonderful Zen garden. Behind the Zen garden wall is one of the most expansive and beautiful bonsai gardens anywhere in California.

Pathways allow you to wander through the subtropical garden located near the top of the hill, down to the Australian garden and through the lily ponds and jungle gardens. The desert garden is tucked into the southeast corner, with trails leading up to the palm garden. Besides having one of the largest collections of camellias in the world, the museum's rose gardens are also quite exquisite and extensive.

Most people come for the art, and it's no wonder, considering the expansive collection maintained inside the three large galleries and a fourth that features changing exhibits. While most visitors flock to view two of the museum's most famous paintings, Thomas Gainsborough's *The Blue Boy* (circa 1770) and Sir Thomas

The Huntington estate includes several buildings.

Lawrence's *Pinkie* (1794), the galleries hold even more surprises. The Huntington collection of American paintings span well over 200 years, with works from the 1730s through the 1930s. Arabella's favorites are housed in the library's west wing and include Renaissance paintings, along with sculpture, furniture, tapestries, and fine porcelain.

Huntington's library houses Henry's collection of rare books and manuscripts and also serves as a research source for scholars from around the world. While visitors will never have the opportunity to view what scholars have access to, what is on public display is absolutely magnificent. There is a rare manuscript of Chaucer's *Canterbury Tales*, a Gutenberg Bible printed on vellum, and the oversize "double-elephant" folio of *Audubon's Birds of America*.

**HOURS:** Tuesday through Friday, noon to 4:30 PM; Saturday and Sunday, 10:30 AM to 4:30 PM; between Memorial Day and Labor Day, daily, 10:30 AM to 4:30 PM. Closed Monday and major holidays.
**COST:** Adults, $15; 65 and over, $12; ages 12–18, $10; 6–11, $6.
**LOCATION:** 1151 Oxford Road, San Marino
**PHONE:** 626-405-2100
**WEBSITE:** www.huntington.org

## San Pedro

# 19 Los Angeles Maritime Museum

**WHAT'S HERE:** Maritime history exhibits on everything from early sailing ships to working underwater

**DON'T MISS THIS:** The bridge of the World War II heavy cruiser *USS Los Angeles*

Beginning in 1941, the Municipal Ferry Terminal served thousands of people needing transportation to east San Pedro's Terminal Island canneries and military bases, and connections to other destinations. The ferry closed in 1963, put out of business by the Vincent Thomas Bridge. Today, the historic ferry building serves thousands of people once again, but now as a museum of maritime history.

The museum features dozens of ship models, some of them significantly larger and more detailed than those in many smaller maritime museums. The models include a twin-mast sailing ship that is perhaps 15 feet long, with sails about the same height. There is also a model of the *SS Poseidon*, built at ⅛-inch scale from plans for the *RMS Queen Mary*. The 22-foot-long model ship, which was used for the 1970s movie *The Poseidon Adventure*, cost $30,000 to build. Propelled by a battery-powered motor, the model's only official cruising was done in a 300-foot-long tank at the 20th Century Fox Studios. But there are a few smaller boats inside the museum as well, including a Yurok Indian dugout canoe and a beautiful 15-foot fishing boat, hand built out of mahogany and camphor wood in Thailand in about 1967.

Inside one of the galleries is the remnant ferry access doorway, and the bridge from the *USS Los Angeles*, a Baltimore-class heavy cruiser commissioned in July 1945. The 674-foot-long ship was smaller than a battleship but larger than a destroyer. She missed action in World War II but spent time off the coast of China and in the South China Sea. The *Los Angeles* served two tours of duty during the Korean War, firing 25,000 rounds from her guns at enemy shore positions, at one point establishing the record for the longest sustained bombardment ever carried out by an American ship. The *Los Angeles* was also the first US Navy vessel to take enemy fire during the war. Refitted several times over the years, the *Los Angeles* was finally decommissioned in 1963, and in 1975 was towed into San Pedro Harbor's Terminal Island and turned into scrap. Various pieces of the ship were saved from the scrap pile and are now displayed in the museum.

The museum also has a large exhibit of maritime-related tools from previous centuries used for repairing ropes and canvas sails, drilling holes, and fixing holes in the wooden hulls. There is navigational equipment such as sextants and quadrants, chronometers and compasses. Working the docks is something seldom addressed in most maritime museums, but here you will find a collection of various dock tools used to help ease the hard work before the advent of motorized equipment and lifts. They include numerous hooks, all with slightly different designs: general cargo hooks, a cotton hook, a dockman hook, and jitney hook. Unfortunately, there is no description of how the hooks were used, but the knowledgeable docents often wandering the floor are available to answer questions like this one.

Other volunteers include the members of the amateur radio club who work on the museum's second floor near an exhibit of several old radio transmitters. There are usually club members at their radios talking on the marine bands to people around the world.

Downstairs, below the ramp to the second level, an exhibit covers the history of the commercial diving business in southern California. The exhibit includes old hard-hat diving suits, pumps, ropes, and other related equipment. With commercial fishing being a major business

The Los Angeles Maritime Museum

for the port, another exhibit documents the San Pedro fishing industry. Outside the museum, there are great views of the busy harbor. And if you happen to get lucky, the museum's World War II-era tugboat may be operating, giving tours of the harbor's ever-changing ship traffic.

**HOURS:** Tuesday through Saturday, 10 AM to 5 PM; Sunday, noon to 5 PM (last entry at 4:30 PM). Closed Thanksgiving and the Friday following, Christmas and New Year's Day, and occasionally on other holidays, so call to confirm.

**COST:** Adults, $3; youth and seniors, $1; children, free.

**LOCATION:** Berth 84, at the foot of 6th Street, San Pedro

**PHONE:** 310-548-7618

**WEBSITE:** www.lamaritimemuseum.org

## *Whittier*

## 20 Pio Pico State Historic Park

**WHAT'S HERE:** Restored home, museum, and gardens of Mexico's last governor of Alta California

**DON'T MISS THIS:** The short video on the history of Pio Pico

Pio de Jesus Pico IV's home and its surrounding ranch were originally named El Ranchito (Little Ranch). When he purchased the land in 1848, his "little ranch" included almost 9000 acres. By 1855, Pio Pico and his brother controlled 532,000 acres, making him one of the richest men in California. Not bad for a man who was born into poverty, only to become Mexico's last California governor.

As governor, Pico supported a California that was free of most of Mexico's control, and that didn't always sit well with Mexico City. After the Americans invaded his country, he fled to Mexico to avoid capture, but he returned following the Treaty of Guadalupe Hidalgo that granted California to the US in 1848. That is when he purchased El Ranchito, became a successful businessman, and even was elected to the Los Angeles City Council. Unfortunately, Pico never learned to speak English, and his dealings with unscrupulous American businessmen ultimately caused him to lose his fortune and his home. He died in poverty in 1894, while living with his daughter in Los Angeles.

Following Pico's loss of his rancho, the old adobe home that he built in 1853 was abandoned and fell into disrepair. The gardens and orchards died, and gone was the home that exemplified the lifestyles of early well-to-do southern Californians. Fortunately, the old adobe was saved from development pressures during the early 1900s, and in 1917, it was deeded to the state of California. In 1927, when the "modern" state park system was formed, Pio Pico became one of California's first state historic parks.

Today, the home has been repaired and portions reconstructed, a job made more difficult because of the serious damage the adobe structure sustained from a major earthquake in 1987 and again during the 1994 Northridge quake. What was considered a "mansion" owned by one of the richest men in southern California during much of the 1860s to 1880s is now a partially restored historic home and museum. The two-level adobe house, something not commonly seen during the 19th century, served as a home for Pico, his wife, and their two adopted children. They hosted many guests on a regular basis. During their stays, and during Pico's more prosperous years, guests were expected to do nothing more than relax and enjoy themselves, and they paid for nothing.

Inside the adobe is a small room where a film is shown about Pico's life. It provides a good overview of the life of the last governor of Mexican California. There are also several exhibits in the main entry room, including a look at all the work that has gone into reconstructing the historic adobe. There are no photographs of the adobe while Pico lived here, so what is known about the interior furnishings is based on written descriptions by those who had visited the home during the last part of the 19th century.

A copy of a portrait painted of Pico in about 1880 is on display. The artist is unknown, but it may have been painted by Paul Petrovits, who, in 1876, filed suit against Pico for apparently not paying him for a portrait that the former governor had ordered. Pico ultimately settled the claim.

The original adobe went through numerous changes, including repairs after the nearby San Gabriel River flooded a portion of the house. Some of those early remodels can be seen, such as the plugged fireplace in one of the rooms. Pico likely made upgrades to the fireplaces, replacing them with cast-iron stoves, a more efficient way to heat the home. Another of the rooms is the small kitchen area that includes traditional Mexican cooking appliances such as the horno oven, located behind the house. Gardens, fruit trees, and a small vineyard have been restored. The grounds also include picnic tables.

Adobe home of California's last
Mexican governor, Pio Pico

**HOURS:** Park is open Wednesday through Sunday, 10 AM to 5 PM; house tours, Wednesday through Friday, every hour from 1 PM to 3 PM; Saturday and Sunday, tours are at 10 AM, 11 AM, 1 PM, 2 PM, and 3 PM. Closed Thanksgiving, Christmas, and New Year's Day.

**COST:** Free

**LOCATION:** 6003 Pioneer Blvd., Whittier

**PHONE:** 562-695-1217

**WEBSITE:** www.piopico.org

# Wilmington

## 21 Banning Residence Museum

**WHAT'S HERE:** Furnished home that the Banning family lived in for 60 years

**DON'T MISS THIS:** The stagecoach barn out back

Andrew Jackson was president of the US when Phineas Banning was born in 1830. Banning, among his many business endeavors, was most responsible for construction of the LA Harbor in San Pedro. He always seemed to know where he was headed and wasted little time moving out on his own. At age 13, Banning left his Delaware home and went to work for an older brother's law firm in Philadelphia. At age 21, he headed to California with his employer, carrying goods bound for the Golden State. Choosing to cross the isthmus jungles rather than sailing around the Horn proved a fatal mistake for his employer, who died along the way and left Banning alone and with no money. Banning still had to sail 3000 miles to his landing point in San Pedro Bay. Soon after arriving in San Pedro, Banning started his own stage and freight lines in the Los Angeles area, gaining both the financial and political clout needed to embark on even bigger dreams.

Over the next 30 years, Banning built his own speculative real estate company and was instrumental in developing the Port of Los Angeles, constructing protective breakwaters and dredging the shallow mud-bottomed basin to a usable depth. He built canals to float his own goods to the railheads that he owned and that connected with the Southern Pacific Railroad's tracks, which he helped bring to the area. Banning also expanded his very extensive line of stage and freight routes between Los Angeles, San Bernardino, and Fort Yuma.

Banning built the finest home on one of the parcels he owned through his Wilmington land-development business. Today, the 23-room Greek Revival home sits near the center of a 20-acre park, and it resides, appropriately, on the lists of city, state, and national historic landmarks. The Banning family lived in the home for 60 years, and since then, the now city-owned historic property has undergone restoration and refurnishing.

The entry hallway extends the length of the home, providing cross ventilation through the first floor during those hot summer days. It was a popular spot in the house during Banning's many parties, which he called "regales." With quality office space near his businesses apparently not to his liking, Banning used part of his home as a very elegant office, befitting his social standing. The restored office contains documents related directly to him, including his commission into the California State Militia of the National Guard, where he became a general. Banning was elected to the state senate in 1865, and his signature, along with every other senator's signature, is on a copy of the document that ratified the 13th Amendment to the US Constitution and freed the country's slaves.

The home's beautiful parlor is both distinctive and elegant, a room that displays family treasures, items that were difficult and quite expensive to obtain before the coming of the transcontinental railroad. The crystal and brass chandelier is one of those treasures that likely came around the Horn by ship, as did the French Rococo Revival furniture, with its fancy scrolls, shell, and floral carvings.

Throughout the home's 23 rooms, it is obvious that Banning enjoyed the fruits of his labor, as he artfully displayed his Victorian-style furnishings. From the hand-carved fireplace mantels and crystal chandeliers, to the dining room's elegant mahogany table, to his master bedroom's huge mahogany bed and the armoire, a present from Mexican General Mariano Vallejo (see Lachryma Montis, page 36), 19th century luxury was ever-present in his life.

As should be expected, the plainest room in the house was the kitchen, which, during the early years, was not even part of the main home, but was later moved in. The original wood stove was converted to gas and an icebox served to keep cold things cold, when ice was available—not easy in southern California. Ice had to be brought down regularly from the high Sierra.

Tours of the home include the adjacent stagecoach barn that contains a large collection of historic wagons and coaches, most belonging to the Banning family. There are also tools used by wheelwrights and blacksmiths to build and repair wagons.

**HOURS:** Tours are Tuesday through Thursday, hourly, 12:30 PM to 2:30 PM; Saturday and Sunday, hourly, 12:30 PM to 3:30 PM. Closed July 4, Thanksgiving, Christmas, and New Year's Day.

**COST:** $5 donation requested.

**LOCATION:** 401 East M Street, Wilmington

**PHONE:** 310-548-7777

**WEBSITE:** www.banningmuseum.org

# Los Angeles County Tours

**T**

## Old Movie Stars Tour

**ESTIMATED DAYS:** 3–4

**ESTIMATED DRIVING MILES:** 180

In LA, many people will try to sell you tours or maps directing you to the homes of current movie stars, but those tours will only let you see the facade of the homes—and sometimes not even that. It's much more fun to tour the interiors of homes that belonged to some of Hollywood's earliest stars. Although it's his final resting place, not his home, the **Ronald Reagan Presidential Library and Museum** (page 217, in the Central Coast region) is a good place to start. The focus here is on Reagan's political life, but there's also much dealing with his movie career. From his Simi Valley museum, it's about 30 miles to Newhall via Hwy. 118 east to I-5 north, where the home of silent western film star **William S. Hart** (page 249) sits atop a hill. His first ranch-house-turned-movie-set is at the bottom of the hill near the parking lot. There's a 10- to 15-minute walk to the top of the hill were his mansion sits. Following the Hart mansion, your next stop is at singing cowboy star

William S. Hart Mansion

Gene Autry's **Museum of the American West** (page 241), about 22 miles away in Griffith Park, near I-5. It's the best museum dedicated to the American cowboy you'll find anywhere, with both the authentic and the Hollywood versions well represented.

Cowboys of one sort or another seem to be the theme here, so it's off to Pacific Palisades by taking I-5 south to I-10, then west to the Pacific Coast Hwy. and **Will Rogers State Historic Park** (page 251). The cowboy philosopher won over the country with his homespun humor—and his ranch house home is where Hollywood stars now visit on occasional weekends with their horses to play polo.

The last stop, **Leo Carrillo Ranch Historic Park** (page 284), will take the longest to get to, as it is south of Los Angeles in the coastal city of Carlsbad, about 105 miles away via I-10 east then I-5 south. This is actually located in the South Coast and Desert region. Once the working ranch home of another cowboy actor, Leo Carrillo (better known as Pancho, the Cisco Kid's sidekick), the ranch features many of the original buildings, including his home, and a visitor center that plays the old *Cisco Kid* television series—originally filmed in color.

# Historic Mansion Tour

**ESTIMATED DAYS:** 4–5
**ESTIMATED DRIVING MILES:** 130

Los Angeles County is California's mansion central. Most remain in the hands of Hollywood stars, movie moguls, and other members of the rich-and-famous club, but several that were private residences are now public museums. Head to Malibu for a tour of the **Adamson House** (page 245), now a state park, but beginning in the 1920s, when it was built, it was the beach home of a very successful landowner and local businessman. The home's extensive custom tile work is exquisite. While in Malibu, stop by the **Getty Villa** (reservations required; page 231), which houses primarily the antiquity portion of the extensive Getty art collection.

From Malibu, it's about 40 miles to Pasadena and the **Fenyes Mansion** (page 253). It's best to refer to a map to get here, and the driving time will depend on freeway traffic. This fully furnished mansion is typical of the early mansions that graced Pasadena's famous nearby "Millionaire's Row." The Beaux Arts mansion was owned by a woman, which was unusual in 1906 when Eva Fenyes had it built. A couple blocks away is **The Gamble House** (page 255), one of the finest examples of Arts and Crafts-style homes. It was designed and its construction overseen by the architectural style's leaders, Charles and Henry Greene, who even designed the home's interior furnishings.

From Pasadena, its just over 6 miles to San Marino to what was once a home but now serves as one of southern

One of several Huntington Museum garden themes

California's finest museums. The **Huntington Museum** (page 259), can easily be an all-day visit. The main house was built by the nephew of Collis P. Huntington, one of the "Big Four" founders of the Central Pacific Railroad. Today, there are few homes that rival the Beaux Arts mansion he had built in 1910.

From Huntington's expansive home, gardens, and art collections, it's time for a 30-mile drive to Long Beach, where two mansions await. But, if you have time, take a slight detour to the City of Industry, about 16 miles away near Hwy 60, to the **Workman and Temple Family Homestead** (page 225). The Temple's mansion, La Casa Nueva, is well worth the time it takes to visit.

From Industry, it's about 26 miles to **Los Cerritos Ranch House** (page 229), located in Long Beach about 1.5 miles northeast from where the 405 and 610 freeways cross. This is one of California's oldest mansions; the two-story adobe was built in 1844. Eight miles away on the opposite side of Long Beach is **Rancho Los Alamitos** (page 227), a 19th century adobe filled with many of the last owner's furnishings and personal items, mostly western-ranch style. Outside, be sure to take time and walk through the expansive gardens. They are quite impressive, especially the cactus garden.

# Family/Kids Weekend Tour

**ESTIMATED DAYS:** 2–3
**ESTIMATED DRIVING MILES:** 20

Kids likely have other ideas about where to go—Disneyland, Universal Studios, the beach—while visiting the LA area, but there are some museums that even the most jaded youngster will enjoy. Anyone even remotely interested in the Old West will thoroughly love singing cowboy Gene Autry's **Museum of the American West** (page 241). And when their energy levels exceed your ability to keep the kids corralled, the **Los Angeles Zoo** (323-644-4200; www.lazoo.org) is literally just across the parking lot.

If that doesn't work, take a trip downtown to Wilshire Blvd. and the **Page Museum at La Brea Tar Pits** (page 235), which is certain to be a hit, with its skeletons and skulls of the thousands of huge animals that were sucked into the depths of the bubbling tar.

From tar pits to pit stops, it's just a few blocks walk west on Wilshire Blvd. to the **Petersen Automotive Museum**

Museum of the American West trail drive cookin'

(page 237). Three floors of exhibits feature cars, trucks, and a few motorcycles, from the automobile's earliest days through some of its quirkiest designs to modern race cars. And because it's in LA, there are a number of movie star cars here—those that have been owned by stars such as Nicolas Cage, and those that have starred in their own movies such as the Batmobile and Herbie.

One last LA adventure for kids is the **Natural History Museum of Los Angeles County** (page 239), which sits in a complex of several other museums. This amazing museum, located about 10 miles away from the auto museum and tar pits, features everything from birds and mammals to valuable gems and the world's rarest shark, a 15-foot-long Megamouth, stuck in a vat of preservative.

A hot rod in the making at the Petersen Automotive Museum

# Los Angeles County
# Travel Information Centers

Los Angeles Convention & Visitors Bureau
www.lacvb.com
213-624-7300

Long Beach Area Convention & Visitors Bureau
www.visitlongbeach.com
562-436-3645 or 800-452-7829

Pasadena Convention & Visitors Bureau
www.pasadenacal.org
626-805-4604 or 800-307-7977

San Fernando Valley Conference & Visitors Bureau
www.visitvalleyofthestars.org
818-379-7000

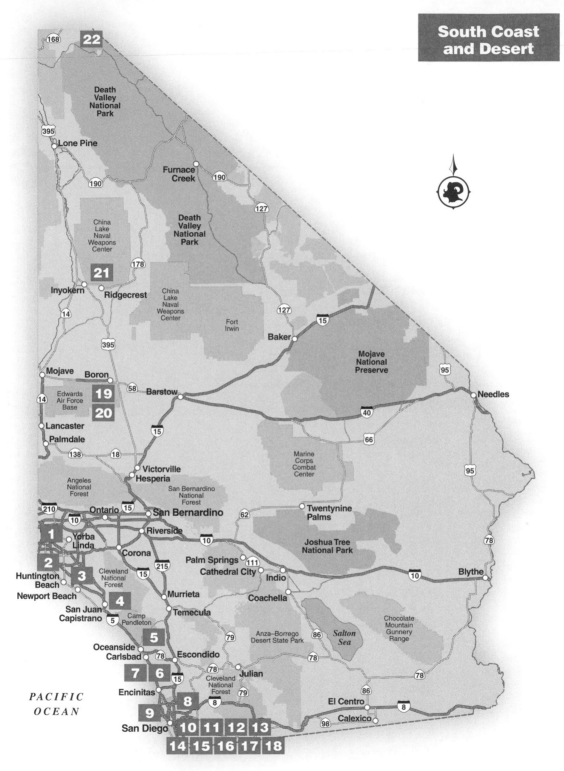

168

**22**

Death Valley National Park

395

● Lone Pine

Furnace Creek ●

190

190

127

China Lake Naval Weapons Center

Death Valley National Park

178

**21**

Inyokern ●

Ridgecrest ●

China Lake Naval Weapons Center

Fort Irwin

127

15

Baker ●

14

395

Mojave ●  Boron ●

Edwards Air Force Base

**19**
**20**

58

Barstow ●

Mojave National Preserve

95

Needles ●

14

Lancaster ●
Palmdale ●

15

40

66

138  18

Victorville ●
Hesperia ●

Angeles National Forest

San Bernardino National Forest

Marine Corps Combat Center

95

210

Ontario ●

15

San Bernardino ●

62

Twentynine Palms ●

78

10

**1**  Yorba Linda ●

Riverside ●

Joshua Tree National Park

**2**

Corona ●

10

Huntington Beach ●
Newport Beach ●

**3**

Cleveland National Forest

15

215

Palm Springs ●
Cathedral City ●

111

Blythe ●

San Juan Capistrano ●

**4**

Murrieta ●

Indio ●

10

Camp Pendleton

Temecula ●

Coachella ●

5

**5**

79

Anza–Borrego Desert State Park

86

*Salton Sea*

Chocolate Mountain Gunnery Range

Oceanside ●
Carlsbad ●

78

Escondido ●

78

**7**  **6**

15

78

Julian ●

*PACIFIC OCEAN*

Encinitas ●

Cleveland National Forest

79

78

**9**

**8**

8

El Centro ●

86

8

San Diego ●

98

Calexico ●

**10**  **11**  **12**  **13**

**14**  **15**  **16**  **17**  **18**

# South Coast and Desert

**M**ost people think of California's South Coast as the surfing capital of the world, but it's much more than that. From a historical perspective, San Diego is where the Spanish established their first mission and presidio. Even after the mission system was essentially closed by the Mexican government in 1833, life in San Diego was slow. A few homes, such as La Casa de Estudillo, had been built in what is today Old Town San Diego State Historic Park. All that changed forever on July 29, 1846 when US Marines, from the sloop-of-war *Cyane*, landed and raised the US flag over the small coastal town.

Although San Diego was slow getting started, it is today the second largest city in California. In 1870, when the city set aside 1440 acres that would one day become Balboa

The *Star of India* is moored at the Maritime Museum of San Diego

Park, it became the first city west of the Mississippi to establish an urban park. Today, Balboa Park is home to most of San Diego's museums, including the Museum of Man, the Air and Space Museum, the Museum of Art, the Automotive Museum, and many more.

North of San Diego, along the Orange Coast, surfing is king, as the International Surfing Museum in Huntington Beach demonstrates. Miles of sandy beaches, combined with warm weather, warm water, and great waves, have made places like Huntington Beach icons for generations of surfers.

While cooling Pacific winds moderate San Diego and Orange Coast's dry weather, the ocean's breezes are absent from the inland deserts. Here, summer temperatures soar into triple digits almost daily, and its thousands of square miles of sand and rock, cactus and scrub brush may see only a few inches of rain each winter. But those few inches can result in explosions of brilliantly colored spring wildflowers across vast expanses of the desert.

During the early years of California's history, the deserts were seen as nothing more than dry, desolate, and dangerous lands that settlers were forced to cross. But once minerals such as borax were discovered, the inhospitality of the desert was overlooked as mines opened in some the hottest lands in the world. The Twenty Mule Team Museum attests to the harshness of the desert and the benefits that mining brought to local economies and distant customers. The modern US military is always in need of places to develop and test new weapons, and the US Naval Museum of Armament and Technology at China Lake provides a look at another use of California's desert mountains. There were a few people who enjoyed 120-degree summer days and chose to live in places like Death Valley. Scotty's Castle tells the story of one of those characters.

From ocean beaches to desert sand and the forest-covered mountains in between, there is something in California's southland for everyone. And there are plenty of missions, mansions, and museums here that illustrate the vast riches that have attracted people here for well over 200 years.

## TRIVIA

1 Which mission celebrates the return of the swallows each spring?

2 Which museum features the works of Jan and Dean, who sold 20 million records between 1960 and 1966?

3 Where can you see America's first successful commercial airliner?

4 At which museum can you board and tour the actual ship used in the movie *Master and Commander*?

5 Which museum features bombs and explosions as part of its day-to-day activities?

6 Name the museum where you can see California's largest model train exhibit.

7 What is California's oldest town and now one of its largest cities?

8 Name California's first mission.

9 Which museum features a car that was driven nonstop across the country in 1952?

*For trivia answers, see page 331.*

# 1 Richard Nixon Presidential Library and Birthplace

**WHAT'S HERE:** The museum covers Nixon's formative years and his life in politics; just outside the museum is his childhood home.

**DON'T MISS THIS:** Astronaut Buzz Aldrin's moon boot tracks in the concrete near the reflecting pool

This presidential museum is unique in that it is right next door to Richard Nixon's birthplace. Far from being considered a mansion, Nixon's small family home, sitting on the exact spot where it was built, illustrates that US presidents need not come from wealthy backgrounds. Whether you remember Nixon and agreed or disagreed with the ways he wielded his presidential power, his presidential library, museum, gorgeous gardens, and childhood home where he was born in 1913 offer a walk through an important and often tumultuous time in American history.

A good way to begin a first visit to the museum is to view the 28-minute movie on Nixon's career, *Never Give Up: Richard Nixon in the Arena*. Nixon wasn't always in the news or one of Washington's power brokers. During his early years in Washington, he was dubbed the "greenest congressman in town." But that changed during Nixon's first term, when he was asked to sit on the House Committee for Un-American Activities, which sought to identify and eliminate anyone believed to have real or often perceived connections with Communism. Nixon came to the forefront of the news when Alger Hiss was brought before the committee.

Historical research requires primary sources such as personal letters in order to more accurately describe events, emotions, and the strategies employed by the movers and shakers. The museum offers several binders filled with primary resources—Nixon's written correspondence, including personal letters to Jackie Kennedy Onassis, to his own daughter on her wedding day, and his words of advice to an up-and-coming politician named Ronald Reagan. For fans of presidential ephemera, one gallery features campaign literature, signs, and buttons from many of Nixon's political campaigns.

Vietnam was a major factor in Nixon's election to the presidency. An exhibit explores some of the political ramifications of Nixon's actions during the war. The exhibit doesn't shy away from the more gruesome and secret operations of the war, from the demonstrations, riots, and Kent State killings in the US to the Cambodian incursions, the 1972 Christmas bombings, and the 1969 My Lai massacre. Videos playing throughout the museum show Nixon in action, including his famous "Silent Majority" speech and how he, if elected president, could bring an honorable end to the war in Vietnam. There is even an exhibit on the US POWs held in North Vietnam.

All heads of state, especially presidents, receive thousands of gifts from other heads of state and from the rich, the famous, and the general public. Nixon was no different. Several of those gifts are displayed and include vases, art pieces, and a jewelry box received in 1973 from Leonid Brezhnev, who, at the time, was the general secretary of the Russian communist party.

There is another special gift that Nixon received. For those who have never seen the original Declaration of Independence in Washington, DC, the Nixon Library offers an opportunity to see the next best thing. In 1820, with the original document deteriorating, John Quincy Adams commissioned the engraving of copies. On July 4, 1823, 200 facsimiles engraved on parchment from a copper plate were issued to various government officials and to surviving signers of the original Declaration of Independence. Only 32 are known to exist, and the one that was gifted to Nixon is exhibited in the museum.

In 1969, *Apollo 11* faithfully took its soon-to-be famous crew to the moon, where mission commander Neil Armstrong first stepped on the lunar surface, with pilot Buzz Aldrin not far behind. Because there was great concern over whether they could actually return safely, Nixon prepared both a congratulatory speech and a condolences speech. Both are on display, and the latter is an interesting read. It says, in part: "In ancient days men looked at stars and saw their heroes in the constellations. In modern times we do the much the same, but our heroes are epic men of flesh and blood."

On the lighter side, there is a story about a celebrity named Elvis Presley who walked into Nixon's White House office with a gun. In this case, it was a chrome-plated, World War II-era Colt .45 that the singer presented to Nixon as a gift. The pistol is exhibited for all to see, including the Secret Service, who were somewhat embarrassed at their lapse in security.

Watergate was Nixon's downfall and one of the last exhibits deals with this presidential and national crisis. The exhibit provides a balanced look at the mistakes that the president and his closest advisers made, along with Nixon's wise decision, facing certain impeachment, to voluntarily step down from arguably the most powerful political position in the world.

Outside the main museum is a beautiful garden and reflecting pool, and, if you know where to look, you can see the cement imprints made by *Apollo 11* astronaut Buzz Aldrin wearing a pair of his original moon boots. A very short walk beyond the reflecting pool are the graves of Nixon and First Lady Pat Nixon, and just past that is the house where the country's 37th president was born.

Frank Nixon built their simple farm home from a catalog kit in 1912, the year before his son Richard was born. With the exception of sprinkler and alarm systems, the house remains as it was in the early 20th century. Many of the furnishings are original to the home and to the family, including the bed where the future president was born and the piano that he played.

The museum is also home to the "Flying Oval Office." The 6-ton Sikorsky Sea King, which carried presidents Kennedy, Johnson, Nixon, and Ford, is on permanent display at the museum. The helicopter was used by presidents

The "Flying Oval Office" during Nixon's presidency

and first ladies, cabinet officials, and heads-of-state on trips around the world, including to Vietnam, so Nixon could have a bird's-eye view of combat zones. Positioned just a few yards away from the front door of Nixon's birthplace, the helicopter is accessible to the public, but it is not wheelchair accessible.

There are additional rooms and galleries to see around the main museum and library, including a full-sized reproduction of the White House East Room, dubbed American's Grand Ballroom. It is the largest room in the White House. There is also a large gallery that features changing exhibits throughout the year.

**HOURS:** Monday through Saturday, 10 AM to 5 PM; Sunday, 11 AM to 5 PM. Closed Thanksgiving and Christmas.

**COST:** Adults, $7.95; seniors (over 62) and military with ID $5.95; students, $4.95; 7–11, $3; 6 and under, free.

**LOCATION:** 18001 Yorba Linda Blvd., Yorba Linda

**PHONE:** 714-993-3393

**WEBSITE:** www.nixonfoundation.org

# 2 International Surfing Museum

**WHAT'S HERE:** Surfing memorabilia from surfboards to the music and guitar of "King of Surf Guitar" Dick Dale

**DON'T MISS THIS:** Video being played from the timeless film *The Endless Summer* and the '60s surfing music

With miles of sandy beaches and waves perfect for surfing, Huntington Beach is also known as Surf City USA, a name the city has now trademarked. During the 1960s, music groups such as the Beach Boys, Jan and Dean, and the Chantays put Huntington Beach on the map and surfing into the world's consciousness, even for people who had never seen an ocean and never would. Therefore, it seems only appropriate that if a non-island city is to have a museum dedicated to the ancient Hawaiian sport of surfing, it should be located in Huntington Beach.

International Surfing Museum

277

When you wind through the side streets of Huntington Beach, don't look for a huge museum structure. There isn't one. Instead, take 5th Street about two blocks back from the Pacific Coast Hwy. to Olive Ave., and look for a quaint little white building with a large surfing-related mural painted on its wall.

Inside the museum, a lot of history is stuffed into a very small amount of space. A bust of Hawaii's famed Duke Kahanamoku is one of the most prominent exhibits. The Duke, a champion Olympic swimmer in 1912 and 1920, began his competitive swimming career in Honolulu Harbor, where, the first time he raced, he beat the existing 100-meter world record. He went on to win gold at the Olympics, and then, with his 10-foot-long redwood surfboard, popularized surfing for the world. The exhibits include photos of the Duke, along with some of his many trophies and surfboards.

If any one thing exemplifies the surf culture, it has to be the music, and surf music takes a starring role in the museum, which has in its collection the very first guitar that belonged to the "King of the Surf Guitar," Dick Dale. You can also see some of Jan and Dean's gold records. With hit songs like *Surf City*, *Little Old Lady from Pasadena*, and *Deadman's Curve*, the duo sold more than 20 million records between 1960 and 1966.

The 1960s surfing craze was the perfect time for a young filmmaker named Bruce Brown to show the magic of surfing on film. The famous poster of three surfers with their boards on the beach, and the setting sun dropping below the ocean, personified the essence of Brown's hit film, *The Endless Summer*. Not exactly rich, Brown and his two surfing companions traveled the world with their surfboards and a single Bolex camera in its watertight case, capturing incredible surfing footage. The Bolex camera resides in the museum's collection, along with clips from the 1966 movie.

As early as the 1950s, kids were attaching metal roller-skate wheels to boards. Skateboarding got a kick start when surfing and surf music became popular in the early 1960s. Those early skateboards gave everyone a chance to dress like a surfer and pretend to experience the thrills of riding the waves, even though concrete walkways were their oceans and slippery metal skate wheels their surfboards. Several early skateboards included in the exhibit provide a quick historical look at the craze that had started to die just as the surfing craze was beginning to subside. But with the invention of those soft and "sticky" urethane wheels in 1972, skateboarding not only got another shot at life, but became and continues to be a multimillion-dollar sport craze.

Many more photos, a relatively new Huntington Beach Surfing Hall of Fame, and several changing exhibits help make the museum a fun place to spend a little time before hitting the beaches. There is a small gift shop, and it's all run by a group of dedicated museum volunteers.

**HOURS:** Summer, daily, noon to 5 PM (opens at 9 AM on Sunday); winter, Thursday through Monday, noon to 5 PM. Call to confirm hours.

**COST:** Adults, $2; 6–17, $1.

**LOCATION:** 411 Olive Ave., Huntington Beach

**PHONE:** 714-960-3483

**WEBSITE:** www.surfingmuseum.org

# 3  Newport Harbor Nautical Museum

**WHAT'S HERE:** Exhibits featuring the history of yachting, primarily in the Newport area, with a special look at the Hollywood stars who have played here

**DON'T MISS THIS:** An opportunity to photograph yourself with a 450-pound black sea bass

The focus of this nautical museum is not what you might expect. It covers yachting, which seems appropriate here, considering that more than 9000 sailboats are registered in Newport Harbor. Over the years, Hollywood stars, including John Wayne, Errol Flynn, Humphrey Bogart, Lauren Bacall, and Jimmy Cagney, have kept their yachts here. Photos of many celebrities and their yachts, such as Cecil B. DeMille's *Defiance* (circa 1930), line the walls, along with shots of some of Newport's earliest yachting events. They include one of the world's largest yacht races when, each April, nearly 500 sailing vessels of all sizes compete for the fastest time from Newport Beach to Ensenada, Mexico.

The museum is in the midst of planning a move (and may have moved by the time you read this) from its dockside location in an old riverboat to its new site down the street in Balboa Village, near the Ferris wheel at the Fun Zone. The existing riverboat museum will also be included in the new land-based museum, and the additional square footage of the new museum will be used for the ever-expanding collections, such as full-sized sailing vessels under sail.

In the existing museum there is a gallery of ship models, many of them famous yachts or larger sailing vessels. All are beautiful and extremely detailed models such as the *Bonhomme Richard*, commanded by John Paul Jones in 1779, and *HMS Victory*, its real counterpart built in 1768 in England. Some of the models are not likely to be seen elsewhere, including one that a prisoner in 1789 made from bone. Another rare model is the 3-foot-long destroyer constructed in 1912 of 22-karat gold. There's also a model of *America*, the sailing vessel that a group of yachtsmen from the US took to England in 1850. They had decided to race in England's first "100 Guinea

The museum's 450-pound sea bass

Race," around the Isle of Wight. *America* won, and from that time on, the race became known as the America's Cup.

Another exhibit describes the history of yachting. The first modern yacht club began in 1720, in Great Britain's Cork Islands, when local yacht owners banded together to form the Water Club of Cork. Soon afterward, other yacht clubs formed around England, and in 1834, Prince Regent spearheaded an effort to establish rules for handicapping yacht designs for racing purposes. In the US, the Detroit Boat Club formed in 1839, and California had its first yacht club in 1869.

Originally the purview of the rich, sailing was brought to the less-well-to-do masses when the Cox brothers of New York designed and built smaller, much more affordable sailboats. That was followed by the invention of the boat motor, bringing boating to those who had no desire to depend on the wind for locomotion. Back on the museum's main deck are several examples of very early 20th century outboard motors.

For those who need a little more action and like to fish, there is a free interactive deep-sea fishing simulator. You can sit in the fishing chair, grab a deep-sea rod and, on a video screen, fight a giant marlin until your arms ache. The museum (both old and new) features a "touch tank" filled with live ocean creatures that will allow kids and parents to see first hand what lies in the fragile coastal tide pools. And for those fishermen who never catch anything worth bragging about, there's an area near the museum entrance where you can stage an "I caught the big one" photo with a 450-pound black sea bass.

The museum also features a gallery of changing temporary exhibits that generally relate in some way to the world's oceans. The exhibits can range from photos of historic oceanic explorations or perhaps a look at the lives of those involved in the earliest days of yacht racing. And with a much expanded dock available, the new museum is planning for many more visits by tall ships, as well as providing information about boating in the area, including where to go to learn to sail.

It is best to check the museum's website for updates regarding its move into the new location and for any changes in fees and hours of operation.

**HOURS:** Tuesday through Sunday, 10 AM to 5 PM. Closed Easter, Thanksgiving, Christmas, and New Year's Day.

**COST:** Donation requested: adults, $5; 12 and under, free.

**LOCATION:** 151 East Pacific Coast Hwy., Newport Beach, on the riverboat in the Balboa Marina. New address beginning in spring 2007: 600 East Bay Ave., Newport Beach.

**PHONE:** 949-673-7863

**WEBSITE:** www.nhnm.org

# 4 Mission San Juan Capistrano

**WHAT'S HERE:** The restored and new mission buildings, in addition to the remnant walls of the original church that were destroyed in the 1812 San Juan Capistrano earthquake

**DON'T MISS THIS:** The only remaining original church in California where Father Junipero Serra is known to have said Mass

The town of San Juan Capistrano, where the mission is prominently located, is best known for the swallows that return on St. Patrick's Day each spring. But less known is that the mission is a wonderful contrast between the old and the new; the old being the crumbling mission, which is open for public viewing, and the new being the amazing reconstruction of the mission that parishioners use today.

The mission was first founded in 1775, but an Indian revolt at the nearby Mission San Diego de Alcala caused San Juan to be abandoned and its new bells hidden. The following year, Father Junipero Serra returned and reopened the seventh California mission on November 1, the Feast of All Saints Day. Thankfully, the hidden bells were still there, and a small adobe church was constructed. That small adobe church still stands, despite two centuries of earthquakes. It is best known as "Father Serra's church" because it is the only surviving original church in California where it is known for certain that Father Serra celebrated Mass.

In 1796, work was begun on a new church that was finally completed in 1806. Unfortunately, its thick adobe walls were no match for the 1812 earthquake, commonly referred to as the San Juan Capistrano earthquake, since the epicenter is thought to have been near the mission. The magnitude-6 quake happened during Sunday Mass, collapsing the mission's ceiling and adobe walls and killing 40 parishioners. The ruins of the great stone church remain today, providing a sense of how large the 19th century adobe church had been and the devastation the earthquake caused. The church was originally 108 feet long and 40 feet wide, with a 120-foot-tall bell tower at its entrance.

Over the next 150 years, efforts to construct a new church were unsuccessful until 1986. Its reconstruction was based as much as possible on the pattern for the original stone church, although so much was destroyed that there was much design guesswork. One part of the restoration that is known to be very similar to the original is the vibrantly painted interior. The bright green matches the green used in the original church, while

Ruins of the Mission San Juan Capistrano's church, which was destroyed by the 1812 earthquake the other colors and the overall motif were copied from similar churches, all originally designed to remind mission settlers of their homelands, which generally were somewhere in Spain.

While most of the paintings, the Italian Carrara marble baptismal, the wrought-iron chandeliers, and the wall murals are reproductions, not everything in the new church is new. In 1775, Father Serra requested that Jose de Paez paint a portrait of St. John of Capistrano, the mission's patron saint. The original painting hangs in the church.

Leave the main church and wander the historic grounds and gardens. The Moorish architecture is reminiscent of most California missions. One, or more accurately, four of the features from the original mission are the bells that were once rung to announce church services and important community events such as births and deaths. Today, they ring to announce the arrival of the swallows from their winter homes in Argentina.

The museum also holds Native American collections such as baskets. There are remnant pieces from the original mission, such as floor tile. The exhibits also include hand tools, spinning wheels, and various documents. One of the most important artifacts is a document signed by President Lincoln. Following Mexico's secularization of the missions, the government assumed control of mission property and disposed of it in 1845. In 1865, Lincoln returned the mission to the church, as declared in the historic document.

> **HOURS:** Daily, 8:30 AM to 5 PM. Closed Good Friday afternoon, Thanksgiving, and Christmas.
> **COST:** Adults, $6; 60 and over, $5; 4–11, $4.
> **LOCATION:** 26801 Oretega Hwy., San Juan Capistrano
> **PHONE:** 949-234-1300
> **WEBSITE:** www.missionsjc.com

# 5  Mission San Luis Rey de Francia

**WHAT'S HERE:** A restored mission and museum, along with the remnant barracks' foundation and the expansive *lavanderia* and garden area a short walk from the mission

**DON'T MISS THIS:** What is likely the oldest pepper tree in California

Father Antonio Peyri was placed in charge of Mission San Luis Rey de Francia from the day it was founded in 1798, and he stayed for more than 30 years. He created one of the largest and most successful missions, designing the original compound, which included a 500-foot square quadrangle. He also built elaborate river- and spring-fed irrigation systems that included charcoal-filtered water, a beautiful sunken garden, and a fanciful *lavanderia* where the Indians washed laundry from water that spewed from the mouths of carved stone gargoyle heads.

The facilities were sprawled across nearly 6 acres and included a large soldiers' barracks, a lime kiln, and an expansive cemetery. The extensive living and support facilities were required to maintain the mission operations. At its peak, the mission managed 3000 mostly Luiseño Indians and 50,000 head of cattle, horses, and other livestock. The mission was completely self-sustaining, growing oranges, grapes, olives, corn, and wheat.

Following Mexico's independence from Spain in 1821, secularization came to the mission in 1833, which resulted in two major events: First, the mission lands that were supposed to go to the Luiseño Indians mostly ended up in the hands of the area's more prominent and well-to-do families. Then, Father Peyri, seeing the end near, resigned and headed back to Spain. He was so loved by the local Indians that a large group followed him 30 miles to San Diego, pleading with him not to leave. After his departure, the mission was doomed.

In 1847, with the US in a war against Mexico, the US Mormon Battalion occupied the mission and used it as an operational base for the next 10 years. The soldiers protected portions of the mission, yet in other areas assisted local ranchers in taking the adobe bricks and other useful building materials for their own needs. Even though the military left, and, in 1865, President Lincoln returned the missions to the Catholic Church, the mission lay abandoned and deteriorating for more than 25 years.

In 1892, a small group of Franciscans from Mexico approached the bishop and requested that they be given refuge in California. He agreed and assigned them to Mission San Luis Rey de Francia. Father Joseph O'Keefe was brought in to assist the new arrivals. What he found at the mission was a mess—crumbled buildings and a nonexistent infrastructure. For the next 14 years, Father O'Keefe worked to rebuild the mission, including the church and the living quarters, on the foundations of the original buildings. Significant restoration has taken place since that time. Some of the best finds occurred in the 1950s and '60s, when archaeologists discovered and uncovered the soldier barracks' foundation and the lavanderia. The original barracks foundation can be seen today, as can the gardens and lavandaria, which are a just short walk across the grounds and down a long, elaborate set of stone steps.

There were originally 80 acres of orchards and vineyards, but those are now gone. Today, inside the main quadrangle, an expansive lawn and garden area are highlighted by what is likely the oldest pepper tree in California. For some reason, the tree is often associated with the mission's first boss, Father Peyri. Sailors actually brought the seeds from Peru in 1830, mistakenly thinking

Mission San Luis Rey de Francia

they were chili pepper seeds, and they weren't planted until after Father Peyri had returned to Spain. The 170-plus-year-old tree has a trunk diameter exceeding 40 feet, and its longest limbs now require support so they don't break.

The mission's museum houses collections from the Spanish, Mexican, and US military historical periods. The museum includes a collection of Indian baskets, and inside a walled enclosure adjacent to the east side of the church is a large cemetery.

> **HOURS:** Daily, 10 AM to 4 PM. Closed Easter, Thanksgiving, Christmas, and New Year's Day.
> **COST:** Adults, $5; 6–18, $3; 5 and under, free; family, $20.
> **LOCATION:** 4070 Mission Ave., San Luis Rey
> **PHONE:** 760-757-3651
> **WEBSITE:** www.sanluisrey.org

# 6 Leo Carrillo Ranch Historic Park

**WHAT'S HERE:** A working ranch where the famed sidekick of television's the *Cisco Kid* entertained many of Hollywood's stars

**DON'T MISS THIS:** The initials "LC" on walls and doorknobs

It's likely that most people today have never heard of Leo Carrillo, but anyone old enough to have watched television during the 1950s will remember seeing him play Pancho in the *Cisco Kid*. He was Cisco Kid's sidekick, and he often got himself into trouble. The series was one of the first to be filmed in color, although it was broadcast in black and white. The ranch's visitor center has all 200-plus of the series' programs available to watch, and one is usually playing anytime you wander in.

Leo Carrillo's entertainment career began in vaudeville during the 1920s, even though his family heritage would seem to indicate that he was destined for bigger achievements. Carrillo was descended from a long line of prominent early California families. His great grandfather was Carlos Antonio de Jesus Carrillo, one of California's governors under Mexican rule.

Gateway to Leo Carrillo's ranch home

While Carrillo spent much of his time in Hollywood, his life centered on the home he helped build in Carlsbad, the present-day location of the ranch. Carrillo first purchased 1700 acres for about $17 per acre in 1937 and later acquired more than 800 additional acres. He was looking to create a real working cattle ranch, but he was going to do it in style. In 1939, he began construction on the main wing of his hacienda. The architecture is a cross of Spanish, Southwestern, and some of his own creation. One thing to look for throughout the ranch are the initials LC—they can be found on everything from door knockers to fence posts. Apparently, Carrillo wanted to be sure that everyone who visited knew who the owner was!

Leo Carrillo did enjoy parties. Many of his fellow Hollywood stars found their way to his home, where they enjoyed horseback riding or sitting by the pool, which originally included a white sand beach. Carrillo brought the totem pole from New York, his home before coming to California, and the big stone barbeque likely served up lots of BBQ from his ranch-raised beef to visitors like Clark Gable, Carole Lombard, and Will Rogers (see Will Rogers State Historic Park, page 251).

There were so many parties that Carrillo's wife, Edith (known as Deedie), had another small house built just up the hill from the main hacienda so she could enjoy a little peace and quiet. She was somewhat reclusive and enjoyed pursuing her artwork alone. Carrillo, who also enjoyed art, faithfully etched the pictographs found on the pueblo-style house's exterior walls.

Carrillo named his ranch "Rancho de los Kiotes," and he ran it like a real ranch. He ultimately had several hundred head of cattle and a number of *vaqueros* (cowboys) to keep it all running smoothly. In what appears to be the Carrillo tradition, following a hard day's work, the vaqueros would gather at the ranch's La Cantina for a refreshing drink or two and talk about their day.

The city of Carlsbad now oversees the rancho, preserving it as a lasting tribute to a man who also believed in the importance of parks and open space. Always a conservationist, Carrillo served on the California State Park and Recreation Commission for 18 years and was instrumental in the state's acquisition of Hearst Castle at San Simeon (see Hearst San Simeon State Historical Monument, page 207).

The park and Leo Carrillo's hacienda and ranch are located in a wooded canyon right in the middle of suburbia. After passing hundreds of fancy tract homes on the hills surrounding the park, its amazing how they all seem to disappear once you've walked from the dirt parking lot down to the visitor center.

**HOURS:** The grounds are open Tuesday through Saturday, 9 AM to 5 PM; Sunday, 11 AM to 5 PM; summer (during daylight savings time) closing time is 6 PM. Access to the interiors of the buildings are limited to guided tours offered Saturday at 11 AM and 1 PM and Sunday at noon and 2 PM.

**COST:** Free

**LOCATION:** 6200 Flying LC Lane, Carlsbad

**PHONE:** 760-476-1042

**WEBSITE:** www.carrillo-ranch.org

# 7  Museum of Making Music

**WHAT'S HERE:** Exhibits that focus on the changing technologies of music from the late 1800s to today, from pianos to electric guitars to the computer age

**DON'T MISS THIS:** The room where you can play many different instruments

Given that so many museums have a "hands-off" policy, it's refreshing to go to the Museum of Making Music, where, in one area, visitors are encouraged to interact (read: play with) "artifacts" in order to explore different music technologies and instruments.

One of the first displays is of a Taylor Liberty Tree guitar. During the Revolutionary War, each of the original 13 colonies had identified a "Liberty Tree" as a lasting symbol of their struggles for independence. The last surviving Liberty Tree was a tulip poplar in Maryland that succumbed to Hurricane Floyd in 1999. Taylor Guitars secured enough of the tree to make 400 special Liberty Tree guitars, which they gave to each of the states, the White House, the Smithsonian, and to other prominent individuals and organizations.

There are five galleries that cover 100 years of musical instruments, beginning with the innovation gallery, covering the years from 1890 to 1909. It features a giant tuba and a 1905 player piano that helped introduce standards for the music rolls, allowing them to be played on the 25 different manufacturers' pianos. There is also a 1905 Steinway piano, signed by Henry Steinway.

Major changes in the American musical instrument industry occurred in the early 1920s. The National Association of Musical Merchants (NAMM) was formed from different smaller organizations, and hence, the big push to expand the reaches of music began. During the late 1920s, new music stores opened and carried just about everything musical. With the introduction of installment plans, a surge of $480 player pianos found their way into thousands of American homes for $10 down and $15 a month with no interest. Such deals spurred significant growth in the numbers of music teachers and in the numbers of people learning to play instruments.

The 1920s also saw significant changes in guitars. In 1929, long before electric pick-ups became common on electric guitars, C.F. Martin made its first guitar designed for steel strings and also

The museum features a walk through the history of musical instruments.

added two additional frets, significantly increasing the guitar's range and setting a new industry standard.

The Great Depression sent jazz musicians underground, but in 1934, Benny Goodman accidentally brought a new form of jazz back to the public. Tired and frustrated as he neared the end of a very disappointing tour, Goodman grumbled to his band to "let it swing." His audience went wild. That was the beginning of the Swing era in music. Interest in live music was spurred further by piano maker Steinway & Sons when, during World War II and the Korean War, the company designed special, smaller, olive-drab-painted pianos and shipped the "Victory" pianos overseas to help improve troop morale. At least one survived and it is in the museum's collection.

The Baby Boom years brought huge increases in musical instrument sales, going over the $1 billion mark by 1969. During the 1950s and '60s, piano makers wanted more sound, and they achieved success when Wurlitzer introduced pianos without strings. They used metal reeds that transferred electrically rather than using a soundboard.

With a push of a button, the museum allows you not only to see the new instruments introduced during each of the 20-year periods, but also hear the new sounds. There are tons of buttons to choose from throughout the museum. The famed Fender Telecaster guitar, the Les Paul guitar, the Moog synthesizer, and more are featured, along with short representative musical samplings.

The 1970s exhibit showcases the introduction of videos allowing the music-buying public to "see" their music in addition to listening to it. Drum machines, electric grand pianos, and mini-Moog came into existence. And those were followed by more technological advances as instruments became louder, fuller sounding, and more versatile.

After spending an hour or so wandering through and listening to the many exhibits, it's time for a real jam session. The museum features a room filled with instruments, from guitars to drums, to synthesizers and even a Mac computer with Garage Band software that allows you to create your own soundtrack. You can try everything, even if you have never played before. Unless you're a musician, you still won't be able to play an actual song, except perhaps on the computer, but at least it's an opportunity to have fun playing with some famous musical instruments. There are also a couple of turntables and a pile of records so you can play DJ and spin the tunes!

**HOURS:** Tuesday through Sunday, 10 AM to 5 PM. Closed Monday and major holidays.

**COST:** Adults, $5; 60 and over, 4–18, and active military (with ID), $3.

**LOCATION:** 5790 Armada Drive, Carlsbad

**PHONE:** 877-551-9976 or 760-438-5996

**WEBSITE:** www.museumofmakingmusic.org

# 8 Mission San Diego de Alcala

**WHAT'S HERE:** The museum features exhibits on the early history of the mission, including the deterioration and restoration

**DON'T MISS THIS:** The open archeology pits

San Diego de Alcala was the first Spanish mission in Alta California, and it was the most troublesome of the 21 California missions to establish. Five separate expeditions left New Spain (Mexico) on different dates beginning in January of 1769. Two were by land and three were by sea, although one of the ships never arrived. Captain Gaspar de Portola led the main land expedition, leaving on May 15 and arriving in San Diego on July 1. Although his ultimate destination was Monterey, he stopped at San Diego, where Father Junipero Serra founded California's first mission on July 16, 1769. Portola established California's first presidio at the same location.

The last time Europeans had been in the area was in 1602, when Spanish explorers sailed through the bay. Thus, when the Franciscan missionaries arrived more than 150 years later, it was literally the first time the Indians had seen Europeans, and it was also the first time they had been exposed to Christianity. Spain was competing with England, France, and Russia for domination of the New World. Without large numbers of Spanish citizens willing to settle these wild lands, it fell to the Church, through its missions, to recruit and convert Indians to Christianity, making them part of this most remote area of the Spanish empire.

The first mission was established near the presidio and coast. Within five years, the site was determined to be unsuitable, and Father Luis Jayme, the pastor, moved the mission to a new location 6 miles away. While most mission Indians, and most California Indians in general, were peaceful, there were occasional attacks on the missions. In November 1775, encouraged by a couple of Indians described as discontents, several hundred non-mission Indians attacked, burning the new mission and killing Father Jayme.

By 1780, a new mission and its support buildings had been constructed on the same site, this time of adobe and in a fort-like quadrangle around a central

The bell tower of Mission San Diego de Alcala

open patio. By 1797, after its slow start, the mission had grown to include more than 1400 Indian converts raising wheat, barley, corn, and beans on 50,000 acres. There were also 20,000 sheep, 10,000 head of cattle, and 1200 horses. As was relatively common in California, an earthquake in 1803 severely damaged the church. Following the 1812 earthquake, which caused additional damage, the padres built thick buttresses at the base of the church that protected it against subsequent earthquakes.

The mission ceased being a profitable enterprise after being secularized by the Mexican government in 1833. After the US took control of California from Mexico, the US Army sent troops into San Diego. They found the mission in severe disrepair, but made enough repairs so it would be habitable as their temporary quarters, where they stayed until 1857. Even though President Lincoln gave the mission system back to the Catholic Church in 1862, over the next 37 years, the mission continued to deteriorate. The slow job of restoration began in 1915, when the Sisters of Saint Joseph of Corondolet established an American Indian school, and work continued through the Depression with CCC crews doing additional reconstruction. Finally, in 1941, the mission reopened its doors as an active parish, a role it continues to fulfill to this day.

The mission's museum is named for Father Jayme, the missionary killed during the Indian uprising. The museum and many of the surrounding buildings offer exhibits including historic photos illustrating the extent of the mission's deterioration and the various phases of its restoration. A photograph from 1880 shows very little of the original buildings remaining, but by 1931, that had changed significantly because the mission had been rebuilt as it appeared in 1813. The mission's exhibits feature hundreds of artifacts related to the mission period, from firearms to tools and even an old gin jug. Apparently, the lonely outpost required a few of its citizens to partake in more than ceremonial wine and prayer. There is also an active archaeological dig site that contains remnants of the mission's original monastery.

The most prominent architectural feature is the bell tower. Its tall, triangular shape holds five bells. The largest weighs 1200 pounds and was cast from five smaller bells that had been sent to the mission in 1796.

**HOURS:** Daily, 9 AM to 4:45 PM. Closed Thanksgiving, Christmas, and New Year's Day.
**COST:** Suggested donation, adults, $3; seniors and students, $2; 12 and under, $1.
**LOCATION:** 10818 San Diego Mission Road, San Diego
**PHONE:** 619-281-8449
**WEBSITE:** www.missionsandiego.com

# 9  Old Town San Diego State Historic Park

**WHAT'S HERE:** A tourist attraction that includes shops, museums, historic adobes, and reconstructed historic homes

**DON'T MISS THIS:** Seeley Stable Museum

In the late 1820s and early 1830s, following the Mexican government's secularization of the missions—which took away their vast agricultural lands and ended their ability to continue operating—settlers and ex-soldiers from the abandoned presidio began building homes and business buildings in what is today Old Town San Diego. The town was small and the living conditions not great, but as the years progressed, especially following the US takeover in 1848, conditions began to improve as the population and related business opportunities increased. Two newspapers were born in the 1860s, and new transportation opportunities such as Seeley Stable became available, yet only seven people considered themselves merchants in the 1860 US Census.

Over the next century, as people discovered San Diego's opportunities—and its great weather—more people came here to live. The city grew rapidly during and following World War II, in time moving the center of the growing city away from old town and closer to the waterfront. San Diego's old town deteriorated significantly until the area became a state park in 1968 and restoration efforts began. Today, the park's historic buildings are surrounded by wonderful restaurants and shops of all kinds.

## La Casa de Estudillo (The Estudillo House)

This adobe home, built in 1827, is one of California's earliest "mansions." The word is used loosely, as these very early adobe homes were considered luxurious at that time. Captain Jose Maria Estudillo, a retired presidio commander, constructed his new home, making additions and improvements for several years. When Estudillo died in 1830, his son, Jose Antonio Estudillo could afford to further improve his family's fancy home, as he had acquired extensive land holdings throughout what is today San Diego County. His acquisitions included Rancho Temecula and Rancho San Jacinto Viego, located north of San Diego near present-day Hemet and San Jacinto. He also owned ranchos near Chula Vista and El Cajon.

The adobe is constructed in a typical U-shape, with a center courtyard garden. Not only are the home's thick adobe walls, varying from 3 feet to 5 feet at their bases, much different from today's construction techniques, so, too, is the layout. The home's 13 rooms, the kitchen, bedrooms, dining room, living room,

La Casa de Estudillo

guest rooms, chapel, and others, are set in a linear fashion around the U, with a covered outdoor walkway connecting them.

In 1887, the Estudillo family's descendents moved from San Diego to Los Angeles, abandoning the house to a caretaker. By 1906, the adobe home was almost in ruins when it passed through different ownerships, including John Spreckles, who owned the San Diego Electric Railway Company.

In 1968, the home became part of the California State Park System and Old Town San Diego State Historic Park. Restoration was begun and furnishings representing the 18th and 19th centuries were acquired and added to La Casa de Estudillo as part of its transition to a historic house museum. There is no known record of the types of furnishings that the Estudillos may have owned, but knowing something of their lifestyle and what was available to them during those times, it is relatively easy to speculate as to what may have been in the home.

The Steinway piano in the main living room was actually shipped around the Horn in about 1853. The maps and wall charts seen in the study would have been similar to those that Estudillo used for his many trips of exploration into the surrounding deserts. The dining room provides a look at the trade industry that early California ranchos and missions depended upon. Those of some affluence imported china, glassware, furniture, tea, chocolate, fine fabrics, and clothes. Californians raised cattle and shipped hides and tallow to Spain, Mexico, and, later, to the eastern US and other countries.

## Seeley Stable Museum

Transportation was critical to the survival and growth of communities in California; San Diego was no different. Albert Lewis Seeley introduced the first commercially successful transportation system to the area in 1867. Seeley had worked as a stage driver in Texas and Los Angeles, so when he moved his family to San Diego, he started his own

stage company. A year later, he won a major government contract transporting US mail and passengers between San Diego and Los Angeles, which he expanded to include stage service between San Diego and Tucson, Arizona.

That same year, he also purchased the Bandini House for $2000, one of Old Town San Diego's original adobes, and he added a second floor. Seeley renamed the home the Cosmopolitan Hotel, and it served as his stage stop and, for the era and location, a luxury hotel. He also built a large stable next door. The original stable is gone, but a historically accurate,

Seeley Stable Museum

reconstructed Seeley Stable, now a museum, sits on the same site. Seeley's business grew and proved very profitable, until the railroads began expanding throughout southern California and into Arizona. By 1887, most of Seeley's stage lines had closed, and he sold his hotel for $15,000.

The main floor of the stable provides a look at some of California's early horse-drawn vehicles. One of the earliest is a buckboard, which provided a much more comfortable ride than some of the larger, fancier wagons. The wagon most associated with Seeley is the mail coach—the Concord "mud wagon" proved to be the wagon of choice for moving mail and goods across the rugged and rocky terrain found throughout southern California's deserts and mountains.

Upstairs features numerous exhibits related to early San Diego and the Southwest. Everything from Indian baskets and pottery to branding irons help give a sampling of what life was like during the late 1800s. There is a saddle collection that illustrates the differences in *vaquero* and cowboy saddles used throughout the Old West. Some of today's cowboy terminology originated with the Spanish words: vaquero evolved into buckaroo; lariat is from *la reata*, a braided rawhide rope; and chaps comes from *chaparejos* or chaparral, southern California's most prominent type of vegetation. There are several items included in the museum that might be seen as curiosities, including an old organ, a chair made from cow horns, and some very early slot machines.

Take time to wander behind the main stable. In the large back courtyard are numerous buggies, carts, and carriages. This is also where the blacksmith shop is found. There is usually a "smithy" working, with the furnace glowing, as he pounds and works the red-hot iron into everything from door hinges to tools.

## McCoy House

This property was originally owned by Maria Eugenia Silvas, a descendent of a Spanish soldier who came to Alta California in the 1770s. The property finally ended up in the hands of James McCoy, and, in 1869, he had a large home constructed on the site. McCoy had come from Ireland and had done well for himself, becoming San Diego's sheriff and later a state senator. Over the years, the property passed through several different owners, and ultimately the house was razed.

In 1995, State Parks archeologists began a dig to recover as much information about the original home as possible. Coupled with historic photos and other research, the McCoy House was reconstructed in 2000. While the home may have been considered a mansion during its heyday, its reconstructed model serves as a house museum. Inside, a timeline exhibit beginning from when

McCoy House

the Kumeyaay Indians lived here continues through several historical periods of San Diego. The timeline includes early Spanish explorers such as Juan Rodriguez Cabrillo in 1542, Sebastian Vizcaino in 1602, Gaspar de Portola in 1769, and, finally, the arrival of the missionaries. It moves through the Californios period, Mexican independence from Spain in 1821, secularization of the missions that began in 1834, and development of huge, privately owned ranchos.

One of the exhibits shows the currency of the day, better known as California banknotes. The banknotes were actually dried cowhides. In order to purchase a "bit" or two "bits" of sugar, the prospective buyer carried the stiff hides with him to the store for use in the transaction. Locally, at one time, a single hide was worth 12 *reales* or $1.50 in silver or $2 in goods

The exhibits describe the value of cattle to the 18th and 19th century California economy. Each cow provided about 200 pounds of tallow, which, after being processed, was transported in cowhide containers called bolsas. The tallow and cowhides were prime exports for the New England shipping industry that arrived regularly, bringing calico cloth and other needed goods. The hides and tallow were also traded for goods from China and Europe.

Prices fluctuated for trade goods, depending on quality and supply, and shipping schedules, storms, ship wrecks, and the whims of traders and buyers dictated supply. In 1830, a single cowhide in trade was worth $2; that's about $37 today. In 1846, a person in San Diego would have paid $15 for a blanket, the equivalent of $278 today; a hat cost $1.20 then, and $22 today; a simple screwdriver that cost $1 in 1846 would run you $18 today; necessities like boots were $10 or $185 today; and a woman's petticoat that cost $45 then is the equivalent of $835 today, a hefty price to pay for fashion.

The exhibits also cover the Mexican-American War and its impacts on California, including the arrival of the Mormon Battalion, following the longest march in US military history. They arrived too late to be of any assistance during the war, but the soldiers were used to dig wells, white wash adobes, and work on various construction projects following the war.

One of the more interesting exhibits in the McCoy House museum is the grog shop. It became a social hub for San Diego, providing news and provisions to the citizens. A grog shop's floor might be made of compacted dirt covered with ox blood to keep down the dust, as smoke from the oil lamps coated the adobe walls. Fabric draped across the ceilings stopped most of the overhead dirt from dropping into customer drinks. Today, they call that "atmosphere."

**HOURS:** Daily, 10 AM to 5 PM. Closed Thanksgiving, Christmas, and New Year's Day.
**COST:** Free
**LOCATION:** San Diego Ave. at Twiggs, Old Town San Diego State Historic Park
**PHONE:** 619-220-5422
**WEBSITE:** www.parks.ca.gov/index

# 10 Marston House

**WHAT'S HERE:** Home of one of San Diego's early leading citizens, who made his fortune in the department store business

**DON'T MISS THIS:** The oak dining room in contrast to the redwood used throughout the remainder of the home

Typical of many homes built during the early 20th century by those of substantial financial means, the Marston House, built in 1905 and located in Balboa Park, incorporated what was considered an innovative design at the time. The home is reflective of the developing Craftsman-style architecture and certainly the most prominent of its kind in San Diego when completed in 1905.

George Marston, the home's original owner, came a long way from his Wisconsin childhood, where he developed a strong sense of good and a love for nature. Both were attributes that would come to serve San Diego well throughout most of Marston's adult life. As his future business thrived, Marston was able to dedicate his money, time, and many talents to improving the city he called home. Besides being the founder and first president of the San Diego Historical Society, Marston was prominent in the development of long-range city planning, and in the development of Balboa Park and other city, regional, and state parks.

Marston's journey to San Diego began when his father, seeking a more healthful climate for himself, moved the family to San Diego in 1870. It was here that Marston began his career in retail, taking several successive jobs, each providing him an education in successful business management. He and a partner soon bought out one of his employer's stores, and his subsequent and continuing financial success allowed him to pursue his civic interests. In 1878, Marston ended his first mercantile partnership, dropping the grocery and hardware business, preferring to focus on dry-goods retailing.

In 1878, Marston married Anna Gunn, a young woman who was born in Sonoma and whose father had come to California seeking gold in 1849. In 1875, Gunn had moved with most of her family to San Diego, where she and Marston met at a town event the following year.

Marston certainly wasn't afraid to take chances. During the 1870s, San Diego was a very small town, with an economy to match. Yet he decided to start a new retail venture, in spite of the fact that there were already eight competitors in town. After his first year in the red, Marston relocated his store to a better site, and financial success followed. By the time the new century arrived, he had moved his business again, this time into a four-story building located at Fifth and C streets.

Marston House

When the Marstons decided to build a new home, they purchased 10 acres near what is today Balboa Park. Marston replaced 4 acres of scrub brush with lawns, gardens, and trees. George was not ostentatious, as an earlier generation of entrepreneurs had been in showing off their wealth. The fanciful Victorian architecture and furnishings were replaced by a simpler Arts and Crafts-style home—its size and elegance subdued.

The 8500-square-foot, four-level home cost only $18,000 to build and is one of the few remaining homes built by William Hebbard and Irving Gill, prominent local architects during the early 1900s. Situated on a slight slope overlooking a canyon and surrounded by gardens, the house has one obvious missing architectural attribute—a main entrance. Gill designed the home with no prominent or obvious "front." Nearly 100 years before the technology would become even marginally popular in California, the home was constructed with solar water heating. A small attic space still holds the system's original large drip pan. The remainder of the upper floor is primarily maid and cook quarters.

When entering the Marston home via the west portico, the light pours in through the glass doors at the opposite end of the house. Walk past the music room and into the main living room, and there you will see wainscot with a series of wooden butterfly keys connecting the two horizontal boards. The keys add a distinctive look but actually serve a more utilitarian purpose—to keep the boards from splitting apart as they age and dry. Like nearly anyone who has designed his or her own home, the Marstons felt the need to improve the living room windows when they moved in, so they had the windows enlarged in order to allow more light to enter the room.

Redwood was used throughout most of the house; one exception was the dining room, where oak was the favored wood. The dining room also features a built-in buffet and a prominent brick fireplace. Something not found in most other homes, except those designed by Gill, were the closet and bathroom floors that were raised 4 inches higher than the main room floors. Gill's thinking was that the rise of floor elevation would help keep excess dirt from being brought in, thus keeping the floors cleaner. Nearly every room has a different wall covering, from the "anaglypta" (an embossed wallpaper designed to be painted over) to the jute and burlap glued to the library walls.

The second floor is where the six bedrooms are located—in addition to four bathrooms and a sitting room. The various smaller bedrooms were occupied by the Marston's children and other family members. The master bedroom is the largest and has its own private balcony looking east over the canyon.

The Marston's enjoyed their home for many years. Anna died in 1940, and George followed her in 1946. The home is now operated by the San Diego Historical Society.

**HOURS:** Friday through Sunday, 1 AM to 5 PM, with tours on the hour (last tour at 4 PM). Closed on national holidays.

**COST:** Adults, $5; 6–17, $2; discounts for students, seniors, and military.

**LOCATION:** 3525 Seventh Ave., Balboa Park, San Diego

**PHONE:** 619-298-3142

**WEBSITE:** www.sandiegohistory.org

# 11 **San Diego Museum of Man**

**WHAT'S HERE:** A broad look at the human species, its culture, technology, and continuing development

**DON'T MISS THIS:** The timeline of human technology, from the first use of fire to the creation of the first modern computer

This museum of anthropology is one of the many museums located along Balboa Park's El Prado walkway. The museum is one of San Diego's oldest, having opened its doors originally for the 1915–16 Panama-California Exposition. Choose whatever descriptive term you like to describe its Spanish Colonial Revival architecture—beautiful, pretentious, flamboyant, grandiose, gaudy—one is likely to fit your first impression of the building. Whatever your taste in architecture, the museum is striking and impossible to miss.

The interior is equally striking, with numerous exhibits, both permanent and temporary, scattered throughout. One of the more imposing is the colorful Mayan exhibit just beyond the main entry in the rotunda gallery. Included are exact replicas of several Mayan stelae—intricate stone carvings that offer a look at the artistry and skills of these ancient people. One of these was carved in 771 AD to acknowledge K'ak'Tiliw and his extraordinary exploits, solidifying the legitimacy of his 46-year rein over Quirigua. Many other Mayan artifacts, such as pottery, are also exhibited.

The museum explores human evolution with several exhibits, including the busts of early pre-humans from Java man to Neolithic man. The exhibits further explore human life, including what it may have been like in the Pleistocene Ice Age.

The passage of time is a critical consideration in all study of humanity, and that subject is explored at a level even kids can understand: Look at the changes we see during a single lifetime or five generations of a family, and then think of the changes that can occur over a million years, the equivalent of 10,000 human lifetimes and 50,000 generations. An exhibit with a million beads helps put things into perspective. Additional exhibits deal with evolution triggered by the environment and the traits developed

San Diego Museum of Man

to help ensure survival. The museum explains the planet's population, how it has expanded and moved, and also how languages have developed and changed.

There is a timeline of human technology development: Fire was thought to first be used 500,000 years ago; the first pottery was made around 12,000 BC, the first form of a compass was invented in 250–300 AD, the first iron nails in 400–500 AD, the first printed newspaper in 748 AD, the concept of plus and minus in math in 1489, the invention of the steam engine in 1775, the discovery of penicillin in 1928, the creation of the atomic bomb in 1945, the invention of Velcro in 1948, and the creation of the modern computer chip in 1971. Then the museum moves to the future of the human species, looking at mitosis (splitting and development of cells), genes and how they might be selected, human reproduction, and the evolution of the human brain. There is even a quick look at the potential development of cyborgs—people with robotic parts, such as strengthened bones and other improved body organs and body parts.

The museum also houses a large collection of cultural artifacts, folk art, and finds from major archeological digs. There are always temporary exhibits that allow either a more in-depth exhibition of the museum's own collections or of major traveling exhibits that can better highlight certain aspects of the human species' development. The museum's website provides a review of current and future temporary exhibits.

HOURS: Daily, 10 AM to 4:30 PM. Closed Thanksgiving, Christmas, and New Year's Day.
COST: Adults, $6; seniors, $5; 6–17, $3; 6 and under, free.
LOCATION: 1350 El Prado, Balboa Park, San Diego
PHONE: 619-239-2001
WEBSITE: www.museumofman.org

## 12 San Diego Air and Space Museum

WHAT'S HERE: Full-sized aircraft, both original and reproductions, from man's earliest flights to the war years to space travel

DON'T MISS THIS: Interactive exhibits where kids can actually "experience" flying

Also located in Balboa Park, this museum is all indoors, except for the A-12 Blackbird and Navy Convair Seadart that reside just outside the main entrance. The Air and Space Museum covers the history of manned flight from a mock-up of Da Vinci's Ornithopter to an *Apollo* service module. More than 60 other aircraft fill the museum's historic timeline of aircraft development; most are originals with a few reproductions mixed in. The aircraft are displayed in the circular exhibit hall that runs counter-clockwise around the museum's main center gallery. Each of the galleries highlights a new and advanced era of aircraft history, from the Dawn of Powered Flight to the Space Flight gallery.

While the Wright brothers may have been the first to prove that extended flight was possible (and full-size reproductions of their early aircraft are displayed), the advent of war proved to be the real impetus for aircraft advancement. Suspended from the museum ceiling is a Thomas-Morse S-4C biplane. With a top speed of 95 miles per hour, this biplane was one of the most advanced US trainers designed in World War I, but the 500 that were built came too late in the war to serve much purpose. With no originals in existence, there is a faithfully reproduced Fokker Dr 1 Tri-plane, one of the most famous aircrafts in history. This airplane is most closely associated with World War I's Red Baron Manfred von Richthofen, although the same model was flown by many of the German air aces. The relatively tiny wood and cloth-covered airplane, with its 23-foot, 7-inch wingspan, could cruise at just over 100 miles per hour and reach an altitude of 20,000 feet.

The 20 years between the culmination of the World War I and the beginning of World War II was a time for flight to move from the military to the barnstormers. The latter excited the general population about the real possibilities of flight, or at least those who could afford such luxury travel. As seen by the many 1930s aircraft in the Golden Age of Flight gallery, aircraft increased in size and power and the old, cloth-covered wings and bodies slowly gave way to aluminum skins.

Engineers made significant advancements in aircraft technology during World War II. With German, British, Japanese, and American war efforts being forced to outdo each other in order to prevail during land, sea, and air battles, cost was seldom an issue. Some of the fastest and deadliest fighters developed during the war can be seen up close. Germany's Messerschmitt 109G (unfortunately, a full-sized mock-up), Japan's Mitsubishi Zero-sen, the American Grumman F6 Hellcat, and the Curtiss P40E Warhawk of Flying Tiger fame are just samplings of the planes displayed. A film shows historic footage of many of the war's most famous aircraft in action.

Three of the museum's largest aircraft fill most of the center pavilion. The Cold War is represented by an F-4 Phantom on the tail of a MiG-17, while a 1940s era amphibious PBY-5A Catalina and a Ford Trimotor—America's first successful commercial airliner developed in the early 1930s—fill much of the remaining space.

The Jet Age Gallery features several early "fast movers" with a MiG-15, an F-86F Sabre, and an A-4B Skyhawk among

World War II-era P-40 Warhawk
of Flying Tiger fame

the collection. The Space Flight gallery includes very realistic full-size mock-ups of a *Gemini* spacecraft and an *Apollo* service module, although both seem quite small considering where they were designed to take their passengers.

The museum also features several interactive exhibits that allow visitors, especially youngsters, a chance to feel what flight is really like, from the Wright brother's primitive airplane to more modern aircraft. Some are included in the entry fee, others are available for an additional fee, and some are changed from time to time.

**HOURS:** Daily, 10 AM to 4:30 PM (open until 5:30 PM during the summer). Closed Thanksgiving, Christmas, and New Year's Day.

**COST:** Adults, $9; 6–17, $4; 65 and over, $7; 5 and under and active miltary, free.

**LOCATION:** 2001 Pan American Plaza, Balboa Park, San Diego

**PHONE:** 619-234-8291

**WEBSITE:** www.aerospacemuseum.org

# 13 San Diego Automotive Museum

**WHAT'S HERE:** Antique cars, from the plain to the exotic, with a look at the changing engine technologies that powered different generations of automobiles

**DON'T MISS THIS:** The car that was driven nonstop across the US and back in 1952

Southern California has always been a focal point for the automotive lifestyle, and this Balboa Park museum houses a broad spectrum of the reasons why that remains true. One thing to remember about many large museums—and automotive museums in particular—is that a significant portion of their collections may be on loan from the vehicle's owners. While many owners enjoy sharing their painted steel-and-chrome treasures with the public, they also enjoy taking them back occasionally for personal tours or other events, or the cars are sold to new owners who have different ideas about what to do with them.

As an example, when this was written, the museum housed a 1948 Tucker Torpedo, one of just 51 built before Preston Tucker and his innovative cars were essentially run out of business. The vehicle is on long-term loan to the museum by its owner, so in a year or two it may not be there, which would be unfortunate because it is a beautiful vehicle. But there are other curiosities in the museum besides the Tucker.

During seven days in 1952, Louie Mattar's specially built car drove nonstop across the US and back, for a total of 6320 miles. The $75,000 car is exhibited along with all the explanations as to how it was done. The 8500-pound car included numerous design changes that allowed the onboard crew to conduct maintenance and repairs, including tire changes, while the car was moving. The car provided cooking facilities and even a shower for its three alternating drivers and crew, and it towed a small trailer that carried 15 gallons of oil, 30 gallons of water, and 230 gallons of gas. When the car's fuel trailer needed to be refueled, they relied on strategically located airfields; while driving down the long runways, the crew would refuel via a gas truck driving next to them.

The auto museum is housed inside what once served as a large, temporary storage and display building constructed for the 1935 California Pacific International Exposition. This planned temporary building still remains standing more than 70 years later. Today, the building is listed on the National Register of Historic Places, and over the years it has served as a Navy barracks during World War II, a storage facility, and an auditorium.

The museum has many antique cars, some elegant, some more common. There is a venerable 1936 Rolls Royce Phantom III, the first-production Rolls with a V-type engine, in this case a 448-cubic-inch V-12. It sold new for $3375; today, the car would cost about $400,000 used, if you're lucky enough to find one on the market. For Bentley fans, there's a 1938 Bentley that cost just $1510 when new, but the resale price is now close to $100,000. There are numerous other exotic and expensive vehicles in the collections, along with the more common US-manufactured cars with the advanced technologies the Big Three automakers introduced over the years.

The advancement in gasoline-powered engines is one aspect of auto technology the museum explores in its many exhibits. There are engines ranging in size from a diminutive two-stroke Vespa motor to a 1963 Jaguar V-12 and the powerful Chrysler Hemi. There is a look at Henry Ford's innovations, such as his 1932 V-8 flathead engine that took up no more space than his old four-cylinder engines, and the 1965 Ford 427-cubic-inch big block engine that helped kick off the US charge toward the big muscle cars of the late 1960s and early '70s.

For the two-wheel enthusiasts, the museum houses a fairly extensive motorcycle collection, including a 1942 Harley Davidson ELC Knucklehead with its 1200 c.c. V-Twin, 75-horsepower engine that had a top speed of 55 miles per hour. That doesn't appear to be as much of an improvement over the 1899 DeDion/Bouton Peugot tricycle on display with its 269 c.c. single-cylinder engine that generated only 2.25 horsepower. But when coupled with its two-speed transmission, it had a top speed of 40 miles per hour. There are Triumphs, a Vincent,

A 1930s-era Bentley (left)
and the Rolls Royce (right)

a 1914 Indian, and a 1942 US Army version of the Indian, one of the 1000 built for the military during World War II.

The museum is a fun look at what has been driving not only southern California, but the world, for more than 100 years. Check the museum's website for current and future special exhibits, as they can change regularly.

**HOURS:** Daily, 10 AM to 5 PM (last admission at 4:30 PM). Closes at 2 PM on Christmas Eve and New Year's Eve, and is closed Christmas Day and New Year's Day.

**COST:** 16–65, $7; over 65 and active military, $6; ages 6–15, $3; under age 6, free.

**LOCATION:** 2080 Pan American Plaza, #12, Balboa Park, San Diego

**PHONE:** 619-231-2886

**WEBSITE:** www.sdautomuseum.org

# 14 San Diego Model Railroad Museum

**WHAT'S HERE:** Numerous large model train setups, including a scale model of the line that passes over Tehachapi Pass by turning "back over itself" to climb the grade

**DON'T MISS THIS:** The interactive train gallery for kids of all ages

This self-proclaimed largest indoor model railroad museum has 27,000 square feet of displays and track layouts. Located on the lower level of Casa de Balboa on Balboa Park's El Prado, the museum is well-signed and easy to find. For model railroad enthusiasts—adults and children alike—there is plenty to see and experience. There are several extensive HO- and N-scale layouts, which are created and maintained by various model railroading clubs.

The museum features scaled versions of some of Southern California's actual train routes, down to rivers, bridges, ranches, and stations. The detail of the exhibits is extraordinary, to the point where a well-placed camera can create a photo that would be difficult to tell from the real thing.

Some of what can be seen includes the O-scale (1/48 actual size) of the Cabrillo Southwestern Railroad, the San Diego & Arizona Eastern HO-scale (1/87 actual size) exhibit, and southern California's Tehachapi Pass. While the Tehachapi's lowest Sierra crossing is at an elevation of just 4025 feet, it is also one of the steepest. When the real railroad was constructed in 1876, the tracks from Bakersfield to the top of Tehachapi Pass had 18 tunnels and a nearly continuous 2.5-percent grade over a 28-mile section that included 124 curves. The real line and the model layout both include the famous Tehachapi Loop, where the tracks cross back over themselves in a helix as they climb the last section of mountain near the town of Tehachapi. For those driving along Tehachapi's Hwy. 58, spotting a real train is easy; it's the busiest stretch of single track in North America. The model railroad version offers a very different perspective on the mountain-crossing line and one well worth seeing.

The museum also features an interactive toy train gallery, where kids of all ages have an opportunity to play engineer. The Lionel type 3-rail, O-gauge trains travel over four separate main lines on a 42-by-44-foot layout, filled with everything from downtown city buildings to people and cars. The experience includes train whistles and horns blowing, locomotive engine sounds, and smoke from the old locomotives. To make things more realistic, a camera transmits an "engineer's view" of the layout to an overhead television screen, allowing visitors a close-up view of the layout. There is also a coal mine section where kids are allowed to operate the coal trains.

For toy train collectors, there is an exhibit of rare American Flyer and Lionel cars from the 1920s through the 1950s. There is also a gift shop for those who care to bring back old memories or create new memories for a younger generation.

For real toy train junkies, the museum is usually open on Tuesday and Friday evenings free of charge. Those are work and maintenance nights for the clubs, so while the trains may not be moving, there are plenty of train experts to talk with about this fascinating hobby. For the evening work sessions, access is through the back door, but it's always a good idea to contact the museum during regular hours to confirm.

**HOURS:** Tuesday through Friday, 11 AM to 4 PM, Saturday and Sunday, 11 AM to 5 PM. Closed Thanksgiving and Christmas.

**COST:** Adults, $5; seniors over 65, $4; students with ID, $3; 15 and under, free when accompanied by an adult. First Tuesday of each month is free to all.

**LOCATION:** 1649 El Prado, Balboa Park, San Diego

**PHONE:** 619-696-0199

**WEBSITE:** www.sdmodelrailroadm.com

One of museum's many elaborate model trail layouts

# 15 San Diego Natural History Museum

**WHAT'S HERE:** Many exhibits here are periodically changed, but they all deal with aspects of natural history, from whales to minerals.

**DON'T MISS THIS:** The mini kiosks that feature California native wildlife in their natural habitats

The predecessor of today's San Diego Natural History Museum—the San Diego Society of Natural History—was founded in 1874, making it the second-oldest natural history museum west of the Mississippi. Although society members had explored and collected specimens since its founding, they developed the organization's first natural history exhibits in 1912, in the newly constructed downtown Hotel Cecil. The society moved the museum to three different locations over then next few years until, finally, in 1933, a permanent home was found in Balboa Park, where much of the existing building was constructed.

With the US Naval presence in San Diego, World War II brought changes once again. The Navy turned the museum into an infectious disease hospital, while the natural history exhibits were packed away to more than 30 locations around the city for safe keeping. Following the end of the war, the museum staff reviewed their plans for the museum's future direction, compared with the collections they had in storage. They decided that the museum would focus its future permanent collections on the southwestern US and northern Mexico.

One of the best things about this natural history museum is that most of what would normally be static, permanent displays are neither permanent nor static. New exhibits and changes to old exhibits bring freshness to the museum. There are, of course, the wildlife specimens, fossils, and large whale bones, but they often come together in changing exhibits that help tell the bigger story about what they are. For instance, one exhibit shows how humans interact with sharks and black bears, and, more importantly, how humans are impacting these animals' existence.

There are numerous fascinating exhibits throughout the museum, and many are attractive to kids. Mini kiosks show southern California wildlife (taxidermy specimens) in their natural habitats, from mountain lions to birds, such as terrestrial roadrunners and endangered beach birds like snowy plovers and least terns.

For those interested in older natural history, there is a great archeological dig

San Diego Natural History Museum

exhibit that illustrates how the bones of ancient animals are located and preserved. And a miniature dig is available for youngsters to try their hands at playing archeologist.

Check the website for current special exhibits that can focus on anything related to natural history, from bugs to wildfires.

> **HOURS:** Daily, 10 AM to 5 PM. Closed Thanksgiving and Christmas.
>
> **COST:** Adults, $9; seniors (over 65), active military, and college students with ID, $6; 3–17, $5; under 2, free.
>
> **LOCATION:** 1788 El Prado, Balboa Park, San Diego
>
> **PHONE:** 619-232-3821
>
> **WEBSITE:** www.sdnhm.org

# 16 San Diego Museum of Art

**WHAT'S HERE:** Art from around the world, including Asian art that is related to many of the world's religions

**DON'T MISS THIS:** The computer search that allows you to see everything in the museum's vast collection, including pieces that are not currently being exhibited

The 1915 Panama-California Exhibition served as the impetus for the creation of San Diego's first art museum. Although planning by local community leaders began almost immediately, it was nearly 10 years before funding, a management plan, a permanent site, and the final building design all came together. The museum opened its doors on Balboa Park's El Prado in 1926, and the collections grew slowly until the early 1940s, when a family donated numerous paintings by masters such as Rubens, Giorgione, El Greco, and Hals. The museum was closed and transformed into a Navy hospital during World War II, finally reopening as a museum in 1947.

A new wing was added in 1975 that significantly expanded the museum's exhibit space. Over the next quarter century, thousands of donations helped to fill that space, including works by Henri de Toulouse-Lautrec and 1400 pieces of South Asian art. Being located in a city of

San Diego Museum of Art

relative affluence has also been helpful; in 1999, a local husband and wife made a donation that increased the museum's endowment by more than $30 million.

From the museum's earliest days, possessing a significant and representative collection of American art was a priority. The curators sensed an obvious dichotomy of direction taken by American artists during the 19th century and their European counterparts. Focusing on prominent American artists such as George Bellows, Robert Henry, and Georgia O'Keeffe, the museum has been able to contrast the work of those who traveled their own paths with regard to style, technique, and interpretation, with those Americans who spent their time in Europe studying the masters.

There was thought early in the museum's history that it should focus its collections on Spanish artists, in keeping with the city's heritage and the museum's architecture. Fortunately, the museum's leadership understood that limiting the collection would be a disservice, so it now includes works of some of the world's best artists, such as Henri Matisse, Ian van Huysum, Salvadore Dali, Pablo Picasso, El Greco, Robert Henri, and Rans Hals.

The museum's collection of Asian art includes many pieces related in some way to the major religions—Islam, Buddhism, Shintoism, Hinduism. The collection ranges from ceramics and sculptures of jade and bronze to paintings and textiles.

**HOURS:** Tuesday through Sunday, 10 AM to 6 PM; Thursdays open until 9 PM. Closed Thanksgiving, Christmas, and New Year's Day.

**COST:** Adults, $10; seniors (over 65) and military, $8; students with ID, $7; 6–17, $4; 5 and under, free.

**LOCATION:** 1450 El Prado, Balboa Park, San Diego

**PHONE:** 619-232-7931

**WEBSITE:** www.sdmart.org

# 17 Maritime Museum of San Diego

**WHAT'S HERE:** Several ships, from sailing vessels to the ferry *Berkeley*, which began service in 1898 on the San Francisco Bay

**DON'T MISS THIS:** The *Star of India*, the world's oldest active ship

It is only fitting that a city so closely tied to the sea throughout most of its history should have an outstanding maritime museum. And for San Diego, it starts with possessing the world's oldest active ship, the *Star of India*. The museum also features several other ships, and most are open to the public for tours. The *Star* began her sometimes less-than-elegant sea career in the Isle of Man, where she was constructed as an iron-hulled ship, an experimental ship at the time. Launched under the name *Euterpe* in 1863, the fully rigged sailing ship set off to prove her mettle, only to suffer a collision and a mutiny. On her very next voyage, the captain died—not an auspicious beginning.

Below the main deck, a museum awaits to tell many stories, not only about the *Star of India*, but also of maritime history. It is not difficult to understand the fears of the thousands of passengers who traveled on the *Star*, poor immigrants fed not much more than hardtack and salt pork during the ship's numerous voyages between Australia, New Zealand, Chile, and California. The *Star* went on to sail between California and Alaska in the early 1900s, working in the fish canning industry until it was retired in 1923. The museum shows everything from how to tie nautical knots to how sailing vessels can sail against the wind.

The *Star of India* is the most prominent vessel in the museum's port facilities, but there are more ships to explore. While only a replica, the *HMS Surprise* offers a close look at what a British 24-gun frigate looked like. And considering the close and small quarters squeezed into its 179-foot hull, it seems a miracle that any of these ships survived the many ocean storms. The Maritime Museum of San Diego purchased the faithfully re-created frigate from 20th Century Fox, who had used it in the film *Master and Commander: The Far Side of the World* (2003).

Ferries remain a prominent part of many maritime transportation systems from Alaska to Seattle and San Francisco, but none is steam-powered, nor does any compare to the elegance found on the ferry *Berkeley*. The *Berkeley*, part of the Maritime Museum of San Diego, is actually a California Historic Landmark and a National Historic Landmark that began service in 1898 on San Francisco Bay. Within the old ferry is a museum that tells the story of maritime history, beginning with the sailing vessels and ending with the obvious presence of the US Navy.

The *Berkeley*'s Age of Steam exhibit includes real steam engines that show how they actually worked in early steamships. Staff demonstrate the workings of the *Berkeley*'s steam engine, which was seen as an innovative approach to getting people and cargo by boat to different destinations at scheduled times, rather than allowing the winds to determine schedules. The Navy exhibit features more than 30 scale models representing a cross section of the ships that have played vital roles in defense of the US.

The maritime museum houses several more vessels, most of them smaller in

Maritime Museum of San Diego

size and scope. One is the shuttle boat *Pilot* that transported harbor pilots to merchant ships from 1914 to 1996, making it the longest-serving boat on the West Coast. Another is *Medea*, a private luxury yacht built in Scotland in 1904.

For those who can still remember the Cold War, the B-39 was a secret naval vessel. It was one of the Soviet navy's diesel electric submarines, classified as "foxtrot" by NATO. She tracked US and NATO warships, including submarines, for more than 20 years. As long as you can climb ladders, duck low, and are not claustrophobic, you can tour this vestige of a previous generation of warships and get a sense of how a crew of 78 submariners could share such small quarters with two dozen torpedoes at depths of nearly 1000 feet.

For anyone wanting a more adventurous museum experience, the *Californian*, a replica Gold Rush-era revenue cutter and the official tall ship of California, offers sailing adventures. The trips can range from a half day to a full week. Check the museum's website or phone for information about when the 145-foot-long sailing ship departs, since its schedule changes.

**HOURS:** Daily, 9 AM to 8 PM.

**COST:** Adults, $10; 13–17, seniors (62 and over), and active military with ID, $8; 6–12, $7; 5 and under, free.

**LOCATION:** 1492 North Harbor Drive, San Diego

**PHONE:** 619-234-9153

**WEBSITE:** www.sdmaritime.org

# 18 San Diego Aircraft Carrier Museum (USS Midway)

**WHAT'S HERE:** A World War II-era aircraft carrier

**DON'T MISS THIS:** The superstructure "island," even if you have to wait in line

Now decommissioned and floating proudly near downtown San Diego, the *USS Midway* served longer in the US Navy than any other aircraft carrier. It was commissioned in 1945, near the end of World War II; nearly 46 years later, the *Midway* was launching hundreds of air sorties against Iraq during Operation Desert Storm.

*Midway* is now retired and has been fashioned into a huge floating museum. There are three primary decks, and exploring them will take between two and three hours, assuming you don't get lost in the maze of corridors and stairways between the decks. With the exception of the "island" that sits above the flight deck, it is all self-guided, but signs and a tour map will keep you on track. The price of admission includes audio headsets that provide plenty of information about the *Midway*'s history and ship operations at identified stations throughout the ship. And since many of the docents working onboard served either on the *Midway* or on other naval ships, they are always willing to provide firsthand information.

During the 18 years of its active sea duty, the *Midway* didn't have a US home port; it was the first US carrier to make a foreign port, Yokusuka, Japan, its home. Serving at the end of World War II, the *USS Midway* was dubbed "Midway Magic" because it always seemed to be on station when other ships were being towed back to port for repairs. The *Midway* served as a test platform when it launched a captured German V-2 rocket in 1946, thus initiating modern naval missile warfare. It also explored new frontiers of warfare while conducting sub-arctic air operations near Greenland.

The tour requires visitors to climb a set of stairs at the ship's main entry onto the hangar deck. For those with limited mobility, elevators operate from the pier to the hangar deck, and from the hangar deck to the flight deck, both of which are wheelchair accessible. Access to other areas of the ship, including inside the island, is limited by ladders with handrails. Once on the hangar deck, the immensity of the ship becomes evident. The deck is full of aircraft (including an A-4 Skyhawk), a gift shop, food service, aircraft engines, a flight simulator, and more. The hangar deck was the ship's workspace, a city within a city with hundreds of sailors repairing aircraft, loading munitions, and moving airplanes up to the flight deck for air patrols and combat missions as needed. The hangar deck also provides access to all other areas of the carrier.

Take one of the ladders down to the second deck for an opportunity to see the galley. The Navy, certainly more than the Army or Marines, brags about having great food and plenty of it. The galley is where 13,000 meals were made every day in order to feed the 2800 crew members, the 1800 air wing members, and the small detachment of Marines who served primarily as a security force. There is also the ship's post office, which conveniently provided mail service regularly by air, an advantage to serving on a carrier. The hangar deck wasn't the only working deck, as the ship's machine and metal shops can also be seen on the second deck.

The flight deck is where the real action took place. Scattered around the flight deck are more than a dozen aircraft of the types that once flew from the *Midway*. They range from an F/A 18 Hornet and F-14 Tomcat to older aircraft such as a Vietnam War-era F-4 Phantom and Huey gunship. It's amazing to think that these big jets were able to land on such a small deck, especially on those moonless nights when storms turned the ship into a wildly moving target.

The one area where access is limited is the superstructure or island, the ship's command and control center. The passageways are narrow and space is at a premium, so the line of visitors is controlled

The *USS Midway*

to limit the numbers inside at any one time. But once inside, you'll learn exactly what life on a ship was all about from the docents.

Back on the hangar deck, there is a great gift shop and, for those whose stomachs can handle it, two flight simulators. One allows you to "jump into" a US or Russian jet and engage in a head-to-head battle; the other allows larger groups to experience what it's like to fly from the deck of a carrier. There is an additional fee for each of these flight simulators.

Beware—parking in the Navy lot directly adjacent to the *USS Midway* makes for a very short walk to the ship, but it is pricey ($5 for the first hour). Street parking, a block or two away (mostly meters), is much less expensive.

---

**HOURS:** Daily, 10 AM to 5 PM (last tickets sold at 4 PM). Closed Thanksgiving and Christmas.

**COST:** Adults, $15; seniors (over age 62), students (with ID), and military (with ID), $10; 6–17, $8, under age 6 and military in uniform, free.

**LOCATION:** 910 Harbor Drive, San Diego Harbor, San Diego

**PHONE:** 619-544-9600

**WEBSITE:** www.midway.org

---

# 19 Twenty Mule Team Museum

**WHAT'S HERE:** The history of borax mining in California's southern deserts

**DON'T MISS THIS:** The case filled with home products that have borax as one of their ingredients

On the surface, there is little to distinguish the small community of Boron from other small Mojave Desert communities, yet buried here is one of the world's largest deposits of borax, or sodium borate. Borax is a crystalline salt with an alkaline taste that once was used in most of America's households as an inexpensive cleanser. Borax is also used as flux for soldering metals and in the manufacture of antiseptics, soaps, glass, enamel, and artificial gems.

The museum's exhibits focus on the history of borax mining in the area, beginning in the 19th century when the famed 20-mule teams hauled borax from the mines in Death Valley to the rail spur. Actually driving a wagon filled with borax over the steep mountain roads and trying to steer a string of 20 mules around tight corners was a challenge for both driver and mule. It took significant coordination and skill to get the outside mules to move faster than their adjacent inside mules when rounding the apex of each tight corner.

In one of those ironies of history, for years, Pacific Coast Borax (now US Borax) had been hauling their Death Valley-mined borax across the top of one of the richest deposits of borax in the world, at what is today the town of Boron. They discovered this in 1927 and soon abandoned their Death Valley operations, ultimately digging the largest open-pit borax mine in the world about 3 miles from town.

Life in the desert has never been easy, but the people of Boron have made the best of things, and the museum documents many of the locals' lives. Life here is not without occasional Hollywood-style excitement. Parts of the movie *Erin Brockovich* (2000) were filmed here (the grocery store and Lahontan Water District office scenes), as were parts of the movie *Carpetbaggers* (1963). The museum features a short film about borax mining.

Outside the museum, there is equipment that was essential to mining operations and also to local farming efforts, as limited as it was in the area. One of the locals constructed a mining exhibit representative of typical small mining operations, including an ore car filled with ulexite from the nearby US Borax mine. Ulexite is a borate, better known as hydrated sodium calcium borate hydroxide or $NaCaB_5O_6(OH)_6 \cdot 5H_2O$. There is also a Fresno Scraper that was used in Death Valley operations to scrape borax ore from the desert floor for loading into transports.

If you have more questions about Boron or the surrounding area, the Twenty Mule Team Museum serves as the Boron Chamber of Commerce office, and the chamber staff are very friendly and helpful.

**HOURS:** Daily, 10 AM to 4 PM. Closed Thanksgiving, Christmas, and New Year's Day.
**COST:** Free
**LOCATION:** 26962 Twenty Mule Team Road, Boron
**PHONE:** 760-762-5810
**WEBSITE:** www.20muleteammuseum.org or www.boronchamber.org

Outside grounds at the Twenty Mule Team Museum

# 20 Colonel Vernon P. Saxon Jr. Aerospace Museum

**WHAT'S HERE:** A look at experimental high-speed aircraft development originally aimed at breaking the sound barrier

**DON'T MISS THIS:** The relatively small engines that powered the X-planes flown by the likes of Chuck Yeager beginning in the 1940s

This small aerospace museum is next door to Boron's Twenty Mule Team Museum and is difficult to ignore, considering the F-4 fighter jet that sits outside the front door. The museum is dedicated to the life and times of Colonel Vernon P. Saxon Jr., an Air Force pilot who spent much of his 30-year military career stationed at nearby Edwards Air Force Base. Saxon, who died of cancer in 1996, the same year he took his last flight, is the only pilot to ever fly a fully armed F-15 in a mission designed to defend Edwards Air Force Base and the Antelope Valley. Actually, it's not as strange as it may seem, considering the amount of military air traffic in the area. In this specific mission, Saxon was assigned to shoot down one of NASA's Boeing 720s, should the remotely piloted research vehicle break formation and fly toward any populated areas before being purposely crashed on remote airbase property during a test flight.

The museum exhibits illustrate many of the firsts that occurred at nearby Edwards Air Force Base. Several milestones in flight history have taken place in the skies over Boron and the Mojave Desert region during the last 60 years. The experimental X-Planes began

flying their high-speed, high-altitude, record-breaking missions in the skies over Boron in the 1940s. The Bell X-1 was the first to break the sound barrier, and the X-15 was the first to fly at hypersonic speed, setting a world speed record for a winged aircraft. There is also a XLR-8 rocket engine on display that powered the Navy D-558 Skyrocket to a speed of Mach 2.5. A variation of this engine—the XLR-11—shot the Bell X-1 and Chuck Yeager through the sound barrier for the first time in 1947. It was also used in the early flights of the X-15.

With Edwards Air Force Base practically next door, Boron continues its connection to aerospace activities. The base

One of the series of engines that powered the early Bell X-series rockets

311

doubles as a back-up landing site for NASA's Space Shuttle program, and the shuttle *Enterprise*, plus others, have paid many a landing visit to this area. The shuttle program is mentioned in the museum's displays.

HOURS: Daily, 10 AM to 4 PM. Closed Thanksgiving, Christmas, and New Year's Day.

COST: Donations accepted.

LOCATION: 26922 Twenty Mule Team Road, Boron

PHONE: 760-762-6600

WEBSITE: www.saxonaerospacemuseum.org

# 21 US Naval Museum of Armament and Technology

WHAT'S HERE: **A close look at the development of the most successful US military weapons, such as rockets, cruise missiles, and bombs**

DON'T MISS THIS: **The video that shows the extensive types of military-related weapons and safety testing that occurs across the base's vast land holdings**

This is a museum for the ultimate military arms techy. The middle of a desert may seem like an unlikely place for a US Naval weapons museum—but the China Lake facility was begun in 1943 as the Naval Ordinance Test Station where the Navy and Caltech scientists were developing rockets for use in World War II. Where else could you find thousands of acres of mountains and valleys, void of human life, and thus reasonably safe to test the hundreds of weapons that have been developed here?

While the military base has existed for 60 years, the museum first opened it doors in May 2000. The museum is temporarily housed in the old officers' club facility inside the base, which creates a bit of a security issue. Be sure to bring ID, as you will be "screened" by the security folks and issued a plastic guest badge with your name printed on it. The process only takes about 10 minutes, and then you're off with instructions to enter the base and drive directly to the museum, about five minutes away. Once you get close, the museum is easy to spot—there are two jet fighters and a Polaris missile standing just outside the museum entrance. Plans are already being developed and funding is being raised to build a new museum outside the base's front gate (tentatively by 2008), eliminating the security-screening process. But the badges are cool souvenirs!

The orientation film is a must, as it provides a close look at the entire base and many of the test facilities used here, such as the 4-mile-long test rails used to try out anything that must go really fast, from rockets to ejection seats. Various ranges are scattered around the sprawling base, allowing fighter jets to attack targets in numerous mountainous terrain situations with new types of rockets, bombs, and missiles under development. Unfortunately, the closest you can get to the test sites is watching the video program that takes you on a tour of the entire base.

In one test area, a large concrete bunker is used by personnel to protect them from drone or cruise missiles, should they decide to ignore their programmed trajectories. The intended target for some of these tests is a mountainside that doubles as a ship. The orientation film includes shots of many of the tests, including many types of missile firings.

The museum features dozens of weapons developed at the China Lake facility over the years. In fact, just about every type of explosive weapon used by the Army, Air Force, and Navy has been developed in some part at China Lake. The primary focus is on aircraft- and ship-launched rockets, and some of the names will be familiar to those who have been involved with any of the military branches, especially during times of war.

One story told about the weapons-development facility and the ability of its engineers and scientists to react quickly occurred during the Korean War. Apparently, the communists introduced new and more heavily armored tanks, which the US rockets merely bounced off of. A request went to China Lake to develop a new rocket that could penetrate the 12-plus inches of steel armor. Twenty-eight days later, the first new rockets arrived in Korea—and they worked extremely well.

China Lake teams were involved in developing the Tomahawk cruise missile that saw significant use during Operation Desert Storm (1991) and again against Iraq. The nearly 18-foot-long cruise missile sits on display in the museum—all 2900 pounds of it. The missiles are often fired from ships or submarines that can be more than 800 miles away from their intended targets.

The most-fired guided missile in history—the air-to-ground AGM-45 Shrike—was developed at China Lake. It's an anti-radiation missile, first fired in 1965, whose sole purpose is to home onto enemy radar emissions and destroy the source. The museum exhibits various versions of the missile, along with inside looks at its guidance systems, rocket motors, and warhead, telling the story about the development and improvements made over the years.

While the Shrike is the most heavily used missile developed at China Lake, the facility's most famous and most

The AGM-45 Shrike missile

widely used weapon is the air intercept AIM-9 Sidewinder missile. It's the one you see in all the movies of US jets firing missiles at enemy jets. It entered the US arsenal in 1956 and has been improved many times since then. The US military uses it on all aircraft that utilize offensive air-to-air missiles. The US has also sold some of the 200,000 produced over the years to other friendly nations.

Beyond weapons systems, the facility designs other military-related equipment. There is a 1-mile-diameter circle where new parachutes and parachute ejection equipment is tested. At this test site, the Naval Warfare Center has developed the parachute-recovery system for the space shuttle's rocket boosters and for the shuttle's pilot-escape systems.

The exhibits are numerous, with enough technical information for any military weapon's enthusiast, but standing next to a Sidewinder or cruise missile can be both exciting and disconcerting, when you know the kind of destruction they are designed to inflict.

> **HOURS:** Monday through Saturday, 10 AM to 4 PM. Closed on some holidays.
> **COST:** Free
> **LOCATION:** One Pearl Harbor Way, China Lake
> **PHONE:** 760-939-3530
> **WEBSITE:** www.chinalakemuseum.org

# 22 Scotty's Castle (Death Valley Ranch)

**WHAT'S HERE:** A desert home lived in and named after a man known as Scotty who never actually owned his namesake home

**DON'T MISS THIS:** The short hike to the top of the hill behind the home

Death Valley Ranch, owned and operated by the National Park Service, is more commonly known as Scotty's Castle. This name comes from a con man of sorts, who was always trying to weasel money out of someone for nothing—and the more the better. And perhaps the most surprising thing is that this magnificent $2 million vacation home, built in the 1920s in one of the most inhospitable places in the world, didn't even belong to Walter "Scotty" Scott, the man for whom it is named.

Scotty was born in Kentucky in 1872, but at age 11, he ran away, traveling to the Nevada Territory in his quest to become a cowboy. He ended up working as a laborer at the Harmony Borax Works in Death Valley and fell in love with the vast desert. He left for a while, spending a dozen years playing the ultimate cowboy in Buffalo Bill's Wild West Show, traveling throughout the US and Europe. It was during this time that Scotty fashioned and honed his skills of removing money from the pockets of the willing. Using a couple of gold nuggets as bait, he conned many wealthy East Coast gentlemen into investing in his Death Valley gold mine, which never existed.

Once again in his beloved Death Valley, Scotty spent his investors' money living it up in the nearby towns and making a name for himself as a great storyteller. Around that time, he met Albert Mussey Johnson, a Chicago insurance businessman and a multimillionaire. Scotty talked Johnson into investing in some of his non-existent businesses several times, with never any return to the businessman. Johnson finally came in person to see Scotty's nonexistent gold mine, and Scotty put him on a mule and showed him many of Death Valley's unique sites, but never a mine. Johnson soon understood that Scotty had found gold alright, and that gold came from other's pockets. But Johnson's poor health had improved in the dry desert air, and he took a liking to Scotty's stories and the wild life he led, so Johnson decided to build a large home in Death Valley instead.

Johnson chose Grapevine Canyon, where an early immigrant had once managed a successful grape, fig, and vegetable farm, mostly because of its substantial water supply. He began construction of his new home in 1925, and since the only local building material was rock and sand, everything else had to be brought in, including the pipe and a Pelton waterwheel needed to turn the generator that provided electricity 24 hours each day.

Spring water was routed into the house to two fountains that allowed water to trickle into open pools, adding humidity to the hot, dry air, helping to cool the home's interior. Johnson had a solar water heater constructed behind the Spanish Provincial home, its 960 feet of alcohol- and water-filled copper tubing allowing the sun to provide plenty of hot water. And unbeknownst to many, Death Valley can get very cold during winter, but the home's massive fireplace provided adequate warmth.

Johnson lost much of his money in the 1929 stock market crash, so he never finished building everything he wanted for his desert "escape." He and his wife continued to visit their desert home each year, but Johnson allowed Scotty to live in the elaborate home as a caretaker year round. The flamboyant Scotty easily convinced nearly everyone, including the newspapers, that the magnificent home was his and that his secret gold mine

Scotty's Castle

paid for everything. Magazines and newspapers began calling the place "Scotty's Castle," something that Johnson quickly discovered. Yet Johnson let the stories continue, saying that "Scotty repays me in laughs." Johnson died in 1948, and Scotty died six years later.

The National Park Service purchased the home in 1970 and offers 50-minute, guided, living-history tours (docents are dressed in period costume) of the home 365 days a year. Since summer temperatures in Death Valley can exceed 120 degrees, November through April is the busiest time for visitors, and sometimes there can be a two-hour wait. Be sure to buy your tour tickets as soon as you arrive, as they are on a first-come, first-served basis.

> **HOURS:** Daily, 9 AM to 6 PM (last tour starts at 5 PM).
>
> **COST:** Death Valley National Park entrance fee: $20 per vehicle (good for seven days).
> Scotty's Castle tour tickets: 16–61, $11; 62 and over, $9; 6–15, $6; 5 and under, free.
>
> **LOCATION:** 54 miles north of Furnace Creek via SR 190 to Grapevine Ranger Station and Hwy. 267.
>
> **PHONE:** 760-786-2392
>
> **WEBSITE:** www.nps.gov/deva/Scottys/Scottys_main.htm

# South Coast and Desert Tours

## Adventure Tour

**ESTIMATED DAYS:** 2

**ESTIMATED DRIVING MILES:** 280

If you like California's deserts, you'll love this adventure. It's a total of nearly 280 miles of driving, so plan on two days to take all this in. Begin at the small desert community of Boron, just off Hwy. 395 near Edwards Air Force Base, home to some of our country's most secret developmental military flying machines. The small town's **Twenty Mule Team Museum** (page 309) will take you back through the history of borax mining (the stuff is used in hundreds of modern products) and the teams of 20 mules that were required to haul the heavy loads from the mines. Directly next door is the **Colonel Vernon P. Saxon Jr. Aerospace Museum** (page 311), an easy way to see some of the aircraft development work that occurs at Edwards Air Force Base.

From Boron, it's about 56 miles north on Hwy. 395 to Inyokern, then 10 miles east to the **US Naval Museum of Armament and Technology** (page 312) at China Lake, deep in the desert landscape. The museum is full of rockets and missiles, and the short film is fun to watch if you like to see rockets and smart bombs in action and all the other testing that goes in the surrounding desert mountains.

Drive northeast about 143 miles through much of Death Valley to **Scotty's Castle** (page 314). If you do this during summer, be prepared for temperatures that may exceed 120 degrees—early spring when the wildflowers bloom is probably the best time to visit. The only advantages of visiting during summer is gaining an appreciation for the natural "air conditioning" incorporated into this fabulous and historic desert home—and encountering fewer visitors.

Colonel Vernon P. Saxon Jr. Aerospace Museum

317

# Family/Kids Tour 1

**ESTIMATED DAYS:** 2
**ESTIMATED WALKING MILES:** 1

San Diego's best museums are within a few minutes walk of each other. It's impossible to miss the **San Diego Air and Space Museum** (page 297) with the impressive A-12 Blackbird spy plane and Navy Convair Seadart "flying" just outside the front entrance. Inside, aircraft represent every aspect of flight, from pre-Wright brothers to space travel.

Not far away, near the big fountain, is the **Reuben H. Fleet Science Center** (619-238-1233; www.rhfleet.org). This place is loaded with hands-on science and technology experiments that kids absolutely love, so plan on spending at least a half day here. Just a few buildings down El Prado (museum row's main street), you will discover the **San Diego Model Railroad Museum** (page 301), one of the largest of its kind in the nation. If by now you've had enough technology, the **San Diego Zoo** (619-231-1515; www.sandiegozoo.org) is about a 10-minute walk away. But that should be saved for another full day because it's too big and too much fun to rush through in just an hour or two.

San Diego Air and Space Museum

# Family/Kids Tour 2

**ESTIMATED DAYS:** 2
**ESTIMATED DRIVING MILES:** 5

California's second largest city is second to none when it comes to museums dedicated to the changes that the human species—and a few dozen other creatures—have experienced through past millennia. The **San Diego Museum of Man** on El Prado in Balboa Park (page

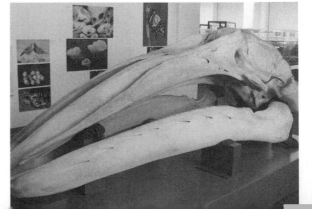

Whale bones at the San Diego Natural History Museum

296) walks you through the very beginnings of the human species, looking at human physical and intellectual changes, along with many of the differences that have developed among our many cultures. Just a few minutes away is the **San Diego Natural History Museum** (page 303), a kid-friendly place designed to help the younger generation experience the natural wonders of the world. The museum features hands-on exhibits that will keep kids and their parents busy having fun and learning at the same time.

When the museum suddenly seems too confining for energetic young ones, jump back in your car and drive about 5 miles to **Old Town San Diego State Historic Park** (page 290). Here you'll discover the roots of the city of San Diego. Today, dozens of shops, a few small museums, restaurants, and a big, grass-covered quad in the center of Old Town give everyone a chance to run off some energy or sit and relax.

## Maritime Day Tour

**ESTIMATED DAYS:** 1

**ESTIMATED WALKING DISTANCE:** About 5 blocks (0.4 mile)

If you can plan your visit for late September through October, do so. San Diego's annual **Fleet Week** (www.fleetweeksandiego.org), which is really fleet *month*, features everything from air shows with the Navy's Blue Angels to special tours through active-duty Navy warships. Anytime you get to San Diego is the right time for a tour of the **San Diego Aircraft Carrier Museum** (page 307), better known as the *USS Midway*. It served from World War II through Operation Desert Storm, and there are aircraft onboard representing every era. Wander down the waterfront a short distance to the ships of the **Maritime Museum of San Diego** (page 305). Here's a chance to tour a variety of sailing ships, ferries, and other boats. Two of the most popular are the *Star of India*, the world's oldest active ship, and the *HMS Surprise*, the replica British 24-gun sailing frigate that was built for the film *Master and Commander: The Far Side of the World* (2003).

Flight deck of the *USS Midway*

# Romantic Tour

**ESTIMATED DAYS:** 2–3

**ESTIMATED DRIVING MILES:** 72

San Diego is a great place for couples who like the arts and love to have fun. At the edge of Balboa Park is the **Marston House** (page 294), a Craftsman-style home built in 1905 by one of the city's early and most successful department store owners. It's just over a mile to the **San Diego Museum of Art** (page 304), which is located in the center of Balboa Park's museum row on El Prado. The museum's elaborate Spanish colonial architecture, along with that of the other museums here, is reason enough to visit. Inside, you can wander among paintings by some of the world's best artists, from Picasso to Dali.

Afterward, drive the 5 miles to **Old Town San Diego State Historic Park** (page 290), where you can visit several small museums, including **La Casa de Estudillo**. This early 19th century adobe was home to one of San Diego's leading families. There are dozens of quaint shops and eateries nearby where you can dine on Mexican (or other) food on beautiful, flower-covered patios or inside brightly painted restaurants. Plan your visit for the first week in May, and you can enjoy the festivities associated with the annual **Cinco de Mayo** celebration (www.fiestacincodemayo.com). A second day's trip of about 65 miles will take you to **Mission San Juan Capistrano** (page 281). March brings San Juan Capistrano's celebration held for the annual return of the swallows.

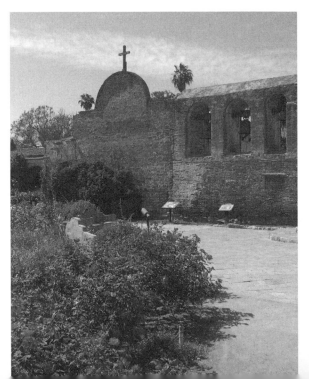

Bell tower at Mission San Juan Capistrano

# South Coast and Desert
# Travel Information Centers

Anaheim-Orange County Visitor & Convention Bureau
www.anaheimoc.org
714-765-8888 or 888-598-3200

Huntington Beach Conference and Visitors Bureau
www.surfcityusavacation.com
714-969-3492 or 800-617-9019

San Diego Convention & Visitors Bureau
www.sandiego.org
619-232-3101

Balboa Park Visitors Center
www.balboapark.org
619-239-0512

Barstow Area Chamber of Commerce & Visitors Bureau
www.barstowchamber.com
760-256-8617 or 888-4-BARSTOW

Boron Chamber of Commerce
760-762-5810

Inland Empire Tourism Council
www.visitinlandempire.com
951-779-6700

Colonel Allensworth State Historic Park

# Trivia Answers

## North Coast

1 Which lighthouse can be visited only during low tide?

*Battery Point Lighthouse*

2 Where can you get up close and personal with a living honeybee hive—and not get stung?

*Humboldt State University Natural History Museum*

3 Where is the only active historic cookhouse for lumberjacks and the public?

*Samoa Cookhouse Museum*

4 What military assignment convinced Ulysses S. Grant to resign his commission early in his career?

*Fort Humboldt*

5 Which museum is devoted to a goofy race that doesn't guarantee the fastest finisher first place?

*Kinetic Sculpture Museum*

6 Where can you see a giant slice of Mendocino County's largest redwood ever cut?

*Guest House Museum*

**7** What fancy home originally came with an octagon-shaped privy?

*Kelley House Museum*

**8** Which fort was built by the Russians?

*Fort Ross*

**9** Which California horticulturist created a potato that McDonald's now uses for its famous French fries?

*Luther Burbank*

**10** Name the childhood pet of Charles Schulz that became the inspiration for Snoopy.

*Spike*

# Shasta Cascade

**1** Name the museum where you can see a 1940s-era iron lung.

*Modoc County Historical Museum*

**2** Which museum has a large collection of famous early California art?

*Shasta State Historic Park Museum*

**3** Name the museum that houses one of the state's largest collections of antique firearms.

*Modoc County Historical Museum*

**4** Which home was built in 1878 by a husband and wife who first passed through the area by way of Beckwourth Pass in 1852?

*Coburn-Variel Home*

**5** What is the name today for the region where the Modoc Indian War took place?

*Lava Beds National Monument*

**6** Name the museum where it is possible to drive a real locomotive.

*Portola Railroad Museum*

**7** Name the park that includes the oldest continuously used Chinese temple in California.

*Weaverville Joss House State Historic Park*

**8** Where can you see a stuffed mountain lion that once ate the local district attorney's dog?

*Plumas County Museum*

# San Francisco and Greater Bay Area

**1** What is San Francisco's oldest building?

*Mission Dolores*

**2** Which museum holds one of California's largest collections of Asian art based on Buddhism?

*Asian Art Museum*

**3** Where can you see the giant wheels that pull all the cables that power San Francisco's cable cars?

*San Francisco Cable Car Museum*

**4** Which museum looks like a big white boat?

*San Francisco Maritime Museum*

**5** Where in San Francisco can you find the remnants of a Cold War missile site?

*Angel Island*

6  **What ship picked up the *Apollo 11* astronauts following their historic first walk on the moon?**

   *USS Hornet*

7  **What is the name of one of the only two remaining World War II Liberty Ships?**

   *SS Jeremiah O'Brien*

8  **On which mansion did carpenters work for nearly 40 years?**

   *Winchester Mystery House*

9  **Which mansion was home to the governor who was in office during San Francisco's great 1906 earthquake?**

   *Pardee Home Mansion*

10 **Which fort was built as part of California's Civil War defense?**

   *Fort Point*

# Great Valley

1  **Where can you see the doll that belonged to Patty Reed, one of the ill-fated Donner Party survivors?**

   *Sutter's Fort State Historic Park*

2  **Which 1860s home featured indoor plumbing and a bathroom with a flush toilet, all rarities at the time?**

   *Bidwell Mansion*

3  **What future Supreme Court justice lived in the Governor's Mansion as governor from 1943 to 1953?**

   *Earl Warren*

**4** Where can you ride in historic railcars along the bank of the Sacramento River?

*California State Railroad Museum*

**5** About which site did legendary musician Johnny Cash write a song?

*Folsom Prison*

**6** Where can you find the very first Pony Car (Mustang) manufactured by Ford?

*Towe Auto Museum*

**7** Name the oldest art museum in the West.

*Crocker Art Museum*

**8** What is California's only town ever founded, financed, governed, and lived in only by African Americans?

*Allensworth*

# Gold Country and High Sierra

**1** Which mansion is a replica of a 17th century Viking castle?

*Vikingsholm*

**2** Who discovered gold on the American River and kicked off the California Gold Rush?

*James Marshall*

**3** Which Lake Tahoe historic site features two homes built by the founders of banks?

*Tallac Historic Site*

**4** Where can you see a wheelbarrow built by the future "horseless carriage" magnate?

*El Dorado County Historical Museum*

**5** What town was commonly known as one of the most notorious of California's Gold Rush towns?

   *Bodie*

**6** Where can you find the largest gold nugget to have survived California's 19th century mining operations?

   *California State Mining and Mineral Museum*

**7** Which Paramount Studios movie features the visitor center at the Laws Railroad Museum and Historical Site?

   *Nevada Smith, starring Steve McQueen*

**8** Around which Gold Rush town did miners take more than $150 million (at $30 per ounce) in gold during its first 50 years of existence?

   *Columbia*

# Cental Coast

**1** Which Pulitzer Prize-winning novelist lived much of his life in the small agricultural town of Salinas?

   *John Steinbeck*

**2** Which mission is located on the San Andreas fault?

   *Mission San Juan Bautista*

**3** Which museum best represents the farming history of the Central Coast?

   *Monterey County Agricultural & Rural Life Museum*

**4** Where did a young career soldier named William Tecumseh Sherman live while assigned to Monterey as a lieutenant?

   *Behind Larkin House in the "Sherman Quarters"*

**5** How many rooms were in the main house when Hearst was finally forced to stop building his castle?

*115*

**6** Which museum features an official presidential jet?

*Ronald Reagan Presidential Library and Museum*

**7** At which mission is California's Spanish mission system founder Father Junipero Serra buried?

*Carmel Mission*

**8** Where was California's constitution debated, written, and signed?

*Colton Hall*

**9** Near which future mission did Gaspar de Portola's expedition first encounter 8-foot grizzly bears, which nearly killed some of the expedition's pack mules?

*Mission San Luis Obispo*

# Los Angeles County

**1** In which mansion can you find tiled floors designed to look like Persian rugs?

*Adamson House*

**2** The owner of which mansion raised shire horses like those used by England's knights?

*Rancho Los Alamitos*

**3** Which museum features the original white Herbie #53 Volkswagen from the 1969 Disney film?

*Petersen Automotive Museum*

**4** Name the second oldest museum in Los Angeles, which attracts thousands of kids each year.

*Natural History Museum of Los Angeles County*

**5** Which mansion was built following a young son's discovery of oil in a field on their property?

*Temple Home*

**6** Name the two museums in the Los Angeles area that were created by a private foundation established by one man's wealth.

*The Getty Center and The Getty Villa*

**7** Where can you watch scientists working in an active archeological pit?

*Page Museum at La Brea Tar Pits*

**8** Which famous "singing cowboy" created the Museum of the American West?

*Gene Autry*

**9** Where is Bob Hope buried?

*San Fernando Mission*

**10** Which mansion was used as an occasional set for the television hit *The West Wing*?

*Fenyes Mansion*

# South Coast and Desert

**1**  Which mission celebrates the return of the swallows each spring?

   *Mission San Juan Capistrano*

**2**  Which museum features the works of Jan and Dean, who sold 20 million records between 1960 and 1966?

   *International Surfing Museum*

**3**  Where can you see America's first successful commercial airliner?

   *San Diego Air and Space Museum*

**4**  At which museum can you board and tour the actual ship used in the movie *Master and Commander*?

   *Maritime Museum of San Diego*

**5**  Which museum features bombs and explosions as part of its day-to-day activities?

   *US Naval Museum of Armament and Technology*

**6**  Name the museum where you can see California's largest model train exhibit.

   *San Diego Model Railroad Museum*

**7**  What is California's oldest town and now one of its largest cities?

   *San Diego*

**8**  Name California's first mission.

   *Mission San Diego de Alcala*

**9**  Which museum features a car that was driven nonstop across the country in 1952?

   *San Diego Automotive Museum*

Mission Santa Barbara

# Index

# About the Authors

Together, authors Ken and Dahlynn McKowen have 50-plus years of professional writing, editing, publication, marketing, and public relations experience. They have more than 2000 articles, stories, and photographs in print, and they are authors or coauthors of *Chicken Soup for the Fisherman's Soul*, *Chicken Soup for the Entrepreneur's Soul*, *Highroad Guide to the California Coast*, and other books.

The McKowens are also the owners of Publishing Syndicate (www.publishingsyndicate.com), which provides writing and editing services for publishers and helpful learning tools for new and established writers. Their company also offers a free monthly writing and publication tips e-newsletter and several writing tips e-booklets. They live with their family in Sacramento, California.

# A Few Organizations that Support California's Missions, Mansions, and Museums:

A nonprofit, privately funded membership organization, the **California Historical Society** is the state's official historical society. Its mission is to engage the public's interest and participation in collecting, preserving, and presenting art, artifacts, and written materials relevant to the history of California, and to support historical research, publication, and educational activities. **www.californianistoricalsociety.org**

The **California Missions Foundation** is a secular, nonprofit organization dedicated to the protection, preservation, and maintenance of the historic California missions and their associated artwork and artifacts, for the public benefit. **www.missionsofcalifornia.org**

The **Historical Society of Southern California**, founded in 1883, is committed to preserving, interpreting, and promoting the history of southern California. The Society informs the southern California community about the continuing study and pursuit of history, and celebrates the diverse dimensions of southern California's past and present, as well as the contributions of its many cultural heritages with a commitment to exacting scholarship. **www.socalhistory.org**

The **San Francisco Museum and Historical Society** is focused on preserving, interpreting, and presenting the historical heritage of San Francisco through regular programs, events, and publications. **www.sfhistory.org**

The **California Association of Museums** (CAM), founded in 1979 by staff and trustees from diverse museums throughout the state, is a nonprofit service organization formed to represent the interests of California museums. CAM assists California museums in fulfilling their missions as educational and research institutions that interpret and preserve art and cultural and scientific artifacts for public benefit. **www.calmuseums.org**